A Good Enough Parent

Bruno Bettelheim is recognized throughout the world as one of the greatest child psychologists of the century. He was born in Vienna in 1903, where he trained as a psychiatrist and received his doctorate at the University of Vienna. He was imprisoned by the Nazis and was for twelve months an inmate of the concentration camps at Dachau and Buchenwald. He went on to found the pioneering Orthogenic School at the University of Chicago, where he achieved remarkable success in healing severely disturbed children.

Dr Bettelheim has lectured widely in Europe and in Israel and is Professor of Education Emeritus and Professor Emeritus of both psychiatry and psychology at the University of Chicago. He won the US National Book Award and the US National Book Critics Award for *The Uses of Enchantment* – a discussion of the vital role of fairy tales in a child's development – and his other books include *A Home for the Heart*, *Surviving and Other Essays* and *On Learning to Read*.

BRUNO BETTELHEIM

A Good Enough Parent

The guide to bringing up
your child

Pan Books
London, Sydney and Auckland

First published in Great Britain 1987 by Thames and Hudson Ltd
This edition published 1988 by Pan Books Ltd,
Cavaye Place, London SW10 9PG
9 8 7 6 5 4 3 2 1
© Bruno Bettelheim 1987
ISBN 0 330 30270 1
Printed in Great Britain by
Richard Clay Ltd, Bungay, Suffolk

To Trude Bettelheim in memoriam
and to our children Ruth, Naomi, Eric

CONTENTS

vii

ACKNOWLEDGMENTS

FIRST I WISH TO ACKNOWLEDGE that the book's title is derived from
D. W. Winnicott's concept of the "good enough" mother. I have adapted
it to both parents, since both are important for their child's development.
My title suggests that in order to raise a child well one ought not to try to
be a perfect parent, as much as one should not expect one's child to be, or
to become, a perfect individual. Perfection is not within the grasp of ordinary
human beings. Efforts to attain it typically interfere with that lenient response
to the imperfections of others, including those of one's child, which alone
make good human relations possible.

But it is quite possible to be a good enough parent—that is, a parent
who raises his child well. To achieve this, the mistakes we make in rearing
our child—errors often made just because of the intensity of our emotional
involvement in and with our child—must be more than compensated for by
the many instances in which we do right by our child. The purpose of this
book is to facilitate being such a good enough parent.

My notions about child-rearing developed over so many years that it
would be impossible to acknowledge all those who influenced them. Most
of these ideas developed in response to problems of child-rearing which I
had to solve, either because I encountered them myself or because they were
presented to me for solution. I am thus unable to express here my gratitude
to all those who in one way or another helped me to form the ideas which
underlie this book. I can, however, be specific in acknowledging the great
help which Joyce Jack gave me in writing it. I am grateful to her for her
unceasing struggle to make it more readable. At her suggestion Katherine

Bernard also read the manuscript and made suggestions which are here gratefully acknowledged.

It was Theron Raines's idea many years ago that I should write a book about raising children, and this was the original impetus for it. Now that it is finished, I am thankful to him for having caused it. While he was its first cause, the second was Robert Gottlieb's interest and encouragement, and his unusual patience in waiting for its completion, which was inordinately delayed; for this I am most grateful to him.

A NOTE TO THE READER

THROUGHOUT THIS BOOK, I have referred to a parent as "he" and "him," unless an example clearly refers to a mother, although I had mostly mothers in mind when writing it and assume that mostly women will read it. Moreover, since slightly more than half of all children are female, it was also difficult to decide how to refer to them. I am convinced that while both parents contribute significantly to a child's being raised well (or not so well), it is the mother, particularly during the early years, who is apt to play the considerably more important role in the process. One way to handle this semantic awkwardness would be to refer to parents always as "she" and "her," while referring to children throughout as "he" and "him," in this way making it easy for the reader to know whether I am speaking about a parent or about a child. But I found it as difficult to think of all parents as female as it was to think of all children as male. Another solution would be to refer to parents and children as "she/he" unless I specifically had a male or a female in mind, but this is not at all in line with my old-fashioned manner of thinking or writing.

But my main reason for shunning these ways of writing was that in writing this book, I felt I was speaking to my readers the way I have been talking all these many years to mothers, to staff members of children's institutions, or to mixed audiences of professionals interested in child-rearing. In speaking to such groups I could never make myself say "she/he" or circumvent the problem by speaking only about "persons." These expressions did not permit the kind of direct personal contact I value, so I have found it wiser to stick to the old-fashioned generic "he," whether I am referring to female or male, child or adult. The generic seems more natural to me, at least so far as children are concerned, because I was raised and spent nearly half of my life in Vienna, where in line with German custom, all children were spoken of in the neuter gender. I wish this were possible also in English, not only for children but also for adults, to make it obvious that one is not just referring to one sex only. But since this isn't possible, I feel it best to use the traditional language, with which I am most comfortable.

PART ONE

Parent and Child

1

By Way of Introduction: The Importance of Early Experiences

Just as the twig is bent the tree's inclined.
—ALEXANDER POPE, *Moral Essays*

THIS BOOK SUMS UP my lifelong effort to discover and test what is involved and required for successful child-rearing—that is, the raising of a child who may not necessarily become a success in the eyes of the world, but who on reflection would be well pleased with the way he was raised, and who would decide that, by and large, he is satisfied with himself, despite the shortcomings to which all of us are prey. I believe that another indication of having been raised well is a person's ability to cope reasonably well with the endless vicissitudes, the many hardships, and the serious difficulties he is likely to encounter in life, and to do so mainly because he feels secure in himself. Although not always free of self-doubt—since only arrogant fools are entirely free of that—whatever happens in his external life, such a person who has been well raised possesses an inner life which is rich and rewarding, and with which he is hence satisfied. Last but certainly not least, to grow up in a family where good, intimate relationships between the parents and between them and their children are at all times maintained makes an individual capable of forming lasting, satisfying, intimate relations to others, which give meaning to his and to their lives. He will also be able to find meaning and satisfaction in his work, finding it worth the efforts he puts into it, because he will not be satisfied with doing work that is devoid of intrinsic meaning.

My concern with child-rearing goes back some seventy years; I began to struggle with the issues it poses first as a teenager and then a few years later as an adolescent. My efforts have continued unabated ever since. During the first years my interest was both theoretical and highly personal; I was trying to comprehend what was involved in the rearing of children as I myself

3

had experienced it, and as I had observed it around me. Although I had very good parents, I nevertheless thought that many aspects of the parenting I received were questionable, and others I rejected outright. In general, I was convinced that many of the ways children were raised could be and ought to be vastly improved, particularly in the light of the then entirely new insights of psychoanalysis.

When I reached my late twenties, some fifty-five years ago, child-rearing became also an eminently practical and immediate problem for me, as I began to devote myself to the arduous task of undoing the severe psychological damage which others had inflicted on some very disturbed children. By applying what I thought were good practices of raising children, which were based on psychoanalytic principles, I tried to heal one and, for some time, two autistic children who lived with me in my home for many years. In the 1940s, under very different circumstances, my efforts—which up to then had been restricted to a very few youngsters in addition to the two just mentioned—were extended to a fairly large number of very severely disturbed children, who lived and were treated and educated at the University of Chicago's Sonia Shankman Orthogenic School. This work has been described in a number of books and many more articles, so there is no need for me to dwell further on it here.

Having three children of my own, I have learned, among many other things, that there are significant psychological and—even more important— emotional differences between the parenting of one's own children and even the most devoted parenting of children who are not one's own. What I learned from all these experiences—what I found useful and what detrimental, and why—forms the basis of this book.

I approached the material also keeping in mind my nearly forty years of experience in conveying to others how best to deal with the problems encountered in raising children. These others consisted mainly of two quite different groups: intelligent and highly motivated mothers of more or less normal youngsters; and the staff of the Orthogenic School, who were devoted to the rehabilitation of children suffering from very severe psychological impairments, through living with them, through educating them in appropriate ways, and through treating them. My efforts were aimed at inducing these adults to deal all on their own, in their own ways, with the problems and issues they encountered with their own children or the children under their care, so that the results benefited both of them. Telling them specifically what to do and what to avoid doing could never resolve the problems, for generalized advice is defied by the uniqueness of each adult and each child, and by the innumerable extremely varied and ever-changing situations in which they find themselves as the adult raises a child and as the child reacts to being raised.

Unendingly varied and complicated as are the moves in a chess game, even chess offers only an extremely simplified metaphor for the intricacy of human interaction. Each chess game starts afresh, and in exactly the same way. The rules are identical for both players; they are unchangeable, clearly understood, and freely agreed upon by the players, who must strictly obey them. And finally, the desired outcome and the reaching of that goal are also clear: the checkmating of one of the kings.

None of this holds true for what happens between a parent and child. Anything that occurs in their relationship is heir to a long and complicated history. Each moment or episode begins differently from all preceding ones—that is, unless both parent and child are already neurotically bound to stereotypical reactions to each other, which doom all efforts at spontaneity and warmth of feeling. There are no agreed-upon rules, although parents often try to impose rules which the child, because of his weakness, may not be able to resist. But such forced agreements only interfere with the child's ability to cope with the problem situation in a way that is constructive to him. This is why in this book I do not wish to offer definite answers but to suggest methods of approach that can promote the parent's and the child's ability to be spontaneous and very much themselves in all that happens between them; this, in turn, will encourage the child's ability to cope with reality successfully on his own terms.

Even if a parent insists that his view of a given issue is to prevail and his rules are to be obeyed, this does not guarantee that the child accepts any of it in his heart. As far as inner experience is concerned, child and parent each follow their own rules, usually without these rules having been made explicit either to themselves or to the other. Further, not only do most parents and children follow their own rules, they can and do change rules easily in the process of interacting without warning one another, usually without any conscious awareness that they *have* changed them, or how. There is no clearly understood and freely accepted agreement on what forms or decides the desirable outcome in child-parent relationships. And the sharpest difference of all between child-rearing and chess: real life is not a game but dead earnest.

Yet banal and oversimplified as chess is as a metaphor for human relations, it can illustrate the fact that in a complex interaction we can never plan much more than a few moves in advance. Each move must depend on the response to the preceding one. Thus it is very important to assess correctly the always changing total situation: an appropriate first move can give at best only an indication of what the right reply to the first countermove may be.

The beginner in chess, who tries to follow his plans irrespective of his partner's countermoves, will soon go down to defeat. And so will the parent who follows a preconceived plan, based on explanations he received or advice given him for dealing with his child. A parent must continually and flexibly adapt his procedures to the responses of his child, and reassess the ever-changing overall situation as it develops. In chess, it soon becomes obvious that it is a blunder to try to follow one's plan without giving the most careful consideration to the opponent's plan, and to every one of his reactions to one's own moves. Such consideration of a child's intentions and reactions is also crucial to parental actions. But the child, when in disagreement with his parents, often hides his true feelings out of his fear about their reactions, so that parents often are stymied there.

The good chess player can contemplate in advance a number of possible moves and likely countermoves, but only because he has learned to reconsider and reevaluate the overall situation after each step. The parent who already can reconsider in this manner his relation to his child hardly needs advice; he will know what to do, and at every action and reaction of the child will constantly reevaluate the situation. So one may say that the parent equipped to make good use of child-rearing advice hardly needs it, while the parent unable to evaluate and reevaluate the overall situation correctly cannot use advice intelligently and successfully. That is why something other than explanation and advice is needed: namely, helping the parent to grasp on his own what may be going on inside his child. If we learn how to project ourselves into the child's mind, while simultaneously trying to understand what motivates ourselves, then we will instinctively choose the best course of action.

Thus this book is based on what I found to be the most effective way of helping others with child-rearing: namely, inducing them to develop their own insights about child-rearing and attitudes appropriate not only to their purposes but also to the person they are and to their child; inducing them to strive to reach an understanding and an attitude which are at the same time of individual and mutual benefit to the parent and to the child.

To develop such insights and attitudes which further the development of both parent and child as persons while advancing the intimacy of their relations, I have found that it is of prime importance to avoid thinking that one knows the right answers, obvious though these may appear to be, before one has carefully examined what is involved in the situation for each party. Further, one should not attempt to understand one's child independently from oneself. If we make a serious effort at understanding ourselves in the context of a given situation, trying to see how we have contributed to it—willingly or unwillingly, consciously or unconsciously—then our view of the matter is nearly always altered, as is our manner of handling it.

It is not always possible to follow this prescription—in the face of imminent danger or some other emergency one has to act immediately. Still, to achieve a long-range solution one must, as soon as calm is restored, first examine one's own thinking and sources of reacting, and then fathom what has gone on in the mind of the child. Striving thus to comprehend one's own behavior and that of one's child around a well-known and now also well-understood situation leads to parental behavior which most benefits parent and child. In fact, it is such self-exploration which often provides the best clues for understanding and helping one's child.

This method of understanding parent-child interactions was implicit in the discussion of some of my previous writings, such as *Dialogues with Mothers* and parts of *A Home for the Heart*. In this book I want to be as explicit as possible in stressing that the only effective way to help well-intentioned, intelligent persons to do the best they can in raising children is to encourage and guide them *always to do their own thinking* in their attempts at understanding and dealing with child-rearing situations and problems, and *not* to rely blindly on the opinions of others.

Through discussing in some depth a limited number of typical problem situations and areas, I hope to show that it is best for parent and child if the adult thinks the situation through on his own and thus discovers exactly what is at stake. A good way to start out is with the premise that whatever the child does, he believes—albeit sometimes quite erroneously—that what he is doing, or is about to do, is the best way for him to proceed in the situation in which he finds himself. The limited number of issues discussed in this book must stand for the enormous range of problems encountered during the rearing of a child. My guidelines are intended to help readers become better able to think through whatever issues concern them at any given moment. From long experience I believe what is presented here ought to be sufficient for readers—if they so desire—to make this method of approaching child-rearing issues their own to the degree that they will be more effective in raising children, and enjoy more satisfying relations with them.

Books telling parents how they ought to raise their children are not exactly a new phenomenon; in fact, they have quite a long history. But only in this century, and particularly since the 1950s, have they been so popular, with large numbers of parents turning to them for advice and comfort when feeling uncertain about how to handle the problems they encounter in raising their children. With the disintegration of traditional modes of family life and of the rearing of children, in the wake of our century's massive urbanization and industrialization, we have lost the security people once derived from long-standing customs, from growing up as part of a large extended family, and from all other experiences these provided.

Thus it is that most modern middle-class persons have not learned very much in their own childhoods about how to take care of children. Matters were different when families were larger and one's kinfolk lived close by; then, much care of the younger children was entrusted to their older siblings, or to some other young relative such as a cousin or an aunt or uncle who was just a few years older and lived with the family, or next door. If there were no blood relations available to take care of younger children, then the children of neighbors assumed this role, as was customary in village culture. By the time most people became parents, they had learned enough about child care to feel secure about raising their own children. When they did feel the need for advice, they could turn to their own parents and relatives, or to their clergyman or physician, confident of receiving the help they required.

Today, however, parents feel that much more is demanded of them if they are to raise their children successfully in a complicated world; moreover, they are obliged to bear this responsibility without much prior experience. Unfortunately, the physical and emotional distance which now so frequently separates the generations can lead young parents to fear—often with some justification—that when they ask their parents for counsel on child-rearing, they may be subjected instead to criticism together with advice which, as likely as not, no longer seems appropriate.

Another significant factor is that many people tend to believe that times are changing fast and that research is constantly yielding new knowledge, so they feel the need to rely on experts. This eagerness to seek "expert" advice can best be understood within the context of the belief that there are no limits to what man can achieve when he tries hard enough and applies himself in "scientific" ways. Reliance on science as the source of progress has replaced an older trust in the wisdom inherent in tradition.

In the field of human psychology, the belief that all is possible, provided one applies the correct scientific methods, has found its clearest and most extreme expression in the tenets of behaviorism, as originally formulated by J. B. Watson. He taught that depending on the conditioning to which a child is subjected in his early years, he can be turned into any one of radically different types of person; therefore, depending on the child's environment and its impact on him, he can become a genius or a villain, or anything else. According to this strange doctrine the newborn child's mind and personality form a *tabula rasa* on which parents, educators, or psychologists

8

can engrave indelibly whatever traits they want. It is not easy to explain why this theory of man as completely manipulable was and still is so widely accepted, usually without parents' realizing it specifically. Actually, every parent's experience indicates that from the moment of birth children differ in their responses, and that at even a very early age they have minds of their own which they often try to assert even against their parents, abortive though such efforts may remain because of the infant's stage of development.

Some people find the behaviorist doctrine acceptable because it holds both that a child's life is an entirely new beginning, for which every type of future development is a real possibility, and that most careful and deliberate training is necessary to achieve the desired ends.

At present, only dyed-in-the-wool behaviorists still adhere to the exaggerated claim that any desired result can be achieved through training, now given the more "scientific" names of conditioning and behavior modification. But little has changed regarding the widespread, basically behaviorist conviction that the child's fate in later life depends entirely on the way he is raised in infancy. Without consciously realizing it, many people adopt and apply to their fellow man this theory derived from the study of conditioned reflexes in Pavlovian dogs and Skinnerian pigeons; they are mostly unaware that these reactions were produced and studied in laboratory animals that were trained to run mazes and thus became, as a result of such conditioning, unable to survive on their own in their natural habitats—that is, were made what in man one would describe as utterly maladaptive and neurotic, incapable of responding spontaneously in their own ways to situations, able to act only as they had been "conditioned" to do.

Behaviorism became the dominant psychological school in the United States during the second quarter of this century, when traditional ways of rearing children were repudiated in favor of a new and more scientific approach which the increasing complexity of life seemed to require. It has remained America's prevalent psychological doctrine ever since, so much so that most people are not even aware that "behaviorism" is the name for what they believe.

This usually tacit, unexamined, and hence uncritical acceptance of behaviorism is antithetical to the principles of very different and much better validated scientific theories: evolution and genetics. Both show, with much incontrovertible evidence, that the human being is by no means completely manipulable; the child's mind at birth is not at all a *tabula rasa*—on the contrary, his very nature severely restricts what later personal developments are possible to him. Genetics demonstrates that much of what a person will be is determined at his conception by the particular mixture of genes which the parents contribute. This mixture is different from person to person (with

9

the single exception of identical twins, who have the same genetic endowment). Through our genes we also inherit the results of the very long process of human evolution. Both genetic endowment and the evolutionary process limit the changes that can be produced in an individual by education or other life experiences.

The Freudian theory of human development, which competes with behaviorism, found a fairly wide acceptance in the United States at the same time that behaviorism was sweeping the country. Freudian theory stresses both the intractability of much of our evolutionary inheritance and the importance of early experiences; though we are unable to alter any of this inheritance, early experiences modify the way it finds expression in an individual's personality. Psychoanalysis adds to the theory of evolution the idea that just as the embryo in the mother's womb repeats in its growth certain stages in animal evolution, so the infant and small child recapitulate important stages of the history of mankind.

Given this unalterable inheritance and these inescapable steps in human development, Freudian psychology is much less optimistic than behaviorism about what may be achieved through child-rearing. It holds that man will always be beset by deep inner conflicts resulting from the discrepancies between what he is by nature and what he himself—or his parents and educators—wish him to be; that he unavoidably has to struggle against selfish, aggressive, asocial tendencies which are as much part of his evolutionary inheritance and his personal makeup as are his desires to form close emotional attachments; that the egoistic drive for self-preservation is often in painful conflict with altruistic tendencies which may require sacrifices for the preservation and continuation of our species in general and through one's children in particular, and for securing the well-being of all those one loves.

Psychoanalytic doctrine is deeply committed to the conviction that how these inherited characteristics will be shaped depends on a person's life experiences. Thus it subscribes to a historical view, according to which later events are to a considerable degree conditioned by what has happened before; therefore, the earliest history of the individual is of greatest importance in respect to what he will be like in his later life, not only because it is the basis for all that follows but also because early history largely determines *how* later life will be experienced. While genetic and evolutionary history creates an individual's potentialities, his early personal history more than anything that follows accounts for the forms these potentialities will take in the actuality of his life. Therefore, respect for the child's unique personality is of paramount importance in all dealings with him. Rather than forcing or "conditioning" the child toward whatever the parent thinks best, the aware and concerned parent will respond sensitively to what best suits his particular child at any given moment, and thus facilitate his becoming the person he wants to be. Such a parent will not only recognize and make allowance for the child's struggles as he grows through certain stages of development but will also give him the kind of support which permits him to find good solutions to them. These stages include the infant's discovery of himself and his steps toward individuation and with it his separation from his mother; the slow move from living by the primitive pleasure principle, which induces him to try to satisfy desires immediately without any regard for consequences, toward the reality principle, based on the realization that he is often much better off if he modifies some of his desires or postpones their gratification in order to gain more important long-range advantages; the acquisition of self-control, as in toilet training; the establishment of the rudiments of individuality during the oedipal stage; his adaptation to the demands made upon him and the internalization of these demands in the form of the superego; and the adolescent developments through which relative maturity, independence, and a unique personal identity are to be achieved.

The child's mastery of each new stage of psychological and social development requires understanding and sensitive help from his parents, so that his later personality will not bear the scars of psychological wounds. The parent must not give in to his desire to try to create the child he would *like* to have, but rather help the child to develop—in his own good time— to the fullest, into what he wishes to be and can be, in line with his natural endowment and as the consequence of his unique life history.

Both theoretical systems—the behaviorist and the Freudian—recognize that changes can and do occur in our attitudes, behavior, and personalities throughout life. But as we grow older, far-reaching changes become much more difficult to achieve, as each year we become more settled into seeing and doing things in customary ways; in short, we become less flexible. Changes that may occur when we are older are likely to affect only limited areas of our personalities and our lives. The importance of early experiences thus rests on the fact that they set the stage for all that comes later, and the earlier the experiences are, the more emphatic their influence.

According to behaviorism, these earliest experiences completely create us as human beings. But psychoanalysis considers them important for a different reason, which has to do with the roles our unconscious and our conscious play in our lives. The conscious mind develops slowly, and in some respects remains always dominated by the unconscious. As long as we live, according to psychoanalytic theory, our unconscious makes us interpret much of what happens to us in the light of our earliest experiences. For example, our unconscious, on the basis of how we interpreted to ourselves our early experiences with our parents, causes us to believe either that the world is basically accepting and approving of us, or rejecting and disapproving. This attitude extends to our belief that we are good or bad persons; it gives us the feeling that we are or are not competent to deal with life; that we are or are not lovable; even whether we will be rewarded or disappointed. Such far-reaching attitudes are formed on the basis of extremely vague feelings which we nevertheless experienced most strongly at a time when, because our reasoning abilities were as yet undeveloped, we could not yet comprehend the meaning of what was happening to us. And since these attitudes which continue to dominate our experiences originate in our unconscious, we do not know what caused them and why they are so convincing to us.

If Freudian theories are correct, it is clear that early childhood experience not only influences the development of self-esteem and the perception of oneself in relation to others, but also determines our interpretation of later experiences and leads us to arrange our life's events to conform to our preconceived notions. Therefore whoever influences the child's life ought to try to give him a positive view of himself and of his world. The child's future happiness and his ability to cope with life and relate to others will depend on it.

Freud said that the most desirable result of a psychoanalytic education— that is, an education which recognizes both the importance of the unconscious and the need for harnessing its forces to serve socially and personally useful purposes—is to enable a person "to love well and to work well." To him this meant the ability to gain the maximum satisfaction available in both the private and the public sphere: to love and be loved by those with whom one shares one's life, and to be useful to society, so that one can take justified pride in what one manages to achieve there, despite life's unavoidable hardships, and irrespective of what others may think of one's accomplishments. One aids one's children in attaining these goals by helping them to develop ways of coping with the vicissitudes of life, so that rather than being defeated, they gain greater insight and strength—particularly also insight into their own inner lives.

Thus, both leading doctrines of child psychology emphasize that much depends on what the child experiences as he goes through the various stages involved in his growth toward maturity, and that a parent's handling of these situations is not only most important, but can be fatal when things go wrong. So now the modern parent is very well informed as to what he should worry about as he deals with the developing child! And, unfortunately, worry he does.

Given these doctrines, and given the fact that most people as youngsters have had no firsthand experience with raising children, it is little wonder that the conscientious parent becomes anxious about failing as a parent and fears that he may harm the child he loves. But parental anxiety—while understandable—does a great deal of harm both to parent and to child. Winnicott, whose concept of the good enough mother I mentioned initially when explaining the book's title, says about the good enough mother that the infant, as he looks into her face, sees there himself—or one might say, finds there himself—because the good enough mother, owing to her deep empathy with her infant, reflects in her face *his* feelings; this is why he sees himself in her face as if in a mirror and finds himself as he sees himself in her. The not good enough mother fails to reflect the infant's feeling in her face because she is too preoccupied with her own concerns, such as her worries over whether she is doing right by her child, her anxiety that she might fail him. The infant who does not find himself reflected in the face of such a mother responds instead to her being worried, and becomes worried about himself. Worse, he sees the face of a stranger where he should find what is most familiar, so he feels lonely rather than deeply connected, as the infant does who finds himself reflected in his mother's face in a positive way.

It follows that to be a good enough parent one must be able to feel secure in one's parenthood, and one's relation to one's child. So secure that while one is careful in what one does in relation to one's child, one is not over-anxious about it and does not feel guilty about not being a good enough parent. The security of the parent about *being* a parent will eventually become the source of the child's feeling secure about himself. Hence my hope is that this book, far from making parents anxious or guilty about what they do in relation to their child, will give them the feeling "That's right, that's what I am doing," or at least "That's what I wanted to do!" In short, I hope that the book will make them feel more secure as parents, less worried about what they may possibly do wrong.

Still, despite the fact that a parent's security about how he deals with his child is so significant for his child's well-being and his own, today all too many parents who are devoted to their children feel that their responsibilities are at times almost too heavy. Even the most normal and unavoidable problems can take on ominous proportions when one believes that one's child's entire future is decided by the way one handles a certain situation. So it is easily understandable that modern parents, who no longer believe man's fate is decided by God's will or is a matter of blind chance, are desirous of receiving the best possible guidance on how to perform the fateful tasks involved in raising their children. The big question becomes: What constitutes this best guidance? Does it consist in an expert's telling the parents what to do and what not to do, or does it consist in helping parents to arrive, all on their own, at sound decisions on how to proceed, decisions about which they feel good?

No book can encompass the millions of problems that may be encountered in child-rearing, nor the unlimited variations in which they can manifest themselves. For his own sake, and that of his child, a parent must solve problems as they occur and in his very own way; otherwise, his solution will fit neither him nor his child, nor will he feel good about it. As to guidance, all that is really possible is to suggest through discussion and by way of some examples how a parent may think about himself and his child in a specific situation.

I feel that a parent's most important task is to get a feeling for what things may mean to his child, and on this basis handle himself in ways that are most helpful to both; if he does, this will also improve the parent's and child's relation to each other. The best way to get this feeling is to remember what a parallel issue meant to us when we were children, and why, and how we would have liked our parents to handle it, us, and themselves. Thus we can put to creative use our own life events, which acquire new and deeper meaning as we recall them and work them through in the light of our own parenthood.

Raising children is a creative endeavor, an art rather than a science. Here an attempt is made to present some suggestions on how to think about this art, and how it may be applied. I cannot tell the reader how to experience this art, nor how to appreciate what is involved in it, for these are far too personal matters to be decided by others, although their views about them may enhance our ability to perform creatively, in our very own ways. Instead, let me suggest how I hope the reader will use this book by quoting T. S. Eliot in *On Poetry and Poets*: "There are many things, perhaps, to know about this poem or that, many facts about which scholars can instruct me which will help me to avoid further definite misunderstandings; but a valid interpretation, I believe, must be at the same time an interpretation of my own feelings when I read it."

The reader who adopts the poet's attitude of self-awareness will find his actions much more interesting and rewarding, and will find raising a child a more exciting, much happier experience for both himself and the child.

2

Expert Advice or Inner Experience?

THE WAYS IN WHICH PARENTS raise their children powerfully influence how the children will develop and who they will become. It is understandable, then, that parents seek the advice of experts, particularly when they cannot decipher the meaning of their child's behavior or are anxious about his future, when they are uncertain whether and how to act, or when their efforts to correct their child's behavior make the child unhappy and arouse his resistance.

But there are other important reasons why, during the last few decades, many parents have sought out and come to trust the advice and recommendations found in child-rearing books and articles. One is the great appeal of the "how-to" approach of many of these publications, as if life were a game that could played "by the rules." Both behaviorism and the trivialization of Freud's theories have contributed to the idea that if you just adhere to certain itemized instructions, certain results will automatically follow.

The "do-it-yourself" experience teaches that when given good blueprints and the right instructions, we are able to construct quite intricate objects to our full satisfaction, whereas without the instructions, we would have fumbled or failed abysmally. This explains the current popularity of "how-to" books and manuals in the most diverse fields, even where the most private feelings and intimate relations are involved. Many people do not hesitate to accept the advice these books offer; the fear of failure is so great, it is no wonder that the desire to do right by one's children has led to a whole library of books offering advice on how to raise them.

Furthermore, there is a near-universal bias in our society toward the idea that there is only one right way to do something, while all others are wrong. And if we follow this right way, achieving our goal is a fairly simple process. Therefore, when things become difficult or complex, parents tend to believe that they must not have used the correct approach, because if they had, things would go easily and successfully. When things go wrong as we are trying to assemble some complicated object, we consult the blueprints and instructions, and often enough we find that we have made a mistake. Once we correct it and do as the instructions advise, the components fit together properly.

It is this double-edged conviction on which the "how-to" manuals base their claim, and of course the successes we have when following such instructions buttress these claims. In fact, the "how-to" movement has shown us that there often *is* a right method of doing things which indeed *is* fairly easy to apply successfully. However, this is most valid when applied to the making of objects, particularly when all that is needed is the correct assembly of already existing pieces. In our society, which in many respects has had its greatest success in mass-producing machinery, people are tempted to believe that the same principles which are so eminently successful in the engineering field should also be applicable to human relations and human development.

Parents who rely on "how-to" books for child-rearing have established unconsciously, or more often subconsciously, a parallel between their most intimate personal interactions with their child and the assembly of a piece of machinery.

Since here, and throughout the book, the concepts of the unconscious and the subconscious are used, it might be helpful to suggest their difference. A person is normally unaware of what goes on in either his unconscious or his subconscious. But the content of the subconscious will usually be accessible to him through a careful examination of his thoughts, feelings, and motives. While the process may be a difficult one, it is possible for him to bring into awareness what goes on in his subconscious. Between his conscious and unconscious mind, by contrast, there is a nearly impenetrable barrier. For what goes on in his unconscious is what is unacceptable to his conscious mind and has therefore been severely repressed. Full awareness of what goes on in the unconscious can be achieved, if achieved at all, only against the greatest resistance. It takes concentrated effort and determination and very hard intellectual work to penetrate this barrier separating conscious and unconscious, and in many cases this may be possible only to a limited degree, or even quite impossible.

In the present example, the idea that they see, and behave in terms of, a parallel between the assembly or functioning of machinery and the functioning of their child might be so abhorrent to some parents that they are simply unable to accept it. For them this parallel, while it does in fact determine their thinking and behavior, remains unconscious. Other parents, pondering the issue carefully and making a serious effort to analyze their thinking and motives, may come to recognize that, unbeknownst to them until then, they had indeed established a parallel between the functioning of their child and that of a piece of machinery. In their case, this parallel was not repressed into the unconscious but had, up to the moment of recognition, remained subconscious.

In either case, parents may speak readily about their wish that their child should "perform" or "function" better than he does—the latter being a popular motive for seeking advice. But parents whose main concern is that their children should live well and enjoy their lives are not likely to refer to their children as "functioning" well or poorly. Actually, it is this subconscious parallel between such noncomparable phenomena as a well-functioning machine and a well-lived life which makes parents dissatisfied with themselves and their children when their child-rearing efforts fail to "produce" exactly the results they intend. They then conclude that there must be something wrong with their "technique" of child-rearing, that they must have applied a "faulty procedure," because otherwise the right results would have been achieved. It is this kind of thinking that leads parents to rely on manuals to tell them how to *perform* better as parents, when the real issue is not to "perform well" but to *be* a good parent.

This is not to suggest that parents shouldn't think about doing well by their children, nor that they should leave such things to chance. Parents ought, through their own behavior and the values by which they live, to provide direction for their children. But they need to rid themselves of the idea that there are surefire methods which, when well applied, will produce certain predictable results. Whatever we do with and for our children ought to flow from our understanding of and our feelings for the particular situation and the relation we wish to exist between us and our child.

Robert Pirsig, in his book *Zen and the Art of Motorcycle Maintenance*, makes the point that even when we are putting together some appliance, obeying advice or instructions robs us of feeling creative about what we are doing. This, so far as the human experience is concerned, is a much greater loss than what we gain in ease when good instructions facilitate our putting things together; so even when all we are doing is putting together an appliance, the feeling with which we endow what we are doing makes an enormous difference in the satisfaction we can gain from it. It is difficult to feel really good about ourselves and our child when we apply in our interactions advice which we were given by someone else. It robs the interaction of the spontaneity that makes for humanly meaningful and hence truly satisfying experiences.

It seems simple to put together a piece of machinery once one has instructions or blueprints to follow. Our expectations concerning the consequences of following the instructions are all positive; we have no anxieties interfering with our ability to comprehend and obey the instructions. And if we get tired, discouraged, or bored because the work turns out to be more difficult than expected, we know that nothing will be lost other than money or labor if we abandon the project; nothing unfortunate will happen if we ask somebody else to finish it for us or if we stop for a while before continuing with it.

How very complicated, by comparison, are parental feelings when we are baffled by the problem of how to deal with a child in a difficult situation. Here we have to act, and yet find it incredibly complex, and often beyond our emotional resources, to conduct ourselves in a manner which meets our own needs and at the same time helps the child to develop his own personality fully and gain, small step by small step, a correct and at the same time positive view of himself and of the world. While it is no blow to our self-love that we don't know how to put some appliance together, we fear that we are inadequate as parents when we are unable to find, on our own, the "right" answers to questions of child-rearing. It is thus with both anxiety and a certain uneasiness that we approach the advice we may find in a book.

The greater our perplexity and need, the greater also is the pressure to find a solution right away. The more perturbed we are, the less we are able to weigh things carefully and the more we wish to be instructed by an authority. Thus willingness as parents to trust what we are told has much to do with our desire to do right by our child, and relatively little to do with the correctness of the instructions these books offer. Otherwise, there would have to be widespread agreement concerning which book to follow and which to reject—an agreement that hardly exists. But paradoxically, the more we want such advice, the less we like it, because our need for it is the consequence of our being confronted by a problem which, deep down, we feel we should be able to cope with on our own.

Furthermore, we often cannot help wondering whether by following the advice we really will be better off, or whether doing so will lead to even greater troubles with our child. This is a valid question, because even if the advice as such is appropriate, for some internal or external reason we may not be able to apply it correctly, and things may get even worse than they were originally! In many complex situations, much depends on how well the advice is understood, how well it is adapted to the unique situation and to the natures of the parent and child involved, and how successfully it is put into practice; in all these and many other respects, there are many possible pitfalls.

The best advice is based on a thorough examination and evaluation of all the specific details, such as the prehistory of the problem area; thus it can never be found in a book. But even when advice is given only after careful analysis of all the particulars, we may be unable to follow it in the way it was meant to be followed. This may aggravate the original difficulty, because we may then feel bad not only about the problem, but also about our inability to make good use of the advice we received. This is enough reason to find the advice unwelcome in retrospect; if we were going to fumble anyway, it would have been better to fumble in our own ways.

Subconsciously we are leery of child-rearing advice even as we seek it. Deep down, we know quite well that much history has preceded the problem for which we are seeking advice; it did not spring from nowhere, and it contains much that is unique to the parent and child involved. While the situation and our behavior in it may have features in common with those an author describes, and even when the problem we are facing is a common one, each of us is a unique individual. Thus no author of a book written for parents in general can know and weigh all the factors involved in our particular predicament. We are quite ready to believe that the advice given may apply to most similar situations, but we are uneasy because we cannot be certain that it is appropriate to ours. We also know that nothing is at stake for the giver of such advice if it backfires, while untold misery may be the consequence for us and our child if our implementation is erroneous or inappropriate, or if the advice or our understanding of it is incomplete.

Here, too, a comparison to following instructions for putting together an appliance may be pertinent. If, as we try to follow such assembly instructions, they appear misleading, incomprehensible, or irrelevant, or if they actually lead us astray, we can put them away or we can object and procure better instructions; we are not any worse off than before. But in dealing with a child, it is much more difficult to undo the damage that is the consequence of bad timing, of unclear or misunderstood advice, or of advice that is entirely off the mark. We know that since we began to follow the advice, things have happened between us and our child to change the original situation; we cannot retrace our steps, or start again where we began.

As we study assembly instructions, few of us are distressed that others may be able to proceed without needing such guidance. But as we read how best to deal with our child, we have the sinking feeling that other parents know and feel secure about these matters while we do not. Why do we have to read up on toilet training, or on eating idiosyncrasies, when other parents don't seem to have these problems? No matter how often we read that other parents *do* have the same experiences and run into the same difficulties, we know from talking with other parents that there are some who don't. There is the child who toilet-trained himself; another who always sleeps through the night; still another who is delighted with the new baby. Thus for every child whose parent is in need of help with a problem, there is another child who didn't create such a problem, or so it seems to the worried parent.

Further, as the parent tries to take in advice, he is humanly prey to unconscious resentment that his child's behavior is forcing him to seek counsel. Often parents, as relatively self-possessed adults, feel that their child should not have run into this particular difficulty, or should somehow have been able to solve this troublesome problem all by himself. If other children can do so, why not ours? Or—worst of all—is it our fault that our child has difficulties where others don't? If we are thinking along these lines, our misgivings make it even more diffucult to take in advice with that equanimity of mind necessary to comprehend it correctly and apply it without distortions.

So, unfortunately, the emotions with which we study advice on how to raise our child are usually mixed or negative. We fear we may discover that we have already done something irretrievably wrong; or that the suggested course of action may run counter to our convictions or to our habitual ways of handling things; or that it may be difficult to conduct ourselves as suggested; or that our child may react adversely if we proceed as advised. Consciously, or more likely subconsciously, we may also be worried that if we act in line with what we are told in a book, we may create conflicts within the family, arousing severe criticism from our spouse or the child's grandparents. Thus our own ambivalence about advice that is not entirely convincing or seems difficult to apply is compounded by apprehension that others may be critical of us if we follow it.

Parents who decide to consult child-rearing books have undoubtedly already considered some potential solutions to their problem of the moment. Even parents who loudly proclaim they "just don't know what to do" have already tried many things and thought of quite a few more. Especially if it is an issue of any importance—nightmares, toilet training, petty theft—we have ruminated over what *might* be the best way to deal with it, and we have also heard the opinions of others.

We also recall the way these matters were dealt with by our parents when we were children, and we know which of their methods we liked or disliked. But whether or not we approved of what our parents did in any particular situation, their method has made a deep and lasting impression, and it continues to carry the aura of parental authority, irrespective of whether we have incorporated their ways of acting into our own or continued to resent them. In any case, our reaction to a book's advice will be flavored by the residue of our past experiences—the "prehistory" of our present attitude to the problem in question.

We *know* that there are many ways to handle any one situation, but only a few which will benefit our child; so it is only natural that we approach recommendations with the tacit hope that these will conform to the course of action which we have already tried, or originally had in mind. Both the satisfaction if this is so and the disappointment when is it not are great. Often, dismay that our own ideas are called into question will seriously interfere with our ability to implement advice in the most intelligent way; we might even subconsciously seek defeat to vent our resentment at the "expert." This is because we have some stake in convincing ourselves that we were right in the first place—that only we parents know what works and doesn't work with our child.

As a matter of fact, most advice on child-rearing is sought in the hope that it will confirm our prior convictions. If the parent had wished to proceed in a certain way but was made insecure by opposing opinions of neighbors, friends, or relatives, then it gives him great comfort to find his ideas seconded by an expert. C. C. Colton (in *The Lacon*) says, "We ask advice, but we mean approbation." This is particularly true when our emotions are strongly involved, as they are in all matters relating to our child.

Parents who are honest with themselves recognize that for every piece of advice found in a journal or book which they accept and act upon, there are also quite a few opposite ideas which they reject. One has only to watch parents selecting from a shelf of books on child-rearing to recognize this. While all child-rearing books are written by so-called "experts," these authors are accepted as experts by some and not by others. The reality is that while there are experts on children and on child development in general, only a person who is intimately familiar with what goes on between a particular parent and a particular child can be an expert on *them*.

All a parent seeking advice can do is to pick from the plenitude of books one in which he finds some statements which are persuasive to him because they conform to his ideas, and hope that the rest of the book will, too. How can he do otherwise? To broaden our views on matters in which we are not personally involved, we might read authors whose opinions are opposed to our own, but where our own child is involved, we like to consult someone who sees things pretty much as we do.

Even advice that is eminently convincing is not always easy to follow if it entails some inconvenience. This holds true not just for advice given by others, but for advice we give to ourselves, or which, objectively speaking, should be fairly simple to follow. For example, every book which mentions the subject advises putting potentially dangerous substances securely out of the reach of children. Yet every day, children are brought to hospitals because they have swallowed such substances. We all have a strong tendency to act like Mary Wortley Montagu, who wrote in a letter to the Countess of Mar: "I give myself sometimes admirable advice, but I am incapable of taking it."

Advice that is in line with parental comfort or views is more easily followed, despite contrary views expressed by some "expert." This is why the advice to let an infant "cry it out" and not to pick him up and cuddle him is still widely followed. It is not so much that this course of action puts less of a burden on the parent, since the child's wailing makes the parent uncomfortable; the problem is that we get annoyed at those who make us uncomfortable, and unconsciously the parent resents the child's prolonged crying and so convinces himself that picking up the child will do no good. Even if a parent who is annoyed by the child's crying picks him up—as he is also frequently advised to do—any benefit to the child may be obviated by the annoyed way in which it is done, which thereupon proves to the parent that picking up the child does no good. While it is easy to go through the motions, it is often very difficult to give comfort to persons who annoy us, even when they are our own children. So if a piece of advice is applied by a parent who resents following it, it often will backfire.

I have met many parents who behaved quite outlandishly toward their children. When asked what gave them the idea of doing so, they nearly always claimed to have read or heard that this was the best way to proceed. It almost always turned out that they had also been given the opposite advice, but to follow it had seemed inconvenient or inappropriate to them, and so they had searched the literature until they found a statement with which they could agree.

In sum, it is difficult to read advice on how to behave as a parent without strong personal reactions, and these reactions interfere with comprehension, not to mention the objectivity needed to avoid projecting into the advice elements not actually contained in it. And once we have sought such advice, it becomes difficult to put it out of our minds. We must come to terms with it, accept it, reject it, make it our own in parts, or at least continue to ponder it. Yet since we sought advice because we were at an impasse with our child—perhaps over his angry jealousy toward a sibling, his fear of dogs or of going to school, his wetting the bed, his overeating or refusing to eat— we lack the time and leisure to consider the advice we receive with the equanimity that would permit us to make wise choices. We are under too much pressure—because our child continues to refuse to go to school or to be afraid of dogs, to not eat or to overeat, to do dangerous things or to ask us to keep him safe from imaginary dangers. Even if our child does not beg us to "do something," we feel compelled to help him, a pressure which is not likely to facilitate our taking an objective attitude toward advice. Should by chance the problem behavior subside for the moment, we continue to worry about what may have brought it on, since we know only too well from past experience that such abeyance may not last, or that the problem may crop up in some other form. So we cannot help mulling over the advice, being bothered by some of its aspects and intrigued by others, which often prevents our objective assessment of how exactly it applies to our problem.

Books often tell parents *how to be* with their child—to be understanding, patient, and, most of all, loving. But much as we want to be, if not ideal, at least very good parents, it is practically impossible to sustain such positive attitudes in crisis situations, when our emotions stir us strongly because we lose patience with what our child is doing or is determined not to do. We cannot understand what makes him so obstinate. We find ourselves unable to love him when he badly hurts our feelings, or when he embarrasses us, destroys some prized possession, spills his food all over us, or vents his rage by hitting or kicking us, or his sibling, literally or figuratively. While sometimes we can take it all in good humor and remain little affected by it, there are other moments when we simply are fed up with our child's behavior, typical though it may be for his age.

Of course, the vast majority of parents love their children most of the time, and would like nothing better than to be able to love them all the time; there is no need to point out how pleasant it is when we are able to love our child without reservation. However, there are few loves which are entirely free of ambivalence. This is true even of the love of a mother for her firstborn son, which, according to Freud, is the most singularly positive and the least ambivalent of all relations known to man. Not only is our love for our children sometimes tinged with annoyance, discouragement, and disappointment, the same is true for the love our children feel for us.

In many situations of conflict, thoughtful parents will tell themselves that all this is a necessary, although difficult, part of the child's growing up, and that they want their children to develop minds and values of their own.

23

Unfortunately such correct insight is of only limited help when parents feel that not only their values but their very way of life is challenged and questioned by their own children, around whom they have built much of their lives in the first place.

What usually does help in such situations is to recall how it was when we wished to behave or actually did behave much as our child is doing now; certainly in the lives of all of us there were times when we exhausted our parents' patience, wanted to defy them or did, and objected silently or openly to their way of life and conduct. If we can truly remember these situations, we will also recall how deeply painful they were for us as children, how anxious and insecure we were behind our show of defiance and argumentativeness, and how we resented our parents' failure to realize all this because they were so wrapped up in their annoyance.

For example, a teenage girl and her mother got involved in an argument which became increasingly more heated and ended with the girl cursing her mother, who was so deeply hurt that she could not shake her feelings for several days. She wondered why she had been affected so strongly. After all, bad as the situation had been, it hadn't been the first time that a violent argument had ended in similar fashion; but she had never been hit so hard before. Finally it dawned on her that this disagreement had somehow evoked in her one of the very few times—forgotten by her until that moment—she had cursed her own parents, when they had severely reprimanded her for smoking. Much to her astonishment, she remembered that at the time, as on similar occasions, although with her swearing she had wanted to hurt her parents' feelings because hers had been so badly hurt, she hadn't believed that she had succeeded. She had been convinced that she wasn't important enough to her parents, hadn't made enough of an impression, for them to be truly hurt by anything she did. Only now, when for days she had felt deeply wounded by her daughter's swearing at her, did she realize how badly her parents must have been hurt when she had cursed them.

With this recollection she realized how she had wronged her parents by thinking them insensitive to her angry outbursts, believing them intent only on having their own way regardless of her feelings. But what was more important now for her relationship to her daughter was that she comprehended how terribly hurt her girl must have been to have been so carried away. Her own wounded feelings receded into insignificance in the face of her compassion for her daughter, whose disappointment in her mother had caused her to burst out swearing at her, not unlike the way she had been deeply disappointed in her parents, who, as she then had seen it, had made much too much of her defying them by smoking surreptitiously.

Thus when we are able to recollect our own emotional turmoil in similar situations—however openly defiant or blasé we pretended to be—and the price this turmoil exacted from us, then our annoyance will dissipate and be replaced by sympathy for our child's inner pain, which he is trying to conceal from us (and possibly from himself) by a show of self-sufficiency or superiority. Our memories of our own childhood will make us patient and understanding; and as we realize that despite our child's obstinacy he suffers now as we suffered then, our love for our child, in whom we now recognize so much of our old selves, will, all on its own, return. But for this to happen, we have to relive such experiences in our mind; merely reading about them will not re-create them in us, because it is the very specifics of our experience which make it vivid enough to be not just remembered, but relived with feeling.

Even if a parent in such a situation, as in this example of being cursed by one's child, is able to follow outside advice that he should keep his cool in times of trouble—and some parents are able to exercise the necessary self-control this requires—in doing so the parent's behavior becomes artificial, even mechanical, because it is not a natural consequence of the parent's inner feelings. Then he appears not more human but less human to his child. It is difficult to remember, and even more difficult to act on, the advice to behave lovingly at times when it is exactly our love for our child that makes us so worried about his behavior. It is just because we do love our children so much that we are so vulnerable—the more deeply we love, the more our feelings can be wounded and our emotional equilibrium, on which our ability to remain patient and understanding depends, can be upset. Were we more indifferent to our children, they would lack the power to make us lose our composure.

Our children are so very close to us because we see much of ourselves in them; to put it technically, as much as they identify with us, we identify with them, usually much more and in more various ways than we consciously realize. We are happy when we recognize in them features we approve of in ourselves. But our closeness to our children comes not only from positive but also from negative identifications. We become very upset when we believe we see in a child aspects of our own personalities of which we disapprove; often these are tendencies in ourselves we have worked hard to overcome. In such emotional constellations, the advice to be patient, understanding, and loving is of no help. On the other hand, realizing at such moments that we see in our child something which is upsetting because we had or still have to battle against the same tendency in ourselves can make us comprehend that we actually are less perturbed about the child than about ourselves; then we understand that the problem lies first in and with us, and only secondarily in the child. This does make it easier to cope and helps us to avoid coming down hard on our child for something that is our problem more than his.

In fact, almost all parents are able to act reasonably, to be patient and understanding, as long as their emotions don't intrude—that is, in circumstances that don't evoke deep personal feelings. But where our child is involved, very many situations evoke such feelings. The trouble is that often when we think we are emotionally neutral and are behaving entirely rationally, we simply are not. An example may illustrate.

The greatest desire of two highly educated parents was that their only child, a son whom they had late in life, should become the kind of person they valued most: a cultured, widely read, thoroughly accomplished gentleman. They could see little good in store for him unless this happened. Still, they accepted his childish ways as long as he was very young and all went smoothly. But when as a teenager he became uninterested in schoolwork, although he continued to make passing grades and caused no special trouble, they became very upset by his passion for sports and his neglect of academic matters. They began to criticize him severely and made it clear how disappointed they were in him. The father particularly, a prominent scientist, fearing for his son's future, put him under great pressure to change his interests. But this failed to produce the wished-for results; what it did instead was to estrange the two, who had been very close until the father began to worry that unless his son took a serious interest in academic matters he would amount to little, or in his eyes, to next to nothing.

The son saw things differently. Neither he nor his father understood that the boy shunned his books because he felt it would be hopeless for him to compete with his father on his own ground, and hence chose to excel where he would not be in competition with his father, namely in sports, which did not interest his father at all. Unaware that this lay behind his lack of interest in what was most important to his parents, the boy experienced their criticism and worry about his future as doubt of him as a person—which it was. This, he felt, placed his very existence in question. The very persons he needed to have infinite trust in him, to believe in him, so that he could believe in himself, made him deeply insecure about himself, made him doubt himself and all he did. This hurt him very deeply and he resented it most strongly, which made it even more impossible for him to be and do what his parents wanted. His need was to become not an inferior copy of his parents but a person in his own right, and this they seemed unable to accept, or to approve of.

The parents were convinced that their motives were entirely rational, that for his well-being their son had to relinquish his present interests and become studious. So committed were they to what they desired for their son that it shed a negative light on all that happened between them and him. The son who, as a child, had loved his parents very much and still loved and admired them was only the more deeply hurt because these loved parents who were so important to him could now see nothing good in him and in what he was doing. He closed himself off from them so that their disapproval would not hurt so much; he became openly defiant, to cover up his deep disappointment in them. The situation at home became desperate for all three, so he spent most of his time with friends who shared his interest in sports, which the parents in turn resented since it took him farther away from them and from what they desired for him.

When the father sought advice about how to handle his son, he was assured that this was probably only a passing phase, that as the boy matured he was likely to recognize the merits of his parents' values and make them his own. But this reassurance fell on deaf ears, and the father finally in desperation sought professional help about what to do to change his son's way of life. He complained to the therapist at great length about his son, wanting to be told how to change him around. Eventually the therapist persuaded him to talk about his own childhood and adolescence and his relation to his own father. As he recollected what he had gone through in late adolescence, the father suddenly realized something that he had entirely forgotten, namely that he had actually undergone the same experience as a son, had reacted to his father as his son did to him. In the earlier generation the issue had been the father's determination that the son follow in his footsteps and take over the family business. Against this he had rebelled; he was determined to follow a career entirely different from the one into which his father had tried to force him, and so he became a scientist. This had led to a long period of estrangement, but eventually, with a heavy heart, the father made his peace with the son's refusal to fall in with his wishes, and eventually took pride in the son's real achievements.

Recognizing the parallel between his relation to his father and that of his son to him, the father was able to shift the nature of his identification with his own son from one based on professional choices to one based on life experiences: on the son's struggle to find a way to become his own man without having to compete with his father. This change was greatly facilitated by the father's belated realization—and until this moment he had been completely unaware of this—that one of the reasons he had not even been able to consider taking over his father's business was his conviction that he could never measure up to his father's success and would all his life continue to feel inferior to him. The eventual recognition of the parallel between his son's experiences and his own permitted the father not only to accept his son's way of life but to have the deepest empathy with the boy. Practically overnight father and son again became very close to each other and could once more love each other openly.

In both cases the fathers were completely convinced that they were motivated by the most sensible judgment of what was best for their child: the father of the scientist believed that the best and easiest way to succeed in life was for his son to take over his father's thriving business; the scientist believed that only an academic career could offer his son true satisfaction in life. What neither recognized was that behind these rational considerations were deep and mainly unconscious motives, the strength of which was taken as proving the merits of the conscious wishes. These unconscious motives were complex and manifold, but the most powerful were, first, an identification with the son and the wish to maintain it permanently by having the son live as the father had; and, second, an even more securely repressed unconscious wish of the father to maintain his superiority over his son, which was based on the belief that he would do not quite so well as the father in the same occupation. Thus both wanted, deep down, that their son be a somewhat less perfect duplicate of themselves, so that the bond between them would never be broken or changed by the father's superiority being put into question. In order to be able to act on these unconscious desires, both fathers needed to convince themselves that they were pressing their sons into a mold because that was what was best for the sons, that they were motivated by entirely unselfish reasons. They needed to believe this to keep doubt from coming to awareness, and to permit them to exert pressure on their sons in good conscience. In both cases the sons felt subconsciously what was taking place; hence their determination not to become secondhand replicas of their fathers.

The wish that a child should follow in his parent's footsteps is not simply due to a desire to maintain permanent parental superiority. It is rather based on a desire to continue a relation to a child in the form in which it was strongest and most satisfying to parent and child. Originally the parent's superior abilities guarantee the child's security and well-being; he loves and admires the parent who satisfies his needs. The child's later refusal to follow the life pattern of his parent thus threatens an old, well-established, and important element of the parent-child relationship: the parent's superiority in dealing with the problems of life, which in infancy and childhood had been an important bond tying the two to each other. How understandable it is, then, that the parent should wish this bond to continue undisturbed, through the child's taking up the parent's occupation, in which the parent is so much more knowledgeable. Since this wish is largely selfish, it remains unconscious and is replaced by the conscious conviction that such occupational choice is what is best for the child.

Matters are often additionally complicated because around the time the adolescent is asserting his wish for an independent existence the parent has reached the age when he begins to fear that his strength is declining. If so, the child's steps toward independence are experienced as a threat to the parent's potency, a threat which could be minimized if the parent's experience in the occupation which the child is about to enter would guarantee the parent's superiority, at least in regard to the child's work.

The jealousy of the mother whose beauty and attractive femininity are declining just as those of her daughter are coming into full bloom is immortalized in the Queen in "Snow White"; and so, similarly, is that of the father figure confronting the strength and achievement of his young successor in the story of King Saul and David. In these ancient stories, King and Queen try to destroy the young who are about to surpass them as age begins to exact its toll.

Modern parents' reaction to their children's coming into the flower of youth at a time when the parents are about to begin their decline is more often to deny that this is so by trying to remain as beautiful, as young, as strong, and as attractive as the child. Getting old is something to be feared in our culture. It does not need to be that, as the example of ancient China demonstrates. There the older one got, the more venerable one became; there parents had no reason to be jealous of their children's youthful successes, nor any need to compete with them in this respect. But our culture is youth-oriented. So anything that seems to threaten it, such as the growing up of one's children, is experienced as a threat to be warded off by trying to be, or at least to seem, as young, strong, and attractive as they are.

While in past times many a mother tried to suppress her daughter's budding sexuality so as not to be threatened by the prospect of the daughter's replacing her, today such a mother is more likely to compete with her daughter in respect to female attractiveness, if not also in youthfulness. Fathers try to keep up in fitness with their sons. Such competition on the child's level makes the parent seem more like an older sibling than a parent. Nevertheless, despite such competition in regard to youthfulness—which puts parent and child on an equal footing—the parent still wishes to retain his parental authority, which is largely based on generational difference and which such competition denies. It negates the parent's generational superiority, which the child needs for his security and for his ability to see the parent as a figure to be respected, not one with whom to compete.

Thus in a relatively new development, the child wishes to have a life of his own, different from that of his parent, which is difficult enough for many a parent to accept; also, matters are made much more complex psychologically when the parent wishes to be part of the child's life by being physically as attractive and proficient as the young are, at the same time expecting to be respected for his superior knowledge of life. This is for both parent and child a no-win situation as long as the parent remains unable to recognize the unconscious aspects of his rivalry with his child. If, on the other hand, the parent can consciously accept what is going on within himself, then, as likely as not, pleasure in his child's accomplishments as he enters the age when he is most attractive in his youthfulness will replace what had been unconscious reactions of jealousy, thinly covered by rationalizations about what is best for the child, and why it is to everybody's advantage when the parent is as youthful as possible.

If we remain unable to recognize what goes on in our unconscious, then our rationalizations—such as that the occupational choice we want our child to make is best for him—are often merely a thin overlay which nevertheless effectively hides the driving force behind our behavior—powerful emotions such as selfish identifications, desire to retain our superiority, even jealousy. Because we wish to do right by our child and to be intelligent, responsible parents, we are easily seduced by the reasonable aspects to disregard the emotional motivators behind our actions. Yet our children, so much more responsive to both their own and our unconscious, and so little moved by rational considerations, feel our emotional involvement quite strongly; understandably they are at times bewildered by it, when the issue seems to them of small objective merit.

If we should admit to ourselves that our emotions often dictate our actions vis-à-vis our child, we would also be much more responsive to his emotional response to us and our desires. While in the heat of the moment we may not be able to muster the patience and understanding we would like to possess, we usually can achieve such attitudes much sooner once we admit to ourselves that we have been carried away by our feelings. But the parent who firmly insists that nothing but logical, rational reasons underlie his behavior is likely to remain intractable.

Many a parent can say with justification—and usually also with considerable exasperation—"I tried and I tried to be patient with my child, but it did not work!" When emotions are not out of control, parents can be patient, but there do come times when emotions get the better of patience. When, on the other hand, we try to be patient because we have been *advised* to be so, regardless of our feelings, it does not come naturally, and then we are pretending with our children.

Whenever we are emotionally involved—and it is rare in an interaction with our child that we are not, at least to some degree—we act not only on the basis of advice received but also as our emotions propel us, and the combination is often unsettling. Fortunately, most of the time we act in accordance with the person we are, in line with what our life has taught us and made us be. Once we realize this and recognize how our own experiences condition our behavior, we become able to comprehend the deeper sources which determine what we do and how we do it.

A child's intuitive understanding, based on innumerable observations of parental actions and reactions in all kinds of situations, gives him a nearly unerring feeling for whether or not his parents act in accordance with their usual beliefs, values, and customary ways of doing things. The younger the child, the more all-consuming is his interest in his parents (and interest in drawing conclusions from his observations, although by no means always the right ones). If he senses that his parents are acting "out of character" (as they might if they follow advice without having first carefully pondered it and adjusted it to their own feelings), he will become confused and regard his parents' unusual behavior with mistrust.

As mentioned earlier, published advice must necessarily be of a general nature, a presentation of abstract concepts and conclusions which may, at best, be based on circumstances analogous to our own, although they can never fully duplicate the specific details of our situation. The same holds true for explanations and solutions volunteered with the best of intentions by relatives or friends. Their suggestions are based on their own experience, which, given the fact that they and their children are different persons from us and our children, does not quite apply to our situations. Each parent and each child is a unique individual; their life histories are unique, and so are their reactions to any particular situation and to each other in it. Furthermore, no set of circumstances is quite like any other set of circumstances. Most family tragedies, big and small, could be avoided if parents could free themselves of preconceived notions about how they or their children "ought" to be or act.

Robert Pirsig is correct—it is "hard to follow [instructions] in such a way as not to make mistakes. You lose feeling for the work." To be told that there is only one way to act robs us of creativity in finding our own solutions. The remedy against the loss of spontaneity, which leaves the parent-child relationship empty and mechanical, is not simply "being shown the overall problem," but being able to comprehend it fully *in our own way*, and on this basis to discover a creative way to resolve it in a manner germane to us. Comprehension comes from within, as we explore the problem and its ramifications, and from our own struggle to find a solution appropriate to our own and our child's personality. This is the theme of Pirsig's book, which describes a cross-country motorcycle trip taken by him and his son. During this journey, which symbolizes the father's own voyage of self-discovery, he tries to comprehend the overall problem posed by his relation to his son, in which is comprised his deeper understanding of himself; and along the way his view of himself changes radically.

Like him, all of us must struggle to understand ourselves better, not the least because our efforts to achieve greater clarity about ourselves make it possible for us to achieve clarity in our relation to our child, with a consequent enrichment of our life. Such understanding of ourselves around some issue of child-rearing cannot be handed to us by someone else, no matter how great their expertise may be; it can be achieved only by ourselves, as we struggle to remove whatever has obscured this understanding from our consciousness. Only our own efforts to achieve such higher comprehension lead to permanent personal growth of both parent and child. But all that any book can do—including this one—is to address some of the overall problems of child-rearing: their origin, meaning, and significance, and particularly, possible ways of thinking about them.

3

Parent or Stranger?

General propositions do not decide concrete cases.
—JUSTICE O. W. HOLMES

JUSTICE HOLMES SAID that general propositions do not and cannot decide concrete cases. He did not for a moment belittle general propositions; but he knew that for decisions on concrete cases a careful consideration of all their intricate details is necessary. Thus judicial decisions require something more than the wise application of general principles; they also demand careful attention to the always unique aspects of the concrete case in point. In the same vein, Freud consistently stressed the importance of an understanding of both psychoanalytic principles and the unique ways in which these reveal themselves in a concrete situation. Psychoanalytic writings, or training, can thoroughly acquaint the student with general problems and the vagaries of human development during life. Such familiarity offers a good chance for comprehending what may underlie the particulars of a situation; but this is only the starting point for careful deliberations of the individual case. The next step for a parent, as for a jurist or psychoanalyst, is to evoke in himself resonances with the overall problem and with the specific, concrete form in which the problem presents itself, so that his understanding will be not only rational but also empathic and emotional.

If advice from an outsider short-circuits this process of discovery, the parent may be seduced into believing that the struggle toward comprehension is unnecessary. But however correctly he may be informed or intelligently advised by being told what to do—as opposed to being stimulated to do his own thinking about it—the telling destroys his spontaneity in confronting the problem and his satisfaction in finding his own method of handling it. This matters a great deal in child-rearing, where complex emotions are involved at all times, and where we cannot help feeling that the best and only genuine solution is *our* solution. Seeking, with the help of others, such as by consulting experts, an *understanding* of the *overall problem*, with which one may well be unacquainted, is a reasonable way to proceed. But *acting* on the recommendations of others cannot evoke in us the feelings of confirmation that well up in us only when we have understood *on our own*, in *our own ways*, what is involved in a particular situation, and what we can therefore do about it.

As we struggle to find the right solution to an impasse, to understand how and why we and our child got into it and what it is all about, we invest much intellectual and emotional energy. Our children, attuned to their parents at all times, are aware of this, and they feel good about themselves in being worthy of such a great investment on our part. This indication of the depth of our commitment to them is often the most important ingredient in reaching them, and with it gaining our goal: a satisfying and hence successful parent-child relationship.

NORMS AND RULES

Being advised that our child's behavior is normal for his age is not very helpful. In addition, the concept is questionable: exactly what does "normal" mean where intimate relationships are involved? It means "average," but no child wants to be "just average"; nor do we wish our children to be just average. Our child, for excellent reasons, should be and wants to be very special to us, not just an "average" individual; he has every right to expect that he is very unique to us. So while the concept of the norm is statistically useful, it is utterly beside the point where the deep feelings between parent and child are at work. A concern with "normality" marks the intrusion of scientific abstraction into what should be a most intimate relation.

When we are happy with our child, we cannot believe for a moment that what he is and does is merely what every average child of his age is and does. Our love for him convinces us that he is very special, not just average. Nor would we be content if our child were convinced that we, his parents, are just average parents, neither better nor worse, neither more nor less concerned with him and his well-being, neither more nor less worthy of his love than are all other adults who in some other respects are, statistically speaking, like ourselves.

On the other hand, to be told that our child's behavior is "normal" offers little solace when our feelings are badly hurt, or when we worry that his actions are harmful at the moment or may be injurious to his future. It does not help me as a parent nor lessen my worries when my child drives carelessly, even dangerously, if I am told that this is "normal" behavior for children of his age. I'd much prefer him to deviate from the norm and be a cautious driver!

Thinking in terms of the norm in relation to our child belittles his singular importance to us, and that of our relationship, because it implies that we are comparing him to strangers. Our child may be average as measured from the outside through comparison with strangers, strangers to the deep intimacy of our living together. It is perfectly all right for outsiders to evaluate our child this way; nobody should expect more of them. But something happens to the parent-child relationship and to the parent's feelings about himself as a parent when he begins to look clinically at his child as would a stranger, assessing what his child has in common with hundreds of thousands of others and in which respects he differs from the norm, as he fits the child into his place in statistical terms.

The psychological studies which establish behavioral norms for various age groups deliberately neglect the innumerable individual differences which make each child unique. When they compare their own child to these norms, parents tend to overlook this, especially when their child exceeds the expectations of the norm. For example, some children easily perform well above average, and then all is well. But there are others who can do so only with extraordinary exertion. It would seem reasonable that parents worry about a child who puts himself under such inordinate pressure. As there are parents who urge the child who performs below the norm to "live up to his abilities," one might expect others to ask the overachieving child to stop doing so, fearing that he pays too high a price for it. But there are precious few parents who do.

One can cite even more telling examples of this attitude. The norms of adolescent behavior include the struggle for independence, the battle against restrictions such as curfews, and the defiance of parental values. Thus should their adolescent child fail to defiantly assert his independence, parents who are aware of the norms of adolescent behavior should be expected to require their youngster to act according to his age norm: to be defiant, recalcitrant, messy, subjected to wild mood swings; and if he does not do any of these things, they should encourage him to act more like a typical adolescent. Again parents seldom do this. When has a parent ever asked his child why he is acting so maturely when he ought to be in the throes of adolescent turmoil? I never heard the parent who requires that his child "live up to his abilities" academically also ask his child to act more adolescent—that is, to react more "normally" and thus negatively to adult requests. More frequently, parents tell their child who acts like a typical adolescent, with some reproach in their voices, that he should "act his age," and by this they mean more like a mature adult, when in fact the youngster acts exactly in line with his adolescent age and behaves in ways which students of this age group have established as the norm.

When our adolescent child defies us, makes us suffer, upsets us with his show of indifference to all we say and stand for, under such onslaught it is difficult to meet his behavior with equanimity because we have been informed that our child is "meeting his developmental tasks in typical adolescent ways" and that his worrisome behavior is but part of the "normal process of growing up and maturing." Being told all that offers little relief when we are anxious about his experimenting with drugs, or doing things which may get him into trouble with the law or endanger him physically—all quite realistic fears. But if we manage to develop the right attitude to his behavior, to have empathy with his state of outer and inner turmoil, then we may be able to help him cope with the difficult vagaries of adolescent life. We can hardly achieve this attitude by comparing our child and what he goes through— and what we go through with him—with established norms. Whatever may be normal for the vast majority, we want our child to be different, so that he will be safe and so that his adolescence will not be such an ordeal for us. As long as he as an individual is incomprehensible to us, no matter what the norm may suggest, we are unable to be truly accepting of him and his conduct, much as we try. And should we, through a sheer act of will, assume an attitude of forbearance and resignation because we feel that we cannot expect him to deviate from the norm of rebellion, our adolescent will realize that this sense of his "averageness" is behind our behavior; he will resent it fiercely, for nothing is more important to him than to be considered unique, different from all others, despite the fact that he is running with his crowd.

Is this, then, yet another no-win situation? Not at all, though it can easily deteriorate into one if our adolescent's obnoxious behavior provokes us either to fight him or to suffer in silence. What we must do is to develop, on the basis of our own inner experience, empathy for the great turmoil and pressures expressed by our child's behavior. We are best able to manage such adolescent crises well when we recall how we suffered in our youth from parallel problems at his age. Often these were more problems of discovering and of being oneself than problems of defying one's parents. Our memories are always of specific situations—how long could one stay out? in whose company?—and never of "meeting developmental tasks," nor of "normal growing up and maturing." Such recollections can induce us to have empathy with our child's troubles. What we remember of issues which we fought over with our parents, or wished we dared to fight over, helps us realize how petty the specific issue itself really is. The important issue is that we too wanted to fight free of our parents, and at the same time to remain close to them;

in fact, we too experienced a whole welter of difficult, connected, and often contradictory feelings.

If we remember all this, how can we not sympathize with what our child is going through? Realizing that what our child is doing is normal for his age leads, at best, to a resigned acceptance of his behavior. But sympathetic understanding derived from our own recollections bridges the gap between us and our child and forges a powerful emotional bond between us.

This all-important empathy springs from both our sympathetic efforts to understand what lies behind our child's behavior and our conscious and subconscious memories of our own parallel experiences which we see mirrored in his behavior. And here it really doesn't matter whether in our day we acted out our desires or suppressed them—just recalling them will help us guide our child through his difficult period in ways he can accept and use, and we can enjoy providing. For a child, or an adolescent, will feel more secure and will more readily accept parental guidance if he senses that his parent is acting authentically, true to his values and convictions and, most of all, on the basis of what he has learned through his own similar experiences.

RULES

The belief that there can be rules for dealing with one's child is inimical to an attitude of empathetic understanding, which can be derived only from our own experiences, which are as unique to us as are those of our child to him. Trust in rules saves us the trouble of having to think through each problem situation and feel responsible for its good resolution. Moreover, since all rules are based on generalizations, they disregard what is individual, and hence make us overlook what is unique in our child and in our relation to him.

In order to avoid having to examine the merits of each case and to argue it anew with the child, some parents like to establish rules, usually relating to how *the child* is to act or behave; very rarely do they feel bound themselves by rules. And some children like to be given rules: not only does it save them, too, the trouble of having to examine each time how they think and feel about a particular situation, it permits them to resent the rule rather than the parent who established it and now enforces it. (It is considerably easier to be angry at an impersonal rule than at someone who is very important to us, about whom we have very strong feelings.) It takes the resentment out of the personal context and relegates it to the realm of abstract considerations, such as the merit of the rule and its applicability in a particular context. But by the same token this takes the relationship between parent and child out of the personal realm and removes it into a theoretical and impersonal discussion, or resentment of rules. The child relates to the rule and what it implies rather than to the parent, the most important person in his life. Going by rules ultimately estranges parent and child.

While in impersonal situations rules have a certain advantage by sparing us the decision-making process, rules objectify and depersonalize. This is what Pirsig had in mind: practical though it may be to go "by the rules" when assembling an object, it is difficult not to become—or at least feel—enslaved by them. Rules are the enemies of spontaneity and positive feelings.

Once rules are formulated and more or less obeyed by the child, it robs parent and child of the real pleasure they both experience when the child spontaneously offers to do a task because he wants to be of help to us, or simply show us how much he appreciates what we do for him by reciprocating. Only compulsive persons like acting on the basis of rules, for their neurotic compulsions do not permit them to do otherwise. The rest of us experience little satisfaction in following rules, neither children in obeying them nor parents in enforcing them. Convenience there might be and frequently is in rules, but pleasure hardly ever; nor does doing things by rules enhance the feelings of parent and child for each other. Rules between parent and child, no matter what their source, objectify and mechanize what ought to be the most personal, the most essentially human, the most spontaneous of relations—the one that can give us new pleasures each day.

SECURITY: A PARENTAL ATTITUDE

In nearly all problems of child-rearing—even when circumstances are beyond the parent's power to influence or control, such as conflagrations, earthquakes, sickness, death in the family—the parent and the child are the problem, and they are also the solution. How the event is experienced by the child, and hence what it means to him, is what the parent can affect. For example, a child may experience a severe illness, even a life-threatening one, as a positive event because of the single-minded devotion and love it evoked from his parents, which brought them more closely together than at any other time.

Whatever the problem, insight into its central emotional and psychological aspects, their nature and origins, will certainly bring us closer to its solution. But to clarify these issues, parents must use their own insight, not that of some other person, such as one who dispenses advice. Freud discovered the fallaciousness of the idea that the insights of the psychiatrist would suffice to ameliorate the patient's problem; even when such insight was completely correct, it failed to benefit the patient. Only if the person himself arrives at insight into what is going on within him will he profit from it. This holds equally true for problems in child-rearing, even when these are rooted in conditions which are beyond the parent's ability to rectify.

During the London Blitz, Anna Freud was much impressed by the fact that while many children were suffering overwhelming anxiety, unable to sleep even during the daytime when all was quiet and showing a wide variety of severe neurotic symptoms because of the bombings, other children were able to take it all in their stride. She recounted how one little girl, beaming with joy, declared one day that she was the happiest person in all of London because while walking with her mother a few hours earlier in Hyde Park she had seen a tree sailing through the air, a most unique and beautiful sight which she alone had had the good luck to witness. That a bomb had exploded nearby and uprooted the tree, the child volunteered only in answer to questions. The danger of it all had made hardly any impression on her, compared with the spectacle that delighted her.

This lucky girl had a mother who, knowing that she was helpless to prevent the bombardment, tried to keep her daughter from being anxious about it. She did not permit the war and its devastations to interfere with the happy relationship which permitted mother and child to enjoy together what otherwise could have been a terrifying experience for both. Typically she remained in her flat even when advised to go into a bomb shelter because, as she put it, she did not want to awaken and frighten her daughter once she had fallen asleep. The fact that the mother also managed to sleep through most of the night despite all that went on also gave the child a sense of security. Had the mother worried anxiously all night long, her daughter would also have been unable to enjoy a good night's rest. Where some mothers might have visited their own terror on their children, this woman conveyed to her daughter only the immense happiness she felt that nothing unfortunate had actually happened to them. This happiness the girl experienced through and with her mother and ascribed it to seeing a tree sail through the air. Where many parents transmitted to their children their feelings about how terrible it was to have to endure the ordeal of the bombings of London, some other mothers like this one impressed their children with their happiness that they were able to *live together* through the bombings. The way in which a parent experiences an event makes for the child all the difference in the world, because it is on this basis that he interprets the world to himself.

Studies of many families during the London Blitz showed a near-perfect correlation between the levels of anxiety in the mothers—most fathers being away on military duty—and those in their children. Those mothers who remained in their flats during the night, sleeping relatively soundly through the bombings, by and large had children who did the same. Those who were devastated by anxiety had children who suffered from even worse anxiety. And while there were exceptions, among the families who could be studied in greater detail it usually appeared that those mothers who before the war had shown high levels of anxiety were those who suffered the most severe anxieties during the Blitz, as did their children. Mothers who in peacetime had been relatively secure, largely free of neurotic anxieties, were those who developed the least degree of anxiety during the bombings, and so did their children.

Parallel findings emerged a few years ago in the study of a southern California community which had been devastated by an earthquake. Some children suffered severe anxieties for prolonged periods, while others who went through the same or even worse experiences showed relatively minor aftereffects. The anxiety of the seriously affected children, although clearly precipitated by the earthquake, had roots antedating the triggering event, and their recovery was easier if their parents did not add their own worries to the children's anxiety.

The behavior of Israeli children in wartime also bears out these findings. These children were exposed to severe bombings and many other terrible experiences. In his study "Children Under Fire," Alfred M. Freedman reports that "parental fear reactions were especially traumatic for small children." On the other hand, if parents were able to keep their own anxiety within bounds and to offer strong emotional and social support, "there was little increase in anxiety among children subject to war stress."

On a personal note, when I was six years old, the four-story house across a narrow street from ours burned down in the middle of the night. It was engulfed in flames which lighted up the entire area, and many sparks flew over to our house, which the firefighters doused with water. I had been asleep. My parents woke me up and took me to the window to watch the unusual and exciting spectacle. Since they were calm and talked with me about the varying colors and forms of the flames, it did not occur to me to be afraid. Taking my cues from them, I felt not unlike the girl during the London Blitz. All I thought about was how nice it was of my parents to wake me up and take me to the front of the house—my room was in the back where I couldn't have seen the fire—so that I could see this rare and exciting spectacle. After the house had burned down, they took me back to my bed and I easily fell asleep.

During the following months, whenever I left our house I was confronted by the ruins across the street. I never felt anxious; it never occurred to me that I might have been in danger, or that our house might go up in flames.

All I thought was that it had been a most unusual experience, and that I had been fortunate to witness it. The security which I had felt emanating from my parents had kept me from feeling any fear.

It is a truism that the anxiety of the parent induces anxiety in the child; however, given the differences between parent and child, the source and nature of anxiety are likely to be different, and anxiety will be expressed differently. It is less easily recognized that if people react with very different degrees of anxiety to the same danger, then these variances must have their origin not in the situation but in something else. For ease of expression we may call this other factor the degree of a person's basic trust or distrust of life, the measure of his optimism and pessimism, the balance of his inner security and insecurity. Investigation in depth always reveals that these basic attitudes are formed long before the event, although the event itself in many cases in susceptible persons induces the overpowering expression of what, without the event, would have remained relatively dormant anxieties. Such people can gain insight into what had caused their original distrust, or deep insecurity and pessimism about the world and their likely fate in it. When this insight is achieved, these feelings are relieved to some degree, and anxiety about the present danger is much reduced. Once one realizes that much of one's present anxiety has less to do with imminent danger than with unsolved early experiences of which one had not been cognizant before, one becomes better able to manage the present situation and help one's children with their anxieties.

Parental anxiety makes life very difficult for parent and child, since the child responds to the anxiety of the parents with even more severe anxiety, and then their anxieties aggravate each other. Fortunately, under normal conditions people don't have to cope with bombings or natural disasters. But whatever the precipitating event, a parent's anxious reaction always creates extreme, even panic anxiety in the child, irrespective of the situation which might have aroused the parent's anxiety. The child responds to whatever aroused the parent's anxiety as if it were truly a world-shattering event.

The reason for this is that a child's shaky security depends, as he well knows, not on his abilities to protect himself, but on the goodwill of others; it is borrowed from the security of his parents. When they suddenly seem unable to cope, he loses whatever small measure of security he has had. His world collapses much more radically than does that of his parent, to whom, however anxious he may be, some coping mechanisms are still available, or who still has some minimal trust that society will come to his rescue, such as that in a conflagration the firefighters will soon arrive, that in an earthquake rescue operations will soon start, and so on. The young child has no such thoughts to give him comfort; security and comfort come only from his parents. If they seem frozen by anxiety or helpless in the face of it, the child feels desperate. Things are made worse for him because his estimation of reality is based on the signals he receives from his parents about it. When these signals suddenly convey to him that there is reason to be very anxious, then he responds not with feelings that would be appropriate to the possible danger but with those which are appropriate to the anxiety he feels coming from the parents. About the causes of their anxiety he is usually very much in the dark, or has only the vaguest notion, which adds to his helplessness. Any anxiety the source of which we are uncertain about is much more upsetting than an anxiety the source of which is known, since knowledge of the danger allows for taking measures to cope with it, at least to some degree.

A homely, everyday example of all this arises from a parent's difficulties in separating himself from his child when he enters nursery school. Separation anxiety is one of man's most basic anxieties; we are all subject to it in various degrees. As infants we fear being deserted by our main caretaker, who is usually our mother. What we experience of how this anxiety is dealt with by a parent will largely determine how we ourselves will manage separation anxiety later on in life. How this works, and that a mother's anxiety is what causes or severely aggravates that of the child, can easily be seen when a child is brought for the first time to nursery school.

Many, if not most, children are a bit hesitant about the new situation of nursery school and initially have some difficulty in separating themselves from the person who brought them there, usually their mother. Still, some children settle in easily, others only with the greatest and prolonged difficulty. All depends on the signals the child receives from the mother; if these convey to him that this is a safe and desirable situation, he soon contentedly enjoys the new experience. If, on the other hand, the child's initial difficulty in letting his mother leave evokes responses in her which suggest to the child that she, too, is worried about what may happen and does not wish to leave him, then naturally his initial upset is deepened. This seems to validate the mother's initial worries and increases them; the child wails and clings to the mother, who becomes more and more insecure about whether he will be able to manage the situation, whether the time was right for him to go to nursery school. Even when the mother openly reassures the child that it is safe to remain in school, the child by then is carried away by his anxiety and will not react to the mother's words, but only to her feelings of anxiety about the separation.

It is much more the mother's anxiety than the child's that keeps the process going. This has to do with the fact that the mother knows something the child has no inkling of: that this separation is only the beginning of a long process which will eventually lead to the child's having a life of his own, independent of his parents, as he progresses through the school years and eventually out into life. It is usually anxious anticipation of the much more severe separations to come which fires the mother's separation anxiety, present all the time in her unconscious as a result of her own infantile experiences. This process and its effects on other children in the classroom may be illustrated by an anecdote which I owe to a teacher of three-year-olds, although it could have happened in any nursery school.

In this teacher's experience, only those children whose mothers have a difficult time separating from them have a difficult time themselves separating from their mothers. A mother who truly feels that nursery school will be good for her child conveys this message through her behavior. She leaves the child on his first day in school without much hesitation, and he is soon happily engaged in activity with his teacher and the other children. But the story is quite the opposite if a parent has inner doubts about leaving her child; she conveys this by lingering on, making a move to leave only to return immediately at the first sign of uneasiness on the part of the child. Soon the child senses that his mother thinks that leaving him is not a good thing, so he begins to cry and to hang on to her. As soon as other children observe this, they become doubtful about being in school, and they begin to cry for their mothers, although up to this moment they have been playing happily.

Particularly interesting to this teacher, and indicative of what takes place in such situations, was the behavior of her own son. One day a mother on bringing her child to school for the first time repeatedly began to leave, only to come back and clasp her child, who with each repetition became more upset and clung more desperately to her. He seemed to sense that she didn't really want to leave him, and obligingly met her expectation of him by not letting her leave. As the child's crying increased and became more frantic, even though she was still right there, other children joined in a chorus of "I want my mommy." Eventually the teacher's son joined in, crying that he wanted his mommy, although up to that moment he had been playing happily, and had never before expressed any anxiety about leaving his mother in the morning when entering nursery school, even on days when she was not one of his teachers. On this day she was his teacher and stood right beside him; she would, as he knew, spend the rest of the day with him in class, and so she was baffled by his crying for her. When she pointed out to him that she was right there, he stopped in confusion; but after only a moment's hesitation he cried even more loudly: "Then I want my daddy!"

When the children observed the mother who could not separate herself from her child because of her separation anxiety, this activated their separation anxiety. In the throes of this anxiety they became desperate about their mothers' absence, because this is the origin and basic form of separation anxiety. The little boy whose mother was right beside him also became engulfed by the general atmosphere of separation anxiety. Since his mother pointed out to him that crying for his mommy made no sense, he had to find some justification for it, which he did in crying for his daddy (although his daddy had never accompanied him to school, nor had he ever cried for him when left at school). It was not his daddy's absence which made the boy cry for him, but his separation anxiety.

Unfortunately, it does not help in such situations for the teacher to confront the mother with her inability to let go of her child, or to impress her with the fact that her reluctance to leave the child makes things much more difficult for him. The mother may make a conscious effort that will lighten the moment, but this will not relieve her anxiety, which may then express itself in more subtle ways. So the well-meant advice to "let go" may help on the surface, but by making the underlying problem less visible, may prevent its solution and create more serious problems in the long run.

It would be better instead to invite the reluctant mother to try to recollect her own first day at school, what her hopes and anxieties may have been, and from what they sprang. Remembering how she felt then and what eventually helped her to let go of her mother will lead her to find all on her own ways to make the experience easier for her own child. She may also realize that her child's attachment to her is not broken because he has entered school; this recognition, as an inner experience, should give even an anxious mother the security she needs to let go of him.

A deeper understanding of the child's anxiety becomes possible when the parent uses the experience as an avenue for discovering how he himself felt as a child in similar situations. Such empathy allows him to understand the sources of his own involvement in his child's attitude toward school. Thus the most useful procedure in such a situation is one which helps the parent recollect his own childhood anxieties. From doing so, he will understand what role these played in his own and in his child's anxiety about separations. But usually a parent can discover this only after he has come to understand the true nature of his child's anxiety, which has next to nothing to do with what may happen in school but only with fear about losing his mother. The details of behavior, unique for each child, offer the best clues to what causes it, but if we can discover these clues (e.g., the little boy's changing his crying for his mommy into "Then I want my daddy!"), we will be able to appreciate what is really going on.

Whether or not parent and child really manage to discover the deepest sources of their interlocking anxieties, the fact that the parent delves into his past to understand his child and the child feels that his parent is doing this to help him brings child and parent much more closely together as they wrestle with the situation. This is why I say that the child and the parent are the problem, but also the solution.

Expert advice will not aid a parent unless he has the appropriate inner experiences; such advice may even prevent him from engaging in the laborious task of discovering the causes of his child's difficulties, and in the process discovering things about his own life and being which bring him that much closer to his child, and the child to him. The right inner experience, on the other hand, will reveal how superficial and impersonal even the best advice is when applied to a complex situation caused by highly personal feelings—a situation that may increase in complexity as new personal feelings are stirred up by it. This is why I wish to reiterate once again that in this book I do not wish to offer "expert advice" but to stimulate the reader to investigate feelings of his own which are involved in child-rearing issues.

4

Their Reasons, and Ours

> The first condition under which we can know a man
> at all is, that he be in essentials something like our-
> selves.
>
> —J. A. FROUDE

ROM THE MOMENT most couples know of the wife's pregnancy, they harbor feelings of hope and also of anxiety. They may wholeheartedly want to have the baby—a rarer attitude than is often assumed—but their anticipatory feelings can still be complex and perhaps ambivalent; and after their infant's birth the same will be true of their feelings for him.

Even before the child is born, parents have expectations—hopes and worries—about their future child, and about what the birth of a baby will mean to their lives. Whatever a woman may have anticipated about motherhood, the reality can change everything. A woman who didn't want to have a child may fall in love with her baby as soon as it is born, unable to understand how she could have had questions about the desirability of being a mother, of having a baby. Another who wished for a child may find it disappointing to devote herself so exclusively—or for so much of her time— to the baby; she may find infant care much more demanding and worrisome and much less rewarding than she had expected.

Here the attitude of the husband-father can make a great difference. If he feels that the baby occupies too much of the mother's interest, time, and energy and forces him to take a backseat in her life, this will be detrimental to him, his wife, his marriage, and the baby. On the other hand, his pleasure in having become a father, his loving support and actual help when the mother feels exhausted after birth and while nursing the baby, are of singular importance in making the addition of the infant to the family a truly happy event.

From the outset, the interplay between parents and child is continuous.

Thus very much depends upon the sentiments with which both parents, but particularly the mother, greet the new addition to the family and the change he makes in their lives. Each event in which they participate, whether great or small in itself, is meaningful as part of their relationship. It is not only the "weighty issues" that count in forming a child's personality and the relationships of parent and child to each other. Often, in fact, incidents which adults consider trifles are immensely significant to a child, providing the parental signals which guide the child's awakening to the world—and this they do, although parents are not aware that this is what they are doing. A parent's words and gestures, his tone of voice and facial expression, can suddenly throw a very different light on things, and so can his lack of response. Not only the parent's overt behavior but what takes place in both his conscious and unconscious mind significantly influence the child, giving him the cues upon which he bases his view of himself and of his world.

As mentioned initially, the goal in raising one's child is to enable him, first, to discover *who* he wants to be, and then to become a person who can be satisfied with himself and his way of life. Eventually he ought to be able to do in his life whatever seems important, desirable, and worthwhile to him to do; to develop relations with other people that are constructive, satisfying, mutually enriching; and to bear up well under the stresses and hardships he will unavoidably encounter during his life. In regard to all this, parents are not just the child's foremost teachers, they are those by whom and through whom he orients himself; all along he observes and studies them to see what they are doing and how they are doing it, and with what openly shown, denied, or even repressed feelings. Thus do his parents show him *who* to be and *how* to be it—the latter always flowing from the first. This knowledge is much more important for the child's present and future existence than the acquisition of specific facts or skills; useful as the latter undoubtedly are, their importance tends to loom too large in the minds of parents.

What are the important steps in the child's growing up, in his becoming ever more himself? Which are the crucial events in child-rearing? Some schools of thought emphasize nursing, weaning, toilet training, how it is done and with what feelings; others stress the importance of the way the child is talked to and played with, bathed, and put to bed. Some find most significant the parent's response to the child's anxieties and problems: how do they help him to cope? There are those who focus on the parents' feelings—their wishes for the child, and their worries; what they dislike in him, and what they enjoy; how they feel about each other and themselves. Not without good reasons did the philosopher Nietzsche assert: "The unresolved dissonances between the characters and sentiments of the parents survive in

47

the child, and make up the history of his inner sufferings." In fact, almost any of these events and conditions in the life of the child and of his family may have a tremendous impact on the personality and perceptions of one child, while the same or very similar occurrences may exercise none or only very limited influence on another. Much depends not only on the situation, on the context within which something happens, but also on the child's age, and on the nature and intensity of the parent's feelings.

The crucial factor is often the way the parent handles himself in a given situation, because this is the child's guide to the meaning of what is happening. The parent's inner attitudes, as expressed in his behavior in situations big and small, are what most affect the child; and it is impossible to judge at the time which event will loom large and which small in the child's experience. Our evaluation of an event's importance can be entirely at variance with our child's evaluation.

This is why a good enough parent is the one whose actions and reactions, whose approvals as well as his criticisms (both equally important and necessary in raising one's child), are tempered by thoughtful regard for his child's perceptions. Good enough parents endeavor to evaluate and respond to matters both from their adult perspective and from the quite different one of the child, and to base their actions on a reasonable integration of the two, while accepting that the child, because of his immaturity, can understand matters only from his point of view.

This is much easier said and understood in theory than it is set into daily practice. Such dual perspective becomes well-nigh impossible to maintain when the issue is one that arouses strong emotions or seems of great urgency to us, either for personal reasons or because it seems of considerable importance for our child's present well-being or his future success in life. We are convinced that our mature view is correct, and it is hard to step outside that frame of reference and seriously consider the matter from the perspective of our child. After all, what possible reason could he have to wish to do such unreasonable, impossible, or dangerous things? What possible motives can he have to desire so intensely, or to be so extremely upset about, what to us is merely a trifle?

The more significant and obvious an issue seems to us, the less we are apt to concern ourselves with possible reasons for the attitudes of our child. We realize that he is often swayed by momentary and irrational impulses, that he tends to act rashly, without concern for consequences—so why should we try to figure out what may underlie *his* thoughts and actions, or take *his* reasons seriously? And if a child's behavior seems outlandish or even perverse, many parents will consider it impossible to fathom his motives.

When a child's behavior is unacceptable, most intelligent parents try to reason with him, explaining his errors to him and expounding the superiority of their point of view. Unfortunately, once he's made up his mind, these well-meant efforts only rarely convince him to change his ways or his mind. The parents may indeed obtain obedience as long as he is little. But all too often, this leads them to believe that since the child now does as he is told, he has made their reasoning his own; or worse, they don't care what he believes, as long as he "behaves." The issue may be settled for them, but it is by no means settled for the child. He may be unhappy about being thwarted; moreover, he may hold a grudge against the parent who forced him to go against what he still considers good reasons, since he had no chance to find out if they were not.

An adult can easily outreason a child without even realizing that he is doing it, the parent's reasoning power being so much greater than that of the child, who is unable to marshal his arguments in a convincing way. But the grown-up's superior ability to argue and his greater command of relevant facts—so convincing to the parent—can be experienced by the child as simply the beating down of his opinion. And many a child, knowing from past experience that his parent will have his way, is angry or unhappy in advance about the outcome he expects, and is prevented by his feelings both from stating his arguments and from understanding those of his parent.

So the child feels outreasoned, and to be outreasoned is a frustrating and debilitating experience. It is a far cry from being convinced—it usually makes us shut up, but we hold on even more stubbornly to our own opinion. The child falls silent, and the parent believes he has won his point. When he asks, the child usually agrees that the parent is right, in order to stop arguments, and all too often the parent confuses compliance with conviction.

Parents are usually unaware that their reasons and behavior make as little sense to their child as his do to them. The more two persons are at cross-purposes, the less each is willing or able to give credence to the other's views and motives, and this applies equally to parents and children. Matters are made even more difficult for them by the fact that until he has reached adolescence, the child is unable to hold two or more differing viewpoints: things are either all one way or all the other. Only a mature mind can understand the varying views that different perspectives can create. So it is the parent who must recognize the wide divergence in perspectives, interests, concerns, and goals between himself and his child, and give his child's views their due, wrong though these may seem on the surface.

Unless at least one side in a conflict is able to consider seriously the other's point of view, there can be no satisfactory solution.

The child's utter dependence on his parent forces him to do as told, and the parent all too readily thinks the child's compliance proves he is convinced of the soundness of the parent's demand. But the child may follow his parent's orders only with great inner reservations, since he has no power to refuse. Being forced to act in opposition to one's beliefs is a very distressing, debilitating experience, even should the outcome of one's actions be favorable; we always think that if we could have acted as we originally wanted, the results would have been better. So the relation of parent and child to each other suffers whenever the parent fails to find a good solution to an impasse which has occurred between them in regard to some matter.

A solution with which both parent and child can be content is possible only after the parent has given credence to the child's wishes and viewpoints—naïve and immature though these may be. Giving credence to our child's thoughts and wishes does not mean we have to accept them as practical, or even meet them halfway when we are convinced that satisfying them would be wrong, dangerous, or impractical. The French have a saying: *Tout comprendre c'est tout pardonner*—to fully understand, to appreciate, the other's views and actions, is tantamount to excusing them. But this does not mean that one has to fall in with them. (This popular saying is derived from Mme. de Staël's "To understand all makes one very indulgent," which, in turn, probably originated in Goethe's "That which we understand we can't blame." Thus, what is required is an attitude of indulgence and an absence of blaming.)

Therefore the good enough parent will examine his child's motives, try to understand his thoughts, appreciate his desires so as to comprehend what it is *he* hopes to gain, and why and how. On the basis of such comprehension, we may be able to show our child on *his*, rather than *our*, terms how his method may be inappropriate to *his* goals, and how he may better achieve them. Then we can elicit the child's best efforts to gain what *he* is after, which he will not necessarily put forth to meet *our* goals for him, reasonable and important though these may seem to us.

To be taken seriously is immensely satisfying to a child, and so is the feeling of being understood by his parent. Since satisfaction is what he is after, receiving *these* satisfactions can be an acceptable compensation for having to modify his behavior.

In fact, most people need to feel that their views have been given full attention before they are willing and able to consider earnestly opposing views presented to them. It requires considerable inner security to be able to consider views opposite to our own, a security that children of all ages are lacking. But it becomes much easier if we feel that the other person is willing to make the effort to understand our reasons and take them (and with it, us) seriously—then we are open to other arguments, and perhaps even willing to accept them.

The most frequent source of discord between parents and children is parental insistence that their child perceive matters as they do and respond accordingly—despite St. Paul's warning that a child can think and understand only as a child, and not as adults do. Terence asserted, even earlier, that there are as many opinions as there are people. It is true: the same phenomenon may appear different even to adults of much the same background, for it is the sum of our past experiences and our particular frame of reference which determine our point of view. And things are even more complicated where parents and children are concerned, because the differences in their experience, objectivity, and understanding are much greater even than those between adults of dissimilar backgrounds. Therefore if we want our child to comprehend something in the way we think is correct, or beneficial to him, we ought to consider what the event or experience may mean to him, given his frame of reference. On this basis we can adjust our own conduct around the event so that it can make sense to him in the way we desire. This is not easy, not even in the most common everyday situations—not even when no external factor comes between us and our child.

We know quite well that we and our children view things from different perspectives, but it remains all too often a theoretical knowledge of which we lose sight whenever we are caught up in a situation in which our perspective and that of our child are in conflict. For example, supermarkets are places where mothers and children can easily get annoyed with one another. If so, usually both are convinced that their annoyance with the other is well justified, while that of the other is unreasonable—a conflict of views which bodes ill for both of them. As Anna Freud remarked, the toddler who wanders off into some other aisle, feels lost, and screams anxiously for his mother never says "I got lost," but accusingly says "You lost me!" It is a rare mother who agrees that she lost him! She expects her child to stay with her; in her experience it is the child who has lost track of his mother, while in the child's experience it is the mother who has lost track of him. Each view is entirely correct from the perspective of the individual who holds it. What actually happens is that mother and child each get attracted, or distracted, by something else: she, intent on the shopping, by the selections she has to make, and he by other things; or, more likely, he is discouraged because his mother is paying less attention to him than to the goods on the shelves. So he toddles off, or lingers on while his mother moves to another aisle. Suddenly aware of her absence, he goes to find her and soon, having moved to another part of the store in his search for her, realizes with terror that he is lost.

The mother understands the child's anxiety, but knowing that they are both still in the same store and that the child can easily be found, she may fail to respond to the *magnitude* of his anxiety; when his fear is translated into adult terms, it is like being suddenly and unexpectedly lost in a complete wilderness. The sensitive mother somehow recognizes this, but it can be very painful for her to realize that she projected her child into such a state of anxiety; it is hard for her to acknowledge that she was concentrating on something—the selection of goods—so unimportant when compared with her child's agony. Furthermore, she may resent his implied accusation of neglect, or feel that it was the child's fault and not hers that he got "lost." So, more to silence her feelings about having paid insufficient attention to her child than out of insensitivity to his feelings, the mother falls back on viewing the situation with the equanimity of an adult based on the resources available to an adult.

While hers is a correct view when seen from her perspective, it does injustice to the child's view, because he was first anxious about feeling lost, and now feels additional desperation about not being understood by his mother. It is this combination which makes such everyday events truly terrifying to the child if we do not react to them appropriately, to his inner experience of them.

Here, as in many parallel situations, if we respond appropriately to the child's terror, all is well, but if we are insensitive to his terror and annoyed that he makes such a fuss and draws attention to us, then the child feels even more lost. He is now not physically lost, but lost because he is misunderstood by the very person whose understanding of him and his needs is his only source of security. Since it was we who chose to take him to a place where so many things attract his attention and distract him from keeping us at all times within his sight, in his view it was all our fault.

Another example may further illustrate the difference in perspectives. A child drops a valuable object, and it shatters. His parent, upset about the loss, lets him see that he is annoyed by his child's clumsiness. But let us consider the incident from the child's point of view. He is anxious about the breakage and the reaction he expects from his parent, which, he knows, will be annoyed criticism. To make matters worse, he knows his parent would not have dropped the object in the first place. Thus his own inadequacy, brought so painfully to his attention, adds a devastating feeling of inferiority and inadequacy to his fear of parental ire. If parents could always keep in mind that this is a child's state of mind, they would not be so annoyed by the material loss. Instead, their hearts would go out to their poor child who is so unhappy about himself, unhappy about what he has done, fearful of parental anger. They would then disregard the breakage and concentrate on assuaging their child's deep distress.

These two very common examples illustrate how differently we respond when we can see things *both* from our perspective and from that of the child.

As a matter of fact, in the latter situation it is he who is more likely to grasp what happened from both points of view, if he can manage to sort out his vague and muddled impressions. Even if he does not wonder why we tempted him to get hold of this enticing object by having it within his reach, he is deeply unhappy about having been the cause of our distress, fearful of our anger, and unhappy about his inadequacy, which the mishap so clearly demonstrates. While we are concerned only with our loss, he is concerned with our loss and unhappiness as well as his own. One may wonder who of the two, parent or child, really shows a higher degree of understanding and maturity in this case.

It is not only different emotional perspectives that are involved, but also very tangible physical differences. Supermarkets are arranged so that their wares are within an adult's easy reach—but not necessarily a child's. What is on the shelves is within the child's sight and hence arouses his curiosity; but it is out of his reach, which frustrates him. And the precious object that an adult can hold securely is simply too big for a child's small hand. As long as our emotions don't get the better of us, we are well aware of these physical differences, and when we are in good contact with our small child, we try to bridge or at least reduce them as much as we can. We stoop down to the child's eye level; we sit on the floor with him—always to his great delight, for he instinctively recognizes our effort to minimalize the emotional and experiential distance between us. Similarly, when we lift him in our arms or let him ride on our shoulders so that he sees things from even higher up than we do, we give him great pleasure, since he can now observe the world from our perspective. Even then, however, important differences remain in our feelings of security; the child riding on our shoulders has lost touch with the safe ground, but we have not.

These are everyday observations. But only if we take time out to look at the world from a small child's point of view do we begin to understand how overpowering everything looks to him: how huge all objects are, how tall and frustratingly out of his reach. Adults see normally onto the top of the table, and all that is on it is within our reach. The small child, unless we lift him up or sit him in a high chair, never knows what is on the table and normally sees only its underside. Even when he is sitting in a high chair, most things on the table are beyond his reach, which often frustrates him. His position in the high chair is somehow precarious, because if he falls from the chair he will get hurt, and he can't get out of it without our help. When we stoop down or sit on the floor, both our adult perspective and the small child's perspective on the world are equally available to us; to the young child only his perspective is available to him, unless we make our perspective also his by lifting him up. He has to rely on our help to see things as we see them, to climb stairs, to cross a street—in all life situations, he must depend on adult assistance. This makes for a degree of insecurity and dependence which is hard to fathom once one has outgrown it, but if we want to be a good enough parent we must understand and empathize with it. If, in the supermarket (an example which is duplicated in any department store), we could for a moment project ourselves into the mind of the small child, we could find it impossible to be cross with him for having been flooded by terror when he lost sight of us. Far from being annoyed with him, we would share his relief that he has been found.

When we succeed in understanding how things look to our child when seen from his perspective, we somehow make his experience our own, not in his but in our way, and thus we gain a deeper comprehension of him as a person. If we do, we then respond to every situation not only in our own way, but simultaneously and vicariously also in his. This permits us to participate in what happens—not as equals, which we are not, but as equally important partners in the common and most important enterprise of our lives, which is living as a family.

Such endeavor at understanding and in a fashion vicariously experiencing what our child is experiencing, and responding to the situation on this basis, has often also the very valuable side effect of bringing to mind significant but long-forgotten similar or parallel incidents of our childhood. It allows us at last to comprehend more fully the meaning they then had for us, the role they played in the formation of our personality and picture of the world. If this happens, we become enriched by a better understanding not only of our child, but also of our own childhood. We may even be able at last to solve previously buried and hence unresolved problems of our own, now revealed under the triple and quite different lights of our child's reaction, of the reaction of the child we were when it happened to us, and of the adult we are now. To the degree we can achieve this, we and our child come closer to each other emotionally and as persons, and we grow able to know and appreciate our children as they are: children.

5

School Performance: A Divisive Issue

Do not train boys to learning by force and harshness,
but lead them by what amuses them, so that they may
better discover the bent of their minds.
—PLATO, *The Republic*, VII

SCHOOLWORK, AN ISSUE AROUND WHICH parent and child are frequently at cross-purposes, may serve to further illustrate how their different perspectives can easily become a stumbling block between them. The same concept or experience may have radically different meanings to each. Many a parent who worries about his child's academic progress is motivated by fears for the youngster's future; however, to the child, the future means tomorrow, or at the most a few days from now. His own school-leaving age, not to mention his adulthood, is an eternity away—incomprehensible and unimaginable. (Even many adults find it difficult to project themselves fifteen years into the future.) Just because the child has no comprehension of the future, what happens right now is all-important to him. Since his parent's dissatisfaction is in the present, it is all-important because of how it feels now; but the source of that discontent—worry about "the future"—makes no sense to the child.

This should not for a moment detract from the fact that for most children to succeed in school, their parents' interest in their learning is of paramount importance. But this interest ought to be with what happens on a daily basis, because this is how the child lives, and this is how he understands his life. The essential ingredient in most children's success in school is a positive relation to his parents and to their involvement in intellectual matters. The child wishes to have access to whatever is important to the parents he loves, wants to learn more about things that mean so much to them. He also wants to please them, to obtain their approval *right now* (as well as that of the teacher, and other persons of importance to him). Applying himself to his studies seems a relatively easy way to gain all this.

The child who does well academically earns many rewards; his parents are pleased with him, his teachers praise him, he receives good grades. Thus if a child who has the requisite abilities to succeed in school nevertheless fails, there must be very powerful reasons at work which cause his failure, reasons which, to the child, are clearly more compelling than the rewards for academic success. To understand them we must find the perspective on academic learning from which failure seems more desirable than success. It is the parental *a priori* conviction that there is no such perspective possible which prevents parents from comprehending why their child chooses failure instead of success. If parents would try to see things from a perspective which makes their child's choice comprehensible, they would understand their child's reasoning and find it logical; more important, the discord between them would be resolved and they would know how to reverse their child's choice so that it would become one more in accordance with their own.

Here is a case in point. Ella was a teenager whose parents were both high achievers to whom their own considerable academic success and that of their children were of greatest importance. However, Ella was a rather mediocre student, very different from her older brother, who was a true scholar, to his parents' obvious delight. Although Ella had previously received respectable grades in all her subjects, she suddenly failed in every one. Understandably, this caused grave concern to her mother, who had worried for years about Ella's indifference to education; she had tried without success to regulate the amount of time Ella spent watching TV, and to get her to read "good" books. Conferences with teachers failed to throw any light on the matter; they too were baffled.

Unhappy and confused about this situation, the mother sought professional advice on how to induce the girl to read good literature and do better in school. She spoke quite freely about her worries concerning her daughter's lack of interest in books, her loafing around with her many friends, her addiction to TV; she also described her own open and severe criticism of her daughter. The one thing she did not mention, until asked directly about the family situation, was that her husband had left the home several months before, to her great distress. This separation was obviously so painful to her that she wished to avoid even speaking or thinking about it, although she was well aware that it had created serious difficulties for her whole family. If possible, she felt her obligation even more strongly than before to see that her children did not go astray. But when she had pressed Ella to improve her performance in school, it had the opposite effect.

It did not occur to this mother that there might be valid reasons for her daughter's behavior, so she did not reflect on what they might be; instead, indolence and the seeking of shallow entertainment seemed sufficient explanations for the girl's extreme behavior.

Had the mother started out with the conviction that her daughter must have as good motives for her actions as the mother had for wishing her to read good literature and to apply herself to her studies, it might have occurred to the mother to ask herself why, when Ella had always gotten passing marks, she had suddenly failed in all subjects, not just in one or another. The mother, in her professional scientific work, was accustomed to consider carefully all the circumstances surrounding an event before she reached any conclusions about its cause. But where her daughter was concerned, she did not ask herself the appropriate questions. What important cause could account for such a radical change in her daughter's school achievement? What other significant events had taken place at around the same time as the academic failure? Had she pondered these questions, it would have been obvious that a great change in the girl's life had occurred, the departure of her much-loved father, and the possible connection between these two events would at least have been suggested.

The mother's own fear that the breakup of her marriage might have destructive consequences on her children, and her determination to prevent them, kept her from perceiving her daughter's true intentions. Her feelings of fear and determination were superimposed on her basic conviction that there couldn't be any good reasons for academic failure. Her low opinion of her daughter's motives, which she saw as laziness, flightiness, or empty-headed seeking of pleasure, and the distress this caused her prevented the mother from looking for a more generous explanation of her daughter's behavior. Convinced that her views of Ella's motives were correct, she simply could not see that Ella wanted exactly the same thing she did: to bring her father back to his family.

Contrary to this mother's idea that her daughter's failure demonstrated that she thought school was unimportant, in actuality the girl had absorbed her parents' conviction that academic success could change one's life and gain one's most important goals. She had therefore decided to use the great significance her father placed on academic achievement to gain what was her most important goal at present: to make him return to his family. Ella was clever enough to realize that if she went on doing passing work in school, her father would interpret this as meaning that everything was fine, despite his departure; thus there would be no need for him to return. Her utter failure—something which had never happened before—might worry him significantly to change matters back to what they had been: he would return home, and she would earn adequate marks again. Her complete failure in all subjects was a device to lure him back, although consciously she was only aware of a feeling that without her father to support her, she couldn't function. Her mother, involved in her own problems, wished only for no more trouble in the family, but Ella was more optimistic: she believed that her father's departure could be reversed, and she set out to achieve this in the best way she knew of. In regard to what was most important, she was in complete agreement with her mother, although her mother could not see this.

Thus, behavior which seems to indicate that parent and child are entirely at cross-purposes can actually be motivated by their seeking the same goal, albeit by very different means. True, Ella may have acted naïvely and immaturely, with little respect for the more distant consequences. But given her age, how could it be otherwise? Also, realistically, what else could she have done to make such a strong impression on her father?

More often than most parents realize, their child's goals are the same as their own. He is so deeply attached to them, his life so intertwined with theirs, that he cannot help but respond intuitively to what goes on in their minds and hearts. Children react often less to what occupies their parents' conscious mind than to what is at work in their unconscious, since children themselves are much more under the influence of their unconscious than adults are. So the child reacts mainly to the parent's unconscious. In his world, where the sun rises and sets with the parent, and where it seems that everything is possible to the parent, what we could call objective reality counts for little.

As deeply as the mother wished her husband to return home, being realistic and knowing the ways of the world, and most of all those of her former husband, she felt hopeless about it. Much as she wanted him to rejoin the family, she felt ambivalent about him because his departure had hurt her so much; she had mixed feelings about her former husband after what he had done. Since she was convinced that nothing would bring him back, it did not occur to her that the wish for his return could be motivating her daughter.

Ella's feelings about her father were not ambivalent, so she responded only to one side of the mother's ambivalence, the one that wanted to see the family reunited; since this side of her mother's ambivalence was in accord with Ella's own desires, she acted on them with great (though unconscious) determination, unable to understand why her mother could not see it Ella's way. Ella, living in the present, did not worry about her future—as her mother so strongly did—but felt real and constant distress about the loss of the father.

From her own experience, the girl did not know her father as a husband, or as an adult male with many interests outside the home. She knew him essentially only as her father; everything else about him carried little reality for her. Now that this relation, so all-important to her, was broken, she could think of nothing else but her wish to restore it. She was not able to see her parents' relationship as it really was; she saw it as the child wishes it to be. Given her perspective, the return of the father seemed much more possible, much easier to effect, than it appeared to her mother, so she set about doing all she could to make her own and her mother's ambivalent wishes come true.

The misfortune in this case was that Ella's mother, convinced that her daughter was deliberately defying her greatest wish for her, could not see that the girl was trying to accomplish what they both wanted most. She could not realize that in the long run, if her husband could at least be induced to function as a father, one failed school term would be a very small price to pay.

The feelings of which we are consciously aware may be likened to the visible tip of an iceberg—its smallest part—while its bulk, like our unconscious feelings and motives, remains submerged and invisible. Ella's academic failure was her response to her predicament, a reaction dictated by what are mainly submerged forces—that is, impulses which came from her unconscious. Thus it would be erroneous to believe that her failure in school was the result of a carefully laid plan of which she was more or less cognizant. The processes by which the unconscious operates are unknown, chaotic, and confused; the motives are very mixed up, often contradictory; and only some of these elements may temporarily come to awareness, in the form of fleeting thoughts which are immediately, or soon, pushed back into the unconscious. She may have briefly thought: "If I fail in all my subjects, that will really show my parents how badly off I am because of their separation; it'll make my father do something about me." But, afraid of such thoughts as much as of the consequences if she acted on them, she repressed them—which did not prevent them from pushing her into the action suggested by the thoughts, without her being aware of what she was doing and why.

Whenever deep emotions or complex feelings move us to action, it is likely that unconscious motives are also at work, that is, motives of which we remain unaware. Our behavior then is "overdetermined," meaning that while we are aware of some of our motives, some others which also influence our behavior remain unconscious, and often these are the ones that primarily move us. In such instances, our actions and our thoughts and feelings result from the confluence of many different strands, the varied residues of much earlier experiences and feelings. Thus, Ella's failure in school, in addition to being unconsciously intended as a demonstration to both parents of how destructive their separation was to her, in all likelihood was in part also the culmination of other psychological processes, some of long standing, going on in her unconscious. If one applies to the problem of this mother and her daughter what has been learned from many similar situations, one may conclude that the basis for Ella's behavior may well be sought in much earlier experiences, antedating the father's withdrawal from his family, which may have simply exacerbated what had been going on in her mind for a long while. Her earlier inability—not refusal, as her mother thought—to be interested in good literature may have been the result of her long-standing perception that her parents were more committed to culture and literature, and all it stands for, than to herself as the person she was. She may have felt that they spent far too much time on what interested them, and far too little on her, so she came to hate what seemed to occupy all her parents' interests to the degree that she was unable to involve herself in it.

Whether it is true to fact or not, all children feel exactly this way at times—that their parents are far more interested in other things than they are in them. Then everything depends on whether the parents' behavior sufficiently counteracts such fearful thoughts of the child, making him believe that he indeed stands in the center of his parents' interest and affection. This is why predominance of parental approval for what the child is and does is so important. Only when he is basically sure of parental approval does the occasional criticism of the child's behavior—which is unavoidable as he is being educated—become bearable without doing damage. The dangers here are either destroying the child's self-confidence and trust in his parents' goodwill, or inducing anger at and rejection of what the parents stand for and defiance of their wishes, which seems to have been true in Ella's case.

The great pity in this situation was that Ella was unable to explain herself to her mother. She did not consciously know why she was uninterested in schoolwork and found the "good" books her mother pushed on her unattractive. But even if she had known the reasons for her behavior, she couldn't have expressed them because she knew they would be entirely unacceptable.

It is sad when parents fail to realize how terribly important they are to their children. If her mother had examined Ella's rejection of good literature from this perspective, she would have had to ask herself: "Why can't my child be interested in something so vital to me and to her father?" And she might have concluded: "Just because it *is* so important to us!" Which might easily have led to the recognition that Ella resented good literature because she wanted herself to be what was most important to her parents. This would at least have suggested a different approach to the problem than haunting the girl with criticisms, for then the mother would have seen how vulnerable her daughter really was, how much she needed her parents' positive attention and affection.

The solution to this, as well as to most other parent-child deadlocks, is *not* to try to make the child obey our wishes, which parents so often see as the only acceptable resolution, and on which they tend to concentrate their efforts. While we may have our way for the moment, we get it by defeating the child, which augurs badly for his self-confidence; moreover, in the end the child may defeat us, not necessarily in regard to the specific issue at hand, but in other and possibly more important battles. And a wedge is driven between us which contributes to our child's eventual alienation from us, as he grows up.

Since the child cannot see beyond the moment, or grasp the idea that there might be other ways to solve a problem than the one he has in mind, it must be the parents who find a solution that does reasonable justice to both their views and those of the child. To achieve this, we must understand and give credence to our child's motives. To discover what these are, we ought to start with the assumption that he, being *our* child, like us can be motivated only by what he considers good causes. (These, of course, are colored by his perspective on things, his age, and the particular conditions of the situation as he sees them.) When we proceed in this way, we give our child the feeling that we are *with* him in trying to find a solution to the issue at stake, not *against* him and his desires. Then we may safely raise the question whether the way he goes about gaining his purposes might not be improved, whether by putting our heads together we might not devise a better way for him to achieve his goals.

To proceed in this manner wouldn't be so hard if we only could be rational in dealing with our child, since the most basic principle in the search for justice is to give the other party the benefit of the doubt. But our intense involvement with our child makes us unhappy if he acts against our wishes. It hurts us so much if he does, that our emotional reaction prevents us from being able to believe that anyone who hurts us could have good motives for doing so. To make things even more difficult, this same close involvement with our child—after all, it was we who set him into this world, taught him all he knows, took care of him day and night—leads us to believe that we already *know* what his motives are. Therefore we feel no need to carefully search for them. A strange paradox—it is the very strength of our love for our child which causes us to be less than just to him. Only when we couple emotional closeness and empathy with sufficient objectivity to view things from his perspective can we discover, or he reveal to us, his true motives. For this we must be able to step—temporarily, for purposes of examination and discovery—outside our own frame of reference into that of our child.

All parent-child situations are loaded with feelings. This is inescapable, but only as it should be, since only parental actions which are imbued with positive feelings for our child convince him of his importance to us, an experience he desperately needs to be able to believe that he can be important also to others. In fact, painful as it is to a child to elicit negative emotions from his parent, it is better than nothing at all. Emotionally cold and indifferent parents are likely to produce either emotionally frozen or violently angry children.

But there are also serious dangers here. Parents who are very upset or angry about something that has no direct bearing on the child may become excited over a minor infraction and thus discharge their pent-up emotions. The child instinctively recognizes what is happening and deeply resents it. Like all of us, he wants to be the recipient only of those emotions which truly pertain to him.

Another pitfall, and one into which otherwise very reasonable and concerned parents often fall, is the situation in which the parent believes himself to be emotionally involved with the child, while the child's perception is that the parent is really not at all concerned with him. This may be the case when a parent strongly emphasizes the need for academic success and overreacts to any academic failure. Our worries about our child's future, about his standing with teachers and classmates, about his self-confidence, maybe even about the family's reputation, can lend a tinge of passion and too strong a fervor to what otherwise would be a perfectly rational desire. Unfortunately, some children experience this concern about schoolwork negatively. Under certain circumstances, our child may come to feel that we are only interested in his academic standing, and not in him as a person. This may induce him to hate these studies, which he believes are more important to us than *he* is. It is but one of many situations in which a parent is sure that all he cares about is his child, while the child is sure that his parents care only for his achievement, not for him.

Here again, if we try to see things from the child's perspective by projecting ourselves into some parallel situation in our own lives, we usually can credit the child's viewpoint. For example, many of us have had the experience on our job that others were interested only in our work achievement, no matter how little merit or pleasure we found in it or how much exertion it demanded. In such circumstances, we feel used rather than appreciated, treated as an object rather than as a subject, as a producer rather than as a person.

But where our child and his schoolwork is concerned, we are convinced that our interest in and concern about his performance is tantamount to concern for him, and we also expect *him* to believe this. But this is not how it feels to him. And it is neither laziness nor lack of interest that keeps him from applying himself to his studies. It is the great disappointment he experiences when he believes that we are more concerned with his performance than we are with *him* as a person. In consequence he may come to resent school and all it stands for, to hate schoolwork to the degree that he is actually unable to do it. Who of us can attend successfully to something we hate?

Another child, who for some reason feels defeated by his parents, may refuse to do well in school as the only way he can do battle with his parents, and possibly inflict on them a reciprocal defeat, equal to that which he thinks his parents have inflicted on him. And yet another, who needs to prove to himself that he is not a puppet whose strings are pulled by parents or teachers, confirms his power by a defiance that takes the form of failure in school.

Although I have said some children "think" that it is schoolwork which causes their difficulties with their parents, actually much more often they harbor vague but nevertheless extremely upsetting *impressions*, so painful and anxiety-creating as to be excluded from conscious awareness. Once repressed, these impressions become inaccessible to the child's conscious mind, but they continue unabatedly to exercise a powerful influence over it. The result is that the child becomes unable to attend to these hated studies, although he has no idea why he hates them so much, or why he has to shun them at all costs, even the most feared cost of severe parental disapproval.

A strong desire which we repress in order to protect ourselves from acting on it continues to exercise its pressure in our unconscious and does so with much greater force, since our rational mind can no longer exercise any control over it. To make things worse, we no longer know why we had the desire, or even what it was. What originally was a wish to act in a certain way now becomes an irrational power compelling us to act in ways we can't explain or control.

This is the strange contradiction which makes repression and its effects so hard to understand; what was repressed, so that it would have no power to induce us to act, becomes the very force that induces us to act. If adults have a hard time understanding this—the workings of the unconscious—how could children possibly comprehend it? If anything, children become even more angry because they cannot stop themselves from doing something they consciously do not want to do, such as defy parental wishes. When their parents reproach them about their schoolwork, for example, it makes them feel truly desperate about themselves, since they cannot make themselves do what would please both them and their parents.

To avoid having to recognize that he cannot make himself do what he would like to do—a most frustrating and truly frightening realization of one's powerlessness to control one's own actions—the child is forced to deny his impotence to himself by claiming that he does not *want* to do what he cannot make himself do. How else can the child explain things to himself?

Freud's seminal paper "Repression," written in 1915, today seems to relate directly to this problem: "In the case of compulsive neuroses, one doubts at first what one ought to consider as having fallen into repression: a libidinal [i.e., a loving] or an inimical striving. This uncertainty is due to the fact that a compulsive neurosis presupposes a regression through which a sadistic striving has taken the place of a tender one. It is this inimical impulse directed against the loved person which is subject to repression. . . ." To which one could add: just because this person is loved so much. The more one loves a person, the greater is the necessity to repress completely any negative feelings one has against him.

Thus if one were to ask a child unable to study—because he originally resented studying and wanted to defy his parent on this issue, but who out of anxiety has repressed this wish to defy—whether or not he loved his parent, he could unhesitatingly say: "Yes." And it would be a true answer, because it was this love which caused his resentment that school achievement should be more important to his parent than he himself. The notion that by not working in school he was defying his parent the child would reject as incomprehensible, because this motivating idea is repressed, and thus unavailable to his conscious mind. If asked why he does not study well, when the parent whom he loves desires it so much, the child, completely baffled by this contradiction, will only say: "I want to study, but I just can't." This is all he consciously knows. No wonder that both parents and children are confused by this paradox.

I mentioned initially that what goes on in the parent's unconscious strongly influences the child; it is also true that the parent, without knowing it, responds significantly to the workings of his child's unconscious. In other situations, parents usually recognize their obligation to accept and respond positively to the child's limited ability and knowledge, and they make all possible efforts to find solutions to the problems which the child cannot handle alone. But when conscious parental anxiety about the child's future because he is failing in school becomes aggravated by the unconscious feeling that this is an act of defiance, then many parents lose their patience. Sensing this unconscious rebellious element in their child's behavior, they tend to exert ever greater pressure on the child. This pressure, and the intensity of the emotions the child feels at work behind it, are taken by the child as clear evidence that only his performance is truly important to the parent, and so his feelings get badly bruised. This experience feeds his unconscious defiance and may aggravate it, so that now he resents not only school, but also his parent. This, in turn, annoys the parent more, and everyone grows increasingly miserable.

Attempts to ameliorate such situations through remedial education usually have little, or at best only limited, effect, since the original conflict was between parent and child, not between child and school. No matter what may be achieved by a professional working with the child to improve his academic performance, the underlying, unconscious conflict will not be resolved; that can be accomplished only by the parent, who must first stop pressuring the child to achieve, and then relieve the child's anxious feelings that his parent is more involved in his performance than he is in him.

Once parents recognize that the child's inability to perform is due to resentment based on a belief that his performance is more important to his parents than he himself is as a person—with unique needs, desires, anxieties—then their efforts to convince him that they are really only interested in him, love him, and want him to be happy will radically change the situation. Their explanation that their worries about his academic performance were only a relatively minor part—and as they now realize an erroneous part—of their great concern for his well-being will be somewhat reassuring. If there is also a change in the parents' attitude which comes with these realizations, this will permit the child to become conscious of what had been his motives in refusing to perform academically. If the parents can now grasp it all, the child no longer needs to keep his motives repressed; what the parents can accept about him the child can accept about himself. So he becomes more or less conscious of what has been going on in his unconscious, and thus his motives become accessible to his conscious control; he is now free to decide whether or not he wishes to succeed academically.

In the theoretical terms Freud used to explain a compulsive neurosis, the unconscious inimical urge to defy the parent has replaced the original loving tendency, which, the child feels, has been thwarted and rejected by what seemed the parent's single-minded insistence on performance. But when the unconscious fear that he is not loved has been removed by the parents' changed attitudes—the demonstration of their acceptance of the child as he is—the loving impulse no longer needs to be repressed and replaced by its opposite, but can assert itself openly.

Even more pernicious than poor school performance is "school phobia": the child's refusal to go to school at all, because the idea of having to go to school evokes unmanageable anxiety. While it may have a variety of causes, the most frequent one, particularly in a young child, is probably the wish not to grow up, to remain forever his parents' little child. Children know that going to school means to grow up, and that this implies giving up more childish satisfactions. But this wish alone rarely provides a strong enough motive for school phobia, unless it becomes combined with the much more potent anxiety that in growing up the child will lose his closeness to his parents, especially to his mother.

Some children who are forced to go to school despite their anxiety about it develop severe psychosomatic ailments, illness being an acceptable reason for staying home. They may develop such symptoms as compulsive vomiting, a drastic expression of the feeling that the idea of school makes one sick to one's stomach, or migraine-like splitting headaches, as if to express that their head can't stand what goes on in school. A girl who had been forced by her parents to go to school despite her desperate pleas to be permitted to remain home became anorexic and through not eating so weakened herself that there could no longer be any question of sending her to school. Usually the symptom the child develops is overdetermined in the sense that it goes back to some other psychological difficulties, which have become merged into the anxiety that prevents the child's going to school. For example, in the case of the anorexic girl, school phobia reactivated severe infantile conflicts with her mother which had centered around forced feeding, the need for which originated in the mother's rejection of her baby; in turn, the infant reacted with a refusal to eat.

In many instances the largely unconscious motive is the child's fear that going to school will mean loss of close contact with his mother. Sometimes this anxiety is aggravated by the notion that younger siblings who are still at home will displace the schoolchild in the mother's love and attention. Illness becomes a way not only to stay home, and thus make sure that one will not be forgotten, but also to get even more of the mother's attention than before; the care the child's illness requires represents a secondary gain, which makes staying at home, close to the mother, even more attractive.

In several such cases, assurance that the child would not have to return to school, when experienced by him as a seriously meant promise the parents had every intention of keeping, was sufficient to make the illness disappear in a relatively short time. It was then replaced by the child's comfortably remaining at home for some time and making adequate academic progress through being tutored, after which he was quite ready to return to school out of his own free will.

This remedy doesn't always work, particularly when the underlying cause is a more generalized severe fear of growing up. In one extreme case a child had been conceived as a replacement for the parents' first daughter, who had suddenly died at age thirteen. The second child, also a girl, knew not only that she was a replacement, but also that her parents wished she would be exactly like her dead sister, whom she had never known. This gave her the idea that she would have to die at the same age, thirteen. She could not help getting older, a process that was symbolized for her by progressing through the grades at school. Saving her own life became an all-consuming obsession, and she did what she could for herself by refusing to attend school, since it had become for her the symbol of getting older. She was cured only by prolonged therapy which convinced her that despite her parents' wishes, she was not a duplicate of her sister but quite a different person.

The tragedy of such situations is that parental efforts to get a child to go to school are viewed by him as proving that they want, if not to get rid of him altogether, at least to stop him from being a child. Efforts to force such a child to go to school are not just counterproductive, they are the worst the parent can do, since to the child it seems to prove how justified his fears are. School, and all it stands for, indeed produces an estrangement between child and parents in this situation. It is essential that parents behave in ways which convince the child that he doesn't need to use such extreme methods— that come what may, he will never lose their love and affection.

In cases of such, or similar, difficulties, parents must develop empathy with their child's predicament and realize that he is suffering from his feelings of insecurity in general and from his doubts of his importance to his parents, as the person he is, in particular. Only this empathy can offer a chance for a solution to the impasse in which child and parent find themselves when the child refuses to go to school or cannot achieve adequate scholastic performance. An important factor which allows parents to develop this empathy is the realization of their tremendous importance to their child. Unfortunately, the child's defiance makes this recognition difficult, since it seems to negate our importance to him. But the very intensity of his refusal to comply with parental wishes should be taken as evidence of the intensity of his emotional involvement in the issue. These emotions express deep commitments, and not just a preference for games and television over "hitting the books." Once parents accept the notion that it is their singular importance to their child that has created the impasse, much of their annoyance at being defied is dissipated, and they can begin to find ways to show him that they do *not* simply identify him with his performance.

But to be able to do so, parents must also have, or develop, trust in their child, an inner confidence that their child will do all right in life. The child needs our trust in him, and in his ability to master life, to give him the confidence to actually do so. Doubts that he will succeed—these are, after all, the source of our worries about his school performance—are utterly destructive to a child who already harbors doubts about parental love. In fact, our conviction that he will succeed is what he needs most in order to be able to do so. It is our trust in our child that creates in him a basic trust in himself, a confidence about his own abilities. Psychoanalyst Erik Erikson has written eloquently and at length about this trust, detailing that its presence or absence determines what the future life of the individual will be.

A child's unconscious need to defy his parents is not only a most frequent but also possibly the most intractable situation in which a child, out of psychological causes, feels unable to do as well in school as he could. If this need is not defused, this defiance may later on be reflected in delinquencies, use of drugs, dropping out.

Of course, there are also other reasons for poor school performance, such as the need to assert one's independence. And the good enough parent will empathize with this need as well. If we as parents can empathize with, for example, the child's need to assert himself by rejecting schoolwork, or his fear that he may become a puppet if he does as others wish him to do, then our attitude toward him will be entirely different from what it is when we attribute his lack of academic achievement to laziness or lack of ability. Empathy changes our critical attitude to an open one: we see that our child's need to be his own person may cause him to want to decide for himself whether or not he will attend to his studies. We wish he would do better, and we try to help him, but at the same time we feel an impulse of pride that he is already stretching his wings—although in an inappropriate way— by asserting himself even against the established authority of the school. We may even decide that his behavior augurs well for his future! Such a positive view will surely counteract any fear he may have that we are more interested in his achievements than we are in him as a person, and will help us eventually to rekindle his interest in his studies. Accepting the validity of his motives, or finding the perspective from which he sees things, permits us to find a way around the impasse without neglecting our own goals. When we approve of his wish for independence, we make him feel good about himself; thus supported by his parent in his major concern of the moment, he may come on his own to see that rejection of schoolwork is neither the only nor the best way to be his own person. On the other hand, this need certainly will *not* be satisfied by putting pressure on him to study, which will only serve to convince him his parents and teachers do see him as a puppet and are trying to pull his strings. Parental acceptance of the need for self-assertion, on the other hand, may help the child find other and less destructive ways to assert himself so that he no longer needs to do so through rejection of learning in school.

When we assume our child believes his own motives are good ones, we nearly always discover that this is true, although these motives may be based on a very immature view of the world; but being a child, what other view could he have? If we proceed on this assumption, we soon discover that our child's reasons and ours, which seemed worlds apart, can in most cases be reconciled quite satisfactorily. This requires goodwill on both sides, and perhaps considerable patience on ours. But these are not so difficult to come by, after we have become able to comprehend what moves our child and able to appreciate it. When we understand what are or what may be his motives, not only will communication between us be easier and more pleasurable for both, but our empathy with our child will result in greater appreciation of him, and therefore in greater pleasure and satisfaction in being his parent.

6

Our Common Humanity

Homo sum; humani nihil a me alienum puto. (I am human; I consider nothing human strange to me.)
—PUBLIUS TERENTIUS AFER

LLA, DISCUSSED IN THE PREVIOUS CHAPTER, is a typical example of a child who truly does not know why she reacts to her studies in certain ways because she has completely repressed her reasons and thus does not understand them herself. Even if she wanted to explain herself, she would be unable to say to her mother, "I hate reading good books because they are more important to you than I am"—not out of fear of any consequences this might have for her, but because her reason is so deeply repressed that it is unavailable to her conscious mind. The same is true for children who don't know why they suffer from illnesses that prevent them from going to school, for the toddler who is too young to be able to tell us anything, and for the older child who, when he is carried away by his emotions—particularly by anxiety—can only scream and cry. None of them can tell us; what then are we to do?

One mother who came to me for advice was quite exasperated by the unreasonable behavior of her little boy. Asked to describe a recent, typical, or drastic example of his behavior, she told how on a visit from their suburban home to the big city he had suddenly started to scream and refused to budge, just as they were about to cross a busy street. It exasperated her because of the spectacle he made of them as she tried to get him to move on to complete their errands. What should she do in such a situation?

I don't like giving advice in such matters, because I believe that in such intimate relations where such strong emotions are at work as exist between a mother and her child, a parent must find his own solution. But I did suggest that she try to imagine—difficult as it is to do so, she being a mature, well-organized adult—what could make *her* suddenly scream, or at least *feel* like screaming, in the same circumstances. It only took an instant for her to realize that she might react this way if she saw something like a serious traffic accident. In a flash she understood that her son must have been terrified by something he saw or imagined. And as she pondered this, she surprised herself by remembering that when she had been about her son's age, she sometimes had been terrified that she might get lost and be unable to find her way back home. It had never occurred to her that her son might have been overcome by something similar. She had been right there at his side; how could he fear becoming lost? But now she realized that her parents' presence had not always been sufficient reassurance against *her* fear of getting lost; even when she was with them she had been anxious that they might somehow get separated and be unable to find each other. That the boy might have feared something similar occurred to her only after she recalled this major anxiety of her own childhood, but once she arrived at this point in her ruminations she felt a deep sympathy for her son in his terror, quite different from her previous annoyance at his "unreasonable" behavior. When I suggested further that her son might have feared not just for himself but possibly for her too, afraid that she might get hurt crossing the street, she immediately understood how alarmed he was at the possibility of finding himself alone in a strange city where he knew nobody, nor his way around, nor how to find his way back home.

Fear of abandonment is a major childhood anxiety, and the child can imagine many ways it can happen. Parents in this mother's situation reasonably explain that there is no danger; but when we are overcome by terror, rational explanations don't affect how we *feel*. The parent's composure demonstrates that he is in command of himself and the situation, but the child's emotions and fears still overwhelm him. And if he thinks his parent does not appreciate the degree of his anxiety, then the parent's unruffled security is not a help but a hindrance. The parent seems to be speaking about an entirely different world; what he says about this other (adult) world does not apply to the child's own world and does not appease his terror.

If we think back, most of us can remember being terrified as children, perhaps when we entered an unfamiliar dark house or slept in a pitch-dark room. When we cried out that we saw something lurking in the dark, our parent explained carefully that there was nothing to be afraid of, but if his tone of voice and demeanor revealed that he thought we were being silly, we were convinced that he simply did not know all the terrors blackness might hold. If, on the other hand, he showed that he empathized with our fear, then we were reassured and our anxiety was reduced, because we felt we were no longer alone with our anxiety.

The parent who remains distant from our terror is not *with* us in the situation; he remains experientially outside of it. But the parent who conveys that he has empathy with our terror, who shows that he considers it legitimate and real, makes us feel that he knows what he is talking about. This is why we can trust what he is telling us. We ought to remember this when confronted with a situation like the one the mother found herself in. If we respond to our child's emotional state rather than to our objective assessment of things, then continuing with our errands will seem not very important, while alleviating his terror will take precedence over everything else. To reduce his terror we will try to soothe him, pick him up and hold him safely in our arms, or in some other way reduce his terror, rather than expect him to accept reasonable explanations at a moment when the degree of his anxiety makes this impossible for him.

When the boy froze in terror, which the unaccustomed bustle of the big city evoked or increased, he was probably more incapacitated by a feeling of complete inadequacy than by specific anxiety about the traffic and possible accidents. A similar feeling may have been the cause of his mother's childhood fear of losing contact with her parents. For a long time, she had no conscious memory of this anxiety, but when she became aware of it, it helped her to recognize the emotions that held her boy in their grip. Years later, she told me that her subsequent efforts to imagine the circumstances that might make her wish to act as her son did, often accompanied by memories of her own childhood, worked very well for both of them. Summoning such empathy would change the situation from one in which she and her son were at cross-purposes to one where she felt, if not exactly as he did, at least strongly *for* him. In short, once she learned to empathize with her son's behavior, she was motivated to strive for an intuitive and emotional, rather than an intellectual, understanding of the forces at work in him.

An empathic understanding of what may motivate our child when he becomes difficult or upset, combined with memories conjured up from our own life, makes an inner acceptance of his behavior possible. Without it, in a situation like the one this child and his mother faced, a parent's reaction will probably be one of annoyance. The irritation will be not just with the impasse of the moment—the child's refusal to move—but more with his inability to function in a simple everyday situation, and also with the fact that our presence and care seem to make so little impression on him. Thus without an empathic and sympathetic response to the child's predicament, our annoyance becomes compounded and things go from bad to worse in our relation.

This annoyance, usually unrecognized, makes it difficult in the heat of the moment to have empathy with our child's point of view. Thus we sometimes fail to help him get hold of himself; our anger only increases his anxiety. But when we are able to recall similar childhood experiences of our own, it is almost impossible to be annoyed. Here intellectual understanding is not enough: we must also open up to our own feelings and memories of parallel childhood experiences to find valid clues about what to do to relieve our child. If we can remember what paralyzed us with fear—an experience every child has on occasion—we may also recall what we wished our parents had done to help us feel better, and this will suggest what might work now.

It is not always possible to remember truly parallel situations; we have lost touch with our early experiences, or perhaps there simply were no similar occasions in our childhood. While this mother could remember childhood anxieties similar to those of her son, Ella's mother could not fall back on such experiences of her own. All she could remember was that reading had been one of the greatest pleasures of her childhood, and this made it impossible for her to empathize with her daughter's opposite reactions.

When our own recollections fail us, we must try another approach, and ask ourselves what might cause us to act as our child does, no matter how different the external details of the situation might be. For example, Ella's mother would have had to divorce her thoughts from books and reading and the high value she placed on culture, which her daughter obviously did not share—Ella's inner experience concerning books was a revulsion. But the true emotional issue between this mother and daughter was not books per se; it was Ella's inability to do what her mother wanted most. Books were only the incidental issue on which the conflict centered.

To develop empathy for Ella's emotional state, her mother would have needed to unearth the memory of a time when she simply could not make herself do something which others did easily, to recover an experience of feeling revulsion toward the object of her parents' wishes. Recalling what she had felt then, speculating on and discovering what might have caused such a reaction in her, she might have said to herself, "*This* is what Ella must be feeling." Then she would have understood how severe and painful the present situation was for her daughter and would have found it impossible to scold her. She could have asked herself: "When I was completely unable to do what my parents wanted me most to do, because although they told me it was enjoyable it only evoked revulsion in me, what did I want them to do to help me with my feelings?" Then she would have had a pretty good idea of what any child would appreciate in similar circumstances. And this would be the best remedy to help Ella overcome her predicament of the moment.

Let us take for example the parent of a boy who has hit another child. Instead of being convinced that it is always wrong to hit out, this parent might ask himself: "What would have to happen, what would I have to feel, in order to make me hit somebody, or at least *feel* like hitting somebody?" Then he would not scold his child, but would realize that what the child needs is help in overcoming his anger, and guidance to see that hitting is not the best way to handle such situations.

Thus the good enough parent, in addition to being convinced that whatever his child does, he does it because at the moment he is convinced this is the best he can do, will also ask himself: "What in the world would make me act as my child acts at this moment? And if I felt forced to act this way, what would make me feel better about it?" If we can honestly answer these two related questions, we will know—with sufficient approximation—what motivated our child, even if he cannot or will not tell us himself; and we will know how we can help him deal with his predicament.

Actually this principle is more than two thousand years old. Terence formulated it in this way: *Homo sum; humani nihil a me alienum puto;* Since I am human, nothing human can be alien to me, which is to say that whatever another human being thinks or does, I ought to be able to find an equivalent of it within myself, at least as a theoretical possibility. If this is true for the behavior of utter strangers, how much truer must it be for one's own child.

It may be difficult to believe that there are situations in life which might make us act as we never thought we would. During my own lifetime, particularly when age and experience had not yet taught me otherwise, I often thought, "I would never do this," but I learned differently by living through two world wars, the collapse of an empire, and two German concentration camps, and by working with a wide variety of psychiatric cases, including criminals and psychotics. Everything that I once believed I could never do I discovered to be possible under certain (usually extreme) conditions; often I would be sorely tempted to engage in some such action, and it took great determination not to do so, and abstaining from it severely taxed my self-control.

Children cannot be expected to have such discipline. We must never be so conceited as to think about anything our child does: "I would never do this." On the contrary, we must believe that if the concatenation of circumstances were the same as his, we would feel exactly as our child feels, and that while we might not act as he does, this is only because of our much greater knowledge of the world and our mature ability to control ourselves. If we accept this truth, it is not all that difficult to imagine what might induce the child to act as he does. Furthermore, if we undertake the mental task of working all this out, we discover fascinating things about ourselves and our child, and about how much we have in common.

. . .

74

For a parent's love to be fully and positively effective it ought to be enlightened by thoughtfulness. Everything we do, as well as how and why we are doing it, will make a conscious or more often an unconscious impact on our child. Even great love can be selfish and carry us away, where more cautious consideration would have made us proceed with greater circumspection. We must know and evaluate our motives and not be satisfied with examining only those of which we can readily approve. We should recognize for whose benefit we really act—our own or that of our child—and the possibility that we may be influenced by concern about the reactions of others—parents, friends, and neighbors. This is not to imply that it is wrong to act for our own benefit when appropriate, but only that we ought to be aware of the fact and not try to fool ourselves, or worse, try to fool our child, into believing that we are acting entirely for the child's benefit.

A child's being put to bed can provide a frequent and homely example of such parental deception. Most parents are usually flexible about their child's bedtime, but they are also quite ready to be inflexible when it suits them. When they are tired at night and want some rest, or time to follow their adult pursuits without being bothered by their child, they tend to insist that he has to go to bed because it is his bedtime, and because he needs his sleep, which he undoubtedly does, as we all do. But there is nothing sacred about any particular bedtime hour, as we know from our own experience, nor about when these necessary hours of sleeping have to start or end, certainly not for the younger child who does not yet need to go to school the next morning. We also know from our experience that when we lose out on sleep one night, we can make up for it the next, and our children can in addition do so by taking a longer nap the following day.

There is nothing wrong with wanting to be freed for the evening. It becomes a problem only if a parent believes that he is sending his child to bed for the child's benefit rather than his own. If the latter is the case, insisting on a set bedtime, rather than being flexible about it, is reflective of taking recourse to rules in order to avoid examining each time the child's degree of tiredness, or of his inner readiness to call it a day. Of this our child becomes aware at quite an early age, exactly at the age when he begins to make a fuss about being sent to bed, which is also the age when he has recognized that we are quite free about when we go to bed, depending on how we feel and what is going on at the time. Usually all the child is conscious of is that he wishes to stay up longer because he still wants to do something or continue to participate in what is going on in the home. But this does not mean that on another level he does not resent our power to force him to do what he does not want to do.

What is particularly obnoxious to a child is being told that he is tired when he does not feel tired. While it is quite acceptable to the child that his parents know better about the world in general, because they obviously do, this does not extend to the child's own feelings; he may not be able to articulate these feelings, but he knows them. Children have a quite subtle sense for whose benefit some action is occurring—theirs or ours. A child can accept—albeit uneasily—that our interests are legitimate, even though their consequences may be unpleasant to him, when we are open about our motives. But most of us are hurt when we feel that we are being gotten rid of, and so is our child. The feeling of hurt turns into anger if someone makes an effort to cover up the fact that we are gotten rid of by saying that it is done strictly for our benefit; and the same is true for the child, even though he may be unable to perceive clearly what makes him feel so hurt and angry and cannot put it into the right words.

When parents, even though they may realize that they want time for themselves, try to deceive themselves that they are insisting on the child's going to bed only because his bedtime has arrived and he needs his sleep, they will be and will sound righteous about it; the more so, the more they wish to hide from themselves that their motives may be in part selfish, and that the child's need for rest and sleep, which is real enough, is a convenient excuse. The child will feel what is going on, and his annoyance with his parents will make it that much harder for him to fall asleep peacefully; it may even give him nightmares as in his dreams he tries to get even for the injustice inflicted on him by his parents, or because he feels guilty about his repressed anger at them.

If, on the other hand, the parents are honest about their need for some time for themselves, they will accept compassionately the child's resentment at this temporary exclusion from their lives. A compromise will be possible— say, another quarter of an hour—and ways will be found to make the banishment more pleasant, such as sitting with him for a while and reading a story, and when he is a bit older, letting him play or read for a while by himself. Efforts will be made to keep the house quiet once the lights are out in his room, so that the exile does not feel he's missing important events.

In other words, we must view this situation both from our parental perspective—we need time for ourselves, he needs a full night's sleep—and from that of the child. The child believes that when people are sent away, it is because they are not wanted, are not liked; my parents are trying to send me away, which means they no longer want me. How terrible not to be wanted by one's own parents, even if it is only for the night! If we put ourselves in his shoes, we will naturally want to dispel these fears, to restore his confidence in himself and us, so that he will fall asleep happily and easily.

Bedtime strife may be annoying, but only rarely does it become a serious matter. Nevertheless, it gives us a chance to ask ourselves how *we* would feel if someone else were to decide that it was time for us to be in bed, whether or not we were ready to go, and this would give us a pretty good idea of how our child feels about it. Understanding his reactions to everyday events, such as our telling him what to wear, when to wash his hands, what to eat, and whatnot, can teach us a great deal about both of us, and about our relation. When, in addition, we ask ourselves how we would react if someone made such requests of us and insisted we do as we were told, we might at the same time wonder what our child thinks are our reasons for doing so. We might ask him to tell us what *he* believes our reasons to be when we are making such requests of him. For many children it would be an entirely new experience to be questioned about their view of their parents' motives, but this will work only if the child feels free to tell us what he thinks—if he believes that we will listen seriously, rather than being bent on refuting whatever he says.

There is hardly a better way to convince our child that his opinions are important to us than to inquire about them, in order not to criticize or refute them but to ponder them seriously. The best result of our being interested in our child's views of why we act toward him as we do, and of our taking his views seriously, is that this will greatly encourage the child's feeling that our views of him are not arrived at arbitrarily. Equity, if nothing else, requires that we take his views of what motivates our behavior toward him as seriously as we want him to take ours. And if we are truly convinced of how much we have in common, of how similar the wellsprings of our actions are— even if we do not always agree with each other on all issues—this will bring us closer to a mutual understanding.

Asking our child what he thinks are our motives is very different from questioning *his* motives, if for no other reason than that we can force him to obey us, while he may need devious maneuvers to get his way. It is this difference in the power to have one's way which makes our inquiries into our child's mind such a one-sided procedure, particularly if we are not fully ready to invite his inquiries into our motives and to reply to them openly and completely. Even if we are, asking a child to reveal his motives and his innermost thoughts to us is a questionable procedure which warrants careful consideration, as the following chapter suggests.

7

The Question "Why?"

Questioning is not the mode of conversation among gentlemen.
—SAMUEL JOHNSON, as reported by Boswell

WHEN I WAS A CHILD, like most middle-class children of concerned, intelligent parents, I must have been asked innumerable times why I did or thought something. And as I recall, I hardly ever felt that my parents were truly interested in my reasons. There were many occasions when the result of my answer to their question was that I was prevented from doing whatever I had in mind and also criticized for the intention. The times of frustration loomed much larger in my mind than the frequent, but less impressive, instances when my parents' response was more positive. In fact, the situation was so little to my liking that when I was asked "Why?" I did not expect to receive an unbiased, fair hearing. This made me hate the question, even in those cases when the outcome was favorable to me.

However, many times my reaction to the question "Why?" was only mildly negative, mainly because I was asked it so often that I took it for granted that this is what adults ask when they disapprove, or are doubtful about what their children are up to, or when children behave in ways that seem inconvenient or inappropriate in some fashion to adults. The frequency with which I was asked "Why?" even about matters that seemed obvious to me I ascribed to the fact that adults simply did not understand children; otherwise there would have been no need for what seemed incessant questioning.

In retrospect, what I remember most strongly is that whenever I was questioned in this way, I felt very much put on the spot, and I resented it. My inner reaction was: "If you would just try to understand me, you could easily answer your own question. The reason you ask me is that it doesn't seem worth the effort to you to think it out for yourselves." Today I could summarize my feeling as a conviction that if those who were questioning me had been sensitive to me and what went on in me, they would not have needed to question my motives. I also remember how hurt I was when an honest answer did me no good, if all I received for it was criticisms. What made the experience painful was that what I said made no difference to decisions which, I was sure, my parents had already made before asking me to explain myself. In short, I was persuaded that "Why?" was usually asked in a critical spirit and with an *a priori* assumption that I could have no valid reason for what I was up to. And whenever my response did earn their approval, I felt they only gave it grudgingly—a conviction due more to my resentment of the question than to a correct assessment of my parents' attitude.

This view of the question "Why?" is common to children, although most parents believe that there is no sting involved in asking it. Parents assume that "why" is a neutral word, but children sense otherwise. The *Oxford English Dictionary* gives as its second definition: "Implying or suggesting a negative assertion" and adds by way of explanation: "('there is no reason why . . .'); hence often expressing a protest or objection." This is exactly how I felt in my childish intuition based on many experiences that whenever I was asked this question some tacit protest or objection was part of the questioner's attitude. This annoyed me, and my explanation took on a defensive tone that was objectionable to my parents.

I think Dr. Johnson's remark "Questioning is not the mode of conversation among gentlemen" expresses some of my childhood feeling about adults' conviction that I owed them an explanation, and perhaps a justification, of my thoughts and deeds. I was supposed to provide answers on request, but my parents explained themselves to me only sporadically, when they felt like it. This disparity was certainly an important element in my resentment.

My reaction was the opposite—one of real happiness—when my parents spontaneously approved of something I did or planned to do, and when they seemed to understand what I was after (and also why) without asking. Then I was delighted to expound voluntarily on my motives and to clear up any small misunderstandings. It gave me great satisfaction and a sense of security to show them that our thinking was identical, or at least parallel in important respects.

When my parents gave me to understand that they had thought things over and considered what my motives might be and were sympathetic even though they could not approve my plans, I often gave them a spontaneous explanation, because I had the impression that I would get a sympathetic, fair hearing. All I needed was to feel that they had seriously considered my point of view; this was sufficient for me. If they then made it clear why they had to insist on their way, I was nevertheless so satisfied by our exchange of ideas and mutual respect that their decision, while not exactly welcome, was at least acceptable. The same decision would have been completely unacceptable if I had been interrogated and my parents had acted as if what I had said made no difference. While even then I nearly always obeyed, I couldn't do so with good feelings about myself or about them; the world seemed too unfair. Even in the many instances when my better sense told me that my parents' decision had been the right one and probably benefited me, this rational insight did little to change my feeling that I had not been treated with the respect I thought I had a right to.

Perhaps an experience I had when I was fifteen may illustrate and in some measure explain my reactions. It made such a deep impression on me that it has stayed vividly in my mind for the more than sixty-five years which have passed since.

I was a very good student, a quiet, introspective, even subdued youngster. But one day the behavior of one of our schoolmasters, which I had found annoying all along—as had most of my fellow students because it was so unlike that of all our other masters, past or present—provoked me so much that suddenly, without forethought, I laid hands on him and, with a couple of other boys, whom my example enticed to help me, pushed him out of the classroom. As soon as we had accomplished it, I was shocked by what I had done; it was so unlike my usual behavior in school and out. I only knew that I had felt so outraged that I had had to do *something*; but of what specifically triggered my action, what motives other than rage had been at work in me, I had not the slightest idea; nor did I know what had caused my rage.

Neither then nor for decades afterward could I understand what had driven me to act so out of character. I had never thought myself capable of such a rash, aggressive, and—considering the setting, an Austrian gymnasium under the old monarchy—unheard-of breach of discipline. I tried to figure out what had induced my sudden rage, since the master had not behaved any differently than usual toward me or the rest of the students. My self-examination was to no avail; but I was unable to alleviate my terror of the consequences by figuring out some excuse for my action. Absolutely nothing came to mind. The school's director, a rather distinguished scholar, was a harsh taskmaster and strict disciplinarian, distant and austere, and I trembled in anticipation of a severe punishment. I expected to be expelled, and perhaps even barred from all the gymnasia of Vienna, which would have had the most drastic consequences for my future life.

The next day at midmorning the director entered our classroom, a rare and always very impressive, even ominous event. As we all stood at attention, he blistered us verbally, accusing the other boys of the crime of not having stopped me, but particularly myself as the leader in this unprecedented and nefarious deed. "Hypocrite" was the mildest name he called me, but the one which seemed to express his deepest outrage, for up to then I had always been, or according to him pretended to be, such a good boy. Listening to his philippic, I grew even more terrified of my punishment, and so, as they later told me, were my classmates.

Having screamed at me and harangued and terrified all of us for what seemed an eternity, he suddenly fell silent for a while, and then added in the quietest voice—a stark and most impressive contrast to the outraged anger of a moment before—words I have never forgotten. He said: "Of course I know that if Dr. X had behaved as I expect all masters of this institution to behave, nothing like this could ever have happened." And addressing me by name, he concluded: "Tomorrow you will stay for two hours after school, working on your own on studies which Dr. X should have made so interesting that there would have been no place for such misbehavior." And with this he calmly walked out. This was my entire punishment, with the exception of the low mark I received for deportment that marking period, when always before, and ever afterward, I received the highest mark in it. Having with reason feared the worst, I was vastly relieved by this incredibly mild punishment, which neither my friends nor I understood.

But what made such a deep impression on me then and ever since was that I was not questioned about my motives. I was not required to make a confession, to repudiate my behavior, or to offer excuses or apologies. In fact the director came right out and told us that he knew what the cause of the incident had been; and while he didn't condone it, he not only understood it, but also to some degree accepted the fact that he or his institution bore some of the blame, having given us a teacher whom he himself could not respect.

This was a tremendous relief. I had speculated all day and during a sleepless night on what I could offer as an explanation—not to mention justification of my behavior, for which I knew there was none—but I could come up with nothing. That this master was a very inadequate teacher was hardly an explanation, particularly since I knew that I really did not care much about that; pretending that this was what had outraged me would indeed have been the height of hypocrisy. I knew that I, like most of my friends, had made fun of his empty, weak, and, worst of all, silly behavior and personality. It had been grounds for teasing him and ridiculing him, which we rather enjoyed; so why did I have to get rid of the source of so much mirth, of a master to whom we all felt very superior, which was a relief from our feeling inferior to most of the others? Why my sudden need to get rid of him?—in which I succeeded, because he did not dare to reenter our class on the day we pushed him out.

My act had been clearly symbolic. But what had been my motives? There I drew a complete blank. I had expected an inquisition into my motives before judgment was passed, and the truth was that I simply did not know why I had done what I did. But I knew that this would be entirely unacceptable to the authorities, and would only annoy those who would decide my fate. Desperate, I was ready to lie, but not even a half-convincing lie came to my mind; I was utterly defenseless. There was just no excuse for what I had done, and knowing this, the director did not try to make me lie to him. It took me a long time to comprehend how wise he had been.

Within a short time Dr. X was dismissed and replaced by a man whom we all highly respected, not just for the excellence of his teaching and for his rectitude in dealing with us, but also for his inner security and for the obvious manliness he exuded, without ever making any show of it. Only years later did it occur to me that the director probably chose this man because he felt we were entitled to be compensated for the bad experience we had had with Dr. X and so replaced him with someone who was his exact opposite.

Before this incident I had been one nameless, faceless pupil among many hundreds, but thereafter whenever we passed each other in the corridors, the director always seemed to recognize me and treated me with cool distance mixed with some small measure of respect, although hardly with friendliness; nor did he ever do me any favors. Years later, it dawned on me that his attitude expressed a wish to let me know that he still disapproved very much of what I had done and hence did not like me, but recognized that my action was quite understandable.

On my part, it took me quite some time to understand his reasons. Even this did not make me like him; he was too authoritarian, and his values were the opposite of mine in respect to politics and education. To appreciate someone whose values were contrary to my own required a maturity of judgment which I did not at this time possess. But slowly, over the years, I achieved it. Gradually I became impressed that this rigid, old-fashioned, authoritarian director had realized on his own what must have enraged me, and had felt no need to corroborate his view either by questioning me or by expecting me to agree to his evaluation of my motives. He was sensitive to the needs out of which I acted, even though I had caused trouble for him in running the school by threatening discipline. That he did not expect me to change was indicated by the insignificant punishment, clearly a token, and by his not requesting any statement of contrition or promise of change or improvement.

The older I got, the more I appreciated that far from questioning me, the director had stated his conclusions without any need or provocation to do so. He understood boys of my age well enough to know what went on in their minds, even when they did not. He disapproved of what I had done, but he had comprehended its essence: everything followed from the fact that Dr. X was such a silly man. He did not probe into my specific motives, partly because he thought them relatively unimportant after he had decided what had been the essential cause of it all, and partly because he probably— correctly—assumed that a boy in my situation was not likely to know what had moved him, deep down.

Although a strict disciplinarian, he knew how to deal with me; he was careful not to destroy my self-respect by obliging me to profess remorse I did not feel but would have been obliged to pretend had he asked me about my misdeed. Indeed, it would have been contrary to the school's goal of instilling self-respect to undermine my own by forcing me to reveal and defend my innermost motives, even assuming that I could do so. Had I been forced by fear of punishment to appear falsely contrite, it would have been tantamount to disowning an essential part of myself. And if I had asserted to the contrary, when questioned, that what I had done was right—unimaginable in the setting of this school—he would have had to punish me in consequence of having obeyed him and revealed myself. This, far from reforming my behavior, would have convinced me that I was the victim of injustice and would have made me hate both school and director.

In the deepest sense the director probably recognized my act for what it was: a symbolic declaration of my need to have good masters I could respect. So my punishment, two hours' detention, was also symbolic, and so was the low grade in deportment in an intermediary report which was never repeated and did not form part of my permanent record. This reflected the director's recognition that my outburst had been an isolated act.

I had to reach full maturity and become an experienced educator and child therapist—and parent—before I fully realized that he had shown me some of the requirements of a wise educator, particularly in tense and difficult situations: we must weigh in our own mind what the child's motives might have been, in order to grasp the reasons for his behavior, what had led to it, what purposes it served. Only on the basis of such comprehension can we decide whether or not we can approve of them, and this independently from our attitude to the action itself, as it is quite possible that we can fully approve of the child's motives but still feel compelled to stop him from what he is doing.

But how does having arrived at an opinion about the child's motives relate to whether or not we question him about them? If we approve of his motives, there is no need for questions. For example, out of a commendable feeling of compassion a child may wish to give away one of our most prized possessions, which we cannot permit him to do. In this case we need only explain to him why he can't give away this particular object, and at the same time express our approval of his motives. If we are in error about some aspects of those motives, he will probably be happy to correct us, for our spontaneous approval will make him feel that he is understood. His good opinion of us will be confirmed and—very important—it will induce him to be similarly open with us in the future.

When parental approval is impossible, it's a different story. Then it is even more important to weigh the child's motives, but the degree to which the child himself may be aware of them must also be carefully considered. If we cannot approve of his reasons, how will he be affected if he is compelled to reveal them? Will we embarrass him? Will he be induced to lie? And when, after he answers our questions, we are forced to be critical of whatever he reveals, will this not convince him that telling the truth has only undesirable consequences for him?

It is again a different situation when the adult not only disapproves of the child's action but is unable to fathom his motives. If our questions yield satisfactory answers, all is well on one level, but on another level it does not take the sting out of our questioning him. The child may believe that we gave him a fair hearing, which is all to the good, and that he can convince us that he is right, but he is left with the uneasy feeling that we failed to understand him in the first place—otherwise why would we have questioned him? It does not increase his respect for an adult so lacking in imagination and so ready to ascribe unacceptable motives to him. Thus, at best, his will be an ambivalent reaction: my parents are fair, but it takes some doing on my part for them to see my point. Why didn't they trust me from the start to know what I am doing?

Of course, there is always the possibility that the child doesn't know his reasons, as I didn't when I pushed Dr. X out of the classroom. If questioning then forces the child to admit this, his parents may not believe him and think he is prevaricating. Now he discovers that his behavior is not only incomprehensible to himself, but even to the wiser and more experienced adults on whose greater knowledge the child's security depends. The result: a further weakening of the child's respect for his parents and a greater reluctance to accept their guidance, since they do not understand him any better than he does himself.

Not just tacitly fearing that he might not know his own motives but having to admit it openly is most embarrassing for a child, to say the least. If he has to recognize this for a fact, how can he ever trust that he knows what he is doing? If he knows so little about himself and the adult does not know much more, how can he ever hope to understand himself and his motives; how can he act more wisely in the future? In being forced to face his ignorance about himself, the child's self-confidence is undermined, and such confrontation also interferes with a good relation to the adult whose questioning has forced the child to make such a debilitating admission.

Also, the child who does not know what motivated him feels, when questioned about it, that he is *expected* to know. Because of this, or because he cannot face up to the fact that he does not know himself, the questioning may induce him to tell a lie. As Oliver Goldsmith remarked: "Ask me no questions, and I'll tell you no lies." To feel forced to lie undermines the child's self-respect, makes him feel a cheat, if not worse; it alienates him from the adult whose questions made him feel bad about himself.

Thus, unless we have independently arrived at an idea about the child's motives, we cannot predict whether or not he can answer our questions truthfully, or we cannot know what bad consequences may follow our interrogation. And if we do know in advance what our child's reaction is likely to be, and think we know fairly well what his motives were, there is no point to our questioning him other than to put him on the spot.

To sum up, if the child does not know his true motives, questioning will make him feel helpless, insecure, and uncertain in the future about the validity of his actions. If we, because we have understood what his motives were, enlighten him about them, both we and he would have been better off if we had done so without first making him lose his self-confidence. If the child's reasons are bad ones in his eyes, he will either lie to us—if not also to himself, which is worse—or he will be forced to disavow his motives, which will not endear us to him, nor will it increase his confidence in his ability to act intelligently.

Fortunately, in my case neither the director nor my parents interrogated me. Understandably, my parents worried about what the consequences of my behavior might be; they speculated about arrangements whereby I could continue my education in some provincial town should I be expelled, as we all feared. Their reaction—their not blaming me and their making positive plans for my future—increased my trust in them; I felt they would be able to work out a solution. The next day, when they learned how lightly I had been punished, they were greatly relieved and saw no reason to ask me why

I had acted so rashly. I'm glad they didn't, because, as it turned out, they had both died before I could have given them—and myself—a satisfactory explanation. More than thirty years went by before I discovered what had goaded me to such an unlikely deed—unlikely as seen from the surface, and incomprehensible from my understanding of myself. Had I been put on the spot, I would have had to tell lies not so much to convince others, but mostly to cover up an ignorance of motives which it would have been devastating for me either to recognize or to reveal openly.

Dr. X had been a simpering fool who spoke with the voice of a eunuch. He could not teach even halfway adequately the elementary aspects of the discipline in which he had earned his Ph.D. We boys were at an age when we had anxious doubts about our budding masculinity and needed suitable masculine figures with which to identify. Dr. X, far from offering a suitable image for identification, increased our anxieties that we might not make it as male adults; he presented us with our worst fears about ourselves—and in the flesh. This is why we hated him, and why some of my classmates gave me a helping hand when I pushed him out of our classroom.

My fellow students were also repelled by Dr. X, but I led the way. What immediate and pressing inner need could have taken me so far from the boundaries of my normal behavior? In fact, something extraordinary had happened just before I acted with this sudden and entirely uncharacteristic violence: my father had suffered a stroke, which completely incapacitated him for some time. Not only was I abruptly and unexpectedly deprived of my most important model for forming my personality; I was also confronted with the possibility—as the only other male in the family—that I might have to step into my father's shoes. This was a terrifying prospect to an insecure teenager already wracked by doubts about his masculinity and afraid he lacked male assertiveness. My father's severe illness (from which, fortunately, he slowly recovered) caused this anxiety to become overpowering and made me fear that I might turn into someone like Dr. X. This was an intolerable thought. Seeing him every day in class increased my anxiety until I could no longer control it. Only by an act of the greatest daring and self-assertion could I attempt to silence my anxiety about myself; and this need was now so great that I could not be deterred by consideration of the likely consequences. It was as if my deed expressed the thought "If you cannot act like a man, I must, although I am much too young for doing so." This was reason enough for my behavior, but also why I couldn't afford to know what caused it. Recognizing the source and the magnitude of my anxiety was impossible, because it would have destroyed what little security about myself I had, when my need was to bolster it at any cost. It would have negated

86

the positive effects of an act which was of such importance to me that I was ready to risk my entire future.

I could fully comprehend the complexity of my motives only after my own psychoanalysis had helped me to uncover certain hidden aspects of my relation to my father. Also I had to gain sufficient maturity and security to understand and accept the extreme anxiety with which I had reacted to the possibility that my father might die when I was still a child. Seeing how long it took me to reach a conclusion convinced me of the undesirability of probing into a child's motives when there is a chance he may not know them. The old-fashioned director, who was completely unaware of psychoanalysis and of the workings of the unconscious, nevertheless knew that it is undesirable, possibly destructive, to probe into a child's motives—particularly so when his actions are very different from his usual behavior, or otherwise extreme in nature. We who are familiar with the role our unconscious plays in pushing us to actions that our conscious mind cannot fathom the reasons for should try to be at least as psychologically sensitive as the director. He realized that my action had been so out of character, and so unusual in all other respects, that I must have had sufficient motives for it. But he was not really interested in my personal motives. He, in all likelihood, was mainly interested in what had been wrong as seen from his perspective, and this was the incompetence of the teacher, of which he was well aware. So he proceeded on the basis of what he thought accounted for the incident. He was interested in what he thought about it, not in what I thought about it.

But by not questioning me about my motives—of which I myself was not cognizant—and relying instead on his estimation of what had been wrong, he gained my lifelong respect, something every parent wishes to achieve in his relation to his child.

8

On Empathy

> Empathy: *The power of projecting one's personality
> into (and so fully comprehending) the object of con-
> templation.*
> —*The Shorter Oxford English Dictionary*

THE DIRECTOR'S TIRADE had been a true expression of his anger. The quiet remarks that followed, about Dr. X's inadequacy as a teacher and leader of boys, represented his evaluation of Dr. X's unsuitability for the teaching profession. He was displeased with Dr. X for his own reasons, but his annoyance with Dr. X made my action comprehensible to him. Thus he felt no need to inquire into my motives, either by speculating or by asking me about them, nor to punish me severely. But his had been an intellectual understanding, not an empathic one—he was far too convinced of his superiority to a mere schoolboy, too removed from his own schoolboy trials and tribulations, for that. My disgust with Dr. X seemed reasonable enough to him; to accept my action as justified he would have had to view us as operating on the same emotional plane—spurred by the same or very similar motives, I in actuality, he in theory, in his thoughts. His conviction of his superiority to me made this impossible.

Empathy, so important for an adult's understanding of a child, requires that one consider the other person an equal—not in regard to knowledge, intelligence, or experience, and certainly not in maturity, but in respect to the feelings which motivate us all. This requires familiarity with the whole range of one's own feelings, not only those of the moment, or those which are typically or habitually evoked in one. An empathic response means an attempt to put ourselves in the other person's place, so that our feelings will suggest to us not only his emotions, but also his motives. When trying to create in us an empathic response we must understand the other from the inside, not the outside, as an interested and even concerned observer might

88

do who attempts to comprehend the other person's motives through his intellect.

The director had tried to understand intellectually what had gone on; he had been very dissatisfied with Dr. X, so he could readily appreciate that I had been too. This was enough for him. To have empathy with what I had done, he would have had to go way beyond that and ask himself why in this case I acted so very out of character, what had driven me to it. Convinced that his understanding was far superior to mine, he found it sufficient to rely on it altogether. Earlier I cited the French proverb which suggests that a true *understanding* of another person is tantamount to *excusing* what he did. Here it may be said that in empathy one *feels* as the other person does; one makes oneself feel for and with him; it is a vicarious experience of what it would feel like to be not just in the other person's position, but, so to speak, in his skin.

Freud spoke of the sympathy that exists between the unconscious of one person and that of another, suggesting that we can understand another person's unconscious only through our own. One cannot adequately explain what is involved in love, anger, jealousy, or anxiety, nor can words really convey what one feels in depression or elation. But if one has experienced these states of being one knows what another person is likely to be feeling. When we feel empathically with another person, we get very close to him; we can understand him much better than if we had to rely only on what he can tell us. Even the great poets must have recourse to symbolic language to convey deep feelings; they speak in metaphors and allegories, because no direct expression is sufficient for their purposes. And to get at their meaning, we have to read not only the lines but also between them; further, we must rely on what their words suggest to our own unconscious, responding to symbols, suggestions, and metaphors.

We should not expect our children to be able to tell us what they feel deeply about, or what is going on in their inner selves, particularly since much of it is not accessible to their conscious minds and they are therefore unable to articulate it. To understand what moves them deeply, we have to rely on our empathic responses to them, our rational mind working to understand what they are trying to tell us by their words and actions, while our unconscious, through "projection into the object of our contemplation," attempts to see them in relation to our own inner experiences, past and present. If we do this, we truly understand them as we simultaneously understand ourselves better. This is why more than two thousand years ago the poet Menander said: " 'Know thyself' is a good thing, but not in all situations. In many it is better to say, 'Know others.' "

To explain the nature and healing effect of empathy, the child psychoanalyst Christine Olden wrote about a violently angry eight-year-old boy. Early in his therapy he dictated a story to Olden which went as follows: "My mother is a stinker. My father is a stinker. My mother is ugly. My analyst is ugly and horrible," and so on. It was a drastic expression of his consuming anger, the reason for his being in treatment. Knowing even then that his analyst would not react to this outburst as would his parents, teachers, and most other people, he asked that another adult be called in to read what he had dictated. This would show the analyst how the world usually reacted to him. The new reader perused his story very thoughtfully and sympathetically. Not getting the shocked and condemning response to which he was accustomed, the boy said provokingly, "That's quite some story, isn't it?" To which the person who had read his angry missive replied compassionately, "This is a very sad story." This unexpected response bowled the boy over, for he saw his story as bitterly angry and attacking. After he got over his surprise, he finally asked why it was sad, and was told that it was so very sad because it showed how little he liked himself—for one must dislike oneself deeply to see only bad in others, and to be so angry at them and the world.

By trying to feel like a person who rages at those to whom he ought to feel closest and most loving, the reader was able to experience herself the inner wellsprings of the boy's feelings. It was obvious to her that only profound sadness could account for it, a sadness caused by the desperation of being unable to like oneself. To be thus understood in his deepest feelings and have them accepted with sympathy—rather than rejected, as usually happened—was the beginning of a change in the boy's views of himself and the world. His analyst's acceptance could not have achieved this, not at this early moment in his therapy, since the boy was intelligent enough to know that to accept him was her job. But that a person who had no such obligation and who hardly knew him could recognize that the issue was not his anger, as up to then all adults had been convinced, but his sadness, this recognition gave him the hope that eventually those most important to him, his parents, might respond positively to his sadness rather than only negatively to his anger. No questioning, however well intentioned, would have achieved this; it would only have corroborated his conviction that nobody understood or wanted to understand him.

Just as I could never have told anyone about the anxieties that caused my violent outburst at Dr. X, so was it impossible for even this very intelligent eight-year-old to trace the sources of his all-consuming rage. The intensity of children's angry feelings is like an impenetrable wall that hides all that lies behind it. We ought to be familiar with this, from the inability of much older angry young people to recognize the true source of their rage. The reason is that persons living under the psychological impact of feelings so violent that they dominate all of their lives—particularly when this feeling is one of anger—cannot think rationally about these overweening emotions. Their anger fills them so completely that they cannot sufficiently distance themselves from it to understand its causes.

To distance oneself from one's all-consuming feelings, to penetrate beyond them to their origins, is difficult even for many mature persons. However, to be able to do so is a good indication of true maturity, since a very important aspect of it is the ability to get, so to say, outside of oneself and one's feelings, even when they are strong, in order to contemplate them objectively. But even young people well beyond adolescence are unable to do so when they feel strongly. For this reason, if we wish to understand our child when he is moved by strong emotions, we must try to comprehend through empathy with him what is going on deep within him, and to respond with our feelings and actions to what we thus discover within ourselves about our child. And to be able to do that, we cannot permit ourselves to be carried away by our reactions to the child's overt behavior.

This boy could only say, "It makes me so angry," the "it" being his unconscious, the source of his rage. Pressed to be more specific, all he could come up with was rationalizations, for the content of his unconscious was unknown to him. He would feel dimly that his rationalizations were empty, superficial, and in the last analysis beside the point; if questioned, the interrogation could only increase his anger, because he would be forced to realize the limits of his self-understanding.

Had I been obliged to explain my attack on Dr. X, all I could truthfully have said was that "something" had made me do it, a "something" which took me years to identify, an anxiety so threatening and unmanageable that I had repressed it into my unconscious. If I had then been pressed to state what it had been, since "something" was no explanation, I would either have become mute—which would have been misinterpreted as obstinacy, not helplessness—or come up with some statement about Dr. X's failings as a teacher. The director and I would both have recognized this as an inadequate explanation. In the end I would have been angry at the director for asking me to do what I could not—explain myself—while he would have been angry at me for stubbornly refusing to admit my real reasons. And pretty much the same thing would have happened had Olden's patient been pressed to reveal the source of his anger. Where the deepest feelings are involved, the understandable wish of parents to find out what motivates their child leads them to press him to explain himself. But since he can't explain even if he wanted to, parents and child become even more angry with each other and lose trust in each other.

Most parents today *know* what was *terra incognita* for the director—that we have powerful unconscious emotions that determine many of our actions, and that it may take years of hard work to bring these feelings to the level of conscious awareness, and that being commanded to do so is likely to make this unconscious material even more inaccessible. Since the reason for the repression of the feelings was that to recognize them was too upsetting or dangerous, being asked to reveal them increases anxiety, and this reinforces the repression. But why do parents have such a hard time in recognizing all this? After all, parents know that they keep some aspects of their lives from their children. I believe the problem—like so much of what goes wrong between parents and child—stems from their conscious desire to be close to their child, and their unconscious feeling that he can only be really *theirs* if he has no secrets from them. Since he is *their* child, there should be nothing in and about him which is hidden from them, including his inner life. They are ready to acknowledge the fact that their child has an unconscious, but while it is all right for that unconscious to be hidden from everyone else, it ought *not* to be hidden from *them*, his parents!

THE ANSWER "I DON'T KNOW"

When we find ourselves at an impasse with our child and are unable to evoke an empathic understanding, we should try at least to respond sympathetically to the child's position. Using our adult resources, we can then offer him a solution to consider, but if he accepts our suggestion, we ought to make sure that he does so not just to please us or to avoid further discussion. For this reason it is preferable to invite him to evaluate our idea and improve on it. This is much more likely to draw out his reactions; moreover, this method sharpens his critical abilities, which a simple question would not. By asking him to react to our idea—"What do you think about it?"—rather than merely to accept it or to defend his own, we will learn much about how his mind works; and by telling us his thoughts, he makes them clearer to himself, as he puts them into words and intelligible sentences.

I have mentioned before that the adult's perspective differs greatly from the child's, and therefore it is often difficult to fathom how he arrives at his decisions. But if we try to see matters from his point of view and then offer our suggestions in ways which indicate that we think somewhat in line with his thoughts and approve, or at least are not inclined to disapprove, of his intentions, he then loves to tell us freely what is on his mind.

But when we are angry, then something in the way we demand an explanation will give him the impression that we are doubtful, if not critical. Any child can read disapproval in his parent's tone of voice, facial expression, body stance, or other subliminal signals which we are not aware of giving but to which he is very receptive. If he fears a negative reaction to what he is about to say, he will be unable to respond to our inquiry calmly and may become so flustered that he no longer clearly knows what his intentions were.

It is a rare child who is so secure about himself and his relationship with his parent that he is free of this kind of anxiety. Whether or not he has been criticized in the past, he experiences *any* criticism as being directed not just at what he thinks or does, but also at the person he is. So most children present their thoughts to adults with some fear that they might be found wanting, or even punished for having harbored such ideas. This fear is the opposite side of the need for approval; the child worries mainly that he will be made to feel inadequate or bad, where he originally was convinced that he was neither—and this as a result of voicing his true thoughts.

Such apprehension makes it hard for him to come right out with his opinions, so he slants them to give his questioner nothing to object to. Often he realizes that he is no longer saying exactly what he thinks, although at other times he is not conscious of censoring his thoughts to make them more acceptable to the parent even though he does. Many adults also are not fully conscious of what they are doing when they modify a story, or why, and the younger the person is, the more frequently is this the case.

Not being conscious of why we are doing something does not mean that we have no feelings about it, although we don't understand them because their rationale has been denied access to our awareness. But the child who, to pacify his parent, withholds or alters his reasons for wishing to do something becomes annoyed with himself and with us, because he cannot be as frank and assertive as he would like to be: high anxiety about our possible reaction simply does not permit this. Afraid we will be critical of what he is about to tell us, he thinks better of doing so and answers our inquiry with an "I don't know." This doesn't commit him to anything, and thus he thinks it cannot upset us. But it usually *does* annoy us, since it is taken as a refusal to answer our question, and because we imagine that our child is either so brainless that he acts without thinking or that he doesn't trust us enough to confide in us. Since we don't like either of these possibilities, we aren't likely to accept "I don't know" as true, and we feel frustrated in our attempt to get to the bottom of things.

Actually, quite often "I don't know" is not just an excuse or an avoidance, but a correct expression of the child's bewilderment. Originally he may have known quite well what he did and why he did it, and he was convinced of the rightness of his action and motive. But when the way we question him suggests our disapproval, he becomes confused. What seemed right up until then now suddenly seems much less so, and so he is stymied.

As parents, we must realize how much we mean to our child; when he senses our disapproval, he at once becomes insecure about his convictions. What previously seemed right now appears to be wrong—not so much because his perception of his action changes, but because it brought on the criticism of his parents. At this point the child no longer knows his own mind: his action was, as he saw it, the correct response to the situation as he experienced it, but it turns out to have been wrong because it causes trouble with his parents. He simply can't sort this out; his immature intellect does not comprehend relativity or differing viewpoints. All he knows is that a thing cannot be both right and wrong; in consequence he is completely perplexed.

So it is that many of our questions, which we asked because we wanted to understand our child, cause confusion for him and ourselves. Since "I don't know" is a statement of incompetence, he resents having to say it, and because he now feels ignorant and inept as a result of the questioning, he blames his confusion on the parent who interrogated him.

The parent in this situation also feels defeated and annoyed when the child answers his query with an "I don't know." In practically all other situations, when our child states his ignorance we are more than willing to enlighten him, since we know that it is in his nature to be ignorant or confused about many issues. Indeed, we usually relish the role of being our child's main source of information. But when a parent who is critical of what his child is doing asks him about his behavior, the parent may reject the idea that the child acted without any reason he knows; the parent rarely takes into account that the child is truly unable to answer the question because his reason is buried in his unconscious.

The child is somehow aware, however dimly, that it is the parent's importance to him which makes it impossible to say anything but "I don't know." He feels the unfairness of being blamed for an empty answer which his parent has provoked. In this respect the child is usually more perspicacious than the parents, who see only the child's frustrating obstinacy in not telling what they wish to learn and not the reason behind it—the overwhelming importance the parents' opinions have for their child, which prevents him from saying something he fears will displease them.

The situation is much the same when our child in our opinion is not performing adequately—in school, for example—and he replies to our query: "I can't do it." While on most other occasions when our child tells us that he can't do something we respond with acceptance and sympathy, here too if we start out with a critical attitude we will get an evasive answer. The child feels our critical attitude and reacts to it—not necessarily consciously—with an attitude of reluctance that provides us with further ammunition for our negative attitude. It seems to him that we won't accept his reasons, so why offer them? Better to claim inability than unwillingness—and of course in many cases the inability is absolutely genuine, although often it is due to unconscious causes.

If we want our child to give us an unadulterated reply, we must let him know that we will respect his answer, a promise that we can convey through our attitude and phrasing of our questions. Then he will feel no compulsion to answer us with excuses or to claim ignorance or inability. Assured of our goodwill, he will be happy to increase it by letting us (and himself) know what is going on in his mind.

Even when we have responded to our child's reasons with empathy for his way of seeing things, there will be times when we cannot subscribe to his views of things or approve of his conduct; but if he is certain of our goodwill, he will be able to take direction in a positive frame of mind. He may not be pleased with our objections, but he won't feel defeated; and if, as we hope, he changes his views and ways of acting, he will do so not out of anxiety, but out of love—not because he fears our displeasure, or maybe even punishment, but because he wants to retain our good opinion of him. It is truly amazing how readily we make considerable sacrifices to gain or retain the respect and goodwill of people who are important to us and who, we feel, are in sympathy with our ways of thinking and doing things. We resent making the same sacrifices if we feel forced into them by persons about whose goodwill we have doubts. The first is a pleasure and thus usually well done, the latter at best an unpleasant chore, and hence more often than not done poorly.

Difficult as it is to avoid situations which may elicit an "I don't know," it is best not to question a child about his reasons. Even if he knows quite well what motivated him, it isn't always advisable to interrogate him, because although there may be no criticism intended, he may believe otherwise. The fact is that it is most children's experience that we rarely ask them to explain conduct of which we thoroughly approve; we ask for reasons when we are dissatisfied, and children know this. For example, most of us are not in the habit of asking, "Why did you work so hard to make such excellent grades in school?" We ask, "Why didn't you do your homework?" not "Why did you come in to do your homework when you were having such a good time playing outside?" We rarely, if ever, ask, "Why are you so nice to your brother?" or "Why did you pick up your room so well?" We may be ready to lavish praise on a well-behaved child, but we are unlikely to question his motives—even though these may be as complex and even questionable as those that underlie bad behavior. So he knows a question usually implies disapproval.

Even when a child feels so secure or is so convinced that he is right that he can explain his motives despite an awareness that we are not in sympathy with them, things are not always easy. For example, we ask our child why he hit another child, and he truthfully tells us that the other child deserved it—"He asked for it." If we push our inquiry, he explains that he was annoyed or provoked by the other child.

Many parents would now respond by saying that one must not permit oneself to be provoked (although they themselves may sometimes find it difficult to meet this prescription), or that annoyance is not a sufficient reason for hitting someone. In civilized society, physical violence is to be avoided if at all possible. But what is possible for an adult is often beyond the ability of a child—to control himself, for example; the difference is maturity, the degree to which we are able to master our impulses. When parents come forth with such pronouncements, all the child learns from the experience is that his parent doesn't understand him, or he concludes: "When I honestly tell why I did something, all I get for it is being told that I'm wrong!" It is amazing how many such experiences the average child collects in a few years' time—and with each one he learns that the consequence of forthrightness is criticism from the person most important to him. If this has been the child's experience, it will be hard for him to resist embroidering the facts to make them more palatable to us, for he is convinced that he cannot afford to tell us the plain truth.

A common explanation for violence is: "He made me do it!" This is not an attempt to shift the blame—as some parents may think—but a true statement of the child's feeling that the other's behavior flooded him with such strong emotions that they overwhelmed his ability to control himself. The parent, who may have observed that the other child did not strike first, may tell his child, "No, he did not!"—meaning that the other child gave no cause; but there was plenty of cause from the child's point of view. An adult, in general, *may* be able to live up to the principle of nonviolence, but is it reasonable to expect a child to have the same self-control?

The trouble here, as in many other situations, is that the parent evaluates the situation from his perspective and decides how he would react, then somehow expects his child to do the same. But the child is much more susceptible to his feelings and much less able to control his impulses. The law takes into consideration a person's reduced ability to control himself; should not we as parents do the same and not expect our children to exercise self-control beyond their age?

If we start out with the conviction that our child's actions are based on good reasons, we can then assume that if he hits another child, he must have been so seriously provoked that, in his view, this was the only appropriate response. If we proceed on the basis of this assumption, we won't have to ask, "Why did you hit him?" because we would pretty well know the answer. We still won't know what the act of provocation was, but we can frame our question accordingly, with sympathy for our child who felt so wronged that he felt physical retaliation was the only possible response: "It's terrible that he made you so angry! What on earth did he do?" The child will feel that we are on his side, and reassured that we understand that the situation did not permit him to act otherwise. There will then be no reason for him not to tell us the story exactly as he saw it. This will avoid the impasse between us, and we will be left only with the problem of making our child aware of an alternative, of a more constructive response to the provocation. If we believe in our child's essential goodness, then we can wait until he is no longer so upset or angry to talk with him about why physical aggression is objectionable and why one should develop self-control. When he is no longer in the grip of anger, the child can listen and take in what we are trying to convince him of.

Is it necessary to add that we shall not convince our child of the desirability of forgoing physical aggression if we ourselves apply physical punishment? If we do, all the child will learn is that physical aggression is all right if you can get away with it, and if you believe you are applying it in a good cause. Since the child is always convinced that his cause was just, he will learn to stop hitting only if we set the example of never using physical aggression in relation to him, not even in what we consider a just cause. This leads us to a consideration of discipline and punishment.

9

About Discipline

Children need models more than they need critics.
—JOSEPH JOUBERT, Pensées, 1842

MANY PARENTS ARE UNDERSTANDABLY CONCERNED about
the best way to discipline their children—how to give them a sense
of responsibility and to teach them to be disciplined in their actions
and reactions. Concern about this is most understandable, given the widespread lack of discipline in society, particularly among the young. Today,
not only are theories about discipline widely varied, the concept itself does
not seem popular. The vast majority of parents who have asked me about
discipline have wanted to hear my opinion on the punishment of children—
such as when and how to punish them—and they nearly always had physical
punishment in mind. These parents, truly wishing to do right in bringing
up their children and worrying about how best to discipline them, had
nonetheless neglected to consider the actual meaning of the word "discipline." Had they looked it up in a dictionary, they would have discovered
that only the last of the definitions given suggests that the word can also
mean punishment. *The Shorter Oxford English Dictionary* defines discipline
as follows: "1. Instruction imparted to disciples or scholars; teaching; learning;
education. 2. A branch of instruction; a department of knowledge. 3. The
training of scholars and subordinates to proper conduct and action by in-
structing and exercising them in the same; mental and moral training. 4. A
trained condition. 5. The order maintained and observed among persons
under control, or command. 6. The system by which order is maintained
in a church. 7. Correction, chastisement; also a beating, or the like." *Webster's New World Dictionary* show that American usage is not very different:
"1. a branch of knowledge or learning. 2. a) training that develops self-
control, character, or orderliness and efficiency; b) strict control to enforce

obedience. 3. the result of such training or control; specifically a) self-control or orderly conduct. 4. a system of rules, as for the conduct of members of a monastic order. 5. treatment that corrects or punishes."

I quote these definitions at some length because they both show that while the word can also be used in the sense of punishment, this is not its most important meaning. The idea of instruction is paramount. The American definitions, when compared with the British, emphasize self-control, and this seems to be what American parents are most desirous to have their children achieve. Thus their problem is how to instruct their children so that they will develop a healthy measure of self-control. Since only the last definitions of this term suggest that "discipline" can also be used in the sense of punishment, and since even this meaning is given only as a special subdivision of a larger one concerning correction, it is very questionable whether "punishment," or "a beating, or the like" are good ways to correct anybody.

The first *Oxford* definition, the original meaning of the word "discipline," suggests further that it is an instruction to be imparted to "disciples"—two words that stem from the same Latin root, *discipulus*, a learner. For most of us, the term "disciple" is associated with Christ's Disciples, who so deeply loved and admired Him, and were so impressed by His person, His life, and His teachings that they tried to follow His example as well as they could. Their deepest wish was to emulate Him, not just because they believed in His teachings, but because of their love for Him and His love for them. Without such mutual love, the master's teaching and example, convincing though they were in themselves, would never have been able to change the entire lives and beliefs of the Disciples. Their story is evidence of the power of love and esteem to inspire us to incorporate another person's values and ideas in our own lives and to emulate his conduct. By the same token, the combination of teaching, example, and mutual love is most potent in preventing us from acting contrary to the value of such an individual. Following this line of thought, the most reliable method of instilling in our children desirable values and the self-discipline to uphold them should be obvious.

The idea of discipleship implies not just the learning of specific skills and facts, but acquiring these from a master in whose image one wishes to form oneself because one admires this individual's work and life. This usually involves sustained, close personal contact, one personality being formed under the impact of the other. Thus it seems that the easiest and best way to become master of a discipline is to be first, and for some period of time, the disciple of someone who has truly mastered this discipline. Given this meaning of the words "disciple" and "discipline," how could one believe that the latter can be *imposed* or *forced* on another person? Any discipline worth acquiring cannot be beaten into anyone; indeed, such effort is contrary to the very idea of discipleship. In fact, the best and probably the only way one can turn oneself into a disciplined person is by emulating someone whose example one admires—not by being instructed verbally, which at best can be only part of it, and certainly not by threats. And if we believe ourselves to be the master's favorite, or at least one of his favorites, we are further motivated to form ourselves in the master's image, or in short, to identify with him.

The younger the child, the more he admires his parents. In fact, he cannot do otherwise; he needs to believe in their perfection in order to feel safe. In what image can he form himself but that of the persons who act as parents to him? Who else is so close and important to him? And if things are as they should be, nobody loves him so well, takes such good care of him as his parents do. Every child wishes to believe that he is his parents' favorite; the fear that he might not be is the root of sibling rivalry, the intensity of which is a measure of this anxiety. Naturally, parents do sometimes prefer one child to the others, although they may fool themselves into believing that they love all their offspring equally. To do so would deny the individual differences of children who, not being alike, cannot be liked in identical ways by the same person. At best, a parent will like each of his children very much—many parents do—but he will like each child in different ways, for different reasons of his own. Most parents are more loving of one child at one time and of another at another time, as each goes through the various stages of development and thus evokes different emotional reactions in his parents. Every child suffers when he feels that he is not the favorite. But if there are enough times when he may rightly feel that he is, this will usually suffice for him to maintain the belief that he is the favorite, at least most of the time; here, fortunately, as in so many other situations, the wish is father to the thought, and the thought fathers the belief. Of course, all this works only if the child's wish to be if not *the*, at least one of his parent's *most* favorite persons, is not too often and too severely disappointed.

As the child grows older, he will no longer admire his parents so single-mindedly; among the widening circle of his acquaintances they will begin to seem less than perfect. However, his wish to be their favorite will continue in full force, although it may be extended to include teachers and some friends, for his earlier need to admire his parents unconditionally was so strong and deeply rooted that it will be powerfully at work in his unconscious for a long time—usually until he reaches maturity, if not longer.

Thus, fortunately, in most families there is a solid basis for the child's wish to be his parents' disciple, to love and admire them, and to emulate them if not in all then in some very important respects; it exists, if not in his conscious, then certainly in his unconscious mind. But we all know families in which this is not the case, where parents indeed do not like a child very much, are disappointed in him, or do not behave in ways that inspire loving admiration. The child who neither admires his parents nor wishes to emulate them may very well find some other person to look up to and in whose image to form himself.

This is the natural consequence of the small child's dependence, his need to be taken care of by someone strong enough to give him security, which persists until he has achieved maturity himself. The danger here is that a child who has failed to acquire self-control at an early age by emulating his parents and has grown into an unruly adolescent will still be propelled by his need for a master he can emulate and may now seek and find an undisciplined master. An example of this is the member of a delinquent gang who is so impressed by its asocial leader that he admires and copies him, with disastrous consequences for the youngster and for society. The discipline with which a member of a delinquent gang pursues the gang's goals and obeys its leader is but another demonstration of young individuals' need to bond themselves to someone they can admire, although they might admire such a person for what most of us would consider bad reasons. On some level, a youngster may know this, however dimly, but his need for attaching himself to someone whom he can admire, and who seems to offer acceptance and security in return, is so great that it drowns out the voice of reason.

It is up to parents to build on the child's need for attachment to promote self-control around particular issues and, even more important, a lasting inner commitment to be, or at least to become, a disciplined person. Even when a child admires his parents, loves them, and, feeling loved by them, wishes to be like them, it is by no means easy to achieve self-discipline; many parents are not that disciplined themselves and thus do not provide a clear image in this respect for their child to emulate. Moreover, many parents try to teach self-control in ways which arouse their child's resistance rather than pleasure in learning it.

There is yet another difficulty: children tend to respond more readily—both positively and negatively—if they feel the strength of their parents' emotional involvement, but disciplined behavior usually precludes a display of feelings, even when we feel strongly about what is involved. It is when parents *lose* their self-control that children are most impressed, for then they are receiving powerful signals. The paradox is that the teaching of self-control requires great patience on the part of the teacher; but patience is a quiet virtue and does not make as deep and immediate an impression as the loss of patience does. It takes what seems to be an infinite number of parental examples of self-control and patience to teach the values of this kind of behavior and to influence the child to internalize these values.

The acquisition of self-discipline is a continuous but slow process of many small steps and many backslides, a process so protracted that in retrospect it may seem to have been unremarkable, as if "natural," and fairly painless. Having forgotten what this process was really like, parents tend to be impatient when their children have a hard time of it. Moreover, they may forget how powerful a motivator the fear of hellfire and damnation once was, and expect their children to acquire self-discipline even without this kind of spur.

If we could only remember our own struggles in this area—how undisciplined we ourselves often were, and how hard a time we had as children in disciplining ourselves, how we felt put upon, if not actually abused, when our parents forced us to behave in a disciplined manner against our will— then we and our children would be much better off. One of the greatest master teachers of mankind, Goethe, warns that only our ability to remember our own undisciplined days will permit us to bear up well under the onslaught of our children's undisciplined behavior. One of his famous epigrams reads: "Tell me how bear you so comfortably / The arrogant conduct of maddening youth?" / "Had I too not once behaved unbearably, / They would be unbearable in truth." ("Sag nur wie trägst du so behaglich / Der tollen Jugend anmassliches Wesen?" / "Fürwahr sie wären unerträglich, / Wär' ich nicht auch unerträglich gewesen.") Goethe could say this with the greatest of ease and enjoy the humor of it because he had achieved true inner security, which made it possible for him to understand with amusement the otherwise "unbearable" behavior of the young. The same feeling of security about himself allowed him to remember freely how difficult, even unbearable, he himself had been in his younger years, something many of us are tempted to forget, if our self-love does not impel us to repress or deny it.

We too should remember how impossible we often were as children and how we then resented it if our parents were not patient and understanding. If we could do that, we would then have much greater patience with and understanding of our children's inability to discipline themselves before they reach maturity; we would bear in mind that, at best, they are able to acquire discipline only very slowly and often only against great inner resistance.

Despite all the difficulties and obstacles along the way, parents are the logical transmitters of the right kind of discipline, since learning it has to start so early and continue for so long. But while parents are content to undertake this responsibility, they are less ready to accept the necessity of teaching it by example. We are all familiar with the old saying "Do as I say, not as I do," but we are still loath to agree that this simply does not work when teaching children. Whether or not they obey our orders, deep down they are responding less to our commands than to their perception of our character and conduct. Our children form themselves in reaction to us: the more they love us, the more they emulate us, and the more they internalize not only our consciously held values, but also those of which we ourselves are not conscious but which also influence our actions; and the less they like and admire us, the more negatively they respond to us in forming their personalities.

A Swedish study, published in 1973, demonstrated persuasively that well-disciplined adults who live in accordance with their values hardly need to preach self-control to their children, and rarely do it. On the other hand, parents who tell children to be disciplined but do not demonstrate discipline themselves are simply ineffectual.

The Swedish government became concerned over the failure of their system, which provides economic security for its citizens practically from cradle to grave, to achieve one of its major goals: the elimination of social disruption. Despite all governmental efforts, youthful alcoholism, drug use, hooliganism, delinquency, and crime were all on the rise as they were in the United States. Although these problems are much less severe in Sweden than they are in the United States, they did motivate the government to undertake a careful study of both well-disciplined, law-abiding youths and of delinquents. It was assumed that youngsters whose parents were poorly disciplined and showed asocial tendencies would show similar tendencies and be prone to be delinquents. But why did some children from affluent backgrounds, where such behavior was not part of the normal milieu, become delinquents, while others did not? This research demonstrated that neither material background nor social class exercised a statistically significant influence on behavior. What was decisive for whether a youngster was likely to develop in asocial or disciplined ways was the psychological and emotional atmosphere which reigned in the home.

The parents who were most successful in raising disciplined children were themselves responsible, upright, self-disciplined persons, living examples of the values they embraced and, when asked, freely explained to their children. They felt no need to force these values on their children, whom they implicitly trusted to become good persons. Indeed, even when these youngsters were deliberately exposed to bad company as part of the investigation, they proved to have internalized their parents' values too securely to be in any real peril. If curiosity induced some of them to join in what a delinquent or drug-using group did, such experimentation was always quite tentative, short-lived, and inconsequential. They found the delinquent or otherwise asocial behavior of such a peer group simply neither attractive nor suited to them; it met neither their needs nor their interests. And the reverse was also true: when delinquents and members of the drug culture were forced to associate solely with "square" peer groups, this failed to produce any significant improvements; they did not even temporarily abandon their asocial ways.

Further, this study found that the problem children did not necessarily come from what one would consider undisciplined or disorganized homes, nor did they have visibly asocial parents—those who did were not studied. Rather, it was found that parents of these asocial youngsters often had discordant relationships because of disagreements over values or, more often, inconsistency on this score; they did not live according to the values which they professed and to which they tried to hold their children. While the parents had tried to discipline their children and teach them what they considered the right values and behavior, the children had not been able to internalize these values precisely because they identified with their parents' inconsistencies. Expected by their parents to be more disciplined than they themselves were, most of the children turned out to be much less so.

Further study also revealed that in respect to whether the children were well protected against falling into asocial behavior, it hardly mattered what specific values the parents embraced—whether they were conservative or progressive, strict or permissive. What made the difference was how closely and well the parents lived by their stated values and by the values they tried to teach their children.

These findings are hardly surprising, considering the well-known fact that the best predictor of a child's academic achievement is the academic level which his parents attained. If the learning of the parents has such impact on that of their children, it is no wonder that, *mutatis mutandis*, the same also holds true for discipline—learning and discipline being such closely related concepts, as the origin and definitions of the word "discipline" make obvious. In respect to learning it has been shown that occasionally an inner need to reject parental values can lead to a refusal to achieve academically in order to defeat the parents, who in all other respects are able to defeat the child; the same can be true in regard to disciplined behavior. A child may simply refuse to emulate the example set by his parents as too demanding. If this happens, everything depends on the parents' reaction to such temporary rejection of what is experienced by the child as too difficult an example. But how compelling is their attitude may be illustrated by the spontaneous angry outburst of a nine-year-old (American) boy who one day blurted out to his father: "I know why you work so hard; you do it because you want to set a good example for your children." His father was amazed—he had no such purpose in mind. He simply lived according to his principles, which made him work well and also when needed hard, for causes he thought worthwhile. Nevertheless, the influence of his example was inescapable. His son could not keep himself from following this lead, working harder than he wanted to, and feeling bad about himself when he didn't. Thus even as he resented his father's behavior, he was in the process of internalizing it.

The boy's naive remark is actually quite revealing. By thinking that his father acted only to set an example for his children, the boy tried to make it unnecessary for himself to internalize these parental values, and therefore he himself could behave in less disciplined ways. Fortunately, his father understood all this and could reassure his son that far from wishing to set an example, and knowing how often it was difficult to live in accordance with one's principles, he hoped that his son, who was so much younger, would be able to take things more lightly, would not work so hard that it prevented him from enjoying himself. He added that he himself had not always been so dedicated—not until he had found work that was meaningful and interesting—and that as a youngster he had liked to take things easy. The boy took his father's remarks to heart and relaxed, but as he grew up, he became ever more disciplined himself. Without being pressured to identify with his father's way of life, he nevertheless eventually made his parent's values his own, although, had he been expected at the age of nine to be as conscientious as an adult of twenty-nine, the outcome might not have been as favorable.

A child will be most impressed by his parents when they act naturally, without regard for effect; and the example of self-respect is so compelling that a child can hardly avoid wishing to emulate his parents. A parent who respects himself doesn't need to buttress his security by demanding respect from his child. Secure in himself, he will not feel his authority threatened and will accept his child—at times—showing lack of respect for him, as particularly young children are occasionally apt to do. He knows that if it happens, it is due to immaturity of judgment, which time and experience will eventually correct. On the other hand, a demand for respect reveals to the child an insecure parent who lacks the conviction that this will be given to him naturally. What is demanded is given grudgingly, if at all, and is always experienced consciously or unconsciously, as stemming from the demanding person's inner insecurity. Who would want to form himself in the image of such a person? Unfortunately, the child of insecure parents often grows up like them. Even if he doesn't internalize and thus adopt the attitude of his parents, the lack of self-confident parents is enough to make the child grow into an insecure person.

Anytime a parent preaches what he doesn't practice, the lesson will fall flat, in the sense that it will not be generalized beyond the specific instance. As a matter of fact, the less deliberate instruction a parent gives and the more he lives consistently by his own values because it comes naturally, the better.

At the beginning of this chapter a remark by the French moralist Joubert was quoted: "Children need models more than they need critics." Probably in his day, as now, parents were quicker to criticize and sermonize than they were to rely on their own effectiveness as models for their children. And indeed, in the short run correction may produce more immediate results; but these tend to be short-lived by comparison to what parental models achieve.

Correcting a child—not to mention ordering him what to do—also has the effect of lowering the child's self-respect, by bringing his shortcomings to his attention. Even if he obeys, he will not profit from correction; the formation of an independent personality will not be encouraged. The principles, or underlying assumptions, of his behavior will alter only if and when he himself realizes that a change will gain for him what he most deeply desires: self-respect.

To be disciplined by others, to accept living by their rules, makes self-control superfluous. When the important aspects of a child's life and behavior are regulated by others, he will see no need to learn to control himself, since these others do it for him. By the same token, he cannot learn self-control before he is mature enough to understand why it is a necessary and advantageous ability to acquire. Punishment may make us obey the orders we are given, but at best it will only teach an obedience to authority, not a self-control which enhances our self-respect. Only after we have reached the age at which we are able to make our own decisions can we learn to be self-controlled; this can be fairly early, but not before we can reason on our own, since self-control is based on the wish to act on the basis of one's own decisions, arrived at through one's own deliberations.

It is instructive to compare the different ways Japanese and Western parents teach their children—control based on parental commands in our culture, self-control based on their own reasoning in Japan. Recently a study was undertaken to discover why Japanese youngsters outstrip Americans academically. Comparison of teaching methods, materials, etc. provided no clues; but when the researchers addressed the question of parental control, it became apparent that there were radical cultural differences that seemed to account for the differences in academic achievement. When young Western children ran around in supermarkets, their mothers—often annoyedly—

told them, "Stop that," if they did not yell at their children. At best a mother would say: "I told you not to act this way!" A Japanese mother typically refrains entirely from telling her child what to do. Instead she will ask him: "How do you think it makes the storekeeper feel when you run around in his store?" or "How do you think it makes me feel?"

Similarly, a Western mother will order her child to eat something, or tell him that he ought to eat it because it is good for him, but a Japanese mother will ask: "How do you think it makes the man who grew these vegetables for you to eat feel when you reject them?" or "How do you think it makes these carrots, which grew for you to eat, feel when you don't eat them?" Thus from a very early age the Western child is told what to do while the Japanese child is encouraged not only to consider the feelings of others—which is very much part of Japanese socialization and much less an important part of Western socialization and hence concerns us less here— but to think out his behavior instead of just obeying orders.

(In relation to the question of academic achievement, which was the focus of this study, it may be assumed that the Japanese child's early acquisition of the habit to think things out on his own stands him in good stead later on, in school, when he has to master academic material. The American child, by contrast, is not asked to base his decisions and actions on his own deliberations; he's expected to do as he is told. Not only is he not encouraged to do his own thinking in situations which his parents consider of importance, but the expectation that he ought to act as he is told may tend to disillusion him in respect to the importance of his own thought processes.)

The Japanese mother expects her child to be able to arrive at good decisions, but she also appeals to her child not to embarrass her—losing face is one of the worst things that can happen to a person in the traditional Japanese culture. Her question "How do you think it makes me—or the storekeeper—feel when you act this way?" implies that by mending his ways the child does her, or the storekeeper, a very great favor. To be asked to do one's own thinking and to act only on its basis, as well as to be told that one is able to do an important person a great favor, enhances self-respect, while to be ordered to do the opposite of what one wants to do is destructive of it.

Equally important in developing self-discipline—and the Japanese are extraordinarily disciplined as a people—is the patience with which a mother waits for her child to make up his own mind. Her patience sets an important example, and also implies the conviction that, given enough time, he will arrive at the right decision all by himself—a conviction which additionally greatly enhances the child's self-respect.

During a prolonged stay in Japan I never saw a child being scolded, nor crying, nor fighting with another child. It was impressive to see a mother teaching her child to step out of his shoes before entering a room. I never observed anyone ordering a child to do so; in fact, the mother typically said nothing, just waited silently and patiently until the child acted. True, she sometimes silently indicated that he was not yet to enter the room. But nearly always nothing was said; the mother's patient attitude as she waited was all that was needed. In parallel situations most Western parents would not show anything like such patience, but would immediately give orders. The child might obey, but his resentment might surface later in the form of unruly behavior. The point is that the parent who is in a hurry *imposes* discipline, whereas *teaching* self-discipline requires time and patience, and trust in the child's doing all on his own the right thing.

Another study in contrasts is the way American (or Western European) parents pick up their child in nursery school at the end of the day, as opposed to the way a Japanese mother does it. (Incidentally, the Japanese mother in question had observed all year long how the other parents behaved, her daughter being the only Japanese child in this nursery.) These parents, as soon as they arrived, immediately hustled their children into their coats and out of the door. Despite the children's obvious wish to linger, they all were gone within a few minutes. The Japanese mother came in and sat down silently, making no effort to attract her daughter's attention. Eventually she spoke softly to the child, but her manner was as unhurried as her daughter's, who continued to attend to the things that interested her. Sometimes the process of leaving took as much as an hour until they left in the most pleasant manner.

Here was a child who could feel that her needs were respected, that her mother did not give her own desire to leave precedence over the child's wish to make a slow transition out of the nursery-school setting to being with her mother. Moreover, the mother was giving her daughter a demonstration of self-control that compared favorably with what the other children had to put up with. This example, more than anything, would teach the child the value of her own self-control.

This ingrained respect for a child's slow development of self-discipline is by no means restricted to the Japanese culture. For example, the American anthropologist Ruth Benedict describes her amazement at the patience with which American Indians wait for their children to get ready, in their own good time, to do as they've been asked. She tells how she could barely contain herself from hurrying a child to do what had been asked of him. But as she moved to do so she felt such disapproval in the Indians present that she desisted. She was ashamed for having shown so little respect for the child's need to proceed slowly, so that he would be able to convince himself that he did the chore because he wanted to, not only because he had been ordered to do it.

Americans are in a hurry; it is part of our culture. But unfortunately, self-control is not learned in a hurry; it takes a great deal of time and patience. Our children are hurried practically from birth. One study, made in an obstetric ward, revealed that even newborn babies are not permitted time to make up their minds but are urged on by their mothers. The most common expression used was "Come on," in combination with other remarks, many of them critical: "Come on, wake up!" "Come on, you have to drink more than an ounce!" "Come on, open your mouth!" "Come on and burp!" "Come on, show off for the lady!"

Behind all this urging and hurrying is not just the mother's impatience and her wish to get the feeding over with, but an inner conviction that unless the infant is pushed or forced to do what is good for him, he won't do it. On the other hand, underlying the Japanese mother's patience is her conviction that her child, being *her* child, when allowed to think for himself, in his own good time will do the right thing—a belief that relieves her of worry over his future, and, moreover, induces the child to live up to her good opinion of him. Most American children, on the other hand, practically from birth on, suffer from their mothers' conviction that unless pushed, or urged, they won't do what is right and best for them. These worries make the child tense and uncooperative, which increases her worries, and so matters get more unpleasant for both.

We cannot copy the Japanese example; our culture, history, and values are much too different. But we can use it to stress the importance, in achieving self-control and self-confidence, of the parents' faith in their own values and confidence in their child. It is the absence of parents' trust and, even more, their doubts about how their children may turn out which make it so difficult for many children to develop sufficient trust in themselves, the necessary basis for self-respect. My parents know best, a child thinks, so if they distrust me, they must have good reasons; they must have discovered some serious flaw in me of which I am unaware: reason enough to develop self-doubt. All this is destructive to that self-confidence and self-respect on which self-discipline can be built! True self-discipline is based on the self-respect it gives us. This is why lack of self-confidence and self-respect are not just detrimental to the ability to develop self-discipline; they make it well-nigh impossible.

Any emotion that has us in its power will shape us—such as a child's love and admiration for his parents—and thus has the potential for both good or evil. The young child cannot distinguish between the morally good and the morally bad. He knows only what feels good and what doesn't, what he likes and dislikes. Thus, filial love will induce him to emulate his parent, whatever the nature of his parent's morals—he will identify with good as well as bad traits.

For example, often children of alcoholic parents who mistreated them when inebriated later become alcoholics themselves, or marry alcoholics. Long before the child understands the connection between alcoholism and abuse, he may have learned to admire his parent's strength and to love him for the good he bestows. Identification with the parent takes place very early in life and becomes so securely anchored in the deepest layers of the developing personality that it can be eradicated only with great difficulties by later experiences. This early identification may motivate a person even as an adult, so that he continues to maintain it, particularly when deep emotions are aroused.

As this extreme example suggests, parents have little power to dictate the aspects of their personality with which their child will identify; hardly any alcoholic wants his child to follow him into alcoholism. Since we don't know which of our traits our child will identify with, we must aim for consistency in our personalities and actions, as the Swedish study makes amply clear. Of course, since none of us is perfect, all we can hope for is that the characteristics which *we* consider desirable will be unmistakably dominant in us, not because we wish our child to emulate us, as the nine-year-old thought was true for his father, but because we wish to be the kind of a person who has these desirable characteristics. If our commitment to be this kind of person is strong, our desirable traits will be so attractive to our child that he will identify most strongly with them. Later, as he grows up, he will judge for himself which of his parents' traits he considers desirable and undesirable, and decide with which of them to identify; but these mature decisions are grafted onto earlier identifications which were made long before the age of reason. Thus we can understand the unconscious attraction of alcoholic behavior to children of alcoholics who, as adults, consciously detest alcoholism; but thus also we see the unconscious attraction of parental discipline for children who identify with that characteristic long before they can consciously appreciate the value of such behavior.

10

Why Punishment Doesn't Work

The power of punishment is to silence, not to confute.
—SAMUEL JOHNSON, *Sermons*

THERE IS A WORLD OF DIFFERENCE between acquiring discipline by identification with those one admires and having regimentation imposed on one—or sometimes painfully inflicted. Forcing discipline on a child is likely to be counterproductive, even detrimental to what the parent wishes to achieve. As for punishment, it may restrain the child, but it doesn't teach him self-discipline; there are much better ways to do that. The parent who gets carried away by the emotions aroused by his child's misbehavior and punishes him would be more hesitant to do so, and be less self-righteous about it, if he would admit to himself that this is what he is doing, rather than camouflaging it as a method of instruction. Otherwise he may fool only himself, and not the child.

What children learn from punishment is that might makes right. When they are old and strong enough, they will try to get their own back; thus many children punish their parents by acting in ways distressing to them. We would be well advised to remember what Shakespeare said: "They that have power to hurt and will do none . . . they rightly do inherit heaven's graces," which certainly includes the blessing of being loved and emulated by one's children.

Any punishment—physical or emotional—sets us against the person who inflicts it on us. And here we must remember that the injury inflicted on feelings may be much more lastingly hurtful than physical pain. A good example of this can be seen in the once common punishment for using foul language: having one's mouth washed out with soap. The procedure is bad-tasting, but only minimally painful; however, the degradation experienced is very great indeed. Unconsciously, the child responds to the obvious message, that he said something unacceptable, and also to the implicit one, that his parent views his insides—symbolized by his mouth—as dirty and bad; not only did he use vile language, but he himself is vile. The punishment rarely achieves the parent's goal: to "clean up" the child's vocabulary. The overt use of bad language may cease, but covert or fantasy use will continue. The child perceives that his parent is very concerned with overt behavior, but seems completely uninterested in what caused the annoyance that compelled the child to use bad language. To the child, the parent seems interested only in what he wants and not in what the child wants—so why shouldn't the child care only about his own desires, and not at all about his parent's?

In therapy children have told me that in response to this punishment they no longer spoke bad words, but instead continuously repeated the words silently to themselves, reacting to even the slightest frustration with streams of unspoken vituperation. They became so negative as to be virtually unable to form any good relations, which only made them more angry and inspired them to think up even worse epithets. In one extreme case, a boy whose silent concentration on angry and violent expressions prevented positive contacts finally reached the point of shunning language to the degree that he could not function at all. Eventually he told his therapist that washing out his mouth with soap resulted in good words being washed out with the bad, so that he no longer had *any* words to converse with.

Of course, each child reacts differently to any punishment, depending on his personality and most of all on the nature of his relationship with his parents, but no punished child escapes the feeling of degradation. I know one girl who managed to defeat her parents' efforts to prevent her using bad words by pretending that having her mouth washed out didn't bother her at all. The parents were nonplussed and gave up. But the relationship was damaged, for the daughter, although pretending not to mind, did mind very much. She felt superior to her parents, who had resorted to such crude methods, but this attitude, while it neutralized the feeling of degradation, impaired not only love but also her ability to respect them.

I am sure that as a teenager I occasionally used bad language, but I can now remember only one single instance. I forget what I was annoyed about, but I said something offensive to my mother. She was shocked and hurt, but she said and did nothing. When she told my father about it, he was visibly upset. He asked me in a very firm voice, "Do I really have to punish you for you to watch the way you speak to your mother?" This was all, but it made a deep impression on me, a much greater one, I believe, than any punishment could have made. The idea that he might have to punish me obviously distressed my gentle father. And so I worried, not that I might be punished—I never was—but that I had upset and worried my father to such a degree. Despite his agitation he had controlled himself; he asked me only one question and let it go at that, without scolding me any further. This did the job—never again did I use bad language to my parents. (I indeed had little reason to do so, but felt no compunction about using it with my peers.) My father's question, which was a warning rather than a punishment, was enough to make me feel that I had done wrong; but because both my parents played down their annoyance with me, I felt I should be able to control myself in my dealings with them. Punishment would not have had this effect; probably it would only have aroused my resistance, for even if a child knows he has done wrong, he feels there must be a better way to be corrected than through pain or mental discomfort. Most children resent punishment, and the more they love their parents, the more they are insulted by such chastisement and disappointed in the wielder of the rod.

Most of us learn to avoid situations that lead to punishment; in this sense, it is effective. However, punishment of criminals shows that it is a very weak deterrent to the person who believes he won't be caught; so the child who was open in his actions before now learns to hide them. The more severe the chastisement, the more devious he will become.

Also, he will learn to express remorse when it is expected of him, whether he feels it or not. In reality he may only be sorry that he was found out and now has to "face the music." Thus we should remember that such an expression of regret, extracted under duress, is an essentially worthless statement made to pacify us, or to get the reckoning over with.

It is much better to tell a child that we're sure he would not have misbehaved had he known he was doing wrong. This is nearly always so; he may have thought, "If my parents find out, they'll be angry," but this is very different from believing that he is doing something which is wrong. Whatever he does seems right to him, at the moment. For example, a forbidden cookie can become so alluring that the intensity of his desire for it justifies the act of taking it. Later, parental criticism or punishment may convince him that the price is too high, and that it would have been better to have left the cookie in the jar; but this is a realization after the fact.

If we tell our child that although we disapprove of what he's done or forbid what he intends to do, we are convinced that he had no harm in mind, this positive approach will make it easier for him to listen to us with an open mind. And while he still might not like our objections, he will like our good opinion of him enough to want to retain it, even if he has to forgo something he liked doing.

A child is rarely *convinced* that something is wrong simply because his parents say it is. It *becomes* wrong to him because he wishes to be loved by his parents, to be thought well of by them. Since the best way to be loved, in the short run, is to do what the parents approve of and in the long run to become like them, he identifies with their values. This identification is thus the result of loving and admiring one's parents, not of being punished by them.

While criticism or fear of punishment may restrain us from doing wrong, it does not make us wish to do right. Disregarding this simple fact is the great error into which parents and educators fall when they rely on these negative means of correction. The only effective discipline is *self*-discipline, motivated by the inner desire to act meritoriously in order to do well in one's own eyes, according to one's own values, so that one may feel good about oneself—may "have a good conscience." It is based on values which we have internalized because we loved, admired, and wanted to emulate people who lived by them—for in this way we hope ourselves to be esteemed by these significant others.

It is not much of a conscience which tells us not to do wrong because we might be punished. The effective conscience motivates us to do right because we know that otherwise we will suffer all the pain and depression of feeling bad about ourselves. In the last analysis, we will *reliably* do right only in order to prevent the pangs of conscience—to feel good about ourselves, not to avoid punishment.

While it is our inner feelings about ourselves which are all-important in this regard, there are also some external ingredients which support our ability to respect ourselves. These include the wish to gain or preserve the esteem of others whose good opinion we value. If we do not value their positive view of us, then what they think is unimportant. They have no power to influence our behavior, even if they have the power to chastise us. All we then do is try to avoid being punished.

Thus, in the last analysis, it is only self-respect that can be counted on to prevent us from doing as we desire, and if this fails to restrain us, then our conduct depends on our calculation of the possible consequences. That is to say, we then live by a situational morality that changes with the conditions of the moment, not one securely anchored in the deepest layers of our personality. Thus a parent's goal in the area of discipline ought to be to increase his child's self-respect and make it so strong and resilient that it will at all times deter the youngster from doing wrong.

I mentioned before, but I cannot emphasize enough, that whatever a child does, at the moment of action it seems right to him, no matter how spurious his reasons or self-deceiving his evaluation of the situation. Therefore, when we reprimand him, we ought also to make clear that we are persuaded he acted as he did only because *he* thought it was justified. This approach is the only one which will safeguard his self-respect and permit him to give us a positive hearing. Although we may be annoyed at the child's having done wrong, we should remember Freud's warning: the voice of reason may be insistent, but it is very soft, whereas the clamor of the emotions is often overwhelmingly loud, so loud as to block out all other voices; and this is especially so in childhood.

The voice of reason needs to be carefully cultivated and made attractive to children so that although it is soft, it will nevertheless get a hearing. Shouting at a child will not get us very far. He may be shocked into obedience, but he—and we—know that he is not hearing the voice of reason. Our task is to create a situation in which reason can be heard and heeded. If we get upset and anxious, we are not likely to speak with this soft voice of reason, and if he is fearful of our displeasure or of actual punishment, he is in no position to listen to this soft voice.

Unfortunately, most of us have forgotten just how overwhelming the desire for a forbidden thing, even such a small thing as a cookie, can be for a child, since we either no longer have such wishes or can easily restrain or satisfy them. The child's desire is so great, however, that it blots out all other considerations. If we want to understand his state of mind, then we have to imagine how we would feel or act—or actually do act—when we are in the grip of the desire to do something against the rules that can easily be done and does no damage to anybody else. Probably one of the most frequent examples of this—which our children can and do observe, even when they don't comment on it—is to be seen in the transgression of speed limits, or in the breaking of traffic or parking laws. The freedom with which we decide whether or not there is any harm in such transgression is noticed by the child, and of course, it's hard for him to accept that the same disregard of rules should not also apply to him. Here, as always, everything depends on what we do, not on what we say.

If we could just articulate the way we rationalized exceeding the speed limit to ourselves, we would know our child's state of mind when he grabbed the cookie. Then we would see that just as we found innumerable reasons to support our disobedience of the laws, so did our child. If we thought along such lines, how harshly could we condemn his misdemeanors? Rather, we would view his misbehavior with sympathy, and find the right words (and feelings) to convince him that what he had done was not for the best. It would make it easier for him to withstand temptation next time, since we had been so nice about it all. But this will work only if we set the example and show that we ourselves are able to resist temptation.

Taking a cookie stands here for many diverse and perhaps more serious transgressions; the more gravely we view them, the less likely we are to think along the lines just suggested, but they apply equally well. Telling our child that, although we disapprove of what he did we realize he thought it was justified, will open a dialogue. However, if we lead him to believe that we don't consider his reasons worthy of our consideration—no matter what they are—he will develop the conviction that we give credence only to our own way of thinking, never to his when it does not accord with ours. In that case, he may give in, but he will become more set against us and our way of thinking.

Telling a child that he did wrong, particularly in an angry and disappointed tone, deflates his self-respect and diminishes his love for us and with it his need to act in ways that will gain our approval. On the other hand, telling him that we are convinced that had he known he was in the wrong he never would have done it, increases his self-respect and his love for us, with all this entails. It is the wish to be loved that induces him to do right in the present. Later on, his self-respect will motivate him, as an adult, to live a moral life.

I do not mean to suggest even for a moment that parents should not reprimand or restrain a child when he does something that they believe is wrong, nor to suggest that they can never be annoyed with him. Any parent who feels deeply about his child will also at times feel strongly about the child's acting in wrong ways. Even the kindest and best-intentioned parent will sometimes become exasperated. The difference between the good enough and the not so good parent in such situations is that the first realizes his irritation usually has more to do with himself than with whatever the child did, and that giving in to it benefits no one, while the second believes his anger is due only to his child and that he therefore has every right to act on it. But surely it is to everyone's advantage if we can keep in mind that when we are angry, we don't reason very well. We are unable to proceed on the basis of a balanced judgment; nor can our child, responding to our emotions rather than to our reasons, listen receptively to what we say. Even if we try to suppress our anger and speak judiciously, he will nonetheless sense our repressed emotions and react to them, rather than to our words. Pretending we're calm when we're boiling inside and would like nothing better than to boil over openly teaches the child that we're dishonest with ourselves—exactly the type of behavior which the Swedish study found so detrimental to the instilling of discipline.

To return to the example of the purloined cookie, how much easier it would be to make the child understand our point of view if we waited to talk with him about it until he was so full he couldn't think of eating. The moment when his desire for sweets is sated he will be able to accept the idea that eating too many sweets is not desirable. The soft voice of reason can easily be heard, because no emotions are causing interference.

All this is so sensible that one may wonder why we do not always follow such procedures. The reasons are obvious and manifold. For one thing, we're unwilling to be satisfied with simply having him desist; we also want him to agree that we are right to make him desist. An example may illustrate:

A mother, whose relationship with her son was generally excellent, had to deny his request for a new ten-speed bike. The teenager was very unhappy, and began to pester her about it, so she asked him to sit down with her and proceeded to explain at length the family's financial situation. The boy listened patiently and tried to take it all in, but afterward he said to his mother: "I don't like the fact that I can't have the bike, but I was willing to accept your no. But asking me to listen to an economics lesson as well is too much!" Fortunately, his mother saw the validity of his point and apologized to him. She understood that rather than making it easier for her boy to accept not getting the bike, she had made it more difficult. Instead of simply having sympathy for his disappointment, she had also wanted him to see things her way, which at the moment was impossible for him.

The trouble is that often, just because we hate to disappoint our children, we fail to experience sympathy for what they feel when we have to deny them something they want. We want them to accept and understand our reasons at a time when their emotional involvement precludes this. Had the mother accepted her son's disappointment as justified at the moment, and waited for the next day to explain the family finances to him when he would have had time to integrate his disappointment, he still might not have been very interested, but he would have felt that his mother was doing all she could to make his disappointment acceptable to him. The mother's lecture made her son feel: "My mother expects me to be much more mature and reasonable than I can be. She wants too much of me; I'm unable to do as well as she wants me to." This feeling is detrimental to his self-respect. But had she postponed her explanations and just given him sympathy at the moment of refusal, he would have felt that his disappointment was acceptable and reasonable, and his self-respect would have been enhanced. Then, if she returned to the issue the next day, he would have been pleased that she hadn't taken his unhappiness lightly, but took his feelings seriously and viewed them as valid.

LEAD US NOT INTO TEMPTATION

Probably no common childhood transgression upsets parents more than stealing, and more disturbing than the act itself is the idea that the child may grow up to be a thief. Thus the parents' reaction is often more commensurate with their anxiety about the future than with the actual misdeed. To the child, who has no intention of becoming a criminal when he takes some small item, this drastic response seems entirely inappropriate, and he is deeply hurt that his parents now think of him as a potential criminal. Generally speaking, he knows that he has done wrong, and is ready to accept his parents' dissatisfaction with him, but only for what he did here and now. He isn't much concerned with the future—first, because he can't imagine it very well, and second, because his mind is fully occupied with the pressures of the present.

This is not to suggest that parents should disregard their child's conduct. Whatever he does, good or bad, their positive or negative reactions strongly influence the formation of his personality. A serious transgression requires an appropriate response, so that the child may learn from the episode. If theft is disregarded, or taken lightly, he may feel encouraged to repeat it, perhaps on a larger scale. So it is important for parents to be aware of what their child is doing, what he has been up to when, for example, he suddenly has a new possession of unknown origin. It is hardly necessary to say that theft must be treated seriously; but equally important is that the parental reaction, to be effective, must be appropriate to the actual deed, and not to what we fear it may augur for the future. In other words, while we do not make light of it, we must not make more of it than the child can comprehend as being justified.

Clearly, he must not be permitted to enjoy his ill-gotten goods. What he has stolen must be immediately restored to its owner, with the appropriate apologies—the necessity of this every child can understand—and if damage has been done, the owner must be adequately compensated. But we ought not to view the act as his having committed a crime; in our legal system a child cannot commit a crime, and we ought not to be more severe than the law. On the other hand, to send him off alone to return what he has taken might not be the best idea. Without our supervision, we can't be sure of the way the restoration is accomplished. More important, in my opinion, is that if we accompany him, he will observe at firsthand how embarrassed we are by his act. For the child who loves his parents, the realization that he has shamed them in the eyes of a stranger is one of the worst experiences he can have.

However, if we also punish him, it may considerably weaken the effects of this distress. In large measure our legal system reflects the common feelings of mankind, and one of these is that punishment erases guilt. Also, our experience with the criminal justice system indicates that punishment is a weak deterrent; it makes the offender so angry at those who inflict it that he can reject the idea that he deserved it, and besides, having paid the penalty he has much less reason to continue feeling guilty. Far better simply to let the child observe the pain and embarrassment he caused us through our behavior to those from whom he has stolen. He will remember it, and will be apt to avoid repetitions.

It may make little difference to us, who fear for the child's future, whether the theft has been from a store or from us, but for the child, taking something from a member of the family and from a stranger are entirely different matters. We can sabotage our own efforts to set things straight if we do not adequately discriminate between these two situations.

There are few children who have never been tempted to pick up small change that their parents have left in open view; or to take it surreptitiously from a purse that has been left conveniently lying around. There are many possible reasons for it. The child may wish to buy something he longs for; he may wish to find out how observant his parents are of their own possessions and of his; he may want to make his parents aware of how desperately he desires something. He may feel a need to keep up with his peers, or to buy their friendship, or perhaps he wishes to punish the person from whom he steals. This is a most limited list of the many and varied reasons a child may be aware of when he takes something. In addition, there can be many unconscious reasons which motivate his action. For example, he may think that he is taking money just to acquire some desired object, but the deed is overdetermined; the unconscious cause of the theft was the desire to embarrass, or punish a parent for not loving him. Some children steal for the excitement they experience when doing so, although they are completely unaware that it is the desire for excitement which drives them on. Or a child may be convinced that he steals only to get some object while unconsciously he is compelled by the need to demonstrate to himself his daring, or his cunning, or he wants to test fate to ascertain that he is favored by it.

When our child takes some of our money we ought to ask ourselves— even before we deal with our child—whether we have been too careless and put temptation in his path. As parents we are often too ready to righteously think that *our* child ought not to be tempted to do such a thing, even though we know that most children take things once in a while. True enough, he should not have done it, but did we do anything to protect him from being enticed? After all, do we not pray to the Lord to "lead us not into temptation" because we know how easily this can happen? Maybe our child would have been able to resist temptation if we had warned him how easily we all are tempted, and how difficult, and therefore how laudable, it is to resist temptation. If we had, perhaps he might have chosen virtue over sin. Virtue unpraised certainly may seem less attractive than sin to a young and inexperienced child whose moral controls are still weak. They may have been further weakened by his observation that his parents are quite ready to indulge themselves by buying whatever they desire, or so it seems to him. While the child's action is clearly wrong, are we not a bit hypocritical in appearing righteously indignant when our child takes some money from us to buy something he desires very much, when all his life he has seen us providing ourselves with small—or not so small—items we desired, whenever we wished to do so?

If we were as serious as we ought to be about not leading our child into temptation, we would be very careful to make the things we do not wish him to have inaccessible to him. It's too easy to say, "I don't have to be careful about putting things away because he oughtn't to take what isn't his"; this is just an excuse for our own negligence.

Maybe I am oversensitive about this issue, but if so, it is the result of personal experience. One day, when I was about ten years old, a person who was then living with us left some change lying around. I was tempted to take some of it, although neither then nor later could I figure out why, or what I wanted it for. I kept the money with me for the rest of the day, fearing that the theft would be discovered, and that it would be apparent that I was the culprit, but also hoping it would, so that the matter would be settled. As time passed, I felt more and more guilty. The next day, some twenty-four hours after I had taken it, I put the money back. I was greatly relieved, but now I wondered more and more why I had stolen it in the first place, since I had had no intention of spending it. I gradually became angry that I had been led into temptation by someone who, moreover, was so careless that he didn't even realize the money was missing. And then, young as I was, I realized that I had wanted to punish him for tempting me, that this had been my motive, since I had no plan to spend any of the money. In my mind I did not forgive this person for his carelessness, first by tempting me to take it, and then by his having made it so easy for me to get away with it.

Thus from my own experience I know that a child may take things in his home simply to punish those who tempt him, or to discover whether they are observant enough to notice what he's up to and caring enough to do something about it. Nobody ever learned about my deed, to my great relief. But the guilt I had felt was so painful that it prevented me for the rest of my life from even so much as thinking of taking anything that did not belong to me.

Had the theft been discovered and had I been questioned about it, I am pretty certain I would gladly have confessed, just to assuage my guilt feelings. But I am sure I couldn't have expressed the fact that I had done it to punish the person who had led me into temptation. And understanding as my parents were, and as ready as they would have been to agree that money should not have been left lying around, I am sure it would not have occurred to them that I took it for any reason other than that I wanted to buy something with it.

I tell this story to suggest that parents ought to be careful not to be satisfied with the notion that their child took something merely to indulge himself. Arriving at such simple conclusions about a child's motive may be a serious error. As my experience shows, whenever a child takes something in his home, his relation to the person from whom he took it always plays a very important role in his action. Thus the child's misdeed needs to be understood also as part of his relation to the person from whom he takes something. For example, he may take from a sibling because he thinks the other gets more from their parents than he does. In this case, he simply feels he is correcting an unfair situation. Perhaps the child thinks his parents have unnecessarily deprived him or in some of their dealings short-changed him in some way, and he goes about restoring the balance by taking something of theirs. Then again, he may wish to signal to his parents a pressing need which he feels they are unwilling to satisfy or unable to recognize. These are but a few possibilities; in actuality the reasons why a child takes something are manifold. For the middle-class child whose needs are fairly well taken care of, the motivation is hardly ever only the wish for material gain. This is why it is so important to find out the whole range of the child's motives. Simply assuming that he acted badly to gain something material is taking too simplistic a view.

The child who wishes to get even or to punish a family member also wishes to gain something for himself, namely satisfaction, but it is hardly ever just the satisfaction of attaining something with the money he took. Here, simply asking *why* he took from one person rather than another may be quite instructive, but we can elicit such important information only if we are not too visibly exasperated, and only if we show him that we have an open mind. Our child, like all of us, is not likely to be able to discover or reveal his innermost motives when pressed by someone who is very angry with him, or who seems to have already decided that these motives are unreasonable.

If we do not genuinely try to understand *all* of the reasons, the overt as well as the covert, then the child will be convinced that we care only about the money and not about him. Clearly, most parents' concern is about their child and his future development, not about their loss, which in most cases is relatively small. But children have a hard time realizing this unless their parents go out of their way to make clear that their greatest concern is not with the theft nor with what it augurs for the child's future, but with understanding the need that motivated his action. Only if he is sure that we care less about his action, or our inconvenience, than about him himself will he be impelled to gain and keep our goodwill, to keep our good opinion of him inviolate.

Taking things such as some money from within the family nearly always indicates that children have very different views of family possessions than their parents do. So much that is around the house is meant to be used freely by everyone that children may have a hard time drawing the line where money is concerned. Seeing that we, his parents, feel free to regulate much of his life, he may attempt to exercise parallel control over us. We decide what he may or may not have, so should he not also decide which of our possessions he may consider his? It makes a great difference to him whether the money he took was just lying around, for he sees that we feel free to handle or even dispose of his things if he doesn't stow them away. And if we've suggested or even demanded that he share his prized possessions with others, he may see nothing wrong with arranging it so that we share some of our possessions with him. Of course, parents who ask their child to share have only temporary use in mind. They would be better off if they would ask the child only to lend a toy to another child, because a loan implies continued possession, while sharing doesn't necessarily imply this.

Still, the main fact here is that we feel free to dictate our child what to do with his possessions, when to let others use them, how to take care of them, how to put them away, even when to get rid of them, not to mention the times when we simply take them away from him for whatever reason. Why shouldn't he think he has the right to do the same with our property? If he does think so, but we don't openly grant him such equality, he may try to establish it surreptitiously. Of course, he is much too young to reason all this out, but these are his feelings, and intense feelings which cannot be fully articulated can often exercise stronger pressure for action than explicit thoughts.

Probably what is most involved when a child "steals" from his parents is his feelings about his family. Since he belongs to his family, particularly his parents, do they not also belong to him? There are many different theories about the origin and purpose of the family. Its main function, of course, is the necessity to provide for the needs of the young while they cannot yet take care of themselves. But there is a theory that the family in its present form originated as a group which shared common property. There were times, and there are societies, in which everything a family owns is common property, to be used by all the members of the family as common usage suggests, and as needs require. If family property will become our portion, why could we not make use of it right now?

Because of his dependent condition, a child often has a keener sense of family—again on an intuitive, subconscious level—than his parents. A more primitive being, he experiences reality in much more primitive and direct ways. It is *his* family; so isn't everything that belongs to the family also his? If he belongs to his parents, and they belong to him, why do mere objects such as money belong to his parents and not also to him? When and wherever all family possessions were really that, possessions of the family, not private property of individual family members, perhaps the sense of family was much stronger and much more secure. With all this in mind, it's a good idea to view and treat a child's taking things from within the family quite differently from his taking the property of strangers. If a child takes from within the family, it should not be disregarded; on the contrary, it will instill in our child a much deeper feeling of family cohesion if we make it clear that—within reason—what the family owns is for *everyone's* use, but that he should not have taken things surreptitiously. What I have in mind when I say "within reason" is relatively small amounts of money, or minor valuables, the expenditure or even loss of which does not jeopardize the family's future. Small losses are very upsetting to parents not because of their value but because they arouse mental images of the child as a future spendthrift, or even thief. This exaggeration of things is not fair to the child, and hence makes him feel that the intensity of our reaction is unwarranted. Such feelings of the child, far from giving more validity to our reprimand, reduce its effectiveness. Things are again different if the child does not know why he took something, when he is motivated by pressures coming from his unconscious. If he repeatedly takes things, does not know why, and, most significant, cannot stop himself from doing so, then he suffers from psychological problems which need to be solved; he needs to be relieved of the inner pressures he cannot control which push him to do things he rather would not. Here, too, the first and most important step leading to a solution of the problem is to discover which unconscious motives account for his actions.

Is, then, a child never to be punished? What about those adults who, reflecting back on their childhood, are convinced that punishment did them a lot of good? And when, as children, we ourselves were chastised, did we not sometimes feel that it cleared the air, and that, much as we disliked the experience, it had some value?

My prime purpose here is not to discuss punishment *per se* as a means of inculcating morality, but—to put it more correctly, psychologically speaking—to analyze the conditions which instill in a child the wish to be a moral, well-disciplined person. If we can do this, then there will be no need to think of punishment. In respect to this goal, chastisement has no merits, but I will go further and say punishing one's child is always undesirable— and this, although it allows the discharge of both anger and guilt.

Unquestionably, when a child has seriously misbehaved and a parent is very upset, punishment may occasionally clear the air. By acting upon his anger and anxiety, the parent finds relief; freed of his upsetting emotion, he may feel somewhat bad about having punished the child, maybe even a bit guilty, but in any case he feels more positive about his child after he has discharged these negative feelings. The child, for his part, need no longer feel guilty about what he has done, since in the eyes of his parent he has paid the penalty, even though the child usually views the penalty as more severe than was warranted by his misdeed. Both parent and child, free of the emotions which stood between them, can feel that peace has been restored.

But is this the best way to attain the long-range goal of turning a child into a responsible adult? Does the experience of seeing a parent act violently or self-righteously produce in the child the impulse to become self-disciplined? And if the parent feels bad afterward about having punished his child—or, as he is likely to put it to himself, about having *had* to punish him, possibly, because of anger, more severely than is justified by the misdeed—will this increase the child's trust and respect for him? Further, is giving way to anger a good example of self-control? Would the annoyed parent not set a better example if he refrained from acting in a way about which he afterward feels some remorse? And a parent who, after punishing his child, does not feel bad about having done it—whether or not he believes he had to do it—is he a good enough parent? And as far as the child is concerned, would it not have been more of a moral growth experience, and a deterrent, if he had had to struggle awhile longer with his guilt feelings? Aren't feeling guilty about a misdeed and the pain of the pangs of conscience which it creates much better deterrents and more lasting ones than the fear of punishment? Acting in line with the urgings of one's conscience surely makes for a much more desirable personality, a more responsible and sturdy one, than a personality which is developed in response to the fear of punishment.

Punishment, particularly if it is painful or degrading, is a very traumatic experience, both because of what it entails directly and because it endangers the child's belief in his parent's benevolence, which is the firmest basis for his sense of security. Therefore, like other traumatic events, punishment can be subject to repression. The pain and resentment may have been repressed, and only the relief which came with the reestablishment of positive feelings, the result of the reconciliation which followed the punishment, is remembered. The memory of the few positive aspects serves to cover up the many negative ones which were so predominant at the time. No child claims, right after he has been punished, that it did him a lot of good; this idea comes much later, when past experiences are seen in a very different light. No doubt the reconciliation which follows makes the chastisement more bearable; this, in a false *quid pro quo*, over time can lead to the belief that the good feeling which the reconciliation inspired was the result of the punishment, which it was not. At best, if there is such reconciliation, physical punishment is less likely to lead to a scarring of the child's personality; but it does not prove that the punishment promoted the development of self-discipline or rectitude.

Any parental act which is meant to be a punishment, however mild, is resented by the child, and the more drastic the punishment, the more severe the indignation it will arouse. Who is likely to emulate or identify with someone he resents, no matter how admirable that person may be in other respects? Thus any punishment, however justified in our eyes and even those of our child, interferes with our main goals, namely that our child should love us, accept our values, and want to live what we consider a moral life. A benign punishment will detract from these goals much less than a severe one, but this does not change the fact that the punishment, being meant and conceived as such by parent and child, will make him less desirous of emulating us and will thus reduce his chance of feeling good about himself and his life in general.

Even when physical or any other form of punishment does not cause permanent psychological injury—which it often does—this proves only that parents who are by and large good enough parents can get away with a lot without doing serious damage to their child. Being a good parent compensates for much that would otherwise impede the child's personality; but the fact that it compensates for many errors we make in raising our children does not alter the fact that they and we would be much better off if these mistakes could be avoided in the first place.

This is why I believe it is always a mistake to punish a child; even if he himself thinks he deserves it, he still feels, when punishment has been meted out, that he has been treated unfairly. He may not make these distinctions clearly, or with conscious comprehension, but his feeling is nevertheless very strong.

Why does a child react this way? First, because punishment threatens the security that rests on his seeing his parent as a protector who will always treat him with tender care; and second, because it is human nature to resent anyone who has the power to punish us. We cannot feel secure, if our security depends on a person whom we resent. Certainly every child often resents certain acts of his parents, but under normal circumstances these resentments, which are due to the innumerable instances in which a parent has to regulate or at least to supervise important aspects of his child's life—in addition to the many more he only thinks he has to—do not compare with the kind of hurt resentments we feel toward those who arrogate to themselves the right to punish us.

The difference between teaching a child proper behavior, or regulating aspects of his life, and "teaching" him by chastisement may seem small or irrelevant to a parent who is convinced that the purpose of his punishment is to teach his child to act better in the future, but as far as the child is concerned the difference is enormous. If he can feel that his parent's intention is to make things good for him, even if he doesn't agree with the correction or prohibition, he still knows deep down that the parent means well; nothing blurs his view of his parent as his main protector. The parent who punishes his child, thinking that he is doing so to protect him against doing things which may have dangerous consequences for him, also believes he is protecting him, but the child feels differently, and a short consideration of our legal system proves him right.

Think of all the safeguards to which every accused is entitled before he can be judged guilty. Not only is he presumed to be innocent until his guilt is proved; he is defended not by himself, but by an attorney who has the same rights, privileges, and prestige as the accuser. Even more important, the case is heard by an independent judge and jury who give the arguments of the accuser and the defender equal weight. But when our child is on "trial," he has to present his own defense, while we find ourselves in the mutually incompatible roles of accuser and judge—and there is no jury at all.

If we, as parents, could only keep in mind the safeguards we are entitled to before we can be judged guilty by society, we probably couldn't find it in ourselves to punish our child for anything, because we would see how we lack the emotional distance and objectivity which are the primary attributes of a dispenser of justice. And as a final word on the subject, the judge who passes sentence never inflicts the punishment himself. Is there not something questionable in our doing both?

So what's a parent to do to prevent a child from misbehaving? Ideally, letting our child know of our disappointment should be an effective restraint, but I doubt that this will always suffice.

As discussed at length, education works best if the pupil is not only very deeply and positively impressed by the person and competence of his teacher, but also wishes to remain in his good graces because of the affection he feels for him, because he loves him and wants to be loved by him. That is why, when given half a chance, the child who has been raised with love and tender care will do all that is possible, within reason, to retain his parent's love, and fears nothing more than to lose him as a protector.

Given this fact, when our words are not enough, when telling our child to mend his ways is ineffective, then the threat of a limited and momentary weakening of our love and affection is the only sound method to impress on him that he had better conform to our request—otherwise we will no longer be able to think of him as highly, or love him as dearly, as he, and we, wish. Subconsciously recognizing how powerful a threat this is, some parents, with the best of intentions, destroy its effectiveness by assuring their child they love him no matter what. This might well be true, but while it may be reassuring at the moment, it does not sound convincing to the child who knows that he does not always feel love for his parents; so how can he believe their assurance of love when he feels that they are dissatisfied or even angry with him? This reassurance actually deprives parents of the best way, the only logical way, of inducing children to mend their ways. Also, most of us do not really love unconditionally; if we are too often and too seriously disappointed, our love wanes. Therefore any effort to make ourselves look better, to pretend to be more loving than we are, will have the opposite effect from the desired one. True, our love for another person can be so deep, so well anchored within us, that it withstands even very severe blows; so can our love for our children. But at the moment when we are seriously disappointed in them our love may well be at a low point, and if we want them to change their ways of behaving, they might as well know it.

Many parents, without consciously realizing it, instinctively know that the threat to withdraw their love is the best and most effective way to correct their child. Therefore, when showing disappointment is not sufficient to induce their child to mend his ways, these parents will convincingly impress upon him that losing their affection is a real danger. When addressing the child's rational mind—letting him know why he did wrong and how he ought to behave in the future—and registering our displeasure with his behavior remain ineffective, then we proceed to impress the child's unconscious with the seriousness of the situation by adding to our words an action which, although it *must* remain mainly symbolic, nevertheless clearly conveys that he is in danger of losing our love. A child who gets this message will correct his behavior for *his* reasons to secure the desired advantage—the parent's permanently undisturbed affection—in the future. The point to be emphasized is that then the child will correct his behavior now and in the future for *his* reasons and not for those of the parent.

The way to do this is to ban the child for a *short* while from our presence. We may send him out of the room or, if possible, send him to his room. Or we may withdraw to our own room. It does not matter in which manner or form the parent clearly indicates: "I am so disappointed in you that at this moment I do not wish to be with you; I feel unable to maintain physical closeness with you." Here, physical distance stands for emotional distance, and it is a symbol that speaks to the child's conscious and unconscious at the same time; this is why it is so effective.

The purpose of sending the child out of the parent's physical presence must never be to punish him, but only to permit both parent and child to gain distance from what has happened, to cool off, to reconsider; all this goes without saying. It all helps. But it is the threat of desertion which, as likely as not, deeply impresses the child. It has been mentioned that separation anxiety is probably the earliest and most basic anxiety of man. The infant experiences it when his prime caretaker absents herself from him, an absence which, should it become permanent and the caretaker is not replaced, would indeed lead to the infant's death. Anything that rekindles this anxiety is experienced as a threat; hence, as long as a child—however dimly—realizes that his very existence is in danger if his prime caretaker deserts him, he will respond to this real, implied, or imagined threat with feelings of anxiety. Even when he is old enough to know that his life is not in any danger, he will respond with feelings of dejection because he nevertheless to some degree still feels as if it were. The difference is that at an older age the fear is not of physical but of emotional deprivation.

Those who in childhood had such distancing imposed on them by a parent whom they loved will recall how lost and lonely they felt when sent to their room. This powerful reaction would be incomprehensible if they had not experienced being sent to their room as a threat of the withdrawal of love, which, in their unconscious, revived separation anxiety. Since on other occasions they liked to be alone in their room and did quite well outside the physical presence of a parent, being all by themselves could not have been the cause of their feeling as if they were actually bereaved. Their feelings were the consequence of their understanding that what was at stake was the potential loss of parental affection, a serious threat to the child, who knows that he cannot manage life should he lose his parent as a protector.

If we should have any doubts that such physical separation is an effective expression of our disgust with the child's behavior, then our children's own behavior can teach it to us. The worst threat a child can think of when he is utterly disgusted with his parents is that he will run away. Children are convinced that this threat will be enough to make us mend our ways—a clear expression of how the child thinks about such matters. Therefore the child understands very well that our threat to distance ourselves physically is a symbol of our distancing ourselves emotionally from him, and such a threat is likely to make a very deep impression on him.

As a *planned* punishment, such physical distancing loses much of its emotional impact, because what makes it work is not the carefully reasoned and executed action, but the strong emotional statement. Such was the impact of my father's question to me upon hearing of my use of bad language to my mother. It was the strongest response that occurred to him at the moment, to convey his disappointment in me. (Interestingly enough, I did not reply, either with an apology or any promise to mend my ways; I was too shaken for that. Instead I went to my room to mull things over. I had to remove myself physically from the strength of my father's feelings; he didn't have to send me to my room.)

To have a strong emotional reaction to one's child's serious misbehavior is only natural; to withdraw one's love temporarily because the child's actions have been such a disappointment that one feels temporarily estranged is the logical outgrowth of one's true feelings. Thus in such a situation, sending a child out of the room, away from one's presence, is an appropriate reaction to one's feelings. That the child experiences it as a punishment is another matter and suggests his correct understanding that the worst a parent can do is to threaten to withdraw his affections. But in the deepest sense it is not a punishment but only a statement of feelings.

Being temporarily banished from the parent's presence unconsciously rekindles the ancient anxiety of the infant that, deprived of his parents, he is lost. The activation of this anxiety in the child's subconscious will make him consciously keenly aware how much he needs his parent, and this will induce him to try to be readmitted into the parent's love. The emotional relief and often the true happiness parent and child experience when, after their short separation, they are again reunited will enhance their relationship.

All this will work well only if the underlying motive of the parent is not a desire to punish the child, but a wish not to become so angered by his misbehavior that anger may lead to a more serious disruption of their basically loving relation.

Parents who wish to punish and hurt their child are able to use any opportunity to do so. So it is hardly surprising that some not so good parents take advantage of the method of withdrawal of love for their nefarious purposes, which they can afford to do because no physical aggression is involved, as it is in corporal punishment. They can hence fool themselves that they were not acting out their hostile feelings but only wanted to correct the child. Such parents punish a child by not talking to him for days and even weeks. This can arouse such anxiety in him that not only does his relation to his parent become seriously damaged—as it was probably all along because of the parent's underlying hostility—but also the child's personality.

A mother went even further in her punishment of her daughter. If she did not behave as her mother expected her, the mother did not talk to her for months at a time; worse, she went out of her way to tell anybody willing to listen about the supposed misdeeds of the girl. In her bitter complaints about her daughter she unconsciously revealed her true feelings, as she also told people that her daughter was not really her child. This must have been how she felt deep down, and it was the cause of her rejecting behavior toward the girl.

Thus all that happens within the parent-child relationship depends on the parent's feelings for his child. The good enough parent will feel bad when he requires his child to separate himself from the parent for a short time so that they both will get hold of their negative feelings and the positive ones will again gain ascendancy. The not good enough parent, when annoyed by his child, will punish him severely, irrespective of the particular method of punishment he applies. He probably will do so because he resents the child, whose presence confronts him with his unloving nature. I do not believe such a parent acts this way because he is evil—I do not believe that such people exist—but, like everybody else, he responds to his inner needs, whatever their origin may have been. A mother like the one who denies being her child's mother does not do so because she is evil—although her behavior has disastrous consequences for the child—but she cannot bear to be confronted by her child with the fact that she cannot love and is a not good enough parent. So she gets even with the child for the inner agonies he creates in her because she subsconsciously knows what a bad parent she is. She punishes her child not for the misdeeds she claims as the cause of the punishment, but because the child makes her feel so bad about herself.

Since this book is written not to detail the damages the not good enough parent inflicts on his child but to advise good enough parents who wish to do right by their child, there is little point on dwelling on how horrible it is for parent and child if their relationship is not basically a loving one.

The good enough parent will avoid punishing his child and will make every effort to have his criticisms of his child be overbalanced by praising him whenever this is appropriate: deserved praise feels so much better to both of them.

Praise, too, is effective less because we are such good judges of objective values and more because it is a statement of our strong positive emotions, of our joy and pleasure in our child's doing well. Our response to his misbehavior should also be mainly emotional, expressing our feelings rather than our objective judgments. Thus praise—symbol of an increase in our love and affection—and temporary withdrawal of affection are the two best ways to influence a child's forming his personality. In praise we come emotionally close to our child and often also physically, too—by, for example, embracing him—and he understands this. The opposite reaction is the consequence of our disappointment in our child. We have every right to feel disappointed, but our disappointment gives us no right to punish. The child knows this; this is why he resents our punishing him yet modifies his behavior to undo our disappointment. When he knows we love him, our disappointment in his misbehavior is understandable to him. By the same token, his love for us is his reason for fearing our disappointment.

Only the example of our own good behavior will induce our children to make such behavior part of their personalities—and only then if we are open about it and neither force our values on them nor expect them to be able to emulate our examples before their own development makes them ready to do so. We must accept it as understandable, and not be disappointed in them, if occasionally they fall into error; and we must at all times retain our conviction of their inherent goodness, acknowledging that it just takes a long time for our example to come to full fruition, as it did in our own lives. The more we realize how true this was for us, the better it will be for them as well as for us, and the easier and smoother will be their development.

And we must be equally honest and open about our emotions, showing through our behavior how deeply we love our children without necessarily always telling them that we do, although this too has its place. We must believe that our love has its best effect through the ways we respond to their needs and help them with their difficulties. When we are disappointed in them, letting them know this also has its place in our relations, provided we don't become critical or punitive, but convey our disappointment through keeping or increasing our distance, because in truth we can't be very close to them when we don't feel like it. This is all just part of being ourselves, not pretending to be better than we are, certainly not making any claim to being perfect, but striving as best we can to live the good life ourselves so that they, impressed by the rewards of living a good life, in their own good time will wish to do the same.

11

Exploring Childhood as an Adult

> We shall not cease from exploration
> And the end of all our exploring
> Will be to arrive where we started
> And know the place for the first time.
>
> —T. S. ELIOT

AMONG THE MOST VALUABLE but least appreciated experiences parenthood can provide are the opportunities it offers for exploring, reliving, and resolving one's own childhood problems in the context of one's relation to one's child. As T. S. Eliot reminds us, only by exploring and reexploring the steps we made in becoming ourselves can we truly *know* what our childhood experiences were, and what they have signified in our lives. If we achieve this knowledge, the impact of these events on our personality will be altered. Our attitude toward our experience will change, as well as our attitude toward parallel experiences with our children. Our growth in self-knowledge must inevitably result in a better comprehension of our children, even more so when the new insights are in consequence of experiences involving these children.

Unfortunately nearly all of our primary experiences are lost to conscious memory, because they happened too early to leave more than the vaguest traces in our minds. We cannot reexperience them, but we can at least explore imaginatively some of their aspects as we observe how our infant responds to his inner processes, to us, and to his world.

For example, if we realize that the infant's waking world consists of only two opposite experiences—happiness and physical well-being, and unhappiness and pain—this can help us also understand the origin and ambivalent nature of all strong emotions. Since it is normally the parents who change the negative state of the infant's existence, such as hunger pains or the discomfort of soiled diapers, into one of satisfaction by feeding or by changing him, he experiences his parents as all-powerful and the source of all happiness and unhappiness; also as all-giving and all-frustrating. Thus ambivalence is built into our unconscious, particularly in regard to our parents. Later on they and their surrogates, our foremost educators, continue to dispense both pleasure and pain, by praising us, for example, or by criticizing and frustrating us. In this way the original ambivalent feelings, so deeply rooted in our unconscious, continue to be fed by the innumerable experiences of daily life.

Understanding this infantile origin of ambivalence, particularly in regard to our parents, can help us comprehend our children better when we are confronted with their expressions of ambivalence about us. The more we can accept their ambivalent feelings in relation to us, the greater chance they will have, as they grow up, to neutralize and control these ambivalences—and the less they will need to blow hot one moment and cold the next. By accepting that the negative aspects of this ambivalence must occasionally be ventilated, we reduce the need for our children to repress them; and the less they are repressed, the more accessible they are to rational scrutiny and modification.

As children, we too were torn by our ambivalent emotions. But when we acted out their negative aspects, our parents' disapproval was usually so strong that we were forced to repress these feelings, which thus retained their full force in our unconscious. When we are confronted as parents with similar feelings in our children, the experience tends to reactivate some of this repressed material. We can accept that our children will have much less control than we do, as long as their behavior does not awaken in us feelings we wish to keep repressed; but when our own repressions become remobilized, then we can no longer deal realistically with the negativism of our children.

That we repress the negative aspects of our feelings about our parents is understandable; after all, we need them and don't want to offend or alienate them by openly displaying our hostility. It is harder to comprehend why we also repress our identification with what to us as children seem negative aspects of our parents. Most of us are quite aware that we have made our own many of the things we like about our parents, but we're *not* aware that we have also identified with and internalized the negative aspects of their attitude toward us. Of this we become cognizant—usually to our great surprise—when we hear ourselves scold our children in exactly the same tone, even with the very same words, that our parents used with us. And this although we had objected to their doing so and have thought that we would never behave to our children in such manner.

On the other hand, when we speak lovingly to our children, we are not at all compelled to use the same terms our parents employed. In our positive expressions and behavior we are quite our own persons and speak very much with our own voice. The reason for this is once again that because there was no cause to repress our positive identification with our parents, it did not become encapsulated in the unconscious but remained accessible to modification as we ourselves developed. The negative identification, in contrast, was repressed and thus remained unchanged.

Very often the relations of the child to the parent of the same sex are more beset by ambivalence than are those to the parent of the other sex. The reason for this is that in relating to the child of our own sex we tend to reexperience some of the more difficult aspects of our own relation to our same-sex parent. Thus it is more likely that a mother will catch herself talking like her own mother when she criticizes her daughter, while a father will find himself repeating in his negative interactions with his son those that took place in his childhood between him and his father.

This is just one example of our tendency to project our own unresolved conflicts onto our children. If we take advantage of the opportunity such situations offer to examine what causes us to behave this way, we may be able at last to solve childhood conflicts we have not resolved before. Such openness to one's feelings will also facilitate our understanding that it is exactly our tremendous importance to our children, and their love for us, that spawns their occasional hostility. It will be clear that when hostility breaks out into the open, what we are being confronted with is but the obverse of their great affection for us. This realization will alter our attitude from annoyance or worse to one of understanding acceptance of the underlying emotional forces, although we still may have to inhibit our child's aggressive behavior. It may even make us recognize that in restraining him, we are reproducing our parents' conduct in parallel situations. Recalling how unfair we thought our parents were will keep us from overreacting to our child's behavior. With such deliberations, things ought to fall into their rightful place, and what now annoys us about our child will not be fed and aggravated by its connection with all the hostile feelings we have repressed into our unconscious. Most of all, as we realize that despite all the aggressive tendencies we had as children, we did grow up to be nonviolent, law-abiding adults, we will be less likely to bear down too hard on our child's aggressive behavior out of anxiety that it will become unmanageable once he is grown up.

The repression of the negative side of a child's ambivalent feelings about his parents, if done too severely, can have the consequence of interfering with the expression of the positive feelings, which are but the other side of this ambivalence. I have known many children who were able to form loving attachments to their parents only after they no longer felt the compulsion to repress all their negative feelings about them.

Of course, if we are able to recognize, through introspection, that our feelings toward our children are also not entirely free of ambivalence, we no longer need to repress whatever negative feelings may well up in us from time to time. The pretense that our child, because of his immaturity and lack of control, is occasionally having negative feelings about us but that we are entirely free of such feelings about him can cause serious problems in the relations.

UNDERSTANDING NIGHTMARES

What has been said about the origins of our ambivalent feelings about our parents holds true, *mutatis mutandis*, for the entire period of childhood. Our earliest experiences, and those of our child, are mostly unconscious and thus not available in direct form to our memory, but later stages of his development replicate some of our experiences that were not necessarily unconscious or repressed by us, or if so, not so deeply. These memories can be recalled more readily, although this may still require considerable effort.

Few of us can remember in any detail the nightmares from which we suffered, as all children do; even those who can recall to some extent the contents of their nightmares and how upsetting they were have little notion what caused them, beyond the obvious fact that the young child feels helplessly anxious about many things which are incomprehensible to him. Not many people realize that a major source of the nightmares of young children is their developing superegos, which try to punish them for their "unacceptable," if not "sinful," tendencies. Among others, these may be sexual urges, or the wish to rebel against authority or to get rid of a parent or sibling. As a forerunner, an early stage of a more fully integrated conscience, the nightmare plays an important role in the personality development of all of us; it had this role in our development, as it now has in that of our child.

Realizing this will help us to treat our child's nightmares with greater care and the respect which a developing conscience deserves. The more we understand about our own nightmares (of which we are not entirely free even in adult life), the better equipped we will be to help our children with theirs. The fact that we have forgotten so much about them suggests that we repressed the childish desires and fears which found expression in those haunting dreams. Underlying such alienation from some of our childhood experiences is the wish not to know what they were all about, maybe even some dim recognition that the terror we then felt has left in us some residues from which we have failed to free ourselves entirely. Witness the unrealistic anxiety many people still suffer, for example, when confronted with harmless animals, such as garden snakes. Their fear is often rooted in forgotten childhood nightmares in which snakes threatened to devour them.

Thus we can use our children's nightmares as an opportunity to explore and reexplore—as T. S. Eliot suggested—what may have been behind our own, and whatever remnants of them we may still carry within us. Then we shall indeed, for the first time, truly know our nightmares and their meaning in our lives. To the degree we achieve this it will be a boon to us and to our children, since we shall then be able, by understanding ourselves, to help them with their nightmares with a personal sympathy for both the immediate suffering and the significance of such experiences in the formation of their personality, a depth of empathy which otherwise might never be available to either of us.

Unlike our nightmares, which we only vaguely recollect, our anxieties about entering school have stayed with many of us; in fact, some people spend a lifetime demonstrating, to themselves much more than to others, that their childish fears of academic and social failure were unrealistic. Because these worries are usually part of our conscious memories, although often only in fragmentary form, we have considerable compassion for our child's anxieties about his first entry into school. Unfortunately, some parents run out of compassion when an older child develops a school phobia for parallel reasons. This is when an understanding based on one's own experiences would be particularly helpful.

These situations stand for many others which may occur in our interactions with our children; efforts to understand the role played by parallel events in our own development always bring about beneficial changes as they provide new clarity about ourselves. We gain a deeper understanding of what certain experiences have meant in our lives and in our relation to our parents, as well as how these experiences now shape our attitude toward what our child experiences and expresses around some similar occurrence. Such understanding permits us to empathize with whatever moves our child, and this nearly always gives our relation greater depth and meaning, making it a more enjoyable experience for both of us. Thus around some common experience, we not only influence our child's attitudes, but we also change our own, because of a better understanding of what similar events meant to us as children.

Children are very sensitive to their parents' reasons for doing something with or for them. Do parents think they *ought* to do this, or do they really enjoy it? Is Mother reading me a story because she wants to quiet me down? Or is it because she thinks it's her duty? Perhaps she thinks I'll enjoy this particular story, or being read to by her, or both? Obviously it is a more rewarding experience for a child if he can sense his mother's desire to give him pleasure.

The child's experience when being read to is radically different from that of the parent, although they engage together in a single activity. However, when parents respond to the story themselves, the two can really share the experience. Perhaps the parent will be moved by the story to recall important memories from his own childhood. I have been told that people who read my book on fairy tales, *The Uses of Enchantment*, suddenly understood why a particular story had been especially significant to them in their childhood. Then it had captivated them in some way, had aroused anxiety or pleasure, or both; but only now did they see why this had been so, with what personal experiences or problems the tale had been connected, so that it became uniquely meaningful to them.

As children these people had wanted a parent to read the story over and over again because, unbeknownst to them at the time but understood now, they had subconsciously hoped that it would convey an important message to the reader. For one it was *The Swiss Family Robinson*; by spinning fantasies about this story, she had found solace from her unhappy family situation. The same book was also very meaningful to another young girl who suffered from the repeated and prolonged absences of her parents, during which she was left in the care of relatives who physically took good care of her but whom she hated, mostly because they took her parents' place. Only as an adult did she realize that she had pestered her parents and relatives to read *The Swiss Family Robinson* aloud to her because she hoped they would get the message that children need to have their parents present. Subconsciously she had hoped that from the story they would understand how much she wanted her parents to either stop traveling or take her with them.

As soon as this woman realized that a child's desire to hear a certain story again and again may derive from his hope that his parent will get the message he thinks the story conveys, reading stories to her own child became a much more rewarding experience for her. Moreover, she began to pay quite different attention to the stories her child requested, for she remembered with particular poignancy how severely disappointed she had been that neither her parents nor her relatives had gotten the message she had tried to send them through *The Swiss Family Robinson*.

Reading stories to her son now took on new levels of meaning for her. Before, she had read to him because she remembered how important this activity had been to her, and she wanted to give him this pleasure. Now it occurred to her that by asking for a particular tale, her son might be trying to give something to her—namely, a message about some matter that was of great importance to him. She enjoyed this demonstration of this confidence in her, his desire to tell her—in whatever roundabout form—something of personal significance.

Her understanding of the importance *The Swiss Family Robinson* had once had for her gave this mother a new perspective on her own childhood. What she had previously recalled and viewed only as an escape into wish-fulfilling fantasies she now recognized as an intelligent, goal-directed action with a specific purpose: to secure relief from a distressing situation, the long and frequent absence of her parents. Before, she had remembered herself as having been unable to improve the conditions that oppressed her, but now she saw that she had actually done her best to persuade her family to change their ways. Thereafter, when she read stories to her son, she always remembered that this was the experience through which she had gained a more positive image of herself as a child, and with it of herself as a person.

What is said here in respect to story-reading holds true, with the appropriate variations, for many other aspects of child-rearing. Comprehending one's childhood experiences as an adult can provide new and important insights. When this happens, both parent and child have a significant experience through what they are doing together; although they are on different levels, the differences are of less importance than the fact that each is beholden to the other for having gained new insights, and for having provided the setting for such growth. The element of equality in such a shared experience is especially important to the child, because each participant becomes provider and beneficiary at the same time.

Many childhood experiences have become, of necessity, deeply buried in the unconscious during the process of developing one's adult personality. This separation or distancing from one's childhood is no longer needed when the adult personality is fully and securely formed, but by then, the distancing has for most people become a part of that very personality. Separation from one's childhood is temporarily necessary, but if it is permanently maintained it deprives us of inner experiences which, when restored to us, can keep us young in spirit and also permit greater closeness to our children.

12

Telling Children About Their Parents' Past

Old, unhappy, far-off things,
And battles long ago.
—WORDSWORTH, "The Solitary Reaper"

IT IS NATURAL for our children to be curious about our lives before they were born, to want to know about our childhoods and past lives. And most of us like to tell our children about ourselves, so that they may feel more in touch with us and understand us better by knowing the experiences that made us the persons we are today. Consciously, our motives are reciprocal: we want to make ourselves better known to our children, and they want to learn more about us. If this is all, then things are fine; but frequently more complex feelings become involved, and then the results can be quite at variance with what was intended and desired.

To illustrate, let us assume that the parent's childhood was very different form that of his child, which is often the case. This increases the parent's wish that his child understand what formed him, and makes the parent's past that much more interesting to the child—but also that much harder for the child to comprehend, since his understanding, like everyone else's, is based only on his own experience. Further, let's assume that the parent once suffered severe deprivations, but has been able to raise his child in relative ease and material comfort. Then such discussions may have unforeseen results. To throw what might happen into bold relief, I will use an admittedly extreme example: the Holocaust. In using it, it is necessary to bear in mind that this case only greatly magnifies what may happen when any parent's life has been much more difficult than that of his child, at least insofar as external conditions are concerned.

To the survivor, the Holocaust must have been the most dramatic, traumatic event of his life, with the most far-reaching consequences for him.

His child will become aware of this at quite an early age—long before he can understand history—because it has had such a powerful effect on his parent. Though curious, he hesitates to ask questions, particularly as he senses the very powerful and difficult feelings that surround this topic.

The parent, on his part, may be reluctant to talk about his experience, partly because these memories are very painful and thus best avoided, and partly because he knows that his child cannot really comprehend the Holocaust, but mainly because he does not wish to burden his child with the thought that his parent had suffered so terribly, nor with the fact that life can have such horrible aspects. If, out of a desire to protect his child, the parent does *not* talk to him about the Holocaust—the significance of which cannot have completely escaped any survivor's child—this silence is interpreted by the child as a deliberate exclusion from the most important period of his parent's life, further cause for worry and wonder. He may also think that his parent's reticence is based on a belief that he wouldn't understand, which, while true enough, gives him the feeling that he is considered incompetent, if not downright unworthy of receiving such confidences.

Thus while the parent's silence about a significant part of his past is based on a wish to shield his child, the child is likely to experience it as a sign of his own inadequacy. In retaliation, he may attempt to balance things out by concealing important aspects of his own life from his parent. Even when the child dimly perceives that his parent wishes to shield him, the positive quality of this protective intention will not be sufficient to counteract his negative feeling of exclusion, alienation, and inferiority.

Things are equally or perhaps even more complicated when a survivor *does* tell his child about the Holocaust. The extreme hardships the parent suffered cannot fail to impress the child with the fact that his own life is so much easier. In consequence, he may conclude that under no circumstance must he give a parent who has already endured so much any more reason to suffer. He might even think it his obligation to make up for the past by giving his parent only pleasure, impossible though that goal is. Then whenever in the process of growing up the child unavoidably does something worrisome or disappointing to his parent, he will feel immediately guilty. This mars the relationship, particularly as the child resents the parent who causes him, although indirectly, to feel guilty. Once more a parent's effort to do right by his child, this time through an attempt to strengthen the emotional bonds between them by taking his child into his confidence and making himself better known to the child, ends up interfering with the good feelings between them!

Such guilt feelings toward a parent create problems enough for the child, but there is always the additional danger that the parent will refer to his

Holocaust experience at a time when the child feels uneasy or doubtful about some act of his own. In such a situation the child may think that his parent deliberately mentioned his past suffering in order to make him feel guilty, or make him show greater consideration for the older generation. Over time the child may come to believe this "emotional blackmail" was inflicted so that he would behave himself and not because the parent wanted to share a very important aspect of his past. Such notions may make him angry that he *was* told about it, resentful even of the parent himself.

These thoughts in a child might be more than empty distortions. Without being conscious that this is one of his motives, a parent may allude to his past to influence his child to behave more thoughtfully toward his parent and be more appreciative of what his parent does for him. And it may also happen that the parent—again without being aware of it—feels some pangs of jealousy of his child, whose youth is so much happier than his own, and resents the severe deprivations he underwent. Emotions like these bring the parent's past vividly to mind, and induce him to speak of it.

While the parent is unaware of these feelings, and would be shocked to learn of their subterranean existence, the child may react subconsciously to what he senses and be resentful rather than pleased to be told about his parent's past. He may even think that only some terrible act of his could have stimulated his parent to speak about these horrible experiences.

Children, being more self-centered than mature adults, naturally tend to believe that they are the cause of whatever their parents do. The child wonders: "Why has he chosen this moment, and for what purpose, to tell me this?" The child may conclude—perhaps incorrectly—that the revelation was provoked by his behavior, not just by his loving curiosity.

Even more ordinary deprivations leave their mark, and if we are not free of resentment—and very few adults who have experienced serious hardships are—unbeknownst to us this attitude will sneak into and flavor our narrative. The child, being more responsive to unconscious processes and less focused on objective content, will sense the resentment and will respond to it vividly, for these are feelings with which he is familiar, while the past is alien to him. Given his self-centeredness, he will think that we are jealous of him because his life is so much better. That is, sensing our feelings of resentment, he will feel resented; next he will come to resent the cause of it all: our telling him about our past.

If, indeed, subconsciously or unconsciously, the parent is bitter over his child's failure to appreciate the advantages which the parent himself could not enjoy as a child, the child will resent being made to feel guilty for enjoying advantages he didn't ask for. He may wonder whether he would have been better off without these benefits—at least he would not be obliged to be grateful for them. Most parents find it very difficult not to react, consciously or unconsciously, to the fact that their child has a better life than they did. And most parents find it even harder to realize that it is nearly impossible for a child to appreciate "advantages" in regard to which he had no choice.

The child who is told of the hardships his parent endured and overcame is likely to fear that he would fail to surmount similar difficulties as well; this makes him feel inferior, if not inadequate. Thinking about how well his parent has done in very trying circumstances, he may feel defeated long before he has the chance to test his mettle, long before he can find out how he might, in actuality, measure up to his parent. He is much more concerned with his present feelings about himself than with what he is being told about his parent's life, the events of a dim and distant past which seems unreal and is hard to visualize.

I encountered such attitudes in Israel in the early pioneers and their children, typically but not only among the founders of the kibbutzim and the generations that followed them. These youngsters openly stated their resentment that all the great deeds connected with the settlement of the Jews and the establishment of the state of Israel had already been done by their parents; they felt there was nothing important left for them to accomplish. But below the surface they also worried that even if equally heroic attainments were available to them, they would not do things as well as their parents. While overtly they admired the achievements of the older generation, covertly they resented being made to feel inferior, and they listened to their parents' stories with considerable ambivalence. A few of the very young children could engage in compensatory fantasies about the great deeds they would do when they grew up, but even they, as they matured and learned to see things more realistically, could no longer maintain their grandiose illusions. Given the relative inadequacy of children's abilities compared to their parents, and the incredible difficulties with which these pioneers had to cope, how could the younger generation feel otherwise?

The Israeli youngsters used to say, "Oh, our parents and their big ideas!"— expressing both a grudging admiration and an inner rejection. The parents, for their part, were deeply disappointed that their accounts of past struggles were not more appreciatively received. Where they had hoped for great interest, if not also admiration, they were confronted with an attitude of boredom. Because they didn't realize that this boredom wasn't due to a lack of interest but was a defense against anxiety and feelings of inferiority, their sharing their past had an effect the opposite from the one they had intended, and they were left with the disappointing feeling that their lives could not really be understood by their children.

But the child's feelings of inferiority are not the only obstacles here. As we recall the past, it's easy to be carried away by the emotions evoked by painful memories. Involved in our own emotions evoked by these memories, we are not then in a good position to evaluate the effect our remembrances can have on our child. Somehow we expect him not only to sympathize with our misfortunes, but also to realize and appreciate how much better off he is. Perhaps he should—but seen from the child's perspective, his life is nothing but normal, which he has come to expect and take for granted. What we have known all our lives cannot be viewed by us as anything except normal. So while he may give lip service to the idea that he is more fortunate than his parents, this is at best hearsay, and like all hearsay, it carries little conviction. Deep down, he does not think that his life is unusually fortunate, although this is what his parent wishes to impress on him.

When a parent expects his child to understand how lucky he is, he is assuming that the youngster has somehow managed to see his own life and his parent's life objectively, although he has no firsthand experience of the latter. Such objectivity is far beyond the comprehension of a child—not to mention the fact that what the adult considers a life of privilege may not be experienced that way by his child. He has his own definition of hardship, which might very well include burdens imposed by his parent's standard of living, about which he has no choice. For example, having to wear galoshes in bad weather doesn't seem like a privilege to the child, who struggles to get them on and off and has to clean them before going inside. Being obliged to wash his hands before sitting down to eat, to brush his teeth, to clean up his room, and to comply with the thousands of other regulations which middle-class life entails—these are the "hardships" with which he is familiar, and he has no idea what his life would be like if he didn't have to cope with them. In fact, to him, the prospect of having no galoshes, or living in a ramshackle house where nothing needs to be put away or protected, may seem romantically attractive, rather than constituting a life of harsh deprivation!

Much of this is illustrated by a story Freud told. When his father related to him a degrading experience with an anti-Semitic bully, mistreatment which he had had to suffer passively, his young son felt no sympathy but only contempt, because his father had not fought back. From the advantageous position in which his father had placed him, Freud felt superior to the older man. If this was young Freud's reaction on being told about the hardships his father had suffered, what can we expect of our children?

For us as for Freud's father, telling our children about our past, with the tacit hope that this will help us forge a closer bond, may instead cause estrangement between us. Is this, then, a no-win situation? Do I suggest that telling a child about the past will always have the opposite effect from the one intended? Fortunately, this is by no means the case. Letting our child know our history, when done with the right feelings, at the right moment, in the right context, can indeed bring us closer together. I elaborated on the possible problems chiefly to illustrate the overall point that the more emotionally sensitive and significant a situation, the more important it is that we handle the situation with care, examining our own feelings and speculating about what the child's feelings are likely to be. All emotionally loaded situations, like strong medicine, have the potential for both good and bad. When correctly applied, and appropriate to the conditions, the propensity for a beneficial effect is there—but the wrong usage may do more harm than good.

"Handling with care" entails a thoughtful consideration of the possible effect of our narrative on the child, given his limited frame of reference. If the story is meant to inspire admiration, there is a danger that this esteem will be tinged by feelings of jealousy and inferiority, and if we realize that what we tell our child may make him feel inferior, out of our love we will temper our presentation to avoid this. As for showing him how much better off he is than we were, realizing that we are in fact trying to make him feel obliged to us should check our impulse. We know from our own experience that while we freely offer gratitude to those who have worked to improve our lot, we deeply resent being expected to be grateful, since that implies inferiority. So we must try not to give our child such a feeling, and this becomes easier if we consider that from his perspective, most of the advantages are given, not chosen, and may not seem like advantages to him.

I have used the example of telling our child about important and difficult past experiences to illustrate the way a situation can backfire, even though there is no disagreement or conflict between parent and child, but on the contrary, a conscious intention to improve understanding. So often parent and child see their experiences, if not also each other, "through a glass darkly," because they view things only in their own frame of reference. Since the child cannot do otherwise, it is up to the parent to try to see the situation from both perspectives. This requires, among other things, that we be honest with ourselves about our feelings for our child and honest with him and with ourselves about our motives; that we inspect our motives carefully so that we are sure that what we are doing is guided by the child's best interest.

This example may also suggest that here, as in all interactions between parent and child, the central issue is the basic context within which such interactions occur: the nature of the parent-child relationship—the deepest feelings each has about the other; how secure each feels within himself, and about the other's intentions toward him; how good he feels in this relationship, and about it; and how parent and child are dealing with the particular problem in hand. As a matter of fact, if the young Sigmund Freud's relation to his father had been better, being told about the father's degrading experience would have evoked sympathy in the son, rather than contempt.

This shows the importance of keeping in mind that a child can see things only in his own frame of reference, which is very different from ours. If we remain aware of this simple fact—although what may be involved in our intercourse with each other may be very complex—then all will be well. We will see our child and his problems clearly—not through a glass darkened or distorted by our self-involvement, by our emotional involvement in our past, or by our anxieties about the future.

PART TWO

Developing Selfhood

13

✦

Achieving Identity

On being asked what was most difficult to man, the Greek philosopher Thales answered: "To know one's self."

A T BIRTH ALL BABIES possess distinct traces of their future personalities, albeit usually only in the merest nascent form. Years of living and experience are required before these first intimations of a future disposition begin to emerge as the outlines of a personality, and many more years will pass before a character has been fully and securely developed—one that will withstand the rigors of life and serve well those who have undergone all the trials and tribulations necessary to become "the lords and owners of their faces."

Achieving one's own identity often involves serious pitfalls and may lead one to make false starts and turns. It is a process that requires one to retrace one's steps, and it is also a path strewn with uncertainties as to which direction to follow. In the course of winning a secure identity, we are projected into deep doubts which we try—particularly when we are young and unsure of ourselves—to cover up and deny by pretending great certainty. Yet hard as it is to become oneself, it is even harder to discover what this self consists of—to recognize what are the essential and what the accidental components of one's personality. Only if we can securely discriminate between these qualities have we achieved our identity.

Just because we all have traits which we don't like or fully approve of, or about which we may have our doubts, knowing ourselves is a difficult achievement. Our detours in the quest for identity may be painful and dangerous. We test ourselves—often without knowing that this is what we are doing—and then must reflect on what these tests reveal about us.

Whatever the particulars of the situation, whatever the age of the boy or girl, the parents' empathy with their child's difficult struggle for selfhood and their sympathy for his attempts to discover, assert, and finally to define and test himself are of paramount importance for the child. He needs their sympathy as an emotional milieu in order to be able to achieve a viable, consistent identity that will permit him to cope with life in authentic ways. The inner attitude toward the growth of one's child toward selfhood ought to remain one of welcome, however troubling his actions of the moment; but its outer expression must change according to the varying forms this search for identity takes as the child matures.

The younger the child, the more this basic attitude must translate itself into parental behavior which unmistakably shows the parents' desire to help their child develop his own identity, such as through an open show of approval and pleasure when the child takes positive steps to assert himself. Active participation of the parents is necessary, because the child's early identity is developed entirely around them; his identity will be of a positive nature only if it is in harmony with parental attitudes to the child. It will be a fragmented identity if the parents' attitudes to their child are partly negative.

When children experience that what they are and do gives pleasure to their parents, this pleases them and makes them feel important, since it is *they* whom the parents recognize as the source of their pleasure. In this way parental approval becomes the incentive for forming a self, permitting children to feel recognizably themselves, different from all others. The important shift from children's feeling that *what they do* gives pleasure to their thinking that it is *they, in themselves* who give pleasure occurs during their first years of life. To speak technically, the parents' pleasure in their child provides him with the experiences he needs to develop his narcissism, that is, the self-love which is the permanent source for the wish to build up a unique personality that suits him best.

Paradoxically, the development of uniqueness begins when the child repeats something he did which gave his parents—and through them, himself—pleasure. This can become a permanent feature of his behavior in order to gain his parents' continuing approval. The enjoyment of this approval is one source of the repetitious behavior of small children. It is most important that parents make it clear to their child which of his actions and behavior give them pleasure, and let their child experience this again and again. He needs distinct and persistent signals to repeat some types of behavior often enough for them to become habitual; parental approval gives him a motive to incorporate such conduct permanently into his budding personality.

Unfortunately, the process that has been described here in positive terms can also occur in negative form. The child who feels that he receives mainly—

or worse, only—reactions of displeasure from his parents will, in self-defense or in retaliation, react negatively not only to them but also to himself. This, too, can become a repetitious and habitual feature of his behavior, a motivating force in the child's developing personality: giving displeasure to those significant persons who create such dissatisfaction in him, but at the same time being deeply disenchanted with himself. The pattern of dissatisfaction and displeasure can then become as much a definite part of the child's character as the wish to give pleasure to himself and to do what provides it.

However, if parents do repeatedly give signals of pleasure and all goes well, in a next step children will begin to give more specific content to their selfhood through partial identification with the parents, selecting characteristics of the personality of each to build into their own. Other traits will be drawn from older siblings, or other significant persons. This incorporation begins with copying—in an age-appropriate way—behavior which then becomes habitual and finally is a motivating force within the self.

To many parents' dismay, the child builds into his personality those aspects of their personalities which make the deepest impression on him, not those which they would most wish him to internalize. These are often traits which the parents themselves do not approve of, but which happen to fit well into the present needs or desires of the child. One major cause of this is that the child is more impressed, and thus influenced, by the emotions he feels coming from his parent or existing in him than he is by the adult's conscious intentions. For example, a parent may be very angry but, convinced that his anger is wrong or irrational, he may control or repress it and belittle the matter that caused it. The child, responding to the parent's repressed feelings rather than to his reasons for repressing them, absorbs into his personality the anger rather than the control. Even a parent's depression powerfully shapes his young child's personality, although this condition may not be viewed as an active force. In fact, a child experiences such depression as actively giving his life a negative direction, through the absence of positive responses to him and his actions. He may remain convinced of the great significance of whatever caused the parent's feelings, and unmoved by the merit of the repression, even though it is the control of such emotions which the parent would like to see the child develop as part of his personality. But this does not work, probably because the child is at this stage much more deeply impressed by the emotions the parent is repressing than by his intellectual act of repression and the reasons for it. Or sometimes this happens because the child, for reasons of his own, needs to respond positively to anger and negatively to its control. Furthermore, we all, but especially children, find it easier to see through the defensive maneuvers of others than through our own.

The precursor of what will later be a person's self—will form his identity—is what for good reasons has been called the body-self. This body-self is the foundation on which all more elaborate and specific aspects of the personality will be built up and which will determine much of the personality's later content and structure, as well as how secure or fragile the structure will be. All the self the infant has is his body; thus the attitudes he develops toward his body are all-important. Whether he perceives it as delightful or disgusting, or more likely something in between, is a reflection of parental attitudes to his body, and predominantly to those of his main caretaker.

Many strongly felt experiences combine to determine the infant's attitude to his body and thus form the basis of his self. This is why it is so important, for example, whether he is being enjoyed while being nursed: whether it is such a pleasant experience that it is taken in a leisurely manner, or whether he is hurried through because the nursing parent is in a hurry to get it over with. A wide variety of experiences enter in the infant's forming a view of himself, a development that comes about through the interactions between himself and his parents, whatever these may be. In the nursing situation, which is so central an experience, it makes a great difference whether the infant is held comfortably or uncomfortably, with what attitude he is burped—what is the reaction to his spitting up?—and so forth. If the parent's attitude is positive, the infant will come to feel that his is a good body that functions well and has reactions which are fully accepted. If, to the contrary, his reactions meet with a negative attitude, he will come to perceive his body as inadequate, if not bad. In the first case his body-self will be invested with positive connotations, in the second with negative ones.

These basic perceptions will be strongly reinforced by many other infantile experiences—being bathed and cleaned, diapered, dressed and undressed, rocked to sleep. Much will depend on whether the parent really loves handling the infant's body in these situations or experiences some aspects of baby care as an onerous, if not downright disgusting chore. If the latter is the case, the baby will not be able to feel good about his body and its functions, and with it about himself.

In all these interactions and in many more, it is not just the adult's conscious feelings which are important but also those of which he is unconscious, very much including those he is repressing because he is bound by a sense of obligation to minister well to his baby's needs, whatever these may be. This latter conviction often inteferes with his ability to face up to what his true feelings would be if he permitted himself awareness of them. For example, he may find stools disgusting because of something connected with his own toilet training. If this is the case, as much as he may try to clean up the baby's feces with a positive attitude, his inner revulsion—of which he may be completely unaware because it has been deeply repressed since he was a small child—will subconsciously be transmitted to the infant. Of course, the child receives these messages only on a subconscious level, if for no other reason than that at his age the elements of conscious, subconscious, and unconscious are hardly separate from each other. Certainly they do not operate separately but as a total unity of experience. He nevertheless responds strongly to the adult's inner reactions, although these may be expressed through barely perceptible facial features of which the adult himself is entirely unaware; or through the way the adult's body stiffens; or through how the whole process is hurriedly done; or through not so much the words which accompany what the adult is doing as the tone in which these are uttered; or by the feelings conveyed through his handling of the infant's body; or by innumerable other signals.

Thus the development of selfhood does truly begin in infancy, when the parents' behavior expresses—or fails to express—their interest and concern for their child's body and for what he can do; their conviction that his body is valuable, worthy of their love and care. Signals are given daily. For example, when an infant throws things out of his crib and expects us to retrieve them so that he can throw them out again, he is testing whether, despite his doubts, it is true that he can act in this world.

It is much more difficult to empathize with our child just a couple of years later during the toddler stage, when he throws temper tantrums and screams bloody murder, instead of gurgling happily as he did when we retrieved his baby rattle for him. Then his unreasonableness, lack of control, and despair make us so distraught that we may fail to recognize that he is after essentially the same thing that he wanted when he played in the crib: to find out what he can do, and what the consequences of his actions will be.

A temper tantrum is the expression of the child's despair of not having a self that works for him. The trouble is that once this feeling has overwhelmed him so that he throws a temper tantrum—or I should say, more correctly, once his despair has thrown him into a temper tantrum—the child is usually overwhelmed to the degree that everything else is blotted out, including recollection of what he wanted and failed to get. The temper tantrum is his reaction to his inability to gain what he desires, but it also demonstrates to him the deficiency of his self. He experiences it as a total collapse. Incapacitated by his rage, he needs the help of others more than ever. His parent's mature knowledge that the child is *not yet* able to do as he desires is of no help to the child, who lives only in the present. What he cannot do now, he believes he will *never* be able to do; this is the reason for his profound and self-destructive despair. It is a self-destructive despair not so much because the child may hurt himself as he throws himself about on the floor, thrashing around wildly, as because when his emotions so overpower him, he not only cannot get what he is after, but has lost control over his own body.

Since this constellation of emotions is behind the temper tantrum, handing the child the object he is after will help mainly in the initial stage of his distress, before despair has blotted out of his mind what triggered his frustration. When the tantrum so overpowers him that he no longer knows what caused it, it is much more effective to distract him, for example by showing him an object he usually desires and inviting him to come and get it. Once he can make a move to do so, the tantrum is over, although his unhappiness over his loss of control may last awhile. The reason is that there is no better way of demonstrating to him that his self—which at this age is so largely a body-self, based on the ability to move in goal-directed ways—has not ceased to exist than to enable him to provide himself with the experience that he can indeed move his body at will, that he can gain for himself things that he desires.

Children traverse an enormous distance in developing their selfhood. Early efforts to be a self by throwing things out of the crib—that is, by showing himself that *he can do things*—are followed by the temper-tantrum stage, which is caused by the failure of his effort to demonstrate to himself that *he can do things for himself*. In the first instance the child has no self yet; through his actions he is merely attempting to form one. As he tests his power to do something—or tries to make sure that he can—his "self" is in the first of several incipient stages of becoming *a true self*. A few years later, his tantrums arise from the fact that he is no longer trying to *be* a self, but is attempting to test what this *self can do for him*. His rage and despair are the consequence when, contrary to his hopes, he is forced to realize that his self cannot do what he wishes to accomplish.

When I speak of being or of having a self, I am referring to the child's feelings—because he has as yet no conceptual understanding of what is involved in being a unique entity, nor in having a personal identity. At this state the child recognizes his "self" when he feels himself separate from others, and his ability to grasp this fact when, for example, he sees himself in a mirror or perceives that he himself is moving his limbs. His having a self denotes a higher state of self-awareness in which he can decide to do something and then do it, without any recognition as yet that all his wishing, doing, thinking, and feeling coalesce into a definite identity of his own.

The problems surrounding the achieving of identity are well known and much discussed. But it is not always easy to apply such knowledge to one's own children when, for example, as teenagers they are convinced that engaging in the silly fads of their age mates forms the very essence of life; or when as adolescents they question, or reject outright, our way of life, fully expecting at the same time that we shall provide them with the wherewithal to live with comfort and ease, and defy our values, although it is these very values which permit them to do so with impunity—for example, our values restrain us from imposing our will on them or forcing them to conform to our desires. If our children's behavior, as they try to find themselves, did not take on such different forms at each stage of their development, often changing almost from moment to moment, it would be easier to recognize the continuity of the process of achieving selfhood. But these sudden, chameleonlike changes make it very hard to realize that their behavior is a reflection of their search for selfhood, and later for personal identity and uniqueness.

For example, they may be "feeling their oats" when they pretend to be much more capable and mature than they are, flaunting the attitude that they couldn't care less if we disapprove of their actions, but expect a few minutes later—if not at the same time—that we will be delighted to attend to their needs as if they were still infants. It is hard to remember, then, that our adolescent child, who is taller and stronger than we are, is acting essentially like a toddler, asserting "I can do it!" or "Let me do it!" while expecting us to do it for him—just as he did when he was learning to tie his shoes or put on his snowsuit. Yet our children need to assert their independence and self-sufficiency at every age, so they can permit and enjoy our taking care of them without any loss of their self-respect.

To become truly oneself, we need experiences, in good measure, both with solitude and with active life and all of its vicissitudes. Unfortunately, in our life with our children we do not always see eye to eye about the right moments, conditions, or amounts of solitude and social intercourse they need. Often when we believe that it would be in their own best interest to spend their time in quiet application, they feel the need for a whirlwind of frantic activity, and when we think they shouldn't isolate themselves so much, they feel, for their own reasons, compelled to withdraw into themselves.

Still, these swings are easier to accept than abrupt alterations between progressive and regressive behavior, when all that has been gained in maturity seems suddenly lost only to be replaced by the most childish behavior. It is difficult to accept without worrying when one's perfectly groomed, lovely child suddenly becomes an utter slob; when the excellent student abruptly loses all interest in his work and spends his time daydreaming. Such sudden shifts usually indicate that below the surface, without our or his awareness, some of the adolescent's most important inner developments are taking place—developments which eat up all the energies he is able to muster.

In psychoanalytic terms, for the transition to each higher stage of development to be complete and successful, a reworking of earlier problems is required at any new level. For example, upon entering adolescence, the child who has already become quite secure within his body reexperiences most of his old insecurities and encounters many new ones as well. The pubertal adolescent's rapid growth makes him uncomfortable with his body, which makes the reworking of old bodily problems more difficult and, at the same time, more pressing.

Oral fixations which seemed to have been resolved in infancy and emotional difficulties experienced during toilet training and the teaching of hygiene which were overcome during nursery-school age, if not sooner, often reappear acutely, many years after they had stopped being problems, either in the old forms or in other, newer guises. The sloppy teenager is now strong enough to act out the resistance against being neat he was forced to suppress as a child. These feelings are reactivated because he needs to free himself of the old suppression so that it will no longer interfere with his becoming a self-determined individual. This is why the old problems now need to be reworked on a higher level so that they take on quite different meanings in the formation of character. If they achieve this new and higher integration, they enrich our character, but if they remain untouched by the developing personality, they peg it to the old immature level. Unless they *are* thus reexperienced and reworked, they remain archaic blocks embedded within a more advanced matrix, alien and alienating elements in the new personality that form fissures within it and make it brittle, subject to rupture at moments of crisis.

Thus all through life, but particularly during periods of marked growth in character development, ancient experiences *ought* to be relived and reworked. But it is hard to remember all this when our adolescent child suddenly and without apparent reason throws a tantrum the way he did as an infant; becomes dirty and as messy as he was years ago; stuffs himself silly, or refuses to eat at all—as if reversion to such infantile behavior were the only way he knew to gain things from us, or disagree with us. But the adolescent needs to resolve these ancient conflicts now on a very different basis, and to give them an entirely different meaning in the makeup of his personality. Doing this work takes time and a great deal of energy, which then becomes unavailable for what a parent may view as age-correct pursuits or behavior. Actually, however, there is no more important pursuit than the overcoming of ancient and pervasive traumas, fixations, and problems: attitudes toward one's body and its functions, relations to parents, one's views of oneself and one's goals for the future.

The hardest thing about coping with this process of self-discovery through regression and progression is that it requires of parents an inner acceptance at all times, but quite a variety of overt responses at different ages and in different situations.

It is not so difficult to realize and accept that the infant who delightedly throws his bottle or rattle out of his crib is trying to achieve a feeling of selfhood; we can thus usually respond to it in the right way. A greater challenge is to respond well when an adolescent throws our values out the window, or into our face, hoping, without knowing that he does so, that we will be as ready—and even *more* important, as glad—to pick up the pieces for him as we were when he tossed his ball on the floor. Thus while at every age for the child to develop well his parents must "pick up the pieces," what this means specifically varies with the age and relative maturity of the child and the state of his relation to his parent.

RESPECT STARTS WITH THE BODY-SELF

Because all later developmental stages of selfhood have their basis in the body-self, one of the best things parents can do for their child is to help him as an infant to develop a healthy and positive attitude toward his body: to make him feel good about what it can do, and at the same time conveying to him how much they love and value it, so that the child will do the same. If a parent succeeds in instilling such attitudes in the young child, it will afford excellent protections against the adolescent's taking dangerous risks with his physical, personal, and social well-being. If a child's body—and of course all the rest of him—has been given love and tender care, then as he grows, discovers, and later establishes his self he will internalize this love and care his body received into respect for it, and for himself as a person. Parental appreciation of the child's body and of what it can and does do becomes eventually translated into the child's appreciation of and respect for his own body, a desire to keep it inviolate, whether from dangers involved in mastering the outer world by risky physical exploits, or in dealing with inner pressures by starving himself, as in anorexia, or through overeating, as in bulimia, or by using drugs, or by acting out sexually.

It was easier to convey such parental attitudes convincingly when even seriously ill children were always cared for at home by their parents. And in a society in which scarcity reigned, providing good food was in itself a demonstration of the parents' great concern for the child's well-being. Here, too, attitudes that in the past could be conveyed through direct action must today be intimated in more subtle, psychological form. But respect for the body and the self are still rooted in the child's perception of the way his parents have treated him and his body.

Thus in the long-drawn-out process of the child's achieving a personal identity, which in its earliest internalized form is not reached until adolescence, the parents' attitudes and actions can be of tremendous help or hindrance. To make each succeeding step constructive in the development first of a self and later of a secure and rich personal identity, a parent must make very clear his approval of such growth toward independence; without it, each level reached may remain shaky, a poor foundation on which to build further.

There are, of course, many problems involved in the child's experimentation with what he can do by and for himself as he begins to master his environment. Toddlers get into all kinds of trouble as they attempt to explore and understand the world. Here, as in so many other child-rearing situations, it is practically impossible to approve of everything the child does, to enjoy and otherwise encourage it, and to avoid all prohibitions. Parental responses can't *always* be positive; there simply *have* to be "don'ts" in addition to the "dos," but even many of the latter are unacceptable to a child, as obnoxious to him as the "don'ts."

What is essential if the child is to enjoy being himself—and to develop his self—is, first and foremost, that his experience of parental approval far outweigh his experience of disapproval; furthermore, approval should be accompanied by open praise and inner delight on the part of parents (and later of other adults significant in the child's life), and on appropriate occasions enhanced by suitable rewards; and disapprovals should be voiced as gently as possible so as to create the minimum of anxiety and discouragement.

This requires a parent to eschew anxiety or annoyance about what his child is doing; or if this is not possible, to make sure that such feelings are commensurate to the actual situation only. In fact, parental reactions often extend beyond what the present conditions may warrant to worries about the future, and this kind of anxiety may provoke an undue severity or intensity of inhibition. This is doubly unfortunate because the child relates only to the present situation, and thinks his parents are doing the same. Also, when a parent's concern is limited to the present problem, and not aggravated by considerations of possible future trouble, it is much easier to think of alternative conduct to propose to the child. I hardly need to mention that any negative attitude to the child's behavior, or plans, ought not to extend to the child himself, nor to his wish to actively explore his world, since only by doing this can he develop his self, his intelligence, and his ability to form judgments.

If for some reason parents do not encourage the development of the child's self but thwart it, then the child may surrender his budding self in order to achieve a pseudo-security through fusion with his mother—or whoever else has taken her place either in reality or in his imagination. Or else, finding the task of developing his own self too dangerous, the child may settle for a pseudo-self, efforts which typically result in later life in a psychotic existence marked by depersonalization. On rare occasions, this may happen through no direct fault of the parents, because of a combination of unfortunate timing and other circumstances.

A case in point: An infant, just after he had truly mastered crawling, as he was crawling on a table, fell off it onto a stone floor, sustaining complex bone fractures that required his being put for a prolonged period into casts which prevented nearly all spontaneous movement of his arms and legs. When the casts were removed, he eventually learned to walk, although he was very anxious and uncertain about it. But his intellectual development was also arrested. Despite the fact that he had learned to talk while he was convalescing, he remained unable to express any ideas of his own; so severely was his intellectual development blocked that by age seven he was considered feeble-minded. Without being truly autistic, he displayed many symptoms of autism, including the absence of "I" from his vocabulary. It took years of therapy to undo this condition, and more years until it became apparent that he had experienced his being put into immobilizing casts as a punishment for having tried to move around and as a warning not to develop any independence—that is, a self.

As usually happens, it was a combination of outer and inner experiences which accounted for such complete arrest in the development of a self. The restricting and painful casts set the stage, but the true cause of the boy's tragedy lay in the attitude of his mother: when he began to try to move after the casts had been removed, this parent—overanxious about a possible repetition of the accident, for which she blamed herself because she had not exercised sufficient care to prevent the child's fall—could not delight in his efforts to move again. She responded to them with great spoken anxiety which expressed itself in angry warnings and an even more impressive silence. All this conveyed to the child the omnipresence of unknown dangers, so great that they could not even be given words. The only safe thing for him to do, he felt, was to give up all initiative in moving, not so much physically as intellectually, because only if he subordinated his self entirely to that of his mother could they each feel relatively secure and he feel accepted by her. The frustrating mixture of the boy's satisfaction in his newly won but still limited ability to move and the terrorlike anxiety this moving about evoked in his mother exposed the boy to such contradictory signals that he did not dare to become a self.

He could not sort out the baffling confusion between his experience that it is advantageous to be able to move and his awareness that his mobility projected his mother, on whom he had entirely and exclusively depended while in the casts, into severe anxiety and guilt. Combined with his at best faint recollection of the event which led to his being immobilized, which he had experienced as punishment for his self-assertion (i.e., moving himself), this paradox created in him unmanageable doubt about whether he should or should not develop a self. As a consequence, he moved only as he was told to, or when he felt absolutely sure that such motion was approved by his mother. However, given his mother's ambivalence and anxiety about his moving about, her approval was a message he rarely received clearly. He could move his limbs, but only rigidly, as if he were an automaton whose motions were externally controlled; his movements did not seem to originate of his own volition and were never spontaneous.

Thus, he acquired locomotion without ever feeling sure that to move his body was acceptable behavior. Unable to move freely, he couldn't develop a body-self based on the ability to decide when and how to move, the sense on which all later selfhood is built. The maternal anxiety which accompanied any moves of his—even those of which she consciously approved—and the guilt his mother felt over his clumsiness, for which she also blamed herself, prevented any enjoyment of his motility, and did not permit him to develop spontaneity in the actions of his body-self. But while one can move without spontaneity, one cannot do any original thinking without it—devoid of it, thoughts remain stereotyped, derived from the outside, inexpressive of any inner self.

This is obviously an extreme example; things hardly ever get so far out of the normal line of development, even when, at a crucial moment, illness or other misfortune interrupts the emergence of a child's body-self. Even in this case, had the mother's anxiety and guilt been less intense, had her pleasure in his recovered mobility been greater and more clearly conveyed, the impact of the original trauma (being put into a body cast) would have been less severe.

A different outcome would also have been possible had the mother's fearful attitudes been counteracted by the response of other significant persons, foremost the boy's father, who, not having been present when the child fell off the table, would not have felt guilty about it, thus his pleasure in his son's becoming bodily active again would not have been an ambivalent message. Moreover, a growing boy naturally tends to identify with his father, whose responses are in accord with the developing tendencies of his son toward achieving an independent self. Unluckily, the father was hardly ever home when the boy was awake and, disappointed in him because of his long illness, had lost interest in him during his long convalescence.

This is but another example of the importance of having two parents on the scene, so that when the relation to one is troubled, the child can find solace in the different responses of the other, and use them to counteract the first parent's negative reactions to him. In this case the mother's overwhelming guilt interfered with her positive feelings for her son, since unconsciously she blamed him for having caused the accident, and resented him for having done so. Matters were made worse because the father, instead of supporting his wife in her distress and trying to alleviate her guilt, which would have helped a great deal, since she looked up to him, added to her guilt by accusing her of having been careless and having caused all the trouble.

When there are two parents who are emotionally involved in the minutiae of their child's life, they are differently involved, being two different persons with different reactions to the same event. Thus, no event need be so completely devastating to the child as may happen when one parent's reactions are not relieved or counteracted by those of the other. And the child suffers less in such situations when the deeply anxious or disappointed parent finds relief for his or her feelings through the spouse's support.

This boy's story is unusual, but I have known other cases in which the inhibition of motility in infancy has led to severe interference with the achieving of a feeling of self. His story suggests the detrimental impact which parental anxiety—understandable as it is in many situations—can have when the toddler's getting into things in his efforts to discover what he can do for himself is thwarted or fails to be validated by his parents' pleasure in his moving out into the world, which alone permits him to begin establishing the rudiments of a self.

THE "ADOLESCENT REBELLION"

Adolescents need their parents to maintain their values, but not to take too active a role in asserting them. The reason for this seeming contradiction is that adolescents need to define themselves not only around their parents and on the basis of parental approval, but also *against* them, because of fear that their parents will dictate their personalities, rather than they themselves. In order to make sure that they are what *they* want to be, to some degree they try to be also what their parents do *not* want them to be, on the presumption that this alone can assure them of their independence. It is this ambivalent and often contradictory wish that makes the life of the adolescent so torn and difficult, and also what makes living with him so problematic for his parents.

And as if this would not make for sufficiently great inner conflict for the adolescent, and this in addition to his conflicts with his parents, he also needs to define himself both positively and negatively as part of the wider world into which he is moving. If parents are too active in encouraging them to do this, adolescents perceive this not as assistance or support, but as an effort to shove them out of the nest.

In order to dare to venture out into the world an adolescent needs to feel that the home of his childhood is still unconditionally his, very much in the same way as the toddler needs to hold on to mother's apron strings, or later on to a "security blanket," a teddy bear, or some other transitional object, in order to feel safe when venturing beyond his crib or bed. Where the young child needs a physical object to hold on to, the adolescent needs the ready availability of the safety of home. There he can be as childish as he wishes, while he tries to act more grown-up in the wider world. If his parents at this time encourage him to venture out, he may think they're washing their hands of him and that there is no longer a safe haven left for him to seek refuge in, when he feels the storms of the world are pushing him helplessly around.

In fact, parents cannot thrust independence on an adolescent; trying to do so only interferes with the process of his gaining it. To try actively to direct the formation of his identity is ill-advised and counterproductive. Any step toward a more distinct selfhood, and with it toward achieving identity, has to be taken all by oneself; if the conditions surrounding one's taking such a step are such as to make one doubt that one has taken it entirely on one's own, then it is experienced as a movement not toward selfhood, but toward greater dependence.

This is why, during the period of adolescent turmoil, it is best when parents can *accept* their adolescent's odd, antagonistic or otherwise unpleasant behavior, *without approving of it*. They should give their adolescent child space to experiment without taking the details of his actions too seriously, and without getting too upset or too deeply involved in what he is doing. Then, when the adolescent comes to realize that such behavior does not really fit his needs or personality, he can believe that giving up his antagonistic attitudes is not due to parental pressure, but is entirely the result of his own decision. Only if he feels this way will he abandon his undesirable behavior permanently. Therefore, beyond trying to safeguard his well-being, it is best for parents to meddle as little as possible with what he is doing, while always gladly offering, without any restrictions, the opportunity to return to being the welcomed child in his own home, as he was before experimenting with his as yet immature and thus often ill-conceived ventures into the wider world.

During this time of adolescent experimentation, parents are well advised to become neither too assertive nor too defensive about themselves and their way of life, nor to yield under the onslaught of adolescent attacks. It is best when they simply hold firm to their values and continue living by them without stressing their superior nature, or being openly critical of the values by which the adolescent is trying to live at the moment. They must bolster their attitude with the inner conviction that their child is inherently good, even though he may not appear to be so at the moment, with the reasonable hope—which to become reality must not be openly expressed—that their consistency may eventually make their way of life more attractive to their child.

This unspoken parental conviction that their way of life is right for them, and their refraining from insisting that it therefore ought also to be right for the child, is what the adolescent needs to protect him from being swept away by his often contradictory emotions, and to enable him to experiment fairly safely with other life-styles. If he is not being deprived of the parental example—or worse, because of their antagonistic attitudes, set against it—he may adapt it to his personality and the conditions of his own life, but only when he no longer fears that doing so will make him a carbon copy of his parents.

One young adolescent, in a period of deep confusion about himself and the world, in despair over what he perceived as his parents' indifference to his struggle to find himself, exclaimed: "You have to have something to push against to know that you're somebody!" He neatly expressed the problem of his age, which is that when one is not yet able to feel oneself "somebody" through inner strength and the consistency of one's personality, one can develop this sense of self best by resisting the strength of something—parental values—that does not push back. Parental insistence would mean that they do not wish their adolescent children to develop their personalities in their own ways; it also would mean that they do not trust that the adolescents will arrive at values with which the parents can be satisfied. But this imaginary wall of parental values must neither yield to the pushing, which would leave the adolescent with nothing to give him the feeling that he is himself, different from all others, nor collapse under his onslaught. If parental values crumble, the rubble of the wall would bury him and fragment his budding personality.

Few of us can discover who we are without also having to ascertain what and how much we can do—not as others bid us, but as we ourselves choose for ourselves. From an early age, children have a need to find out what their bodies can accomplish in a larger sense, and for them specifically. The desire and need to demonstrate to ourselves that our bodies serve us well and compare favorably with others' explain one major source of the pleasure many of us derive from sport and athletic activities and from looks and appearance. Athletic activities always involve some risks, which escalate as the child becomes older and stronger.

In adolescence, when the main developmental problem is to discover and affirm one's identity, youngsters have a special need to test their bodies, because the results are immediately available, measurable, and visible. Evaluating the merits of one's other achievements is by no means so simple and is certainly less direct. It is much more difficult for an adolescent to base his self-esteem on nonphysical qualities, and the results are much more tenuous and subject to doubt. For example, when a child wishes to believe that he is a considerably better person than his age-mates, or even his parents, this is not easy.

Parents and educators tend to think that academic achievement can and should give an adolescent feelings of worthiness, merit, and self-esteem. But while this works to a considerable degree for the younger child and may later work for the mature adult, it rarely does for the adolescent. The reason is that in his efforts to become and be himself he has to fight free of adult domination, including the imposition of adult values, which, while reasonably acceptable to the young child because of the security which comes with such domination, is obnoxious to the adolescent. The more he feels dependent for his self-esteem on the evaluation of adults, the less he feels himself a person in his own right. Thus it is counterproductive for him to base his feeling of self-worth on adults' estimation; it pushes him back into childhood attitudes from which he is desperately trying to free himself.

In efforts to reassure themselves of the superiority of their bodies and (by implication) their selves, adolescents who are uncertain about their value in other respects may be tempted to engage in potentially dangerous ventures— reckless driving, rock climbing, ski jumping. Failing to find more positive ways of affirming their value, they may engage in delinquent and even criminal acts. In this way they declare their superiority to a society whose standards they disparage because they are convinced that society disparages them, which in some ways may be true. Thus in their case a desire to get even combines with a need to excel in some way, pushing them to ever greater extremes of daring. I have heard more than one juvenile delinquent say: "If I can't stand out by being the best, at least I can do it by being the worst." Leaders of violent gangs assert that they have to be more outrageously violent than the rest to establish or keep their domination.

The need to defy parents or society is an important element in the formation of the delinquent personality, but in the last analysis it is lack of self-respect which causes delinquent behavior. Delinquency and reliance on drugs for escape from the feeling of worthlessness are desperate efforts to silence the inner voice which tells a person that he is no good and is a nobody, notions that frequently originate in childhood experiences in which a child was made to feel that his body and with it he himself were not valued.

14

Play: Bridge to Reality

Man is only man indeed when he plays.
—FRIEDRICH SCHILLER

"CHILDREN'S PLAY should be regarded as their most serious actions," wrote Montaigne. If we wish to understand our child, we need to understand his play. This is why in this and the following chapters so much space is devoted to a discussion of play and games. Most parents realize the importance of play and would agree that play is not only an enjoyable but a serious and significant pursuit of children. They gladly provide toys and play materials, encourage and help their child to use them, and make arrangements for him to play with other children. Play activities change as children grow in understanding and different problems begin to occupy their minds. Through play, they begin to comprehend how things work: what can or cannot be done with objects and how, and the rudiments of why or why not. From playing with others, they learn that there are rules of chance and probability, and rules of conduct which must be followed if we want others to play with us.

The lesson children can learn from play which is possibly of greatest value is that when they lose, the world does not come to an end. If the child loses this game, he may win the next one, or the one after that. Through defeat in play and games which can then be performed again and won, children come to see that despite temporary setbacks in life they may still succeed, even in exactly the same situation where they have experienced defeat. Of course, for a child to learn this, his parents must not emphasize winning but rather the enjoyment of the game. They must show him that losing is as little a demonstration of personal inferiority as winning is of superiority. The British, who as a nation are known for their fine sense of sportsmanship, have high admiration for the good loser. They know it's easy to be a good winner and bask in the smiles of the world and fortune. But to accept a loss in good grace and not permit it to defeat us, to concede that it was justified by the rules of the game, is not only praiseworthy in itself, but protects the loser against the sapping of his self-esteem. Our children would be much better off if our attitudes about losing were similar.

Freud regarded play as the means by which the child accomplishes his first great cultural and psychological achievements, and that through play he expresses himself; this is true even for an infant whose play consists of nothing more than smiling at his mother as she smiles at him. He also noted how much and how well children express their thoughts and feelings through play. These are sometimes feelings of which children themselves would remain ignorant or overwhelmed if they did not deal with them by acting them out in play fantasy.

Child psychoanalysts have enlarged on Freud's insights, which recognized the manifold problems and emotions children express through play; others have shown how children use play to work through and master quite complex psychological difficulties of the past and present. So valuable is play in this connection that "play therapy" has become the main avenue for helping young children with their emotional difficulties. Freud said that the dream is the "royal road" to the unconscious, and this is true for adults and children alike. But play is the "royal road" to the child's conscious and unconscious inner world; if we want to understand his inner world and help him with it, we must learn to walk this road.

From a child's play, we can gain understanding of how he sees and construes the world—what he would like it to be, what his concerns are, what problems are besetting him. Through his play, he expresses what he would be hard pressed to put into words. No child plays spontaneously just to while away the time, although he and the adults observing him may think so. Even when he engages in play partly to fill empty moments, what he chooses to play at is motivated by inner processes, desires, problems, anxieties. What is going on in the child's mind determines his play activities; play is his secret language, which we must respect even if we do not understand it.

Even the most normal and competent child encounters many difficulties which present him what seem like insurmountable problems in living. But by playing them out, one aspect of the problem at a time, in the way he chooses, he may become able to cope with very complex problems in a step-by-step process. He usually does so in symbolic ways that are often hard even for him to understand, reacting to inner processes of which he himself is unaware, processes whose origin may be deeply buried in his unconscious. This may result in play that makes little sense to us at the moment, or may even seem ill advised, since we do not know the purposes it serves or how it will end. This is why, when there is no immediate danger, it is usually best to approve of the child's play without interfering just because he is so engrossed in it. Efforts to assist him in his struggles, while well intentioned, may divert him from seeking, and eventually finding, a solution which will serve him best. Our interposition is more likely to divert the child from his own purposes, because our suggestions are apt to make good sense on a conscious level and hence be convincing to a child, who is easily influenced and unaware of the unconscious pressures he is trying to cope with. But in the course of giving reasonable advice, we may prevent the child from mastering the psychological difficulties which beset him.

A four-year-old girl reacted to her mother's pregnancy by regressing. Although she had been well trained, she began to wet again; she insisted on being fed only from a baby bottle and reverted to crawling on the floor. All this greatly distressed her mother, who, looking forward to the demands of a new infant, had counted on her daughter's relative maturity to make this easier. Fortunately, she did not try to prevent her regressions, something which would have been difficult, as the child was not just playing at being an infant again, but insisted on acting like one.

After a few months of this regressive behavior, the girl replaced it with much more mature play. She now played "good mother." She became extremely caring for her baby doll, ministering to it in a variety of ways and much more seriously than ever before. Having in the regressed stage identified with the coming infant, in what was now clearly play she identified with her mother. By the time her sibling was born, the girl had done much of the work needed for her to cope with the change in the family and her position in it, and her adjustment to the new baby was easier than her mother had expected and feared.

In retrospect it can be seen that the child, on learning of her mother's pregnancy and that a new baby was to join the family, must have been afraid that the baby would deprive her of her infantile gratifications, so she tried to provide herself with them. She may have thought that her mother wanted an infant, which she no longer was. So she may have decided—if one can call an unconscious reaction a decision—that she herself would again be an infant. Then there would be no need for her mother to acquire another, and she might give up on the idea.

Permitted to act on notions like these, after a while the girl must have realized that wetting herself was not as pleasant as she might have imagined, that being able to eat a wide variety of foods had its definite advantages when compared with drinking only from the bottle, and that walking and running brought many more satisfactions than did crawling. From this experience she convinced herself that being more grown-up is preferable to being a baby. So she gave up pretending that she was one and instead decided to be like her mother—in play to be like her right now, and in imagination to become at some future time a real mother. Play provided the child and her mother with a happy solution to what otherwise might have resulted in a difficult impasse.

At four, the girl was at an age when she could act both the infant and the mother, and believe it. Older children cannot regress so easily and openly, nor can they believe even in play that they are really parents. A good solution for many of them when they can no longer permit themselves to pretend to be what they are not is to act out these roles in a play they put on as actors, or in a puppet drama. As actors and puppeteers they are able to act out things in ways which protect their hard-won maturity while at the same time allowing them to be as childish as necessary, or more mature than they really are. Thus children, left to their own devices, often find solutions to problems which oppress them. But they will not be able to do so if we, thinking we know best at what and how they ought to play, interfere for our own reasons with what the child is trying to do for his own reasons.

It is not only such problems in living that children try to master through play. Often it is part of their effort simply to understand the world. The little girl who ministers to her dolls as her mother does to her and the little children who play at working as their parents do are trying to understand their parents, first as persons but also through their occupations by copying their actions. The younger child who in play copies older siblings is trying to understand them and, at the same time, what it means to become older.

A child's own play efforts can indeed be self-healing, as when children take care of dolls, or of stuffed or real animals, as they wish their parents would take care of them, and thus vicariously try to make up for felt deficiencies. Unfortunately, adults often fail to recognize the significance of children's play, and therefore feel free to interfere with it. Insensitive to the deep meaning that apparently nonsensical, repetitious play can have, they may deprive their children of the chance to spend endless hours doing what seems like the same thing over and over. Only rarely, in fact, do children repeat exactly the same play procedure in exactly the same detail. Careful observation reveals minuscule changes in the pattern, reflecting the variable directions play takes if left to its own course. And when there is no variance—when the play is completely identical from one day or hour to the next—this fact in itself carries a significant message. True repetition in play patterns is a signal that the child is struggling with matters of great importance to him, and that while he has not yet been able to find a solution to the problem he is exploring through play, he is continuing to seek one.

First and foremost, children engage in play because it is enjoyable in itself. This is so obvious that it seems hardly worth mentioning; yet the pleasure derived from being able to function is among the purest and most important of all. We enjoy the experience that our body is functioning well. Pavlov speaks in this connection about what he calls a "muscular gladness," and before him Harvey remarked that there is a "silent music of the body." Children as they exercise their bodies feel such an exuberance that they often cannot remain silent but loudly express their joy in what their bodies can do, without knowing that this is its cause. The young in particular need to have their fill of it. Even young animals—particularly young mammals—play as they exercise their bodies. While we cannot be sure whether and to what degree they exercise not only their bodies but also their minds when they play, there can be no doubt that for humans of all ages, both are involved. Psychologists speak of the pleasure inherent in functioning (*Funktionslust*)—the pleasure we derive from the experience that our bodies and minds are operating and serving us well forms the basis for all feelings of well-being. Solitary play provides us the satisfaction gained from the experience of functioning well, but through playing with others we can derive life's other great satisfaction: that of functioning well with others. The very foundation of this experience is created through play, when a baby plays with his parents and is delighted by it, but in the long run he can have pleasure only if his delight is validated for him by that of his parents.

The greatest importance of play is in the child's immediate enjoyment of it, which extends into an enjoyment of life. But play has two additional faces, one directed toward the past, the other toward the future, like the Roman god Janus. Play permits the child to resolve in symbolic form unsolved problems of the past and to cope directly or symbolically with present concerns. It is also his most significant tool for preparing himself for the future and its tasks. Long before these psychological meanings and unconscious aspects of play were discovered, there was general understanding that it was the child's way of making himself ready for future pursuits. This preparatory function can also be observed in the playful behavior of young animals as, through it, they acquire skill in using their bodies for specific purposes, such as hunting and eluding pursuit. Play's function in developing cognitive and motor abilities has been explored by Karl Groos (the first investigator to study it systematically), Piaget (to whom we owe our best understanding of what the child learns intellectually from play), and many others.

Many children who do not have much chance to play and who are only infrequently played with suffer severe intellectual arrest or setbacks, because in and through play the child exercises his thought processes. Without such exercising his thinking may remain shallow and undeveloped. Also, language development is advanced if the adult engages in prolonged conversation with the child on an appropriate level while they play together, at a time when the child is most receptive to such conversation. Through playing with language, the young child explores what one can do with it; for this reason, too early insistence by the parents on the correct use of language can reduce his pleasure in his creative use of words. (Teachers of culturally deprived children have found that encouraging them to create poetry was most beneficial in stimulating their intellectual development, because while doing so, they played with language and used it creatively in new ways. The experience often made these children more optimistic—directly about what they could do with words, indirectly about what they could do in the world.)

Play is crucially important, because while it stimulates the child's intellectual development, it also teaches him without his being aware of it the habits most needed for such growth, such as stick-to-itiveness, which is so important in all learning. Perseverance is easily acquired around enjoyable activities such as self-chosen play. But if it has not become a habit through pleasant activities, it is difficult to achieve it through more difficult endeavors, such as schoolwork. It is best to learn at an early age, when habits are formed and when the lesson can be assimilated fairly painlessly, that we rarely succeed at a thing as easily or pomptly as we might wish. It is through play that a child begins to realize that he need not give up in despair if a block doesn't balance neatly on another block the first time around. Fascinated by the challenge of building a tower, he gradually learns that even if he doesn't succeed immediately, success can be his if he perseveres. He learns not to give up at the first sign of failure, nor at the fifth or tenth, and not to turn in dismay to something less difficult, but to try and try again. But this he will not learn if his parents are only interested in success, if they praise him only for that and not also for tenacious effort.

Children are very sensitive to our inner feelings. They are not easily fooled by mere words. Thus our praise won't be effective if, deep down, we are disappointed by the length of time it takes them to achieve their goal or the awkwardness of their efforts. Further, we must not impose *our* goals on them, either in thought or in action. Gregory Bateson and others have demonstrated how destructive it is for a child to receive contradictory signals from his parents. Exposed to one message from verbal statements and a contrary one from subliminal signs (which the speaker himself may be unaware of making), the child becomes utterly confused, for what he is told is the opposite of what he senses is the truth. This will as effectively prevent him from persisting in the face of difficulties as will criticism for his failure or praise only for success. A parent's understandable ambitions for his child and the desire that he should succeed can often be impediments to the child's ability to develop persistence in the face of difficulties.

Here, as in so many other situations, a parent's deep inner conviction that his child will eventually do well, however long it may take, is the best protection against the need to push him to achieve, or the tendency to be disappointed when he fails, as well as against giving false praise which the parent doesn't really feel is deserved. The child knows very well whether his efforts, although they end in failure, are praiseworthy or not; and if we give him praise which he knows is undeserved, it tells him that we have a low opinion of him because we believe that he can do no better. The parent's inner faith in his child and what he is doing may move mountains, including those of the child's doubts about himself. Laying his self-doubts to rest permits the child to try and try again without experiencing destructive feelings of defeat.

Many teenagers and adolescents (and older persons too) refuse to persist at tasks which do not come easily; they feel that they are failures because success eludes them, as it does nearly everybody who does not persist. Actually they only pretend to refuse; in fact they are unable to stick to tasks which are difficult at first because of deficiencies in their early play experiences. As small children they missed sufficient chances to learn as a matter of course that it takes many and sustained efforts to succeed—probably because deep down their parents were primarily interested and involved in their success, but not also in their many and often clumsy attempts to achieve their goals; or perhaps the parents in their own minds made too little of their child's goals as compared to those the parents had in mind for them. This attitude comes through to the child whether or whatever he is told about it.

It is reported that Einstein was still unable to speak at the age of three. He preferred communicating with—and, if adults were receptive, through—building blocks and jigsaw puzzles. One may assume that even at this age his thoughts were of a nature which could not be communicated or made comprehensible through the language of a three-year-old. Late in life, he made two statements which illuminate what he thought about the value of combinatory play (as in jigsaw puzzles) for the development of the mind. "Man," Einstein wrote, "seeks to form for himself, in whatever manner is suitable for him, a simplified and lucid image of the world and so to overcome the world of experience by striving to replace it to some extent by this image." What Einstein seems to be saying is that children overcome the defeatist experience of living in a world they cannot master by creating a more comprehensible world which they *can* comprehend, that they do so in a manner uniquely *suitable to them*, and that only they can know what manner this is.

Elsewhere Einstein wrote: "Taken from a psychological viewpoint, this combinatory play seems to be the essential feature in productive thought— before there is any connection with logical construction in words or other kinds of signs which can be communicated to others." Thus it is clear that through such play, whether with Tinkertoys, Erector sets, or a wide variety of other (best if self-chosen) play material, or with puzzles, children acquire the habit and the enjoyment of engaging "in productive thought." Doing these things, they learn how to make logical constructions at an age when they are as yet unable to do so with words. The jigsaw puzzle is a very good tool for learning, long before children can put the idea into words, that by arranging seemingly disconnected pieces in the correct order, one can arrive at an image of wholeness which is much more than its parts.

Repeated efforts, some of which are failures but which finally lead to success, not only show children the necessity of perseverance, but also teach them to trust their ability to succeed. It is this trust which, once acquired, makes it possible for them to keep at a task until it is mastered. Such trust further convinces us that if we do persist, many goals which for a long time seemed far beyond our reach can be achieved. In this process, the child acquires and improves skills of thought and manipulation as well as the habits of perseverance, patience, and application which help to make more complex learning possible. No television program can develop such an attitude of tenacity in the face of obstacles; neither can it convince children of their ability to create wholeness out of seemingly disjointed parts. While series such as *Sesame Street* keep children fascinated and in the process teach them things that require no special effort to master, television generally offers little material to build on later, when hard work is required to cope with more complex challenges.

A prodigy like Einstein may, without assistance, create out of the most disparate pieces "a lucid image of the world" and make "logical constructions"; but even an average child can do this if guided by adults to play in the right way—that is, if he is allowed to learn how things can be constructed out of building toys, or how puzzles can be put together. If child and adult enjoy doing such things together, soon the child will make his own constructions, which, to him, will be a lucid image of the world. But to be fully meaningful, these have to be his own inventions; our role can only be to give him ideas on how to go about it. This is why it is best to limit our participation to handing him the pieces or helping him if he requests aid. The reason for this is that most of us lack the patience needed to wait until a child finally succeeds; most of us are usually too committed to reaching the goal, and too little accepting of his endless meanderings on the way to it.

Mostly, children need time and leisure to concentrate on their play, and the opportunity and encouragement to go about it in their own way. If we are too eager for our child to achieve what he is trying for, he will be discouraged that he couldn't do it sooner and on his own. If we try to direct the construction, the result will be—at best—a compromise between his "simplified and lucid image of the world" and the adult's image of the world, which is much too complex for a child's comprehension, no matter how we try to "keep it simple." Thus patience and correct timing in playing with children and in letting them do things all by themselves are highly important; and our approval and delight in our child's play activities—whether or not we understand their meaning or purpose—are crucial to his motivation.

Some parents (usually for reasons of which they are in most cases completely unaware) are not satisfied with the way their child plays. So they start telling him how he ought to use a toy, and if he still continues to suit his own fancy, they "correct" him, wanting him to use the toy in accordance with its intended purpose, or the way they think it ought to be played with. If they insist on such guidance, the child's interest in the toy—and to some extent also in play in general—is apt to wane, because the project has become his parents' and is no longer his own.

As if this were not bad enough, there may be serious consequences later on. Such parents are likely to continue to direct and dominate the child's activities, motivated by the same inner tendencies which did not allow them to fully enjoy his play as *he* developed it. But now everything is happening on a more complex intellectual level. The parents may then try to improve the child's homework by suggesting ideas that are much too sophisticated, and in any case are not his own. In consequence he may lose interest in developing his own ideas, which pale by comparison to his parents'. What he wanted, in talking with his parents about his homework, was appreciation of his efforts, encouragement that his own ideas were valuable, and not a demonstration by his parents that his ideas were not good enough. Such parents would be most astonished to learn that their efforts to help were the cause of his unwillingness to be interested in his homework, if not of his refusal to do it at all. But this is the consequence of his having been repeatedly disappointed in his own attempts because his parents' ideas have been so much better than his.

Einstein, in his remarks about the importance of play in developing the ability to form logical constructions and create one's own image of the world, may also have been thinking about what is required for this to happen: the child as much as the adult needs to be given plenty of what in German is called *Spielraum*. Now, *Spielraum* is not primarily a room to play in; while the word also means that, its primary meaning is free scope, plenty of room— room to move not only one's elbows, but also one's mind; scope to experiment with things and ideas at one's leisure, or, to put it colloquially, to toy with ideas. This phrase correctly suggests that the creative mind plays with ideas as a child plays with toys; this is generally recognized. It is less commonly known that when a child plays with toys, he explores and forms ideas, although he is not yet able to put them into words. As the creative adult needs to toy with ideas, the child, to form his ideas, needs toys—and plenty of leisure and scope to play with them as he likes, and not just the way adults think proper. This is why he must be given this freedom for his play to be successful and truly serve him well.

TOYS AND PLAYING "GROWN-UP"

Toys have always represented inventions and mirrored the symbols of society's technological progress. Today's cars, trucks, airplanes, and space ships fill the same role in our children's play as the toy chariot did in ancient India or Greece. The popularity of toy construction sets, airplanes, walkie-talkies, moon buggies, and so on attests to the child's interest in objects that are artifacts of adult life. It is very important to children that their parents share their feelings of delight in playing with these toys. For children the delight comes primarily from fantasies of being great pilots, musicians, painters, explorers, inventors, dancers, or truck drivers right now, while the parents' enthusiasm tends rather to be based on their projections of their child's future.

Unfortunately, to the detriment of such shared fantasies, many parents are unable to spontaneously enjoy their children's occupational fantasies because they have already made up their minds about what they consider the appropriate future for their children. In this case, identification with the child can prove harmful if it restricts his freedom of choice. Usually, it arises partly from the parent's desire for vicarious gratification, through his child, of his own unattained wishes, and partly from his inability to conceive of the child as possibly wishing for something other than what he, the parent, considers most desirable for him.

Many children of white-collar, middle-class parents are particularly disadvantaged in this regard when compared with children of blue-collar parents. When a fireman watches his child play with toy firetrucks or a carpenter observes his child nailing a few boards together, the adult can feel an immediate pleasure in the child's activity because of the gratification that comes from seeing the child emulate him, and this despite the fact that such a parent may hope that his child will surpass him. The hope for a better future for his child does not interfere with the pleasure of seeing that what the parent does for a living is important to his child. If so, the delight the child derives from thinking that he is working at the same tasks as his parent and that the parent derives from thinking that his child values his work highly can together make for a very special emotional bond between them.

While the same holds true for the physician's child who plays at being a doctor and for the scientist's who makes experiments, things were probably simpler when a child automatically followed in his parent's occupational footsteps (for girls, of course, this usually meant homemaking). His play was based on observing and copying his parent's labor, in preparation for doing it himself. Then later, as he helped his parent with the actual work, it was easier to become proficient at tasks for which his play had already prepared him. So pervasive was this pattern that many students of play concluded that play's main purpose was to learn future roles. However, this is too narrow an interpretation; it ignores others of the manifold meanings of play, although it is an important dimension.

Now the emphasis has shifted from the preparation for specific adult roles to a more general anticipation of becoming a grown-up. As in times past, play still helps in developing cognitive abilities, social and physical skills, such as bodily coordination, and the manipulation of tools. Play still anticipates future occupations but no longer isolates and defines *the* occupation which will fill out the child's adult life, such as farming or home-making. Rather, play now suggests the wide variety of possibilities open to the child. As children play with animals and dolls, with trucks and airplanes, with doctor's and nurse's kits and construction sets, they fantasize about these activities, exploring how it feels to be a mailman or a physician, an inventor or an astronaut, experimenting imaginatively with possible adult roles. This is particularly important today when so many career opportunities beckon and a wise choice is difficult to make. Having mentally tried these possibilities on "for size," the child will be in a better position to choose satisfactorily.

All this works well, however, only if we do not interfere too much. We may be tempted to belittle some of the options our child experiments with because the particular occupation does not appeal to us. The opposite procedure—overvaluing some choices because they appeal greatly to us—is equally harmful. In either case, it is a mistake to react to a child's tentative exploration of an occupation as if it were already a definite choice. The mother who decides that her daughter will *certainly* grow up to be an animal breeder or a vet because she likes animals so much does the child no favor. Nor does she help things by being convinced that the *only* good life for her daughter is that of a homemaker, a figure skater, or a lawyer. All children need their parents to encourage them in the idea that they are preparing themselves for a good life whether they are single-mindedly devoting themselves to the care of hamsters, or whether they suddenly tire of these pets and turn just as single-mindedly to dance or sports.

FANTASY AND PLAY

Through his imaginative fantasies and play based on them, a child can begin to compensate to some degree for those pressures he experiences in life and those which originate in his unconscious. Through his fantasies he becomes better acquainted with the contents of his wishful thinking, as well as some of his asocial desires. As he acts out angry and hostile fantasies in playing war games or fulfills his grandiose wishes by imagining himself to be Superman, the Hulk, or a king, he is seeking the vicarious satisfaction not only of unrealistic daydreams, but also of being in control of others in order to compensate for those feelings which are the consequence of his being so largely subject to the control of adults, most notably his parents.

Here there emerges a most significant difference between fantasy and play. In his imagination the child can be absolute despot with no limitations on his rule. But as he begins to play out his fantasy, he soon learns that even absolute rulers are subject to the limitations of reality. Once he has, for example, made a law, he has to obey it—the other children will insist on it. If the "pretend" king is too capricious, the game will disintegrate and His Majesty will be in for a rude awakening. He will soon learn that even the most powerfully imagined emperor can retain his throne only as long as he enjoys the good will of his subjects, that he can play the sovereign to his playmates only if he makes such play attractive to them. No such restrictions apply to his free-floating fantasies.

When I speak here of the child's fantasies, I am thinking not only of the very young child, but also of those considerably older. The biographies of creative people of the past are full of accounts of long hours spent sitting by a river as teenagers, thinking their own thoughts, roaming through the woods with their faithful dog, or dreaming their own dreams. But who today has the leisure and the opportunities for this? If a youngster tries it, as likely as not his parents will fret that he is not using his time constructively, that he is wasting time daydreaming when he should be tackling the serious business of life. And this although the development of one's inner life, including one's fantasies and daydreams, is among the most constructive things a growing individual can do.

The days of most middle-class children are filled with scheduled activities—Boy and Girl Scout meetings, music and dance lessons, and organized sports—which leave them hardly any time to simply be themselves. In fact, they are continuously distracted from the task of self-discovery, forced to develop their talents and personalities as those who are in charge of these varied activities think best. This includes school, which now begins at an age which used to be considered too early for formal schooling. Television provides today's children with ready-made fantasies, but what makes it even more pernicious is that having had insufficient leisure to develop a rich personal fantasy life—which requires ample time to emerge and grow—these youngsters must rely on the medium to fill a need they cannot meet themselves because they have been deprived of adequate opportunities to explore their impulses freely in dreaming up a world of their own creation. Modern life conditions and parental attitudes deprive our children of those long hours and days of leisure to think their own thoughts, an essential element in the development of creativity. It simply cannot be acquired in half-hours stolen away from other things deemed more important by those who direct their lives.

Goethe, in speaking about another great poet, Torquato Tasso, but simultaneously referring to himself, makes this point by asserting that talent is best nurtured in solitude. He knew and wanted us to know that the poetic imagination, like all other meaningful and rich fantasy life, can emerge only out of long hours of more or less playful and uninterrupted concentration on one's inner life.

When the modern child seems to be lost in daydreams, many a concerned parent may suggest (or insist) that he use his time more purposefully and tell him how to do so. This is inadvisable. Not only does it show a disregard for the importance of the child's fashioning his own inner life in order to become an authentic individual (which requires a vast amount of energy, although the work is invisible), but it conveys to the youngster the feeling that to do so is wrong. The parents may pay lip service to the wish that the child should become a real person, but without allowing him to concentrate his energy on this difficult endeavor—energy which is then unavailable for anything else—he won't be able to achieve this wish.

It is in large measure the child's not having had sufficient leisure to develop his own rich inner life that causes him to pressure his parents to be entertained, or makes him turn on the TV. It is not that the bad money of such mass-produced entertainment drives the good money of inner richness out of circulation; it is that the child has not been given the chance to create his own good currency of a rich inner life. Thus in a vicious circle, lack of chance to spend much of his energies on his inner life and absence of sufficient time to do so cause the child to turn to readily available stimuli for filling an inner void, and these then prevent him from being able to develop his inner life. Not having had sufficient opportunities to develop the appropriate skills to dream up an elaborate "secret garden" of his very own, the child falls back on the empty busyness the parents provide or insist on, or upon even emptier entertainment, which prevents such a private "secret garden" first from being created and then from being filled with the beautiful flowers of his own imagining, which, as he grows older, could grow into more mature images that give deeper meaning to his life.

Of course, it is much less demanding to have one's time organized by others—with acceptance or resentment, as the case may be—than to develop in the slow and difficult process of trial and error one's own initiative in organizing one's life. Initiative is poorly developed in children who are forced to rely on others for the organization of their lives.

When the child visibly makes many false starts and falls into many errors in organizing his life, the parent's fears tend to take over. He then deprives the child not just of the opportunity for self-development but, worse, of the necessity to do so on his own. Without opportunity and necessity, most children will not develop their own initiatives in organizing their lives, and the parent's unspoken conviction about the child's inability to do it becomes a self-fulfilling prophecy. It must also be remembered that initiative is not developed and tested on the basis of those rare occasions when a child, by chance, has an opportunity to be really himself for a short period of time, particularly not when some organized and demanded activity is always looming in the background. Initiative will not grow on barren soil, even though there are occasionally rare children who somehow possess such initiative and go about living their own lives despite all obstacles. It is a lot of trouble to learn to live by one's own initiative, and it requires much courage and determination, which many children can muster only if they have to. If not, they will let others take care of these matters; at the same time they are likely to resent it, and in the end be deeply disatisfied with themselves, their parents, and their lives.

Without question, there are certain dangers inherent in letting a child develop his initiative. Nor will it do to encourage a child to do so, as some parents try. In such circumstances, the child's actions may seem to be due to his own initiative, but he knows that they are not—he is doing what his parents expect or demand of him. Therefore, all a parent can do is to be aware of the existence of such dangers when the child begins to develop his initiative in truly running important aspects of his life; the parent can then do his best to minimize the bad consequences of such initiative. When a child is able to develop his initiative while he is still little, these dangers are relatively small and are easily prevented from having dire consequences. On the other hand, sometimes an adolescent will suddenly take his life in his own hands, in ways which are resentful, defensive, and aggressive. If this is the case, usually such a person has been deprived of any true development of initiative, and then the chance of his making serious errors, of courting much more severe dangers, is often quite great.

Given enough opportunity to spin out their thoughts, most children soon begin to use fantasy play to bring order into their chaotic inner world, or to free themselves from its undesirable outcroppings. By doing so, they begin to increase their capacities to cope with reality. All children try to flee into a world of fantasy when reality becomes unmanageable, but only those who are seriously emotionally disturbed try to escape into it permanently. For normal children, fantasy play serves as an effort to separate out the inner life of imagination from the outer life of reality, and to gain mastery over both.

More than anything else, fantasy play—as opposed to pure fantasy— builds a bridge between the unconscious world and external reality. Through play, fantasy is modified to the degree that the limitations of reality become visible by means of the play activity. At the same time, reality is enriched, humanized, and personalized by being infused with unconscious elements coming from the greatest depths of our inner life. In fantasy, in dreams, in the unconscious, everything is possible. Nothing has to follow in any orderly sequence; nothing contradicts anything else. However, if the unconscious is uninfluenced by reality, it remains asocial and chaotic. On the other hand, reality free of fantasy elements remains harsh, cold, emotionally unsatisfying even as it seems to meet our needs. Clearly, our inner and outer worlds must be integrated in a harmonious way if we are to have a satisfying life.

Today many people suffer because, in their lives, the worlds of fantasy and reality, which for our greatest well-being must interpenetrate one another, remain apart. In earlier times, when myth, religion, and a wide range of magic beliefs were an important part of life (as they still are in large parts of the world today), this dichotomy did not exist to such a debilitating extent.

Our children have no less capacity for fantasy than other generations. The problem today is that personal fantasies are not permitted sufficient room to develop and are continuously infringed upon by the impersonal, deindividualized fantasy products of the mass media. With it, our children's uniquely personal fantasies and speculations fail to animate their "real" lives. Also, the emphasis on practicality and reality interferes with our children's chance in home or in school to engage in fantasy play of their own creation. And even if they are encouraged in this activity, they usually are much too soon asked to talk about it or to express it in some other form, long before it is ripe enough for expression. As the child reveals his fantasy, adults are often too eager to influence him by asking questions or stating their approval or delight, which eliminates the child's need to gain clarity about it for himself. In any case, the fantasy is aborted before it reaches full bloom. If this happens repeatedly, many children become disillusioned about their own fantasies, not because of lack of adult interest, but because of too much and premature interest. Efforts to help him improve his fantasies make him feel that they are no longer his own.

Unfortunately, it has become fashionable in certain circles to call almost any unstructured activity of a child "creative." This uncritical acceptance of fantasy as reality prevents the building of a bridge between the two worlds. Children test the limits reality imposes by playing out their fantasies. For example, if a child is annoyed at a person, he imagines tearing the person's head off. This does not matter in fantasy, because in the next moment he can affix the head again, and everything is fine. But in reality, of course, things are different.

There is a familiar fairy tale about a wife who is given three wishes and squanders one by asking for some sausages. The husband becomes angry at such a foolish wish and without stopping to think, he wishes the sausages onto his wife's nose. When they appear there, he realizes how careful one must be with one's wishes, and what may happen when they become reality. There is nothing he can do but waste the final wish by asking for the removal of the sausages from his wife's nose. And so the couple learn what happens when fantasy is subjected to the tests and limitations imposed by reality.

A child learns the same important lesson when he goes beyond the fantasy of tearing off a head and actually decapitates his toy animal. He is submitting his fantasy to the limitations of reality, thus visualizing what his wish is all about—which he cannot do, so long as it remains mere fantasy. He quickly learns that a head cannot easily be restored to its body. With such experiences, his vengeful fantasy—"I'll tear his head off"—slowly changes. He realizes: "Right now I want to do something drastic, but I know I really won't, because I have learned that that would cause irreversible consequences." The desires of the unconscious thus become tempered by the impact of the limitations of reality as experienced in play. The extreme ideas embraced by some young people and their belief that these can be realized in short order show how little opportunity they had as children to learn through play to respect the limitations reality imposes on the realization of fantasy.

INTEGRATING INNER AND OUTER WORLDS

For many human experiences, there is an optimal period when they best further our development; if we do not experience them at such time, they may never have as constructive an impact on our personality formation. The play age is the correct time for building the bridge between the world of the unconscious and the real world. In fact, this is the main developmental task of this stage. Later in life, when the two worlds have been too long separated, it may be impossible to integrate them—or at least to integrate them very well. This is why some people who have failed to achieve this integration escape into a drug-induced fantasy world, while others undertake strenuous intellectual efforts to achieve such integration, for instance through psycho-analysis. Remedial efforts are not even a second-best way to achieve inte-gration, but if this developmental step fails to take place, life itself may come to be experienced as profoundly unsatisfying.

Imaginative play is so very important because it provides the primary means for integrating inner and outer worlds. Through it, also, a child constructs a bridge by which to pass from the symbolic meaning of objects to active inquiry into their real properties and functions.

An example may illustrate. When a child builds a tower of blocks and then knocks it down, it is not simply that after he has acted "constructively" for a time, his destructive drives have gained ascendancy and found expres-sion. There is a much deeper meaning to his activity. In the building part of the play, he has labored subject to the limitations imposed by reality upon his imagination—his internal reality. Even while he asserted his dominance over the blocks by making them fit *his* design, he still needed to make allowances for the nature of his materials, for gravity, for the laws of balance and support. In revolt against these restrictions, he destroys the tower—not so much to give vent to his destructive tendencies as to reassert his dominance over a reluctant medium. Thus what goes on is much more significant than the mere alternation of constructive and destructive action. What the ex-perience really mirrors is a crucial learning experience about inner and outer reality, and about mastery.

The child learns from his play experiences that he can be master su-preme—but only of a chaotic world. If he wants to retain at least some mastery over a structured and organized world, he must forgo his "infantile" desire for total mastery and arrive at a compromise between such wishes and the hard truth of reality—i.e., the limitations of building with blocks. He learns that a wish to exert total mastery leads to chaos (pushing down the tower of blocks), as he repeats the experience again and again.

Eventually, after repeated play, the advantages of a compromise in which inner reality takes cognizance of the nature of external reality become so obvious that it is accepted as the right order of things, first and for a while only reluctantly, but finally willingly. Only through such experiences does the child learn to temper his inner demands in the light of what is feasible in the world he lives in. Play is the process by which he acquaints himself with both sets of realities—inner and outer—and begins not only to make his peace with the legitimate demands of both, but also to learn how to satisfy them to his own and others' benefit.

15

*Understanding the Importance
of Play*

*Should we not seek the first traces of poetic activities
already in the child? Perhaps we may say: Every child
in his play behaves like a poet, as he creates his own
world, or to put it more correctly, as he transposes the
elements forming his world into a new order, more
pleasing and suitable to him.*

—FREUD, in "The Poet and Fantasy"

MOST PARENTS WANT to raise their children well, and they do all they can to nurture the skills and attitudes they believe will lead to personal satisfaction and success. In some areas, their encouragement comes naturally, without any special effort. For example, many parents find it easy to implant an interest in reading, sports, or music in their children merely by living their own lives and doing what interests them most. But when it comes to reinforcing the earlier and more basic ability of sticking to a task even when it is demanding or frustrating, parents may not recognize that playing with their child is a crucial factor in developing this trait. The underlying reasons for this are fairly obvious. Parents read because they enjoy it, and the same goes for music or sports. Thus when they read to their children, listen to or make music with them, play ball with them, they encourage an interest in reading, music, or sports through spontaneous and largely unconscious attitudes. But being adults, they are seldom personally committed to playing with toys in the same way, so there is no automatic support through normal parental predilections for most of the child's play activities.

Parents' inner attitudes always have a strong impact on their children, so the way parents feel about play, the importance they give it or their lack of interest in it, is never lost on their child. Only when parents give play not just respect and tolerance but also their personal interest will the child's play experience provide a solid basis upon which he can develop his relation to them and further to the world. This point is easily understood, yet somehow parents often fail to show a real commitment to children's play activities, despite ready lip service and the purchase of toys.

For example, we sometimes refer to a task beneath our interest as "mere child's play." The phrase is indicative of the gulf that separates the grown-up's world from the child's world, and of a certain amount of inadvertent contempt toward play. All too often parents look on play as a "childish" pastime—and this despite their understanding of its important place in the child's life.

However, this was not always so. The separation of the child's world from the world of adults is a comparatively recent development in human history, and was slow in coming. Until the eighteenth century, and until even more recently in large parts of the world, children and adults played the same games, often together. So there was an immediate understanding between adult and child not only as they played together, but as they observed each other engage in something which was personally meaningful to both.

PLAY AND GAME

Most adults find it easier to involve themselves directly in complex and adult games, like chess or baseball, than in play on simpler levels, such as stacking blocks or riding a hobbyhorse or toy car. Although the terms "play" and "game" are often used interchangeably, they are not identical in meaning. Rather, they refer to broadly distinguishable stages of development, with "play" relating to an earlier stage, "game" to a more mature one. Generally speaking, "play" refers to the young child's activities characterized by freedom from all but personally imposed rules (which, unless the child is compulsive, can be changed at will); by freewheeling fantasy involvement; and by the absence of any goals outside the activity itself. "Games," on the other hand, are usually competitive and are characterized by agreed-upon, often externally imposed rules; by a requirement to use the implements of the activity in the manner for which they are intended and not as fancy dictates; and frequently by a goal or purpose outside the activity itself, such as winning the game. Early on, children recognize that there is a much greater opportunity for pure enjoyment in play, whereas considerable stress may be felt when playing games. A four-year-old, for example, when confronted with an as-yet-unfamiliar play situation asked, "Is this a fun game or a winning game?" The attitude with which he approached the activity depended on the answer he was given.

An easy distinction between play and games can be seen in these two typical examples. There is a clearly defined difference between a play activity in which a small boy's toy automobile flies through the air, knocks down tall block buildings, and then becomes the recipient of his whispered confidences and a game such as Monopoly, in which a piece of metal is a marker, all moves of which are dictated by an elaborate set of rules covering every contingency and providing for a specific goal—winning. It makes sense to speak of the "rules of the game," but play has no rules, aside from those the child wishes to impose on his own activities, and which he may vary from moment to moment, as he desires. Actually, it is the child's spontaneous fantasy as expressed through his play which determines what is going to happen next. The play proceeds not in line with objective reality or the logical sequence of events, but as free associations of the moment may suggest. There is, of course, a continuum from the free-play activity to the well-structured game, and some activities partake of aspects of both play and game.

Many languages have only one word for what English designates with the two nouns "play" and "game," and even English has only one verb— "to play"—for both activities. We play at playing, and we play a game, but there is a difference. As noted earlier, play proceeds on a more primitive level, and games require a more mature level of understanding. Games, with their definite structure and their competitive aspects, are naturally closer to our adult ways of spending time, and thus they evoke more immediate empathy in adults. We enter into their meaning and importance quickly. If we could be as emotionally involved in a child's play as we are in those games we also play, we would find in ourselves a spontaneous feeling for play's importance which provides an emotional bridge between age groups.

Relations were probably easier in many ways, and more meaningful and enjoyable for both children and adults, when they played the same games, even though the internal meaning the play had for each was not identical. The same play could signify for the child, for example, an exploration or reconstruction of his world, while for the adult it might be mainly recreation. But what was important about children and adults playing the same way— although with different inner meanings—was that they were equally serious about what playing meant to them, and equally convinced that this play enriched the life of each. That they both played in the same way gave the play a special significance for children, while it permitted adults an inner participation in their children's activities, which made for a special bond between them.

Today, there are relatively few games which are enjoyed as much by adults as they are by children. More often than not, children are experienced as intruders when grown-ups reluctantly feel obliged to make allowances for the child's presence and perhaps let him participate. When I was a child in Vienna, things were often different. One of the most common and popular leisure activities of adults was cardplaying (it was Freud's main recreation, for example, during the working year). My father spent many of his relatively few leisure hours playing cards with relatives and friends. As they played for hours, I watched them, which they took for granted, since I did not interfere with the game—it was too important to them and to me. My kibitzing changed nothing in the way they played and interacted with each other. They played for insignificant stakes, but when my father won, he gave me a share of his winnings. Small as it was, it added to my interest in the game and increased my watchfulness. That these adults were so serious about a game I also played with my friends was important to me, and so was the fact that they enjoyed it as much as I did. Of course, my friends and I knowingly, and probably more often unwittingly, copied our parents' behavior during our card games, making jokes and emulating other types of behavior we had observed. It was from my experience of playing the same card game that I spontaneously understood its importance for my father; and it was from his experience that he had full understanding of and empathy with what playing this game with my friends meant to me.

With our common interest in and enjoyment of card games, it was only natural that when the occasion arose, such as a rainy vacation day, my father would play cards with us children for long hours, often the same games he played with his friends. However, this was an entirely different experience, even though the game was identical. When my father played with us, his role and attitude was that of a parent who enjoys what he is doing because it is enjoyable to his children. This made it very different from the experience when I watched him play the same game with his friends—then he was every bit as serious about it as I was when I played with *my* friends.

It is from experiences like this that I know the difference between a parent playing with his child—important and enjoyable as this is for both when all goes well—and a parent and his child, each entirely on his own, playing the same game with contemporaries. When parent and child, each for his very own reasons, are engrossed in the same play, this can form a bond between them which is truly *sui generis*.

DIMINISHING AWARENESS

It was not so long ago that adults still instinctively understood children's play and enjoyed it themselves. As recently as a century ago, Blind Man's Buff and similar games were a favorite recreation for all ages. Blind Man's Buff is mentioned as a game enjoyed by both children and adults as early as six hundred years ago, in the *Romance of Alexander*. Shakespeare refers to it in *Hamlet*, Goldsmith in *The Vicar of Wakefield*, and Dickens in *The Pickwick Papers*. It is mentioned by Rabelais and in *The Pentamerone* as being played by the royal household. Many artists, including Goya, depicted it. Pepys told that on December 26, 1664, he finally went to bed, but his wife and members of his household continued to play Blind Man's Buff until four in the morning. In a later century, Mrs. Tennyson reported in a letter that her husband, the Poet Laureate, enjoyed playing it with Jowett and the poet Palgrave during the Christmas festivities of 1855.

Part of the enjoyment of Blind Man's Buff and similar games is that they provide exciting yet safe exercises in disorientation, excursions into a world of darkness rather than blindness. The game existed in many forms, ranging from the primitive to the quite sophisticated, which made it attractive to both young and old. In some variations the players remained absolutely silent but had to stay in their places, and the blindfolded person had to locate one of them by touching him. In other variations the players moved about so that the "blind man" could not be sure where they were, although he was given verbal clues when the players called out to him. There were versions in which no change in environment was permitted—things and people remained in the same places—but the blindfolded person, having been twirled around several times, had to reorient himself and locate a target which he had previously fixed firmly in his mind (as in Pin the Tail on the Donkey). But whatever the variations of this game most adults today would consider taking part in it beneath their dignity. Grown-ups in previous times enjoyed it very much, but adults nowadays tend to avoid play that seems to them pointless and hence "childish."

But just how pointless are such activities? Perhaps they appear meaningless to us today because by avoiding them we have lost a spontaneous understanding of their inherent significance. Only by empathetic participation can we understand many forms of play. If we didn't know from our own experience, as spectators or participants, what football and baseball are all about, batting or kicking a ball around a field could seem a pointless and senseless activity. The same holds true for moving markers around a board, and even for dice—one of the most ancient of toys, enjoyed and played by young and old all over the earth. Only after we have involved ourselves in these games do they begin to make sense to us.

The same goes for much of our young child's play. Were we to join him wholeheartedly at it, our participation would soon reveal how meaningful play can be for those who take it seriously, but as long as we consider ourselves outsiders, it seems a silly and random activity. In fact, however, such games as Blind Man's Buff and many others deal with very significant experiences, and this is why both children and adults have played such games with great relish for centuries past.

On the simplest level, games like Blind Man's Buff and Pin the Tail on the Donkey represent attempts to get along without sight, allowing the player to test the extent to which he can safely rely on his sense of direction. In Blind Man's Buff the blindfolded player feels his way from object to object and is momentarily lost when moving in the empty spaces between them. This is the same experience we have when we grope around a dark room at night. Fear of the dark is one of the oldest and most pervasive terrors of man, and surely it was even more intense, even among adults, in the centuries when artificial lighting was not readily available. But even now, all children are terrified of being "lost" in the dark, or of being unable to find their way when there is no light. Games like Blind Man's Buff repeat this experience in a playful manner, permitting the child to feel that he can master his anxiety about darkness. The merriment that erupts when the blindfolded player touches another player mirrors the relief the anxious child feels when, in the darkness of night, he finally gets in touch with his parents. The game reassures him that he can count on being able to do so.

As adults we seem to have mastered this fear; most of the time, all we have to do to escape the darkness is to switch on a light. Perhaps we have lost interest in playing Blind Man's Buff for this reason, and we no longer empathize with the younger child, who is still in the throes of his night fears, if not also in terror of darkness, and to whom such a game has much to offer.

When we play blindfolded, we also test the good intentions of others; we need reassurance that our fellow players will not take undue advantage when we cannot see what they are doing. Thus the game gives us assurance about our environment: the trustworthiness of people and the permanency of objects. It poses and answers a question that is most basic to feeling secure in this world: Do we have to be on guard, on the lookout all the time, or is it safe to believe that things will remain essentially the same and predictable?

A basic rule of such blindfolded play is that objects must remain in place, although people may move about. There is good reason for this rule, which teaches an important lesson for life: in large measure, security in the physical world depends on the permanency of objects. We can find our way around because physical objects—doors, stairs, tables, and chairs for the small child, streets and houses, mountains and trees for the older—are reliable landmarks. On the other hand, people are not fixed in location; security regarding them does not come so easily. What other experience could teach this lesson so directly, simply, and convincingly?

The lesson inherent in a game like Blind Man's Buff is one that every child needs to learn in order to overcome his primal anxiety—fear of abandonment and of darkness. For a long period, the infant wants his mother to be near him all the time: only her physical presence, as if she were an object, offers reassurance. Eventually a feeling of security based on the mother's reliable care of the infant will suffice; he will be satisfied with the feeling that she will always return when needed. This permits him to feel safe even if his mother is not always physically present.

Similarly, fear of getting lost, of becoming disoriented, is another basic anxiety of the young child. In a game like Blind Man's Buff we do become disoriented, but instead of this being a destructive experience, it offers us the pleasure of seeing things immediately rearrange themselves when the blindfold is removed. And the general jollity relieves our momentary anxiety as we realize that to some degree, we were mistaken about where everybody was located.

Games like Blind Man's Buff help children confront problems that are of central importance in learning about the world. In fact, by the time these problems are encountered in the relatively sophisticated context of an organized play experience, they have already been explored by him countless times in more primitive settings. For instance, practically all children sooner or later try walking around a room with their eyes closed in order to find out whether objects remain in place even if they are not closely watched, and also to learn what types of things are stationary and what types of things may not be. There are almost endless variants of this experiment. In one, the child closes his eyes and wants an adult to hold him by the hand as he walks about. The question posed here is: "Can I trust you to look out for me, or must I be on guard myself all the time?" Sometimes the child closes his eyes but at the crucial moment opens them a bit, peeking. Now he is asking: "Do I have to watch all the time, or can I let my attention wander and trust my instincts to tell me the right moment to pay careful attention again?"

In yet another version of this experiment the child walks around with his eyes closed, and adults are told to warn him before he runs into an obstacle. Here the question is: "Am I well enough protected to risk exploring the unknown, as represented by what I can't see?" The child's delight when we always warn him in time demonstrates how important the reassurance is to him. He comes to realize: "Even when I do not see danger, my parents like guardian angels watch out for me." One child, beset by sleep-interrupting night fears, conquered his anxiety by playing this particular game over and over. During the day he repeatedly tested whether his parents would watch out for his safety when he himself could not see dangers. Since they did provide him that important reassurance, the child could relinquish his night-time wakefulness and sleep soundly again.

DESTRUCTIVE PLAY—OR IS IT IN TRUTH CONSTRUCTIVE?

When parents have an inner spontaneous empathy with the very special meaning play has for their child, this in itself does a great deal for the child and their relationship, even if the adults spend only limited amounts of time in play. What he needs most is their emotional commitment to the importance of his play, so that it can be fully significant to him. His frequent demand that we play with him represents his effort to gain, from our active participation, a sense that what he does is also important to us. If he gets this emotional message—if our conscious and unconscious interest in and respect for his play quiets his conscious doubts about it—the child will need less of our participation to remain convinced that we truly believe his activity is important.

A famous literary example from the mid-eighteenth century may illustrate that adults need not directly participate in a child's play in order to reinforce its importance, as long as they enjoy it, approve of it, respect it. Goethe's earliest memory—one which he considered so important that he used it to introduce all his other recollections by putting it at the beginning of his famous autobiography, *Aus meinem Leben—Dichtung und Wahrheit (Out of My Life—Poetry and Truth)*—was of throwing first his own toy dishes and then his mother's dishes out of the window. He wrote: "On a beautiful afternoon, when all was quiet in the house, I fooled around with my newly acquired pottery dishes and pots, and since nothing came of it, I threw one piece of pottery out into the street and rejoiced that it so amusingly shattered. The brothers von Ochsenstein, seeing how much it delighted me as I merrily clapped my hands, called out: 'Go on!' " And go on Goethe did, as he first tossed out all his play dishes, and when there were none left, continued to do the same with his mother's crockery.

Freud, in his paper "A Childhood Memory out of *'Poetry and Truth,'* " suggests that Goethe was symbolically acting out his anger at his sibling and his wish that the hated usurper should be thrown out of the house. True enough, but I believe a great deal more can be learned about play in general from this first recollection of one of the world's greatest geniuses.

To begin with, Goethe stresses that at first his play with his pottery got nowhere, suggesting that his first action failed to meet inner pressures with which he needed to cope at the time. Only when he hit on the idea of tossing a dish out into the street did his play become meaningful. This is a typical example of the way children begin to play rather aimlessly, not quite knowing what makes them occupy themselves with some particular thing. It also shows us how the most common everyday objects can help the child to act out—and with luck solve—some of his deepest and most exigent problems, provided he is given ample and free scope to use these objects as seems best to him—never mind what their *intended* use is. And it shows us how, when left to their own devices, children can change what begins as aimless play into something that is most meaningful. Like Goethe in this example, whenever truly important issues are involved the child does not know beforehand what he is going to play out, or why; he has no conscious plan. If he did, then his play would serve conscious and not unconscious needs; and since these unconscious needs are unknown to the child, they are usually unknown to his parents also. Thus they cannot *plan* play for a child which will meet his most pressing needs.

Only at the moment when the first piece of crockery crashed onto the street and shattered might little Goethe have had the lightning realization "This is what I wanted to play!" and *delightedly* clapped his hands because of the sudden shock of recognition that this was what fit his needs, released and relieved the pressure of feelings which threatened to suffocate his emotional life, and freed him of his angry dejection. If anyone had tried to explain all this to the little boy, he could have comprehended none of it, although he grew up to be one of the most brilliant men who ever lived. At other moments and in other contexts he might have been able to understand that he was angry at this sibling who, he feared, had replaced him, and that his wish was to get rid of the intruder (many a child tells his parents that it would be best to take the new baby back to where it came from). Although he acted out these unconscious desires through play, he would have been astonished if the unconscious sources of his play had somehow been brought to his conscious attention. Worse yet, this would have destroyed at once all that he had tried to achieve through his play. Probably he would have dissolved in desperate tears, denying all that he had been told. The end result might have been that he would have repressed his unconscious feelings much more deeply, so that they would have become entirely inaccessible to symbolic expression and relief, and might have done permanent damage to his future emotional development.

Following Freud's analysis of this story, we may assume that the first motive of Goethe's play was a symbolic expulsion of his sibling by throwing things out of the house and into the street. But as most important psychological phenomena are overdetermined, we may also speculate that throwing his dishes (which, as his possessions, in a way also symbolically stood for him) represented his feeling that he had been thrown out of his home by this sibling, that his security had been shattered, as his dishes were shattering.

The approval of the von Ochsensteins, prominent citizens of his native city and esteemed friends of his equally prominent family, may have been what permitted the child Goethe to expand on what he was doing by also throwing out his mother's crockery. In this way he punished her symbolically as the cause of his distress, and thus relieved himself of his anger at her. The continuing approval of these important adults and their amusement at his action restored his confidence that he was still deemed very worthwhile, that his anxiety that he was forsaken was not as justified as he had feared. He had found an audience beyond his parents, and it convinced him that his way of dealing with his severe distress was indeed a good way to cope symbolically with what so deeply perturbed him. Freed of much that had oppressed him, he could join his neighbors in their enjoyment of it all. Having relieved himself through play of much that had deeply distressed him, with this outside encouragement he could successfully go on with his life. It was the first of many experiences which showed Goethe that he had it within himself to cope with even the most difficult and painful vicissitudes of life, a justified self-confidence which was part of his greatness. But none of it would have happened had these adults not buoyed him up when he most needed it.

As Goethe writes, "My neighbors continued to signify their approval, and I was delighted to have amused them." These adults, as was typical then, were much more accepting of a mischievous child than we are today. It was their understanding and appreciation, not their direct participation, that enabled Goethe to master through symbolic play an experience too overwhelming to be coped with more directly. Their approval permitted the play to move from a cry of distress—Goethe's feeling that "I have been thrown out"—to an act that reassured him "that what I am doing is appreciated." As his mother's dishes crashed into the street, the open incitement and enjoyment of his neighbors allowed Goethe to feel: "I can punish my mother for having given me a competitor; and by destroying her dishes, she won't be able to feed him; others can understand that! Despite what I'm doing, or perhaps because of it, important adults approve of me." This was exactly the assurance Goethe most needed at this critical juncture of his life.

Like most self-invented symbolic play, Goethe's act, as previously suggested, had meaning on many different, important and urgent levels, whereas play material created by others can only rarely fit so well the always-changing demands of the moment. Goethe's play expressed his feeling that he had been thrown out; his wish that his sibling should be thrown out; his punishing his mother by throwing her dishes out. But on still another level, Goethe probably wanted to get rid of *all* the dishes, so that he would no longer be fed from them, or be expected to eat from them. His sibling was being nursed, and his play expressed also his own desire to return to an earlier feeding situation that his competitor was now privileged to enjoy, and for which he envied him.

Today many parents would be appalled by such "destructive" behavior. They fear that if permitted to proceed in such a way without being stopped or at least corrected, the little boy will grow up to be uncontrolled, perhaps even destructive and violent. As we know, exactly the opposite was true in Goethe's case. Fortunately for him, his parents were so convinced that their son would become a very fine person that such an idea did not occur to them. Nor did this idea occur to the neighbors; otherwise they would not have encouraged Goethe's play, which without this encouragement would not have been such a success. And Goethe, having been able and permitted to act out his annoyance drastically in his own way and with such approval, was also able through these actions actually and symbolically to get rid of his anger to some degree when it was at its height. All this having been done, he could later form a very positive relation to his surviving sibling and of course went on to lead a justly admired life.

The neighbors and the family encouraged Goethe's "destructive" behavior because they must have felt and understood, on some level, its significance. In fact, they often recalled it with pleasure. In ending his account of this event, Goethe writes: "In recompense for all this broken pottery we had at least a funny story to tell, which amused until they died most especially the neighbors who had incited me."

As if to emphasize the importance of adult empathy with the play of children, which alone permits it to attain its full positive meanings, Goethe followed this story with a description of the way he and his sister played at the feet of their grandmother, or, when she was ill, by or on her bed, and how important it was to them that she always enjoyed and encouraged their play in a soft, friendly, benign manner.

How likely is it that such an experience could be repeated today? However much we might claim to be concerned with helping our child resolve severe emotional impasses, if it came right down to it, we would probably be just a bit more concerned with the dishes than with the child, and worried that if destructive behavior like that remained uncurbed, it would lead to terrible consequences.

Goethe's story suggests that in times past, people knew that children need to get things "out of their system," and that spontaneous play is one of the best ways to do so, although nobody ever talked about it in this manner. Today, the adult need to "get things out of one's system" is perhaps commonly accepted, but when children try to do this and get angry—which they often do get, because they are so often frustrated in their attempts to arrange things to their liking, or just do things—they are corrected by adults. Destructive outbursts like Goethe's do not now meet with an attitude of pleased enjoyment, as was his; with us such destructive play evokes opposite adult attitudes of inner criticism, if not also of open disapproval.

The result is that such events, instead of becoming happy memories enjoyed by children and adults alike all through their lives—forming a strong bond between them because of the child's feeling of heightened self-esteem and well-being due to the adults' approval of his actions—are most likely now to become angry or guilt-laden memories that drive parents and child apart. Today if a child were to throw dishes out of a window deliberately and systematically, such behavior would most likely be rejected and provoke severe criticism, as well as punitive sanctions. The behavior certainly would be stopped long before it had run its full course, more often than not without the adult's trying to understand the child's motives. Frustrated in their unconscious intentions and reproached for their actions, our children usually learn to repress whatever feelings cause their destructive impulses and forget the whole incident. But the angry feelings do not go away; they either find an outlet in more devious ways, where their meaning cannot be so readily understood and where the action is so removed from what caused it as to provide little relief, or the anger is repressed and continues to work in full force in the unconscious. In cases of sibling rivalry, to which Goethe abreacted by breaking the dishes, repression may result in a lifelong animosity to the sibling because the childish hatred could not be resolved in an angry reaction. The opposite was true for Goethe, who, having purged his anger at his sibling in one big and oft-remembered act, could develop an excellent relation to him, which was greatly helped because his angry reaction was viewed so positively. It is fairly easy to get over one's anger when expressing it has such favorable consequences; it is impossible to do so when one has to repress it.

Feeling understood during a very difficult moment in his life added to Goethe's conviction that even in bad situations, life can still offer compensations. The episode became a shared memory that strengthened the bond between adult and child. If this happened today, the event would either be forgotten or repressed; recalling it would bring only unpleasant memories. Or it would be remembered as an occasion when the child acted foolishly and destructively, which would make the memory damaging to his self-esteem. If he also recalled his parents' negative attitude to what he had done, this memory would easily revive the feeling of anger and rejection he had experienced. It certainly would not strengthen his relation with them, but rather weaken it.

I have known many children and adults who suffered deeply because their parents considered their play or some other behavior very foolish. Not knowing any better, they continued to accept their parents' evaluation of their actions as correct, although they did so nearly always with considerable resentment. In consequence they thought of themselves as being in part—and in a few extreme cases, quite—foolish persons. but even when they had thus adopted their parents' views, the fact that the parents had let their child know of their low opinion of him was always deeply resented. As adults, many of them were ashamed to recall what they had come to consider as their foolish actions when they were children, while others looked back on themselves with an attitude of superiority—how silly they had been! This attitude they assumed in an effort to compensate through the present feeling of superiority for feelings of deep inferiority which their parents' view of them had instilled in them.

When they were able to analyze more deeply the meaning of the behavior which had been regarded as foolish by their parents, the analysis revealed how meaningful it had been. Then they recognized with great relief that what they had done had been far from foolish. However, this did not suffice to free them of their feelings of inferiority, which had been caused by the belittling attitudes of their parents. They finally recalled how angry they had been and how deeply hurt they were, not so much because their parents had seriously misunderstood them but because the misunderstanding clearly reflected the low opinion their parents had harbored of their own child.

We ought to assume that whatever a child does, however outlandish or foolish his behavior may seem on superficial observation, he has excellent reasons for engaging in it. If we start out with this assumption, we will search for its meaning, and the more incomprehensible the behavior the more seriously we then search. While we might not quickly or fully understand it on this basis, we are much more likely to do justice to it. This will be of great benefit to our child and will aid our understanding of him. It will greatly improve our relations to each other. By contrast, if the adult's attitude to significant childish actions is to dismiss them as pranks, or to inhibit or punish the child, then we should not be surprised that adolescents reared in this way consider that nobody over thirty makes sense.

How much have we all lost since Goethe's time by this shift in attitudes regarding play—children and adults alike!

16

Play as Problem-Solving

While just this or that poor impulse,
Which for once had play unstifled,
Seems the sole work of a life-time
That away the rest have trifled.
—ROBERT BROWNING

I N THE DAYS WHEN parents and children played the same games, they
shared a virtually automatic understanding of the purposes of play: to be
both meaningful and enjoyable. This is still true concerning the most
primitive, earliest, and hence most important play, that of the infant—and
woe unto the child if it is not.

When a baby tosses a rattle out of his crib and his mother hands it back
to him, in their moment of mutual delight the mother hardly notices the
fact that in this new achievement, her infant is asking himself some very
important questions: "Can I influence my objective environment without
dire consequences to myself? Can I safely assert my will and manipulate
objects without suffering for it? Can I rid myself of something that annoys
me? Can I relinquish control of my belongings temporarily without losing
them altogether?"

The mother's response to these questions will be affirmative if her pleasure
in the baby's new skills moves her to applaud his act and guarantee its
repetition by returning the rattle. But the answer will be negative if she
becomes impatient or annoyed and thus gives him the feeling that his manipulation of objects is naughty; and if she simply refuses to return the toy
to him, it teaches the child that manipulation of objects leads to permanent
loss, both objective (the rattle is gone) and subjective (the effort leads not to
interpersonal satisfaction but to interpersonal frustration).

The knowledge which the infant seeks through his play is so crucial that
he needs to repeat the same action-query many times to feel sure of the
answer; thus his persistent repetition of the play. Without being at all aware
of it, he seeks first answers to some of man's most profound philosophic

inquiries: "Is there a thing Me? How can I be sure of my existence? Can I do things? Can I be certain of regularity, permanency, predictability in my world and my person? What is the world's intention toward me?" All these issues are investigated and partially answered on the level of his growing comprehension of the world through his play and the response of others to it and him.

Some of these questions he explored earlier when he closed his eyes, or turned his head away, and discovered that he could make things become invisible. Initially this action probably gave him his first indication of the basic difference between self and nonself: when he closed his eyes or turned his head away, he remained the same as before, but what had been in his field of vision disappeared, hence it had no permanency but he did. Thus closing the eyes and turning the head are important stepping-stones in the separation of "I" and "Not-I," and in the psychological formation of a self.

Since by turning his head the infant can make things seem to disappear, he learns to turn his head when he sees something unpleasant and wishes to deny its existence. Later, when speech develops, the concept of NO will be formed out of this reaction. That turning the head in this way is the precursor of NO can be seen from the fact that in our culture, shaking the head from side to side is always tantamount to saying NO.

In its earliest form the game of Peek-a-Boo consists of one person moving in and out of another's field of vision by means of the second person's eyes being covered and uncovered in short succession. The source of the infant's enjoyment lies in the happy discovery that the other player, although temporarily invisible, has not disappeared. In more advanced versions, approach and withdrawal are added, and it becomes Hide and Seek. In such play, the nature of human relations becomes apparent to the child: even before he can put it into words, he understands that although people remain constant and the same, we may either come closer to the other or distance ourselves more from him. Finding out that not only can he himself make another person disappear by turning his head away or closing his eyes but that the other can also remove himself at will is one of the greatest disappointments of infancy and something which the child therefore tries to master through a variety of play experiences.

Freud described a small child pushing a toy under the bed and then pulling it out, again and again in seemingly endless repetition, trying in this way to reassure himself that things which disappear are not necessarily gone forever but can return, can even be retrieved by the child's own efforts. This particular child's anxiety had been aroused by his mother's absence. His game reassured him that just as his toy could disappear and then become visible again, so too could his mother go away for some time and then return to him. The essence of the play lay in his attempt to convince himself first that even though he couldn't see his mother, she wasn't gone forever, and second that while he had no control over events brought about by others, such events need not be as destructive to him as he had first feared. He also learned that he could indeed have full mastery over events he himself caused, and, equally important, that there is a difference between events he could produce himself and others which are beyond his direct sphere of influence. Being able to effect the former takes much of the sting out of the latter. Many other self-invented play activities serve similar exploratory and reassuring purposes.

Different from such self-invented solitary play are the games a mother plays with her baby. These are an infant's first introduction to his culture and also to the communicative process. As the mother plays Peek-a-Boo and Where's the Baby with her infant, there comes a moment when the child begins to comprehend the communicative nature of the game and joins in on his own. Delighted by the realization that his mother plays the game with *him* because she enjoys *him* so much, and that she wants him to enter into the play, he does. This starts the communicative process by which he discovers the other—his mother—and simultaneously, himself. This discovery forms the basis of our conscious interactions, albeit in the most rudimentary form; it is the essential basis on which all later communication will be built, since it requires the notion that one person can meaningfully interact with another person. Although mutuality begins in the nursing situation, what happens there is largely unconscious. In Peek-a-Boo and similar mother-infant interactions, mutuality becomes a conscious experience. The infant's happy facial expressions and noises evoke additional pleasure in the mother and motivate her to continue the game with greater enthusiasm. He realizes that what he is doing is the cause of this and that he has communicated something to her—something to which she has responded, and responded in the way he desired.

How important such play is in establishing selfhood was demonstrated to me by an eight-year-old autistic girl. As often happens, the severe pathology of her case permitted observing a phenomenon also seen in normal behavior but as if it were under microscopic enlargement, or thrown into bold relief by a bright light. This girl had been virtually mute all her life. She completely rejected all efforts to reach her physically or verbally, and was unresponsive to all aspects of her environment. She resented all efforts to make contact with her; if one reached out to her actively, she responded with angry, terrified withdrawal.

It took more than a year during which we carefully respected her wish to be left alone, while still trying to take tender, loving care of her, before she moderated her total isolation and permitted occasional approaches, although she did not respond to these in any discernible way. Of all the many and various ways in which we tried to reach her she finally responded only to one: a simple game which combined features of Peek-a-Boo and Where's the Baby, in which I eagerly "looked" for her and expressed my delight when I found her. Although she was right there all the time, I pretended for a time not to see her, so that I could rejoice when I "discovered" her. Eventually she actually hid behind a curtain, even peeked out from behind it, mimicking what I had done innumerable times in my play of finding her. As we were once more playing this game for quite some time, she permitted me to hug her. At this, I proclaimed louder my joy at finding her—and my pleasure was indeed great and genuine, especially because she had allowed such close bodily contact without immediately shrinking from it. We continued the game, and she continued to permit herself to be hugged; as I thus held her gently, she suddenly uttered a complete sentence, her first ever, telling me what she wanted from me.

This American girl, who had been brought to Vienna for psychoanalytic treatment, had by then been living with us for a year and a half. Since she was mute, there had seemed no point in talking with her—and in front of her—in English; so since the time she had come to Vienna she had been spoken to in and had heard only German. Nevertheless when she uttered this, her first sentence, she said in perfect English, "Give me the skeleton of George Washington." The tragedy of her life had originated in the fact that her father was completely unknown, not just to her but also to her mother, because of the strangest of circumstances. The mother, who became aware of her pregnancy only after she was in her fourth month, had tried to get rid of the fetus. After the child was born, she wished that the girl had never been born, so that her own life would not have been destroyed—as she saw it—by this child. Only after the girl was five years old and clearly autistic did the mother become guilt-ridden and try to do the best she could for her daughter. Her desperate efforts to secure treatment for her by the best experts in the United States proved futile, since the girl was universally declared hopeless, so she finally came to Vienna and Anna Freud, who told her that only living in a psychoanalytically organized environment might offer hope for her girl, the environment which we created for her. It is completely unclear how she got sufficient knowledge of her history to know that her problem was due to the fact that she had no known father. Still, in her sentence she told that what she needed was a father, and as an American girl with no known father she could think only of the father of her country as a solution to her problem. Since the unknown father was "the skeleton in the closet" of her life, she asked for his skeleton.

It is important to note that in telling me what she wanted to give to her, she not only spoke for the first time in her life, but spoke in a complete sentence, referred to herself by means of the personal pronoun "me," and addressed me by my name. These details are remarkable in view of the fact that autistic children, even after they begin to talk, do not use personal pronouns. Thereafter she never stopped talking altogether, although for quite some time she used language only sparingly.

This girl—who until then had refused any contact with the world—achieved the rudiments of a self first through Peek-a-Boo and through playing it recognized the other, to whom she communicated something of greatest importance to her. It was by means of Peek-a-Boo and the other game in which I "searched" for her that she realized that *she* was the one who was hiding, that it was *she* who was being searched for, and found. Playing these games enabled her to find herself and at the same moment to find the world of other people—through play she had joined the world. Also through play, she became able to hope that what she desperately needed could be given to her.

A feeling of selfhood and the experience of being able to communicate and to receive communication are acquired through playing such simple games, but they also serve other important purposes. They teach a child that even when he and his mother are temporarily out of sight of each other, the interruption of visual contact does not mean that their emotional contact is also broken. His mother's frantic quest in Where's the Baby and her delight in finding him clearly demonstrate to him that out of sight does not for a moment mean out of mind—on the contrary, losing sight of the baby only increases the desire for his presence. It provides him with the much-needed assurance that contact will not be lost, whatever may happen. On the strength of this knowledge he learns that he need not cling to his mother at all times; he can safely let her out of sight for a while. And his mother's pleasure when she finds him, and his in being found, adds a positive dimension to his daring in leaving her or permitting her to be invisible for a moment.

As Peek-a-Boo reassures the child that he won't be lost or forgotten, so are other anxieties assuaged by games which demonstrate the integrity and importance of all the parts of his body; for example, This Little Pig Went to Market, which involves touching and naming the toes or fingers. This game conveys to the child the information that his body is in good shape; nothing is missing or liable to be overlooked. Even more important, it assures him that the various parts of his body are emotionally significant to his parent.

In addition to quieting anxiety about disappearance, games in which the child can take a more active role, such as Hide and Seek, also serve to enhance his mastery of himself and the world. Hide and Seek is one of the most ancient and pervasive games known to mankind. All efforts are bent on searching for the player who is "it." This convinces him that even if he is not visible, he has not been forgotten; and that it is important to one and all that he be found, because the activity—and, in the transferred sense, life—cannot go on without him. Such is the dignity and reassurance that "simple" play can confer on participants.

In the more primitive hiding game Where's the Baby, the child waits to be found, although he may help out by shouting, "Here I am!" In Hide and Seek and its related variants, his success depends on his getting to safety (called home, home base, or house) through his own efforts. What he learns through this more advanced play is that he can afford to venture out on his own into the world, risking exposure to its dangers (as represented by the pursuer and the strange hiding places), and return again safely to the permanent security of home base. He can test his skill, luck, and daring out there, confident that somehow he will again be able to reach safety. The game even provides a built-in consolation prize: should he be caught, he does not lose out or have to leave the game, but becomes instead the powerful and active pursuer in the next round.

INCREASING MASTERY

Through play, more than any other activity, the child achieves mastery of the external world. He learns how to manipulate and control its objects as he builds with blocks. He gains mastery of his own body as he skips and hops and jumps. He deals with psychological problems by reenacting in play those difficulties he has encountered in reality, as when he inflicts on his toy animal a painful experience that he himself has suffered. And he learns about social relations as he begins to realize that he must adjust himself to others if satisfying play is to continue.

Many life experiences which would be commonplace to an adult are overwhelming to a child. Adults have learned to know, accept, and even anticipate them. None of this is true for children; for them, many experiences are entirely new and unexpected. Even events that have become well known to a somewhat older child are exciting or overwhelming to the young child because of his inexperience. Only rarely does a grown-up encounter the unusual, the very exciting, the threatening and unexpected occurrence. But such events are the rule rather than the exception for the young child, even though the occurrence itself may seem ordinary, innocuous, or even pleasant to the adult observer.

As one grows older, the difficult experiences of the past serve as preparation for those encountered in the present; this renders the present more predictable and tolerable, as well as less exciting. As we repeatedly live through experiences, we learn to master them, however overwhelming they may have been at first. This is why a child repeats over and over again in play an experience that has made an overpowering impression on him. Through repetition he tries to familiarize himself with it and develop the tolerance that is the direct consequence of undergoing the same course of events repeatedly, and the mastery that is the result of being in active control rather than a passive subject over whom others exercise their power.

A child can be bowled over by genuinely exciting or threatening events, but also by experiences that seem neutral or positive to adults, such as a visit to the zoo. Observing the animals is interesting and enjoyable for both adult and child, but to him it also poses questions: What are the similarities and what are the differences between animal and man? What in us is animalistic and what specifically human? To the child, who in many ways feels much closer to animals than do adults, these are absorbing and entrancing problems. If a child has a chance to play with baby animals, he may be stimulated to think about the all-important problem of what the essential differences between adults and children are. In which ways are they alike and in which different? Not that he formulates or analyzes such questions consciously, deliberately, or thoroughly. If he could, he would soon arrive at answers, and repetitions of the experience would not be necessary. Given his age and ways of thinking, he wonders about these issues piecemeal, randomly, as his observations stimulate his thoughts. But it is these and similar questions which, without his being able to express them, nevertheless preoccupy him and entice him to further observations, although he has little idea how they will eventually add up. Nor will these questions permit him to arrive at clear-cut answers, but the inability to solve a problem is no reason to abstain from the effort. It is one of the hardships of childhood that a child can't avoid the struggle, despite the fact that he is only rarely able to achieve the solution.

Often it is not so much the complexity of the occurrence itself that confuses a child, but the implications of it. The experience itself may be baffling, but far more so the ramifications, and it is these which he tries to master through many repetitions, both in reality, by repeated visits to the zoo, and in play, by reliving the experience at home with his toy animals. Much of the appeal of stuffed animals derives from the opportunity they offer to play out and ponder such problems in safety and at leisure. This is an additional enjoyment which children derive from toy animals, on top of the pleasure of being able to control and to master the animals, whereas a child is fearful of the same type of animal if it is alive. As is true of other play, here too one of the primary values of the activity for the child is that it allows him to feel in control of what frightens him in reality. A real bear presents a potential threat, but with a teddy bear he can do as he likes. The bear's power is thus in his control. The teddy bear protects the child and threatens his enemies, as the real bear has threatened him. Visits to the zoo have the additional importance of convincing the child of the power of the animal which his toy animal represents, and this reinforces the latter's significance. Teddy bears are an invention of this century, so one may wonder whether stuffed animals could have had equal importance to children in the past, before zoos permitted them familiarity with the animals these toys represent.

Through play, which does not need to conform to reality in all details, a complex experience can be broken up into manageable segments, each of which can be relived and thus understood and mastered without undue anxiety. In this manner, one piece at a time, the child can assimilate an event with which he could not come to grips all at once. If the experience was a bad one, it can be neutralized through play; if it was one in which he felt disagreeably dominated, it can be transformed into one in which he is in control.

For example, a child may repeatedly put blocks, toy figures, or other small objects into a truck or box, only to spill them out, put them back in, and spill them out again. A problem with which he may thus be struggling in symbolic form is the one posed to him by defecation: "How is it that something put into my body, such as food, comes out of it, often in small pieces? Does it mean I am losing something permanently from my body?" Putting his blocks into a truck and spilling them out again shows him that, contrary to his anxiety, nothing gets permanently lost in this process. A truck is good for this play because it moves about easily, as the child does, and it carries within its body the small pieces that get spilled out, as he carries food within his body, only to spill the contents of his bowels into the toilet.

This play is meaningful also because during toilet training, and later when he is reminded to use the toilet, the child feels like a passive object, pushed to perform as his parents dictate. In contrast, in his play he is totally in charge; he decides when something is to be put into the truck, and also when and where it is to be spilled out. It is but one example of many other activities in which, through his play, he tries to compensate for the countless situations in which he feels controlled or manipulated by his parents— situations that are frustrating and debilitating to his self-consciousness. This compensation the child can achieve only through self-chosen free play, not through play suggested or directed by adults in which he would again feel manipulated.

Many repetitions of this filling and spilling sequence may be required before the child is able to cope in symbolic form with the question that has perturbed him and in some cases can occupy his mind to the exclusion of nearly everything else (i.e., whether or not he loses valuable body content when he defecates). Such interior problem-solving underlies his persistence in playing such games. He is not at all conscious that he is trying to solve a problem; all he knows is that the play is very important, and meaningful, to him. However, if one tried to make him understand what he is symbolically acting out and attempting to deal with in this manner, he probably would not be able to understand what we were talking about. To most children the idea that they might be playing out feelings about toilet training is so unacceptable as to be unbelievable; nevertheless, they would stop the truck game in disgust. Others, having less deeply repressed their interest in the process of elimination and in their stools, would understand the explanation quite well, but they too would no longer be able to use this play for solving the problem that concerns them deeply. The reasons would be the same: the parental injunction against interest in or play with his feces has been adopted by the child, so he can solve problems of defecation only in symbolic form. The explanation destroys the symbolic nature of the play, and the child becomes unable altogether to continue dealing with the issue that perturbs him.

Then the two closely connected problems with which he tried to cope symbolically through his play—"Am I losing something of value when I defecate?" and "Am I in charge of my defecating?"—may remain unresolved and continue to plague him in his unconscious for a long time, since no solution could be found at that level. Of course, some children may return to their efforts to cope with these problems in some other symbolic form through different play, but often the substitution will not be nearly as effective as was the original play.

To sum up, play is an activity with symbolic content that children use to solve at an unconscious level problems they are unable to solve in reality; through play they achieve a sense of control which in actuality they are far from possessing. The child knows only that he engages in play because it is enjoyable. He isn't aware of his *need* to play—a need which has its source in the pressure of unsolved problems. Nor does he know that his pleasure in playing comes from a deep sense of well-being that is the direct result of feeling in control of things, in contrast to the rest of his life, which is managed by his parents or other adults. This pleasure is particularly keen when the play puts the child in control of an activity that represents symbolically an activity in which he strongly resents being controlled.

It is important that a child be able to conquer reality through play. However, even more crucial to his development is the freedom to transform an event of which he was the passive subject into one in which he is the active instigator and controller. For a sense of well-being, and even more for self-respect, everyone needs the conviction that he is to some degree master of his fate; this is even truer for children than for adults, simply because so many decisions in a child's life are made for him. Such a conviction is a prerequisite for a child's development of the belief that he has an important stake in the world and can to some extent shape his own life in it. Self-determination is hardly within the capacities of the young child in reality, but in play, he can accrue this power to himself. And since the line between fantasy and reality is not yet clearly and definitely drawn for him, play works for the child and strengthens his capacities and understanding. What would be a debilitating flight into fantasy for the adult is actually a strengthening experience for the child, who is at the proper age to achieve mastery through play and in fantasy.

Since the child often cannot really know what will be done to him, many events not actually painful will nevertheless make him fearful. After such an event, a child will typically play out the experience in fantasy. Following a visit to the dentist, for example, the child might play at fixing another child's teeth, telling him to keep his mouth wide open, as he himself was instructed, and inserting little pieces of cardboard to take X rays. If no other "patient" is available, a toy animal will do. The many hours a child may spend in such play is a clear indication of how much actual time he would have needed in the dentist's chair in order to truly understand what was done to him and why, and to deal appropriately with all the emotions the experience aroused. Just as we can understand and analyze events that move too fast for our comprehension by watching them in slow-motion replays, so the child learns to understand and analyze, through long hours of repetitious playback, events previously beyond his comprehension.

Older children, having a much larger backlog of either direct or analogous experience, can to some degree master events in anticipation. For example, a ten-year-old has sufficient experience at first or second hand to understand an explanation of what will happen when a tooth is pulled, and he can begin to comprehend and assimilate the event before it occurs. This is entirely beyond the capacities of very young children, for whom all meaningful mastery is achieved after the event through play. For example, it is impossible to prepare a small child for hospitalization. Even if he understands the words of the explanation, they have no concrete reality for him, because he has no experience of hospitals on which to draw. When the event happens, it is overpowering, and his mastery of it requires subsequent play repetitions, first of details and then of the experience in its entirety.

Most parents do attempt to prepare their children for traumatic experiences such as hospitalization. Unfortunately, their verbal preparations usually are effective only in allaying the parent's own anxiety about the event. It would be much better for the child if his parents *played* hospital with him beforehand. Although this cannot give him true mastery of the event, it can at least make some of the particulars less surprising and distressing.

After hospitalization, the child needs to play out, time after time, single features of his experience. Then gradually he will be able to master it altogether in play. He may begin by giving his teddy bear an endless series of injections, focusing so much on that one detail that his parents may mistakenly conclude that he remembers only being given shots. But slowly, as he achieves mastery of this one aspect, he builds up enough assurance within himself to go on to another. Then he may play out the care of the nurses, each detail one at a time, repeating the process again and again until the events begin to lose their anxious connotations. Thus he eventually comes to feel: "I can understand it. I know what it's all for and about." As he plays out each part of the event, one at a time, his understanding of the segments eventually leads to a grasp of the larger picture, which initially was much too complex for him to understand. And as he actively inflicts on his toys in play the procedures he suffered as the passive subject, he begins to realize that he need not always be the helpless victim, but can do unto others what has been done to him. Thus through play the child's passive suffering is turned into active mastery.

Traumatic events in particular can best be mastered through play. For example, a small child cannot conceive that surgery is needed to safeguard his health or his life. It is terribly threatening for a child even to consider that his life may really be in danger, or even that his leg will be incapacitated by a cast for a long time in order that he can walk well in the future. The fact that a child undergoes such an experience without incident does not mean that he has accepted it, much less accepted it as important to his continued well-being. In this situation he cannot afford acceptance, because that implies that the experience may happen again—a thought much too frightening to be entertained. It is much easier for him to accept such events as being necessary for others, or for toys, since then they do not carry the same personal immediacy. A child may pretend that this toy dog has hurt its leg, and unless the leg is straightened by heavy bandaging, the poor thing will never again be able to run fast. Or he can play that unless Monkey's teeth are fixed, Monkey won't be able to bite into a hard apple but must live on Jell-O and soft bananas. Playing out one's own traumas with toys slowly dispels the massive anxiety that interferes with an understanding of the experience. Once such medical attention has been understood as unavoidable yet beneficial for the stuffed dog or toy monkey, then the application to oneself comes on its own.

So a child will act out his trauma a hundred times with a toy, assuring the stuffed animal over and over again that the treatment will make it well. Listening to his own reassuring voice, the child eventually convinces himself. But first, parental reassurances are absolutely necessary, since only with these in mind can the child reassure the toy. As in so many other play activities, it is the parent who must take care to set the process of acceptance going in the child.

THE PRIMACY OF PLAY

The more opportunity a child has to enjoy the richness and freewheeling fantasy of play in all its forms, the more solidly will his development proceed. Later encounters with learning, games, and sports will strengthen and enhance his knowledge and mastery of the world. But for games and sports, or even for learning to be fully meaningful, his prior experience with play must already have provided a firm foundation. This is why culturally deprived children who had little chance to play and were little played with by parents have such a hard time in school—without the experience of succeeding in play, they do not trust themselves to succeed in school. For this reason, it is not sufficient for parents to wait to share in play activities when they reach a more formalized stage. The older child's activities may offer more intrinsic interest to a parent, but by that time it may be too late. Both kinds of experience—play and games—are necessary for growing up well. Children lose out on a great deal if TV viewing or even activities such as academic learning prevent them from having rich experiences with both play and games. The ability to enjoy games builds on the play experience.

For example, there is little wrong with a game such as Go to the Head of the Class; it is entertaining and educational. But it won't help a child master the school experience; it merely repeats and formalizes that experience. Mastering the school experience needs to be accomplished through the more imaginative channels of early play. A child just entering kindergarten may line up his stuffed animals in a row and "teach" them. Or he may conduct "classes" for his preschool siblings. By doing so, he is actively learning to master an experience which he has been passively subjected to during the school day. He acts out the teacher's role, which makes her more acceptable and understandable as a person, an instructor, and an imposer of discipline. If he can play the teacher, he will find it easier to tolerate the teacher-student relationship and can therefore use positively most of his experiences in school.

The value of fantasy repetition in mastering difficult reality experiences is nowhere more clearly demonstrated than in playing school, and here the parent, if he plays his child's eager pupil, can prove a great boon. Parents are the ideal "pretend" pupils, because they can demonstrate to the child that even adults can accept passive learning without losing face. But if parents aren't available as pupils, the young child is probably better off teaching his dolls or stuffed animals than trying to teach his younger siblings. The danger is that if the younger children fail to learn, the child who plays teacher may feel defeated; and if they object to his overbearing or impatient behavior, he will have difficulty mastering in play what he may have experienced in reality.

Here again, parents should avoid becoming conscious educators. For example, parents may want to help a child learn the multiplication tables— a difficult task for many a youngster to solve. The parent asks: "How much is six times seven?" When the child does not come up with the right answer, the parent corrects him, which gives him a feeling of defeat and failure. The child's experience could be quite different, however, if the parent were to reverse roles and ask the child to pose a problem. When he asks the questions, the possibility of defeat is obviated. After the parent has given the right answer so often that he's sure it is firmly engraved in the child's mind, then the time has come for the parent to make an occasional "mistake." The more outrageous the mistake, the more it will be enjoyed by the child, who will not believe for a moment that 6,742 can possibly be a correct solution to six times seven, though he might discover both the problem and the right answer within the number.

Such play puts the child into the driver's seat; through it, he becomes much more active in learning, which is as it should be. No longer is he the passive supplier of correct answers—instead, asking the questions is a pleasant game. Eventually this can be varied by parent and child taking turns at asking the questions, but only with problems that the child has fully mastered so that no experience of defeat is possible.

The child who has to think problems to pose to his parent is much more concentrated on this activity—which includes figuring out whether the parent is giving the right answer—than the one who has been subjected to an examination camouflaged as help in learning the multiplication tables. No matter what the specifics of the situation, any parent who concerns himself with helping his child to play out school experiences, whether real or imagined, instead of trying to teach him, will be aiding his child's progress in school most productively.

Practically any human activity can lend itself to misuse in the service of defensive pathology, or for compulsive purposes. But the fact that it *can* do so has little bearing on its real nature. We know that very neurotic children develop play rituals to feel protected thereby from terrible dangers which otherwise might befall them. But it would be erroneous to conclude that this is the universal rationale for ritual play.

For example, we probably all recall the walking rituals of our childhood. We walked along ledges, stepped only on certain squares of the pavement, or made ourselves walk as close to the walls of buildings as possible. Perhaps we had to step on all the cracks in the sidewalk, or on none of them; or we had to set one foot exactly in front of the other at every step, or after so many steps to turn ourselves around, repeating some secret formula. Walking play like this is of such ancient nature and universal persistence that it has outlasted empires, social systems, and religions. Despite this fact, spontaneous childhood rituals have been little studied.

There seems, in fact, to be serious misapprehension about the true meaning of walking rituals. Psychoanalysis tends to explain them as compulsive efforts to bind anxiety, but this interpretation—while pertinent in some instances—fails to do justice to the importance of this play for all children. Walking rituals appear to be a normal and ubiquitous phenomenon, despite the possibility of neurotic elaboration. These rituals seem simple at first glance but have some remarkable aspects. One is their widespread appearance and persistence at a certain age level, without social pressure or adult encouragement. Equally interesting is the fact that most children, after they reach a certain age, spontaneously give up this type of play, with the notable exception of pathologically compulsive children, who may carry obsessive behavior into adulthood.

Walking rituals may be better understood as an experiment in and demonstration of self-mastery, a proof of one's capacity to command one's own activity. The child learns that he has some control, if not yet of the outside world, at least of his own actions within it. Rituals like these are completely the child's own spontaneous invention; the very essence of the activity is that the rules must be self-chosen and self-imposed. Details may be copied from other children, and may change from moment to moment as the walker decides. What must never change is that the rules are self-set, and that the child is convinced that obeying them will achieve "magical" results. Anyone else's notion about the rules of play will be rejected. If his pattern is to step on none of the cracks, the child will respond with an incredulous stare to a suggestion that he pervert it by stepping on all the cracks.

The "magical" dimension of the play is in the feeling the child gets from it that although he is a mere child, subject to the restrictions of the adult world, he suddenly becomes his own master. He himself has set his task; and he also executes it by himself, with no one's help. What greater magic is there than to use a simple device meaningless to anyone else, and by that very device deliver oneself from a life of bondage to a life of freedom? It is a wonderful secret, all the more exciting because no one else can guess at it, especially adults.

Within a young child's reality such activities are not childish, but are the most mature of all for one reason: they permit him to be captain of his fate. The feeling of potency the child derives from this sense of self-mastery convinces him that he is master, in a fashion, of his seeming masters—the adults who don't even know what he's really doing. Hence the rhyme "Step on a crack, break my mother's back." That which magically gives the child power over himself at the same time gives him power over his parents.

17

Play and Reality:
A Delicate Balance

Of all people children are the most imaginative. They
abandon themselves without reserve to every illusion.
—J. B. MACAULAY, *Milton*

PLAY HAS VERY IMPORTANT MEANINGS for children, but wise parents will not attempt to structure a carefully organized play program for a child as though it were a well-balanced diet. In play, spontaneity and inner direction are of supreme significance; without them, much of the value of play is destroyed. I emphasize this point because faulty understanding of the unconscious meaning of play and misapplication of certain insights derived from the use of play in child therapy have made it more difficult for adults to take play as seriously as it must be taken if the child is to be understood on his own terms.

For example, in psychological treatment a child might be encouraged to shoot a toy pistol at a figure; this may be done either to free his aggressions or to discover their source and intended goal. But this occurs in the presence of an adult acting as a therapist, in an "as if" therapeutic situation. If a parent encourages his child to shoot at someone, or even at himself in a normal play setting, it is a mistake—he is not taking the child's play seriously enough. If he did, rather than just pretending to do so without paying close attention to what the play is all about, he could hardly encourage such an unequivocal show of aggression against others, not to mention against himself.

Another common mistake adults make in reacting to child play is taking it as not "for real." But in more than one sense, play is the child's true reality; we have to respect it as such. This is why we ought not to encourage our child to shoot at anyone. But this caution refers only to our *encouraging* our child to do so. We may very well give him a toy gun to use as *he* likes, or sees fit, be it for his protection or for aggressive play, but whether, when, and how to use this toy should be entirely the child's own decision. Our giving him the gun implies our permission to use it as he wishes, when and how he feels a desire or need to do so, but no more. More important, it also implies our confidence that he will use it appropriately, even wisely, in a way that he thinks to be appropriate or wise, as seen from his perspective.

Incidentally, this holds true for all toys we give to a child. Our providing him with such play material should be no more than a statement on our part that it is all right with us if he chooses to play with it; our gift should never be the result of our wish that he should play with it, or play with it as the manufacturer intended. These attitudes not only rob his play of spontaneity, which would be bad enough, but control that which should help him assert his freedom, be in charge, in relief from the rest of his life, which is controlled by adults.

Children have a need to rid themselves of their aggressions, at least through symbolic play, and it is sufficient permission to do so when we give them toys suitable for that purpose. If we encourage a child to play aggressively, we exercise—however subtly—control over the activity, which is likely to increase his frustration or aggression and with it the need for discharge, rather than freeing him of that need. On the other hand, if his aggressive play is directed toward us—as it might be, if for no other reason than that he wishes to discover what our reaction might be, rather than because he wishes to hurt us, even in play—and if we do not react appropriately to what he does, then we effectively demonstrate to him that we take neither him nor his aggression very seriously. If we show a contradictory approach to the play by initially intellectualizing ("Let him work off his aggressions") and subsequently attempting to render the activity harmless ("Even though you've just 'shot' me, it means nothing"), then such attitudes destroy the serious qualities that play has for the child.

But when a child "shoots" his parents, should they shoot back? Certainly not; counteraggression by an adult—whether in play or in earnest—has never yet proved beneficial to a child. Nevertheless it is not much help to him to let him shoot us with his toy gun without our giving an appropriate reaction. The reaction, of course, must be not to his action as such, but to his intentions. Only our on-the-spot assessment of what motivated the action can tell us whether the best response is an admiration of the child's assertiveness—what a powerful warrior he is!—or a playful dramatic collapse to the floor, or a shadow of anxiety, or a question about how he will manage with us out of the way. By the way, a well-placed question such as this one is much more effective in convincing a child that shooting and killing are detrimental to his well-being than any theoretical discussion of the evils of war or violence.

This is because the child lives in the immediate present and within the limited confines of his direct experience. Wars, even those he sees on the TV screen, take place in some far-distant place and have no bearing on him that he can understand. And should we succeed in impressing on him the tragic consequences of war, the primary effect will be to infuse him with an overwhelming sense of powerlessness. After all, the youngster is smart enough to figure out that he has no effect on what is going on somewhere far away in the world. But shooting at his parent is something he *can* control, and really do something about. Almost any child realizes that however angry he is at a parent, however much he may want to get rid of him at the moment, he does not want to lose him forever. Children are acutely aware of how much they need the care and protection of their parents, and how deeply they would suffer were their parents to turn in retaliation against them, or to disappear permanently.

Charity begins at home, and so does learning about aggression. A child will understand that shooting and killing people is wrong when the parent who was playfully made a target inquires who is going to pour the milk in the future or go to the store for ice cream. Such a question can convince a child of the need to keep his aggression under control in his own best interests, as no abstract description of the horrors of war could do. To be told that what we want to do—shoot the gun—is wrong annoys and frustrates us, and puts us on the defensive. But realizing things on the basis of one's own experience and interest—that is, a parent who has been shot can no longer serve the child—makes the learning become positive.

Whatever the parent's response to being "shot," he must take the play seriously, and not respond with sermonizing or counteraggression. On the other hand, when children play shooting games among themselves, counteraggression is an age-appropriate response which does little harm and perhaps some good. While the child may discharge some aggression by shooting at his playmates, he also accumulates a great deal of new anxiety when other children shoot at him. A buildup of such anxieties created by shooting games eventually may impress on him that everybody loses in a free-for-all, since the shooter is also the target. However, this important lesson goes by the board when adults, trying to be "nice," let their child riddle them with "pretend" bullets without showing any appropriate reaction.

Some adults may overreact to this type of shooting play. Parents who fall into this trap are usually more concerned with their own feelings about aggression than with helping a child master his aggression through such play, as opposed to merely repressing it. This is also true for sexual or other types of anxiety with which many children try to cope through shooting play. So when they forbid it they block the safe and necessary outlet it can provide.

At the same time they rob the child of the valuable lesson that if we try to shoot others, they will shoot back, and everybody will lose.

Some parents, out of their abhorrence of war and violence, try to control, or forbid altogether, any play with toy guns, soldiers, tanks, or other toys which copy and thus represent implements of war. While these feelings toward violence are most understandable, when a parent prohibits or severely criticizes his child's gun play, whatever his conscious reasons for doing so, he is not acting for his child's benefit, but solely out of adult concerns or anxieties. Some parents even fear that such play may make a future killer of the child who thoroughly enjoys it, but the pitfalls of such thinking are many and serious.

First, as playing with blocks does not indicate that a child will grow up to be an architect or builder, as his play with cars and trucks does not foretell the future auto mechanic or truck driver, so his playing with toy guns tells nothing about what he will do and be later in life. Second, one may reasonably expect that if through gun play a child feels he can well protect himself and if he discharges much of his aggressive feelings, then less of these will accumulate and press in later life for dangerous ways of discharge. Shooting games provide outlets for accumulated frustrations and thus are apt to reduce them. Hence the child's aggressive and hostile feelings can be more readily controlled by him than when a parent prevents their discharge, rendering reduction through symbolic play impossible. Such prohibition also leads to additional frustration and anger which accumulate because the child is prevented from using an outlet that he sees freely available to other children and is suggested to him by the mass media.

Since in regard to violence the issue is control of aggression versus its discharge, the best way for parents to deal with this problem—whether or not it is one in their estimation—is to do everything in their power to prevent their child from experiencing frustration or accumulating hostile feelings. While it is impossible to shelter one's child entirely—for all life, and particularly that of children, is full of frustration—one can try not to add to it, such as by prohibiting play the child wishes to engage in.

Third, and by far the most important attitude because it is most pernicious in its consequences, whether spoken or implied, is parental fear that the child may become a violent person, perhaps even a killer. This thought is far more damaging to the child's emotional well-being and his sense of self-worth than any play with guns can possibly be. This is particularly true because of the importance to him of his parents' views of him. After all, a child gains a view of himself primarily from his parent. It is apt to make him very angry at them and the world for holding such a low opinion of him, and this increases his propensity to act out his anger, not just in symbolic play but in reality, once he has outgrown parental control. He knows that he wants to play with guns, and if his parents think that this presages a future killer, his image of the kind of person he is, or may develop into, is in danger of becoming seriously distorted. As the example of Goethe has shown, a child's need to discharge aggression has little to do with war, or even violence on the streets, but usually mostly with events taking place at home, such as jealousy of a sibling or anger at a parent. Hence, permitting a child the opportunity to discharge his anger symbolically at some third party—at other children, perhaps, with whom he plays Cops and Robbers—is much preferable to his having to repress his anger. If then there is no permissible outlet for it, it will continue to fester within him.

Girls are as subject as boys to all kinds of frustrations, very much including sibling rivalry and anger at their parents, and so it would serve them equally well to be able to discharge their anger through symbolic play, as with toy guns. Furthermore it would prevent their feeling frustrated because an important type of symbolic play available to boys is not available to them. By playing with guns they too would get things out of their system. They would realize that boys are not advantaged in comparison to girls in this respect.

Often a child's desire to play with toy guns is mainly motivated by his wanting to be able to protect himself symbolically. If his parents prevent him from doing so, he feels deprived of a chance to protect himself by those who ought to be his natural protectors. And if his parents seriously fear he may become a killer because of these normal desires—self-preservation, ridding himself of hostility, acting out aggression in play so that he won't have to do so in reality—then their outlawing not only such play but also the desire for it becomes by virtue of their convictions a devastating attack on the child's own person and an indictment of his present and future existence.

After so much has been said to suggest that parents should not prohibit symbolic play which has such an important role in the child's dealing with inner pressures, it still might seem necessary to stress that there is no point in forcing any play activity on children, nor in encouraging them, for example, to play with toy guns or other war implements. Whether they wish to do so, and when, should be left entirely up to them, girls and boys alike. But when they wish to engage in such play we should accept it as such: play that is at that moment important to them and that foretells nothing about their future lives. As always, what is most important for the child's present and future being are the inner convictions of his parents about him, such as that he—whatever he plays at the moment—is a very fine person now, and will be no less fine once he is grown up. More than anything else, this will help the child feel so secure within himself that he will feel little pressure to act aggressively against others.

The more seriously children explore *all* possibilities which appeal to them, and the more their parents support *all* such efforts, the better able they will be later on to decide what suits them best. Many children spontaneously limit their own play to one or a few related areas, for a time or even for years. A permanent occupational choice may come out of it, and if so, memories of happy childhood play can add permanent zest to one's activities. But more frequently a child's preoccupation is due to the need to work at some problem, and when it is finally solved, the preoccupation vanishes; it has served its purpose. By having concentrated on it, the child seems to have gotten this particular type of activity "out of his system." Later on, when he has entered an entirely different career from the one his childhood play might have suggested, there will be no regrets, because he will have had his fill of the other activity.

It is often hard to imagine and impossible to predict how a child's continuing concentration on some type of play can anticipate and prepare him for what seems like a quite different profession or avocation. Only in hindsight can one realize how goal-directed the child's activities actually were. For example, from infancy onward a girl surrounded herself with a wide variety of stuffed animals. She was inseparable from them, spending her days playing with them to the exclusion of all else, so much so that when she entered school she could work up no interest in learning, not even about animals. When she became a teenager, she carefully kept all of her stuffed toys but shifted her interest to caring for real animals; she then spent all her free time, as well as hours she should have spent at school or doing homework, hanging around an animal hospital, where she soon became a welcome helper. She cleaned out the animals' cages and did other menial work she would never have done at home, and she played with and took excellent care of the animals. At that time both she and her parents were convinced that she would become a veterinarian. The parents encouraged the idea, pleased that their daughter was finally occupying her time constructively and preparing herself for a profession of which they (although with some inner reservations) could approve. So she went to college to become a vet. However, when she had nearly completed her studies, she suddenly dropped out of college and returned to her earlier habits, being and working around animals in rather random fashion, though always concerned for their welfare. When thirty, this woman suddenly abandoned her lifelong fascination with, and devotion to, animals; she finally had gotten her fill of them. She returned to the university to become a social worker, and she now concentrated on working with very ill people. Only then did she realize that all her dedication to animals had been a displacement, because until this time she had never trusted herself to be able to care for and minister to people. With animals, she had worked out her anxiety that she was unable to care well for other people.

Now the progression from infatuation with stuffed animals, to that with real animals, to working in a caring capacity for people at last became clear to her, and to all who had followed her development. What now seemed so obvious, however, had by no means been obvious before. Subconsciously she had prepared herself with animals and tested her ability to take care of these "stand-ins" before she finally could do what all along had dominated her unconscious life: take care of people.

Not often is it so obvious that the child's play and the adolescent's preoccupation are but preparation for an adult profession. However, in the lives of many who have the opportunity to organize their own existence, childhood play is in some fashion significant in laying the foundation for what would later on become a major interest.

As long as a child is little, the question of what he will eventually choose as an occupation remains remote. What counts when he is young is how well he is able to enjoy his play—not as preparation for future roles, but for what it means at the moment. More than anything else, gaining full satisfaction out of an activity in line with one's age development holds out the promise that one will continue to like what one will do in life. For a child to gain such feelings of pleasure and self-worth from play, he needs his parents' consistent corroboration of the importance of his play activities. So it is crucial to his well-being that we not deflate him through indifference or lack of understanding, or discourage him through critical attitudes which often have more to do with our adult worries about the future than with what he is doing at the moment. All caring parents have concerns about their children's future, try to plan for it, wish to be able to help them achieve their goals. But today many parents go way beyond such normal solicitude in being anxious about their children's future. If they are, however much they may try to keep it secret from their children, the children feel it and usually feel it keenly. Whether such anxiety is openly expressed or kept secret from children, in their minds this creates severe self-doubt which can become so ingrained that even marked success in later life does not eradicate it. Inner security is the result of early perception that our parents approve of what we are doing, and this is translated in the subconscious to mean that we are doing well as persons. Thus when a parent shows he is pleased that his child is playing well—that his play is important, purposeful, meaningful—this increases the child's feeling of self-worth and with it his security about himself and his future. This is why nothing is more vital to our children than that we truly feel, and communicate to them, our conviction of the importance their play has for them, and hence for us.

Since many of us as adults can no longer involve ourselves spontaneously and directly in a young child's play, as earlier generations could, we must use other avenues to compensate; our understanding must make up for what we have lost in immediacy and spontaneity. A fuller appreciation of the far-reaching importance of play and of what is inherently involved in it can transform an intellectual understanding of its theoretic significance into that emotional commitment to play activities which all children need from their parents.

TOYS AS SYMBOLS

There are many contributions that only parents can make to their child's play. For example, no teacher, and certainly no age-mate, can be as deeply and personally involved in play that seems to relate to the child's future as are his parents. Play is anchored in the present, but it also takes up and tries to solve problems of the past, and it is often future-directed as well. So a girl's doll play anticipates her possible future motherhood and also helps her to deal with emotional pressures of the moment. If she should be jealous of the care a sibling receives from their mother, doll play permits her to act out and master her ambivalent feelings. She deals with their negative aspects by mistreating the doll, who represents her sibling. In this symbolic way, she can punish her sibling for her jealous agonies, of which he or she is the innocent cause. She can make amends for her negative attitudes to her sibling and satisfy the positive elements of her ambivalence when she takes good care of the doll, just as mother does of the sibling, and in this way free herself of guilt and identify with her mother. In addition, the girl also identifies with the doll, and thus vicariously receives the care her mother lavishes on the sibling. Thus in a myriad of ways doll play is most closely connected with a girl's relation to her mother.

It is a misfortune for boys that they are only rarely offered opportunities to play with dolls and even more rarely encouraged to engage in it. Many parents feel that doll play is not for boys, and because of this they are usually prevented from dealing with issues such as sibling rivalry and problems of family constellation (among many others) in this convenient symbolic way. Perhaps if parents could see how eagerly boys use dolls and doll houses in psychoanalytic treatment—certainly as eagerly and persistently as girls do— to work out family problems and anxieties about themselves, they would be more ready to recognize the value of doll play for both sexes. For example, in dollhouse play, boys—as eagerly as girls—put a figure representing their sibling out of the house, put a figure representing a parent on the roof or lock it into the basement, place the parents together in bed, seat a figure representing themselves on the toilet or have it mess up the house, and in countless ways visualize, act out, become able thus to deal better with pressing family problems.

When given the freedom to do so, both boys and girls use dolls to great advantage in working through unsolved problems; they reenact experiences from the recent past or from infancy, or fantasy experiences they wish they'd had, or cope with whatever other residues of the past they need to master. Some parents, especially fathers, think that doll play is contrary to masculinity, which it is not. There is a great deal in a boy's past experience (just as there is in a girl's), such as the way he was fed, held, bathed, or toilet-trained, which he can best master through doll play or play with dollhouse furniture, such as tubs and toilets. There are for him, too, present problems such as sibling rivalry. And while child care will probably not play as central a role in his future as in that of a girl, it may be a very important aspect of his life as a father.

If parents are worried that doll play may feminize a boy, all they need for reassurance is to watch how boys play with dolls, because it is very different from the way girls play with them. Unless a boy has already embraced femininity by reason of severe neurosis, he does not handle dolls or play with them as a girl does. His approach is quite distinctly masculine, typically much more aggressive and manipulative than that of girls.

True, boys' doll play is usually shorter-lived than girls', and not quite as significant an experience for them; but this is no reason that they should lose out entirely on what it can offer them. Actually, toys viewed as typical for boys, while they may offer a chance for working out problems of the present and anticipating the future, are much less suitable than dolls for mastering difficulties of the past. If parents feel relaxed about their son's playing with dolls, they will provide him with valuable opportunities for enriching his play life. For this to happen, it is not sufficient that parents simply refrain from disparaging such play; because of the still-prevalent attitude that doll play is only for girls, both parents need to feel positively about a boy's doll play, if he is to be able to take full advantage of it.

Today, when it is relatively rare for a parent to become as engrossed in the same play activity as his child does, there are still toys which evoke deep feeling in a parent, as they do in a child. Dolls are probably the best example of this.

Whether a mother merely watches her daughter play with dolls, encourages her in it, or actively participates, she is often deeply involved on many levels. She may reexperience aspects of her own childhood doll play and her own mother's involvement in such play and in herself, simultaneously feeling what it now means to be the mother of a little girl who plays with dolls. The child as she plays with her doll feels in some way the strong emotions which reign in her mother's conscious and subconscious mind, and experiences a closeness to her mother based on the deep emotional involvement they *both* have in the girl's doll play. This closeness gives the play a special significance and depth of meaning for the child which it never could attain without the mother's involvement. The mother need not be always physically present, nor when she is present must she be so personally involved on many levels; it is enough if the child carries a mental image of her mother's involvement. One such experience with her mother can make such a lasting impact that the child will carry this image within her and reactivate it whenever she plays with her doll—it is that meaningful. She will continue to react to the emotional signals she has received from her mother and combine them in her doll play with other feelings which originate in her own past and present experiences of being mothered and playing at mothering. Important as her feelings are about being mothered and about someday becoming a parent herself, her doll play could not attain the same depth of meaning if her mother had not been on occasion deeply and personally involved because of the recollections it evoked in her.

PARENTAL IDENTIFICATION

Few other types of play can quite compare with doll play for eliciting deep parental involvement. Still, there are many other aspects of children's play which can affect a parent deeply, through recollections and other feelings it activates, particularly when a child's play reminds the parent of having played with the same toy, or having played in similar fashion. Also, the older the child gets, the more easily do play activities echo not only the parent's own childhood experiences, but also his present hobbies or recreations. For example, the teenager who can play a serious game of chess has an experience very similar to his parent's in doing so. Empathizing with a child's joys and sorrows in school or on the playing field and reliving one's own experiences there is a common occurrence of parenthood; and it applies equally when a few short years later, one's child goes through the throes and thrills of his first love. But by then, the youngster's personality is largely formed, and he is struggling to fight free of being dominated by the parent. By the teenage years, the youngster is—or should be—too distinctly his own person for a parent to see or project much of himself and his own past into his play. While the teenager's play—and other experiences—may evoke in the parent parallel experiences of his own life, he can no longer identify with his child as he could several years earlier.

Only during the early stages of personality formation, which is typically the age of most intensive doll play, can a mother fantasize that her daughter is like herself as a child, that the little girl will develop as a mother exactly in the way she hopes for, and avoid the pitfalls and dangers the mother herself perhaps couldn't evade. Parents know that their children will most likely have a life quite different from their own, that only so long as the children are small can parents fully identify with them, and relive some of their own childhood experiences in play.

But as long as we can identify with our children in their play through such memories, this makes the play uniquely meaningful to both parent and child, and while our children are still very young, we can imagine that they will follow our common course in their future development.

Such positive identification with children's play was much easier when the life activities of girls and boys repeated those of their parents. For example, playing with a hobbyhorse—like the doll, a very ancient toy—had an entirely different meaning in an era when horses were the principal means of transport and traction, not to mention their role in warfare. The child riding a hobbyhorse emulated important adult activities on a size-appropriate scale, and the parent watching him knew that he was preparing for important aspects of adult life. This knowledge could easily induce fantasies about the child's future, and parents might have recalled the fantasies they entertained when they rode hobbyhorses. Such parents could also muse on the difference between these fantasies and the present reality, exactly as modern parents may respond to their children's doll play or "astronaut" play.

Today, even if an adult is very fond of riding, it is now a leisure activity, which reduces its serious meaning. No longer is riding a horse or using it for work an important dimension in the life of most adults. With the exception of the slim ranks of cowboys and jockeys, it is a rare parent who, watching his child ride a hobbyhorse, thinks with pleasure about how well his child is preparing for success in life, or of how that life will resemble his own. Today parents accept the fact that it is unlikely that their children will follow in their footsteps.

With the older child, things may be somewhat different. Seeing a youngster at a computer, or playing a musical instrument, permits a parent to have pleasurable fantasies about the child's future. Still, for most parents, their children's academic achievements seem most likely to offer promise for future success. For this reason, many parents (without actually realizing their motivation) today push school achievement on their children at much too early an age, in nursery school, and even before! Parents believe this will promote their child's progress once in grade school, but for everything in life there is a right and a wrong time; if we push a child to perform, or to succeed, more often than not this has the opposite effect. Teaching reading or math to children is unsuitable for most of them before the age of six or seven. While a child's intellect can be stimulated at earlier ages, this is beneficial only if it is done in an age-appropriate fashion.

Unconsciously, through exposing their child to early academic experiences, parents wish to be able to anticipate their child's future success; they derive pleasure from such thoughts, and they tend to allay any fears they may harbor in this regard. The main trouble with such early efforts is that they are premature, and thus often counterproductive. While it is true that most children can learn to read, write, count, and do simple mathematical computations at an early age, these activities usually have no intrinsic meaning for them, aside from the fact that performing them pleases their parents. The result may be that such academic activities will later continue to remain void of meaning for such children. However, it is only such intrinsic meaning that will motivate the child to devote himself to the kind of learning offered in elementary and high school. If a little child is pushed too early to do schoolwork, he does it only to please his parents. If so, later, when he is in conflict with them, he may be tempted to hurt them through academic failure. The less intrinsic meaning academic learning has for a child at first exposure, the more likely he is to abandon it later. It is much better to delay exposing the child to intellectual learning of an academic nature until he is mature enough for it, and his intellect sufficiently developed, for what he is learning to have considerable intrinsic meaning to him.

Many parents who wish to teach academics to their children at an early age try to do so in a playful manner, but for the child this is not play, although he may enjoy the parental attention. Some parents unconsciously view their child so much as part of themselves that they cannot imagine that what gives them pleasure, such as academic prowess, could have a very different effect on their child. The same phenomenon explains why other parents push athletic achievement on their children. They genuinely enjoy it and hence cannot comprehend that while the child enjoys giving pleasure to his parent, the activity may involve too much pressure, tension, exertion, and anxiety about failures for the child—that it is just too demanding a task for him. The child then faces a dilemma: he resents being put under pressure, but giving pleasure to his parent is so important to him that he cannot afford to let the parent know his true feelings.

Parents who do not consider that the child's pleasure may not be parallel or equal to their own can create serious problems for him. An example of this can be observed in roughhousing play between parents and children. Children usually enjoy such play, but only up to a point. Most infants and small children enjoy being thrown up into the air and caught, if this is done with moderation and great care, and not for too long. Such limited play reassures them that they can safely lose contact for a moment with their parent without danger; further, it gives them confidence that their parents can turn potentially dangerous situations into safe ones. But some parents, carried away by the pleasure such roughhousing gives *them* and unable to imagine that something so enjoyable to them may be frightening to the child, go far beyond what is pleasurable for him. And when things get too exciting for the child, the excitement can become overwhelming and arouse fears.

There is also the kind of rough-and-tumble in which a parent wrestles his child down or shadow-boxes with him, enjoying his own strength and superior athletic abilities; often he firmly believes that what he enjoys so much his child must enjoy equally. But the child's pleasure soon becomes mixed with the experience of inadequacy in relation to the parent, anxiety about his comparative weakness and his utter dependency on the parent, and fear that the parent will become dangerously carried away by his dominance. So what began as an enjoyable experience ends up overwhelming the child with anxiety and feelings of defeat. The parent feels confident in his knowledge that he will not take advantage of his superior strength and believes that what he knows, the child knows, too. But this is not the case; all the child knows is that it has become too much for him.

This is why a parent's participation in play which his child has chosen all on his own is so much safer and more rewarding to both parents and child. If, in addition, such play stimulates parental recollection of similar childhood play and permits happy fantasies about the child's future, then it provides an eminently constructive and happy experience for all concerned. A mother's playing with her child at dolls is a paradigm of such play. The loving manner in which a girl takes care of her dolls seems to promise to her parents that she will be a good mother and gain much satisfaction, fulfillment and pleasure from it.

Parents who make a positive investment in their children's play instill in them the secure feeling that when they are grown up, they will be well able to meet the tasks of adult life. This confidence is born at the moment when the child feels that he is playing well, and his parents' satisfaction is an important element of this feeling. Parental encouragement of play and parental commitment to play's immediate importance for children solidifies the role of play in preparing the child for the future.

Until very recently, when a girl played with dolls or at taking care of a house and a family, she was much closer to the activities that filled much of her mother's adult life, and to what both her parents expected her future would hold. Today, with work outside of the home having become a central role in most American women's lives, this is no longer true; and it is even less true now for boys who play with soldiers, trucks, or toy trains.

In their typical play, most boys are apt to manipulate toys which represent objects (cars, airplanes) and do so aggressively, while girls tend to play at taking care of toys (dolls), which represent people. Thus a boy may be more apt to get lost in abstractions and relate aggressively to the world rather than caringly. But this does not need to be so; if the boy's parents relate caringly—rather than critically—even to the boy's aggressive play, then such caring attitudes will instill parallel attitudes in the boy. And many a little boy is as tender as his sister when he dresses and undresses his stuffed animals, bathes them, and puts them to sleep.

Therefore I believe these sets of characteristics are not wholly or even primarily sex-related, but basically a question of cultural conditioning. In imitation of her mother, a girl's play is much more directed toward caring for people, and it is personal interactions that determine the nature of much of our day-to-day reality. Furthermore, under modern conditions of life the girl has much more opportunity to watch her mother in her mothering and homemaking activities and help with them, even if these are done only after she comes home from work, than a boy has for observing his father and participating in his central adult activities. Helping his father with the chores around the house on a weekend or going with him on a fishing trip cannot compare in intensity and importance with watching one's mother every day, or at least every evening, and helping her with her chores. Even if the mother is gone much of the day, the little girl gets the same opportunity to observe her usually female caretaker. Recreating in play what her mother does and helping her out with it in actuality provide yet another set of experiences to anchor a female firmly in everyday reality and prepare her to cope with its demands.

The better a child comprehends his parents' occupation as meaningful on a level he can understand, preferably from his own experience, the more he will emulate in play what he considers to be important aspects of his parents' lives. From their own experiences, children know how important the work of some adults is, such as that of teachers, ministers, physicians, and nurses. Children whose parents are not engaged in occupations like these will nevertheless play at being doctors and nurses, partly because it permits them to explore each other's bodies, and partly because of the importance these professions have for them when they are ill. Although all children play at these occupations, if one or both parents are engaged in such work, this will make the play much more significant for both parent and child, because it facilitates mutual identification.

The child of an artist, say a painter, can observe what his parent is doing, and can believe he really understands what his parent is working at if he also paints. And that parent will be much more involved in his child's dabbling with finger paints or brush than many others. With the computer fast making it possible for many more parents to work at home, one may hope that much of the damage which industrialization did to the intimate life of parents and children may be partly undone. Although what a parent does with the computer will be a closed book to the small child, as he grows older, he will be much better able to understand the work life of his parent.

It is to be hoped that future social development and technology—such as the computer—will permit parents to do more of their work at home. If so, their work, about which most children know only from hearsay, would become much more real to them. Even more important, their parents at work would become to them as real as today only their parents at home or at leisure are. With it the lives of parents and children in their entirety would become real to each other. It is to be hoped that this would help parents to understand and accept that the child's world of play is as real and important to the child as is the world of work to the parent, and that therefore it ought to be accorded the same dignity.

18

Parents and Play: The Double Standard

Children begin by loving their parents; after a time
they judge them; rarely, if ever, do they forgive them.
—OSCAR WILDE, A Woman of No Importance

CERTAINLY PARENTS ARE HAPPY to see their children absorbed
in play. But are they equally happy to become engrossed in the playing
themselves? If a child's play is pleasurable to a parent chiefly because
he can then pursue his adult activities without feeling bad about neglecting
his child, it does not take the child long to realize this. He soon learns that
to his parents play itself is not very important, but his being out of their way
is; this lesson simultaneously diminishes him and his enjoyment of play,
and reduces the capacity of play to develop his intelligence and personality.

The true test of a parent's belief about play is reflected not in what he
says, but in how he behaves. The fact is that parents often behave incon-
sistently. Sometimes all goes well: the parent is not doing anything of particular importance, his child asks him to play, and the parent obliges, at
least for a time. The child wants him to admire what he has built, and the
parent again obliges. But if the parent is occupied with something that
demands his attention, usually his response to the request is: "Not now; I'm
busy." If the parent is in a good mood, he may preface his refusal with an
apology or promise to make up for it later, a pledge not always kept. Parents
tend to assume that if a child doesn't repeat his plea, he has either solved
his problem or forgotten about it. But many a child hears the statement "In
a few minutes" as a brush-off, and he's not all that eager to earn a second
brush-off by repeating his request.

Such parental behavior suggests to children that their activities rarely
seem as important to us as our own, and hardly ever more important. There
is nothing very much wrong with that—if both parties are equally seriously
engaged, why should parents drop what they are doing to join their child?

The situation is different, of course, when there is an emergency, but in such cases, the transfer of our attention is virtually automatic. This is very important for the security of the child, and so some bright children test how reliably they can depend on it by claiming that an emergency has arisen. Others, without necessarily wishing to ascertain how dependable their parents will be in a crisis, pretend an emergency exists to bring a parent hurrying to their side when they have a great desire to tell or show the parent something of importance. But this only works a few times; then the parents cease to respond, and make no bones about their annoyance at being taken advantage of in this way, as in the fable where the child cries "wolf" once too often. This is understandable. But is a parent really being taken advantage of when a child goes to great length to signal how important it is that the parent come to him, emergency or no emergency? Or, to put it differently, is only what *we* consider an emergency—such as an actual danger or mishap—truly an emergency? Or is a child's need to reassure himself of his importance to us, and of the importance of what he is doing, not also an emergency?

If a parent is just a bit more patient with a child's claim of emergency when all he needs is to convince himself that the parent is ready to drop everything and rush to his side when he feels a need for it—even though we may not believe his urgent demand is justified by the situation—then the child will be able to feel more secure about his importance to the parent. This improvement in the child's inner security will be reflected in a parallel improvement in his relation to his parent, which will express itself in much better mutual relations. Such a result may well be worth the inconvenience caused by our responding to what the child feels as an emergency even though, seen from our perspective, it was not that at all.

Children appreciate our prompt attention during emergencies; however, they also know that most of the time it is only an emergency that brings us quickly to their side, not interest in their play. They would much prefer that we would always drop everything for their sake, but as they grow and mature they should learn to accept that it is unreasonable to expect that if two people are importantly engaged one will always quit what he is doing to join the other.

But what happens when a child is deeply engrossed in play and the parents are ready to go out? They call him to come and get dressed. Or perhaps they want him to greet a visitor, or come to the table for lunch. His answer is, as ours would be in an analogous situation, "Not now; I'm busy." Are we prepared to honor our child's statement, as we expect him to honor ours? Or do we insist: "You come here, *right now*"? If we do, then we have once again succeeded in impressing on him the conclusion that we do not take his activities as seriously as we do our own. Worse, we have demonstrated that we do not take his activities seriously at all, when they conflict with our plans.

Although it is not an ideal criterion, the fact is that many people gauge the value of others, as well as themselves, by what they do. If their activity is viewed as significant, then they feel significant too. Such an assessment may be unfair and disregards a lot: a person should be judged by the kind of human being he is, not by his job or status. But since many adults evaluate themselves and others in this way, how can a child be expected to do otherwise? This may be an immature way to evaluate a person, but the child *is* immature; he has not yet developed a clear sense of "what I am" as distinct from "what I do," and his feeling of it is fragile and beset by great insecurity. If what a child does is not viewed as important, then often he comes to feel that he personally is thought to be of little consequence as well. Thus a parent's attitudes toward a child's play will strongly influence his later feelings about his own ability to be important and do significant things.

If we truly took our child's play as seriously as we take our own tasks, we would be as loath to interrupt it as we are reluctant to be interfered with when we are working. This is the pattern demanded by consistency and a sense of fairness; and one reward for thus respecting our child's play is that it enhances his own sense of play as an important activity in the whole context of family life.

This is not to say that parents always take play lightly. After all, we want our children to enjoy themselves; we buy them toys and take them to the playground; we are conscientious about providing opportunities to play. Unfortunately, however, most parents devote themselves seriously only very selectively to a few aspects of their children's play, and what they choose is more likely to be activities in which the child engages when quite a bit older. But underlying attitudes are largely formed early on, and the older child may already be suffering from the consequences of having his earlier play taken lightly. For example, if a chess-playing father and child are in the middle of a good game, or if a father is involved in his son's Little League activities, the call to dinner is hardly ever answered promptly. The parent who fully participates in his child's activity because of personal involvement has a perfect understanding of how important it is—and this participatory attitude is very different from being involved only as a parent. In the first instance, the parent will join his child in protesting that the game simply cannot be interrupted; in the second, he will insist that the child interrupt what he is doing and obey the call to come to dinner right away. The child observes this difference and is dejected when he realizes how rarely we take his play really seriously, and do so only when it is also important to us, never mind how important it is to him.

What a child explores in his various disorientation games, as exemplified earlier by Blind Man's Buff, is of course no longer so important to adults, who have long since attained a good degree of mastery of this kind of confusion. Therefore we cannot expect to experience again the deep satisfaction our child derives from his investigation in play that answers these compelling issues of his life. But if we truly comprehend what such play means to him, then we can at the very least participate vicariously in his pleasure. We can enjoy his capacity to provide himself with meaningful experiences and feel respect for his attempts to find answers to the existential questions which beset him. Indeed, the issues of permanency of object and the intentions of others are among the enigmas of the play age, and are by no means limited only to early childhood.

Despite the importance of our encouragement of play, it is never beneficial for parents to play with their child strictly out of a sense of duty. To play because one "should" is simply not the same as playing together with one's child, or even appreciating the importance of his play. This confusion about the parent's intent is precisely what mars so much of the child's play. Many adults, whether parent or teacher, tend to play with children for purposes outside the play; they may wish to distract, entertain, educate, diagnose, or guide them. But this is not what the child desires. Unless the play itself is the thing, it loses much of its meaning to the child and adult participation becomes offensive; the child can guess the adult's purpose and becomes annoyed at the pretense of wholehearted participation.

The use of educational toys, so dear to the hearts of many parents, may serve as an illustration. There is really nothing much wrong with educational toys—*if* the emphasis is entirely on the enjoyment of play and not on the intent of educating. Such toys become problematic, however, when parental emphasis is placed on what using the toy supposedly teaches the child, rather than on however the child himself wants to use it. Educational toys become absolutely deadly when the child is expected to learn what they are designed to teach, instead of learning what he wants to learn by playing with them as his fancy of the moment suggests. A child must be able to use any toy the way he wishes to, not as the parent, teacher, or manufacturer thinks it ought to be used.

It is amazing what an infant can learn just by playing with the cardboard core of a roll of toilet paper, and how constructive, imaginative, and educative a child's play with empty boxes can be. In earlier days, when twine came on wooden spools, young children used the spools as blocks and gained as much pleasure and learning from them as they do now out of specially constructed building blocks. Indeed, they probably got something more out of playing with spools than they do from blocks, since they knew that the wooden cores had an important function in the adult sewing enterprises of their mothers. Thus both child and parent found something important represented in wooden spools, whereas blocks are important only to the child.

Some parents spontaneously realize the value of having a personal investment in their child's play objects, although they are not always consciously aware that this is what motivates them. Instinctively they add a new measure of mutuality to their child's pleasure, without setting out purposely to do so. With their greater leisure and their own enjoyment of craft activities, these parents may have the time and inclination to fashion toys for their children, thereby duplicating what their own parents or grandparents did out of necessity. Such parents create an experience through which they become emotionally involved in the toy they have created with their own hands. They get enormous enjoyment not only from the task, but also from imagining how their child will play with these toys. The meaning the parents have invested in the toy remains active as they play with their child or watch his play.

Other parents make the production of toys a common project. For example, with the child's help they collect scraps of wood. In doing so they both contemplate what forms they will give these bits and pieces. Together they sand the wood, and perhaps the child invites some of his friends to help with this labor and with the painting and the shellacking that follows. From then on and ever after these blocks are very special to child and parent. No store-bought blocks can compare in importance with these visible and tangible examples of the child's and the parent's common investment in a toy.

What counts here is mutuality: both parent and child are invested in the blocks, although out of quite different motives. This common bond of emotional investment can go a long way toward making up for the fact that the parties are not equally involved in the child's play with the product of their labor.

WHEN PARENTS BECOME CONSCIOUS EDUCATORS

On the other hand, such parallel investment in play can work well for a time and then backfire through adult motives. The following story is an illustration of the point, and it involves a partly happy but much more unhappy memory that haunted a highly successful man all his life. The man's father was very much involved in stamp collecting, so the youngster needed little urging to become an avid stamp collector too. As a boy, he was naturally intrigued by his father's absorption in the activity, and the father encouraged his son's interest. For a period while his father worked at the desk with his own stamps, the young boy had a wonderful time sitting on the floor fooling around with *his* stamps, weaving all sorts of fantasies around them, convinced that what he was doing was every bit as important as what his father did, if not also the same thing. It made him happy to be and act like his father; this was the happy part of the memory. Parent and child were engrossed in the same activity, each in a way appropriate to his age.

But then the father began to insist that his son become "serious" about what he was doing, and learn all that was involved in the lore and science of stamp collecting. This was a terrible shock and disappointment to the boy, who up to this moment had believed that what he had been doing *was* very serious. Now he was no longer permitted to indulge his fantasies as he organized the stamps in his own way, but was told he should be systematic in a mature way—the father's way. What had previously been a strong bond between father and son quickly became a source of mutual irritation, with the father insisting that the boy handle the stamps in the "right way." This demand made no sense to the boy, since it required too much of his young patience and much more knowledge than he possessed.

As long as he was free to weave his daydreams about the stamps and his father was equally involved in his own thoughts about stamps, each could enjoy what he was doing. But when the father turned conscious educator and tried to teach not by the example of his serious involvement, which had been the source of the boy's interest, but by pushing the boy to go about stamp collecting in an adult way, their common activity became a source of great conflict. The boy felt (rightly) that he could never satisfy his father's requirements, and the father felt that his son was not getting all he should out of stamp collecting. Decades later, the boy—now a fully grown man— was still sad that a common activity which for a time had been and could have remained a deep bond between him and his father had become instead a source of deep disappointment.

Many a parent, like the father in this story, gets carried away by his child's questions on how to do a thing, or by the wish to see his child do well. He tends to answer the child's questions in great technical detail, mistakenly trying to teach higher skills and minutiae rather than helping the child find his own age-appropriate level of doing and understanding. The child does want to acquire expertise but can do so only bit by bit in his own way, and in his own good time. Forcing premature professionalism on children can sour their original interest in an activity, since it is no longer enjoyable for them on their terms.

The real tragedy—a tragedy that is repeated in many more ways and many more times in children's lives than parents realize—is that the father's intentions were good: he wanted to make stamp collecting something he and his son could really share. The boy too was motivated by the desire to do something that would tie him more closely to his father. But when the father gave the child the impression that what he was doing did not come up to the father's standards, the boy became disappointed, not only in stamp collecting and what it could offer, but in himself, because he could not live up to his father's expectations.

They continued to work together on stamps, but only for a short while. The father became frustrated because his efforts to teach the boy the proper way of collecting stamps got nowhere and led only to mutual dissatisfaction. The boy felt even more frustrated, because now he no longer could enjoy what had been his greatest pleasure in life. Even worse was the disappointment in himself. Up to the moment the father decided his son should become more "serious" about stamp collecting, the boy had felt great about himself; but now he felt inferior, unable to achieve what was expected of him.

Years later, after his father's death, the son became much more successful in his profession than his father had ever been. But he still had a hard time fighting his feelings of inferiority, the seeds of which, he was convinced, had been planted in this shattering experience. Afterward, he could never again trust himself when he thought he was doing well. Most of his memories of his father were a combination of a nostalgic desire for the paradise he had enjoyed before his father became convinced it was time to introduce him to the adult levels of stamp collecting, and his resentment over being suddenly criticized and made to feel inferior. He could not shake this feeling precisely because he had felt so good up to the time his father had impressed on him that he was not doing well enough. The tragedy mentioned before was a double one—the father's, because his effort to tie his son closer to him led to mutual estrangement; and the son's, because his sense of being so close and happy with his father ended suddenly, and he was thereafter deprived of this feeling which had sustained him up to that moment. From then on, even thinking about collecting stamps made him feel dejected.

We would all like to believe that later on in life, our children will remember our efforts to teach them to do things well; this hope is often the motivation behind parents acting like conscious educators, as the father did in this example. But given the insecurity that all children feel, it is unfortunately more likely that the pain of parental criticism will make a much stronger and more lasting impression than the parent's conscientious efforts to teach the child how to "do things right." Children always take such criticism from their parents personally, since they do not have the advantage of adult objectivity.

What happened around stamp collecting in this example can also happen in innumerable other situations, such as when a parent starts coaching his child to make him a star in the Little League. In the process of serious goal-oriented coaching, something is likely to get lost—the fun of the game, at least. And paradoxically enough, intense parental attention of the wrong sort can sow the seeds for a later unhappy development. The conflict of motives between parent and child that begins in play, when the parent's motive overrides the child's, can develop later in what has been called the generation gap. And this can happen with parents who are convinced that there will be no gap between themselves and their children, since they have always taught their children what the children wanted to learn. Certainly they want to learn, but at their own pace. In their fantasies children want to do just what their mothers or fathers do—but their fantasies of what their parents do are very different from the reality. Children can't understand this, but parents must. Thinking that the fantasies aroused by some activity, or the actions themselves, can be the same for parent and child denies a real dimension of the age difference between the two.

Thus, there always have been and always will be play situations in which an adult cannot fully share in this child's enjoyment of the activity itself. We cannot feel the same delight a toddler does when he drops little plastic balls into a milk bottle hundreds of times, or when he pushes a little truck back and forth, or pulls a toy about the house with the unending attention such important activities fully deserve in his eyes. These are the situations when only our appreciation of the importance the child's play has for him and our pleasure in his delight can form the bridge between parent and child.

In certain ways, however, there isn't much difference between a child's endless repetitive play behavior and an adult's preoccupation with throwing a fishing line into the water in what (to the uninitiated) may seem a long monotonous sequence. How does casting—to the fisherman a most interesting, purposeful activity—differ from a child's endless repetitive play behavior? Certainly there are rather refined skills involved in this adult pastime, and considerable knowledge of fishing lore. But the child, on his level, brings comparatively as much expertise to bear on his own pursuits, and finds the minute variations of pushing or pulling a truck as engrossing as the fisherman finds the various ways of throwing out his line.

Perhaps we should bear this analogy in mind as we watch what seems to us monotonous play. It may serve to remind us of how meaningful certain repetitive behavior is to adults, although we call it "sport" rather than "play." At the very least, when we watch our children play we can take pleasure in their enjoyment and in their intelligence, persistence, skill, good looks, or charm. As long as we take delight in our children for whatever reasons that are natural to us, our children will interpret our happiness as delight in what they are doing, since they themselves are delighted with and by their play, and even more so by our approval of them and their endeavors. Different though our thoughts may be, both child and parent thus will have a common emotional experience that forms a bond which, when well nurtured in many experiences, will endure as long as they live.

PLAYING TOGETHER

Despite everything that has been said, it is obvious that parents cannot always have direct empathy with their child's play experience. But certainly it can help parents to become aware of the different needs, anticipations, and desires a child brings to his play, as long as the parent realizes and accepts the fact that divergences between parent and child do exist. And the greater the parent's emotional involvement in play, the more beneficial it is to the child, and to the relation with each other.

Almost any mother can recall with pleasure the elaborate fantasies she acted out with her dolls: how tenderly she ministered to them, with what fierce anger she occasionally abused them. Such a mother will provide her own children with dolls; she may even create beautiful wardrobes for them. But how many hours is this mother willing to spend playing dolls with her child? Mothers nowadays believe themselves to be too busy with more important things to be bothered with play. When acting this way, they deprive themselves of experiences which, would they permit them to sink in, might turn out to be considerably more meaningful than they could possibly imagine. For example, if a mother took the time to play with her daughter, she would surely be fascinated by the stories her child invents around her dolls and the kinds of experiences the child makes them undergo. It might even bring back to the mother stories she herself had woven around her own dolls, and she might discover previously unknown or long-forgotten aspects of her childhood. If she thinks along these lines, the parallels and differences between her fantasies as a child and those of her daughter will tell such a mother much about her daughter, and give her a direct feeling for how the daughter experiences herself. It is too bad that many mothers have forgotten so thoroughly the great joy and pleasure they felt when they asked *their* mother to play with them and she did so, and the lost feeling they experienced when she wouldn't join in.

Here is a very important aspect of play, one that is frequently overlooked: it makes a vast difference to the child and his play if he can share his experiences with an adult who is able to remember childhood experiences around the same play. There is ample room in most children's lives for play with other children, both spontaneous and as organized in nursery schools or playgrounds, and also for solitary play. That is, there would be ample room for play at home if television did not take its place. But parents, even those concerned about television, often fail to ask themselves carefully enough why their child seems mesmerized by it. The most common reason for this fascination is the child's desire to escape solitude and be in contact at least with imaginary characters on the screen, when real people are not available. Unless his relations to his parents are badly disturbed or his ability to relate seriously impaired—both ominous signs of emotional disorder—any child would much prefer to interact with real people in a real setting than with imaginary figures on the television screen. Solitary play, which parents often try to promote in place of television, cannot satisfy this need, nor can it take the place of people, even imaginary ones if no real ones are available.

When people who grew up before television was omnipresent in homes reflect back, they realize that they were able to fill out their empty time with play, and they wonder why modern children seem unable to do so and turn on the television; but they usually forget to ask themselves what they might have done had television been available to them. In all likelihood they too often felt the need for give and take with people, and when it was not available they turned to play and fantasy of such interactions with people, as in doll play, or play with soldiers or other toy figures, only because imaginary interactions with people, as through television, were not available to them. Also, before television was an outlet for this need, perhaps these children may have insisted more strenuously that their parents or siblings play with them and thus eventually gained their true desire. Many modern children, turned down by their parents, do not continue to insist that their parents play with them, but dejectedly turn to television as the second-best opportunity for interaction with at least imaginary figures. Unfortunately these children are seriously deprived of opportunities to forge bonds of intimacy with the most important persons in their lives—their parents—around play activities equally engrossing and meaningful to both parent and child.

Since many children now go to nursery schools at a much earlier age and have the opportunity to play there, why can't this experience make up for playing with the parent? The most obvious answer is the most important one: because these other playmates are not parents. Nothing anyone else says or does can compare in significance to a child with what his parent says or does. The young child cannot help seeking his parent's approval; nothing bolsters his self-esteem more than a parent's approbation. Furthermore, nothing plunges him into deeper despair than a parent's lack of interest or criticism. The younger the child, the more this is true. Therefore, only some kind of parental involvement in the child's play can make it seem truly important and worthwhile. Without it, play is "kid stuff" without much relevance, something a nursery-school teacher or baby-sitter does because it is her job and it keeps the children quiet.

A child doesn't want to be "kept quiet." He needs and wants to do things that are important to him. For example, it is always exciting for the young child to investigate the contents of a purse—but nothing can compare with turning his *mother's* purse inside out. Fascinating as adult secrets are in general, none are more interesting than those of one's parents. The child is curious about the contents of his parents' drawers! What other people do, what they have, how they organize things—all these become important as the child begins to learn about the differences in how things are done by his family and how they're done in other households. But first he wants to learn how things are done at home.

For example, however innocuous the contents of his mother's purse may be, the child's explorations of it are exciting and important play to him. Her purse must be terribly important, he reasons—look at the way she always carries it with her, clutching it so that she won't lose it. If we appreciate our child's investigations as such, we can take pleasure in his avid wish to find things out and be gratified by his interest in us and our possessions. But we can also go beyond this to understand the deeper and often symbolic, unconscious meaning his search has for him. Children themselves are doubtless unaware of the motive of their explorations, but we can guess the hidden meaning behind the child's great and natural desire to investigate the contents of his mother's purse and of the parents' chest of drawers. Psychoanalytic investigation has shown that such exploration, particularly of a mother's purse, has a great deal to do with a youngster's sexual curiosity. But it is sexual curiosity on his own level—not about sex as we might consider it.

It is worth pointing out in this connection that play with guns, especially with water pistols (and this is true primarily for boys if only because girls—much to their detriment—are given less opportunity for such play) often has to do with the child's efforts to understand the function of the male genitals. And this not in terms of adult sexual knowledge but along the lines of little boys' and little girls' direct knowledge of what the penis is there for—urination. In terms of the young child's experience, that's about all there is to it. Since girls are as much interested in it as boys are, toys which squirt water (including water pistols) are of great interest to both sexes. Similarly, both boys' and girls' fascination with their mother's purse is unconsciously connected with their curiosity about what may be hidden inside the vagina, and the secrets that might be found there. Children usually gather that in some obscure way *they* were found there—who knows what other secrets might be discovered? Again, the sexual organ is seen not in adult terms but from the child's own points of reference. All children are curious about what sexual organs are there for, how it should be that they come in two interesting varieties. This is what they try to explore, and need information about—not about what adults do when they engage in sexual activities.

If we give tacit approval to our child's investigation of drawers and of purses, and also to his play with toys that squirt water, we are also giving him implicit security in regard to his age-correct sexual curiosity. We imply that sex is a matter of legitimate interest to him. Being critical of such behavior—angrily snatching a purse away so that its contents won't spill out, or prohibiting or showing annoyance at play with a water pistol or a toy that squirts water—is sex-inhibiting, and just at the age when freedom to explore would count most. If exploring mother's purse or drawers is wrong, how can trying to understand the function of her vagina be all right? Such inhibiting actions will have unfortunate consequences no matter how seriously parents tell their children that sex is "normal" or "pleasurable" or whatever terminology they employ in hopes of preventing future sexual "hang-ups." To tell a child that his later sexual behavior will be pleasurable or approved of is of little help if he is made to feel guilty about his present symbolic sexual exploration. To him the prohibition can only mean that it's wrong to try to understand sex or to master sexual problems on the play level. From this it follows (in his mind) that any type of sex is wrong, no matter what parents may say in their conscious efforts to provide "correct" sex information. Only information that is given in age-correct form is comprehensible to the child; what would be age-correct information for an adult is therefore not correct for a child.

But if, through our attitudes to his symbolic sexual investigations, we can show the child that it is all right with us, this gives him the feeling that sex is an "all right" aspect of human life. If we foster a positive attitude when the child tries to explore, then the young child who has only the foggiest notions of what sex in general is all about will come to a more complete understanding gradually; the feeling of sex being "all right" he will have gained from our positive attitude to his infantile sex activities and symbolic sex explorations, and this will extend to and be supported on each new level of age-appropriate sexual awareness.

19

Proving Oneself Through Contest

"Now we shall see who is stronger, I or I."
—Holofernes in Nestroy's play *Judith and Holofernes*

A CHILD BECOMES FAMILIAR with material things and their properties as he plays with them; thus he masters objects and they become acceptable to him. This is why playing with his food is so important to the infant, and why he tries to feed the person who is feeding him. Through handling the food it becomes familiar to the infant; it becomes truly *his* food. The more he mashes it, the safer he feels it is and the more pleasant to ingest. By feeding his mother, he demonstrates to himself that he is not just the passive recipient of food but also its active dispenser; mastering the process of feeding makes eating all the more enjoyable.

Who feeds whom is one of the first contests the child engages in; it is based on the most tender, happy feelings. An infant who has negative feelings about his food or about the person who feeds him—although at an early age he can hardly separate the two—will resist being fed and fight those who try to make him eat; moreover he will have no desire to feed others.

Around the infant's first relation, which is to the mothering person, and around the earliest experience, which is that of being fed, the most positive contest can occur, or the most negative, culminating in the infant's refusal to be fed. The positive playful contest is desirable and beneficial, and the negative contest is destructive, but both are efforts at self-assertion. If he is not defeated in these contests, either type can add to the child's self-esteem. However, when he *is* defeated in these early contests, the experience will have serious detrimental consequences for his self-esteem and ability to relate to others.

When self-esteem is the result of contests in which the competing partners are positively related to each other, then there are no losers but only winners.

When the child, because he enjoys being fed so much, wishes to provide his mother with the same experience, both are winners. These contests will have only happy connotations; they form the basis for good relations with others. In contrast, it is very difficult to develop any self-esteem even around successful self-assertion through fighting against undesirable experiences, such as when the infant spits out food which he is fed in a manner unacceptable or offensive to him. Whatever esteem can be gained from such negative self-assertion will have, at best, defensive connotations and become the basis for efforts to retain and strengthen it in solitary ways, rather than through good relations with others.

Another major source of self-esteem is the infant's experience that he can do things—handle objects, make them do as he desires, and make his body do things for him, such as when he learns to crawl. Here, as throughout childhood, fundamental to the infant's self-esteem is the approval, admiration, and love of the people most important to him. Later the child's knowledge and mastery of objects become relatively secure through play, and he understands better what he can do. He becomes progressively more interested and better equipped to enjoy also the more advanced forms of mastery games can provide—a mastery achieved through contests. Engaging in solitary play and playing games with others will henceforth alternate, depending on opportunities and the needs or predilections of the moment.

The older the child gets, the more his development of self-esteem rests on succeeding in real and game-situation contests, very much including those in which he competes with his own past performances, or in which one aspect of his personality competes with others for dominance. It is then that games become ever more important as experiences, and for the development of the child's personality. Through playing games he can demonstrate to himself and others how much he can do, how well he can perform intellectually and physically. Through his victory he will gain admiration—or so he hopes—which will increase his self-esteem.

While play can be and often is solitary, games imply some sort of companionship, as indicated by the Old Saxon and Gothic word *gaman*, meaning "fellowship," from which the word is derived. The modern word "game" can refer to any kind of playing, but its particular meaning, according to *Webster's New World Dictionary*, is "any specific amusement or sport involving physical or mental competition under specific rules" and, to emphasize that these are two very different kinds of competition, there is added in parenthesis "Football and chess are *games*." *The Shorter Oxford English Dictionary* expresses the same idea by offering this definition: "A diversion of the nature of a contest, played according to rules, and decided by superior skill, strength, or good fortune." Thus contest is the essence of games, and winning is the desired goal; this much is clear. That the child tries to gain and prove his competence through competing is hardly surprising, since both words are derived from the same Latin source, *competere*, which has among other meanings that of "to strive for (something) together with another."

What is not so obvious is that often the most important element of competition in games is the inner contest between different aspects of one's personality. If the particular mastery one seeks to attain through playing games is over oneself—and with it the self-esteem which can be derived from it—this goal is camouflaged by competition with others, whose main importance is then to serve as a foil or standard against which the individual measures himself. The feeling of self-esteem which one gains through games involving some contest—having played well and won—is usually much more important than the defeat of the competitor, and is often the main incentive for playing a game in the first place.

Consider the contests in which young children engage, particularly during the earlier stages of game-playing. They stare at each other, and the first to wink or laugh is the loser; they compete to see who can hold his breath longer; or they squeeze each other's hand to see who can suffer the pain without flinching. On the surface, it seems that the purpose of such contests is to win out over the other, but on a more important level, the mastery which is sought and tested is over oneself: to find out about and demonstrate one's endurance, to control one's involuntary emotional expressions and physical reactions. Much more significant than showing superiority over the antagonist is the self-esteem one achieves through such mastery over oneself.

Some children keep score on their ability to exercise this type of self-control, and they know very well that the issue is the ability of their mind, or will, consciously to dominate the spontaneous reactions of their body. These games are so common that one may assert that all children, at one time or another, engage in games whose main purpose is to test themselves and their performance. I knew one six-year-old, for example, who kept score through checking off one of two columns which he had labeled "Me" and "My mind," indicating that for him the issue was not whether he or his partner won, but how well his mind could control his body.

DEFINING THE SELF

There is a world of difference between obeying the command of another and controlling oneself. Toilet training—because it is so fundamental a socializing experience—may be used to illustrate this point. On the surface it seems that a child becomes trained because his parent wants it; but things don't really operate that way. No matter how much the parent may want his child to become toilet-trained, if the child refuses, then toilet training breaks down. Toilet training as the result of a pact with the parent—"I obey, and you will love me"—is highly problematic. Some children who give in to parental pressure then develop neurotic traits.

The most successful toilet training seems to be the result of a child's pact with himself: "I will control myself, so that my parents will like me better and so that I can be proud of myself." This attitude is the only one that is truly effective. The "do it for Mother" request, while a necessary starting point for such self-restraint, will lead to an ultimate failure in personality development if it does not culminate in the child's pact with himself—"I want to train myself"—which ultimately results in self-esteem based on "I did it all by myself." Thus while Piaget is correct in suggesting that the pact with oneself derives from others, from their wishes, and from a desire to please them, I believe this is only the starting point.

Psychoanalysis tends to see the development of the self as coming about from the continuing relationship to the mothering person, and this is undoubtedly true. Much more questionable, however, is the facile notion that a child becomes socialized primarily to please his mother. Normal human development requires an integration of two experiences: first, of pleasing oneself, *and* also of pleasing others. This can be observed in the behavior and experience of a very young infant. He drools, blows bubbles, sticks out his tongue to please himself and to gain information about what his mouth can do for him. The experience is filled with functional pleasure for him and, like all play, is directed toward gaining more control and mastery.

The enjoyment the mother derives from watching her infant's pleasure and the way she responds to his gurgling noises with sounds of her own transforms his solitary play into a mutual activity in which each partner sparks a reaction in the other. In that sense, it mirrors the dynamics of most games. But in this one, as when the infant feeds his mother, nobody loses; rather, both win. As mother and child repeat the experience again and again, reaffirming the integration of pleasing oneself and pleasing others, the child grows strong in his conviction that such pleasing and being pleased are interrelated, not disparate facets of life.

CONTESTS WITH THE SELF

The games a child plays with himself, in which he imposes strict rules on himself and rigorously obeys them, always precede his insistence that others obey the rules. Such games are of enormous importance in preparing the child for playing successfully with others. Not all games children play by themselves fall into this category, but many serve exactly this purpose. This is true of the games of not budging or flinching, mentioned earlier, or those which require conquering a sense of revulsion, etc. There are striking similarities between these and such ritual games as commanding oneself not to step on cracks, or to hop on one foot for some self-imposed distance, although these games center less on demonstrating self-mastery and more on providing the experience of triumph over an obstacle. The essence of these games is that the difficulty is self-imposed and the consequence of the play experience is an enhancement of the self.

A psychological comparison of games in which the rules or obstacles are self-imposed with others in which the rules are externally determined suggests a two-step process in personality development. The individual self develops in comparative isolation, while character, or social personality, can be achieved only through interaction with others. Obeying a self-imposed rule in a staring contest or meeting other such challenges enhances the development of self-respect and feeling of self-mastery. Obeying the preset rules of a formal, organized game leads to the development of the individual into a social human being. Goethe, in a saying which I have previously quoted in part, beautifully described this two-pronged development necessary for achieving full humanity: "Talent is best nurtured in solitude; character is best formed in the stormy billows of the world" ("Es bildet ein Talent sich in der Stille, und ein Charakter in dem Sturm der Welt").

Learning both to control and to demonstrate aggression is the underlying purpose of many games, particularly those involving physical contact. All contact sports require that aggression be kept within the boundaries set by the rules of the game, although aggression has been kindled both by the competition inherent in the game and by having to withstand the aggression of the antagonist. He, in his turn, must also limit himself to what is permitted by the rules; nonetheless, his actions are experienced as threats to one's body and to one's feeling of competence; thus they increase one's aggressive tendencies, which makes self-control both more difficult and more necessary.

There are many games that can be played alone or with others; but whether or not competition with others is involved, there is always competition with oneself, and one's self-esteem is always at stake. Throwing a ball against a wall and catching it, or shooting baskets, whether engaged in for pleasure or to increase one's skill, can still evoke quite angry and aggressive feelings when things do not go well. This aggression has to be kept under control, as children soon realize—or else they make even more errors. This is certainly true in golf, for instance. Such play is clearly designed to prove oneself, and perhaps to impress real or imagined spectators. This can be true even when children play with toys like yo-yos. Many jumping-rope games are clearly ways to show off and improve one's skills as well as compete with others. There are many active games in which no bodily contact is permitted which nevertheless are highly competitive, such as tennis or basketball, and of course physical-contact games such as football or wrestling are also very competitive. Still, even those games which clearly involve winning out over one's competitors are frequently engaged in not so much to be victorious over others as to compete with and prove oneself to oneself, and to impress others (whether present or absent) whose admiration and approval enhance one's self-esteem.

THE MEANING OF VICTORY

In the courtly tradition, a knight who entered a tournament made it clear that he was competing primarily for the favor and admiration of his lady and to prove his manliness to her. At the same time he was proving his manliness to himself and others, so that he himself could feel secure about it. Only secondarily was his purpose that of defeating his opponent. Similarly today, the main value of a trophy won in competition is the pleasure of displaying it to attract the admiration of others, who thus continue to enhance one's self-esteem. While in the heat of the contest one wishes to defeat one's opponents, once victory has been won, the opponents become by comparison relatively unimportant, unless by chance some personal enmity was at work. Whether openly acknowledged or hidden, whether it is success in a mental or physical contest, victory is experienced by a child as a vindication of himself, and as a gift he offers to his parents or others whom he wishes to value it and him highly. Thus do games allow children the opportunity to demonstrate their worth, by showing themselves superior to others.

Psychoanalytic investigation has shown over and over again that a child's rivalry in games is a projection of his rivalry for the love of his parents, or others who stand in their place. Competition in class, particularly in the earlier years, is not for grades *per se*, but for the approval of the teacher because of the buttressing of self-esteem it provides. The other children serve only as a convenient foil to cover for the real object of competition. Teachers, at this age, are in many respects experienced subconsciously as stand-ins for parents, and doing better than other children is most desired because winning out over them gains the child parental approval and affection.

There are no fun fairs without games of skill and of chance. In the first, one competes with oneself in respect to some aptitude. (Other games combine skill with the unleashing and controlling of aggression, as in throwing a ball at targets which are knocked down, or destroyed, such as clay figures.) But games of chance exercise an uncanny attraction, particularly to children, because they are so insecure about whether they are worthy of being loved or chosen by fate, fate being but another stand-in for parents. And this is why it is so important to children that the gum-ball machine into which they drop a coin should return something wonderful to them. As negligible as the object the machine dispenses may seem to adults, to the child it is of greatest importance as a demonstration that fate has favored him.

Video games, which presently are so popular, and pinball machines, which they have largely replaced as prime game-playing machines, owe their appeal to a combination of skill and chance. Winning, or at least doing well, in these games is desired as a demonstration of skill and, by implication, worthiness, but it also suggests one's superiority to real or imagined competitors. Unconsciously, winning is also taken for a demonstration that fate favors one, an idea that adds considerably to the feeling of self-confidence which one seeks to attain. No wonder, then, that these games are played with great intensity and persistence by persons or age groups who are insecure, such as teenagers and adolescents, who try to compensate for their feelings of inferiority and to quiet inner doubts through demonstrations of both their skill and their luck.

THE ROYAL GAME OF CHESS

In the first chapter, chess was used as a metaphor for human relations. Here I would like to stress that this, the most intellectual, complex, and refined of all games, from which chance is entirely eliminated, is essentially a war game. In chess the fighting spirit, without which success is not possible, must be sublimated to the utmost degree; otherwise it interferes with the high measure of concentration, planning, and foresight which are at all times necessary.

If a parent plays chess, the young child will emulate what he sees. The complexity of the game is still far beyond the ken of the young child, but he will play with the chessmen long before he is able to play chess, manipulating the pieces, placing them here and there, as his fantasies about the king, the knight, or the queen dictate. As he grows up, he moves from play expressive of and ruled by fantasy to playing chess by its definite rules. If, as an older child plays chess, he continues to indulge in fantasy speculation—for example, if he wonders about the marital relations between king and queen, or about the status of the pawn in the kingdom of the chessboard, so like his own in the realm of his family—he will not be able to concentrate sufficiently on the game to play it well. From this he will learn that for success within a given framework, one must pay due attention to the demands of that structure.

Then, as the child really learns to play chess, he will place and move the pieces as the rules and strategy, both his and his opponent's, dictate. One observes here the modalities of play and game: the child's play involves his attempts to establish harmony within himself only; in games, he attempts to harmonize with the requirements of the game, and with what the strategy of his opponent requires. In the first instance he establishes internal order; in the second he accepts and works within the external order to achieve his goals.

Chess is perhaps the outstanding familiar example of the pure game of the mind. One master player, Richard Reti, has gone so far as to suggest that chess symbolizes the victory of mind over matter because it is usually necessary to sacrifice pieces (to give up matter) in order to execute successfully a higher design. This suggests that for Reti at least, the associations attached to the playing of the game led to a more refined view of the world.

More important is what the game of chess (like other games, but as distinct from play) can do for the development of personality. Chess contains a strong competitive and thus aggressive element, but by virtue of its organization and rules, it forces the player to resist giving in directly to aggressive tendencies and instead sublimate them to a high degree by bringing ingenuity, application, and patience to bear on them. That is, he learns not only to control and master his aggressions, but to make them serve a socially approved enterprise.

Anyone who has experienced the pleasure inherent in playing a good game of chess knows the deep satisfaction with oneself that such sublimation of the desire to overcome one's opponent can provide. The satisfaction of playing well—that is, in sublimating—is hardly even affected by losing the game, as long as it was interesting. The rules of chess actively encourage an interesting game for both parties, by permitting the weaker player a handicap of one or more pieces. Thus the player of stronger skills need not be bored by a routine game and certain victory; the weaker player may win because the handicap has equalized skills.

The qualities which in the game of chess are developed into highest form are common to all games; they are what make games so important for the growth of a child's personality. Games teach impulse control, by permitting safe symbolic discharge of aggressive or negative emotions, while encouraging and rewarding such sublimation. But each particular game also has its own specific psychological or symbolic meaning.

Although chess makes the highest demands on man's rationality, it would not exert such fascination if it were not also full of symbolic meanings that exercise their influence on the players' unconscious, although most people have no inkling why they are so fascinated by the game.

There has been considerable speculation concerning the psychological meanings underlying chess. One suggestion is that chess permits symbolic exploration of oedipal or family conflicts. In this connection it may be mentioned that the lowliest figure, the pawn, symbolic of the child in the family, not only can overcome any figure (all pieces can do that), but on reaching its goal, can change itself into the most powerful figure of the game, and this is its unique prerogative. Just as the pawn can become queen or bishop upon reaching its destination, so does the child look to the day when he will arrive at his destination and become powerful in his own right as adult and parent.

King and queen may stand symbolically for parents, but it was only in fifteenth-century Italy, with its religious cult of Mary, that the most powerful figure was renamed the queen. Until then this figure had been the vizier—the actual ruler in several oriental countries where the king was merely a figurehead. The other pieces, for instance the bishop or the rook, may also be likened to important adults who, though powerful within the family and in relation to the child, are nevertheless subordinate to the parents.

However, all these rather obvious psychological connotations of the pieces seem insignificant when compared to the essence of chess—that one must understand its rules and the infinite variety of moves and countermoves. Each kind of piece moves in ways unique to it and shared by no other kind. The game requires an understanding of the assets and liabilities of these specific moves. Thus it teaches symbolically how one must know and use one's particular talents and one's place in society to realize one's special opportunities to the best advantage, with due respect to the complex matrix in which this game—representing life—unfolds. One must be able to estimate the likely countermoves of one's opponent, as in life we must consider and anticipate the likely reactions to our own moves, a skill most important for successful living with others.

Chess is a prime example of how games can teach the skills needed in life as they simultaneously meet conscious and unconscious needs. Regardless of the level of complexity or the specific nature of a game, all games teach the necessity of knowing and following the rules of the game. And living by *some* rules—ideally rules that are moral, self-chosen, self-imposed, and attuned to one's society—is what defines man as a social being. It is the condition through which he is lifted from solipsistic isolation into successful living with others.

20

*Unconscious Sources,
Real Achievements*

*There can be no recreation without delight, which de-
pends not always on reason, but oftener on fancy; it
must be permitted children not only to divert themselves, but do it after their own fashion.*

—JOHN LOCKE

PLAY AND GAMES SERVE all kinds of needs; the younger the child, the less he knows of his own inner life. He is unaware of many of his more complex needs, even though these may express themselves through activities in which he openly engages. As he becomes able to do more on his own, fewer of his needs are satisfied only by other persons, nor are they any longer satisfied mainly in fantasy. He begins to deal with his desires in some measure in reality. This requires that the satisfaction of his needs be altered and modified in terms of reality, which makes what is at stake more visible and tangible. This, in turn, makes it possible for the child to gain conscious understanding, at least to some extent, of what is the nature of a particular need and what is involved in its satisfaction.

In this way a process gets under way that eventually will determine success or failure in life: whether (and to what degree) we can modify and sublimate inner pressures so as to relieve them, and satisfy our needs in reality—and this not only in the immediate present, but also in the longer range. The more we become able to achieve permanent advantage, the more the pleasure principle is replaced by living in accordance with the reality principle. To the degree this becomes possible, to that degree we become able to husband energies originating in the unconscious and make them serve us construc-tively in terms of reality, thus enhancing our ability to master life. Playing games helps develop this ability and adds a social dimension to it.

In his play the child tries to relieve inner pressures, to gain pleasure, to escape displeasure; and if this is not possible in reality, he escapes into fantasy and tries to achieve in imagination what reality has denied him. As he matures, more and more of his activities are compromises between what his desires and needs demand and what is given in reality, hence possible in and allowed by it. This includes more and more not only physical but also social reality. In short, growing up in this world and becoming able to make a go of life requires learning to cope with reality in all of its aspects. Playing games permits the child to acquire this ability, small step by small step, and to do this in often pleasurable ways which not only encourage such learning, but make it psychologically possible because the enjoyment of the game makes bearable the management of frustrations which are also involved in it, such as the possibility or actuality of losing. This would be unbearable did not the game itself and the social interactions during and around it provide compensations.

As discussed before, in play the child tests his ability to satisfy inner needs in reality; but if reality does not lend itself to this, or demands too much conformity, the play stops and the child retreats into fantasy. True, imaginary satisfactions make frustrations imposed by reality a bit more sufferable. Still, there is a great difference between whether the child remains occupied with pure fantasy where no learning takes place, or acts out his fantasies to some degree also in reality, as he plays with blocks and doll figures, or by using a play house. In the first case, no allowances are made for reality; in the second, the child is learning to use features of reality for fantasy purposes. The more advanced his play becomes, the more appropriate are the elements of reality the child uses for his purposes—as we all must learn to do in life if we wish to be able to gain our goals in realistic ways. None of this is learned, however, when the child retreats into solitary fantasy without acting it out in play. Such withdrawal into fantasy and with it into potentially dangerous (because isolating) self-absorption is not possible in game-playing, because the social context within which it is played mitigates strongly against solipsism. An example may illustrate this process.

Whenever the circumstances of a child's existence—that is, his day-to-day life at home with his parents—make him unhappy (and given the conditions of all our lives this is frequently the case), he tries to compensate for it by wish-fulfilling fantasies of a very different life which would make no demands on him and satisfy all his desires. This imagined life must also occur within a family home, since the child cannot think of it in any other way, nor how his needs and desires could be met except within a family setting. So he fantasizes about a different home not only in which his needs are immediately satisfied, but also in which he can freely act out his anger if this does not always happen. In the next stage, fantasy alone is not enough; the child wishes to fabricate this imaginary world in which he is in control of all things. Some implements, a cardboard box, a few blocks are sufficient to suggest this home. As the child's ability to manipulate objects increases, objects such as blocks are more elaborately arranged, and others such as dolls or toy furniture are placed within this structure, thus becoming an ever better replica of a real home. More complicated life activities are carried on in this play setting, such as parties for dolls and toy animals, using toy dishes and imaginary or real food. The child learns to make use of what reality offers in the way of toys, and arranges and uses them with increasing appropriateness.

Still, all this is only play, because the child can alter things from moment to moment, pretending that a doll is now a parent, then a sibling, and at another time himself, and so forth. All this changes when the same wish for an ideal home and for having life under the child's entire control is played out as a game, that is with other persons. Then pretending that a block is a bed, then a stove, and finally a car will not do. Rather the child and his friends will perhaps collect material from which to build a treehouse, with a real table and real chairs in it, or some structure of this sort. Or he and his playmates will construct some hideaway in a corner of the home, preferably somewhere away from his parents and their reality, in a secluded place in the basement or attic. There, together, they act out a way of life of their own, now that they have a home of their own. But not only will this secret home they have constructed for themselves have to be arranged according to the objects they have managed to collect, it will also have to be planned and arranged to please all of the participants. Thus consideration for the ideas and desires of others becomes part of the planning: the child in playing games learns to cooperate with others so that the play will be a success. If all goes well, more and more elements of reality will be incorporated into this make-believe home. The children may no longer be satisfied with setting up parties for themselves or their dolls or stuffed animals, with mudpies for food and empty cups standing for liquids drunk out of them. Instead they will raid the refrigerator and eat sandwiches and cookies; they will drink real drinks and enjoy them in their private abode, which then takes on even more features akin to those of reality. More and more aspects of reality will enter into their play until the children, by now older, start giving real parties for their friends. In this process the child learns to follow the "rules" of the social game, exploring and learning which of his friends are compatible with one another, and why they are or are not. He may learn certain social graces—to call his friends to invite them, or even to write and mail invitations in good time; to buy and prepare supplies, even to save or earn the money to buy them; to set the table and plan and prepare games for entertainment; in short, to play the host, and to play it well, and even to clean up afterward.

The basic development sketched here is one that, *mutatis mutandis*, also takes place around many other games children play. Starting with Candy Land and Chutes and Ladders, simple games which nevertheless require ability to count, to wait one's turn, to move only as far as the cards or the dice permit, the child moves on to Parcheesi, Chinese Checkers, and eventually Monopoly, which require him to choose from a variety of strategies and take into consideration the plans of one's opponent; and then to ever more difficult and complex games such as chess, each demanding more planning, ingenuity, and foresight than the preceding ones.

In many ways, other early learning is analogous to this progression from fantasy to respect for reality, from very simple to ever more complex and more reality-oriented play and from that to games requiring the participation of others. In this process the child takes important steps in his socialization and incorporates significant aspects of his cultural inheritance. Chess, for example, is a sublimated form of combat, and Monopoly a not-so-sublimated simile of capitalistic enterprises. There are games such as Cowboys and Indians which copy historical events, and others copy travels, discoveries, and so forth.

In his spontaneous play, when the child rolls an empty cardboard toilet-paper core back and forth, he rediscovers the wheel; if he does not discover gravity in block-building, he finds out its effect and learns to counteract it through adequate support of the pieces so that they will not immediately tumble down. When he plays with his trucks, he repeats important achievements in transportation. Thus in the development of his play he duplicates man's great cultural acquisitions. The same is true when he masters man's greatest cultural achievement: literacy. In the life of mankind, literacy—reading and writing—did not begin as a utilitarian skill; nor should it in the life of the child.

Many games which are not systematically instructive are nevertheless effectively so: many games require counting and also some reading, such as that of instructions. Other games parallel school learning, as in Spill and Spell where reading is of the essence, and where practice and mastery of spelling proceeds in much more enjoyable ways than in class. And, while it is not widely recognized, it is hardly surprising that academic learning, too, mirrors and parallels the development which is characteristic of play and games.

MAGICAL DIMENSIONS

Learning to read, so basic to all academic achievements, illustrates not only these parallels, but their importance if intellectual subjects are to be learned well and to attain deep personal meaning. The child who through playing games of progressively greater complexity has mastered the knack of controlling to some measure the largely chaotic tendencies of his unconscious and that of harnessing its energies for largely conscious and reality-oriented purposes will find it relatively easy to apply the same skills to the learning of reading. But unless he has learned and expanded this technique in playing, he will not be able to apply it to learning to read, and reading may then seem a dry and unsatisfying enterprise, if not downright impossible, or so unpleasant as to be avoided. Whether it is a question of play and games or of academic learning, success in mastering such ventures requires that the unconscious is ready, able, and willing to invest its energies in the activity. This is particularly important in the beginning and in the early stages of intellectual efforts, before they have proved their merits, but it is also true throughout their later development. No matter what the "real" merits of an intellectual activity are, to be fully enjoyed and appreciated it must offer in addition pleasurable or otherwise desirable satisfactions, very much including those of an imaginary, even seemingly magic nature which appeal to our unconscious and meet some of the needs originating in it.

Adults are usually unaware that learning to read, which they view as a rational undertaking and a typical ego achievement, can be mastered well only if the child intially, and for quite a while afterward, experiences reading both as fantasy satisfaction—as in his play—and as a very powerful magic. The child who greatly enjoys hearing stories that stimulate and satisfy his fantasies will also wish to know how to read these engrossing tales to himself when no one is available to read them to him. But if he did not experience the pleasure of being read to, he will not be easily interested in learning to read. Lacking this experience he will doubt that learning to read is something he wishes to do, and the hard labor involved in learning it will not seem worth the effort.

But even being read stories which they much enjoy will not be sufficient motivation for most children to engage freely and eagerly in the difficult task of becoming literate. For this the example of their parents' interest in reading will also be necessary, or at least very helpful. If his parents are interested in reading themselves and derive meaning and enjoyment from it, this will be a strong incentive for a child to emulate them. If reading is important to his parents, it will be to their children, notwithstanding rare exceptions such as those discussed earlier in which literacy became the battleground on which the child tries to defeat his parent. In most cases children wish to be able to understand what is an important aspect of their parents' lives, and to participate with them in it. Without a positive parental image of the merits of reading, the child may fail to develop an interest in it.

At first acquaintance, literacy appears as sheer magic, and not as being of any practical use. This is as true for the young child as it was true for mankind. Originally, reading and writing served religious and magical ends. We know, for instance, that Homer had heard about writing, although at the time he composed his oral epic the *Iliad*, Greece was nonliterate. It simply did not occur to him that the writing about which he had heard some vague talk could be used for utilitarian purposes. He describes the processes of making meaningful signs on tablets and deciphering them as essentially magical acts. When Homer thought about writing, he thought about it as actually conveying secret power, not merely information. This was not just because the oral tradition of the Homeric era and the extensive reliance on memory which it required rendered literacy virtually unnecessary. It was also because this idea was common to preliterate societies, which ascribed to the written word the magical power which is implied and reflected in the Scriptural statement "In the beginning was the Word, and the Word was with God, and the Word was God."

For centuries, the power of the written word remained a secret conferring special privileges on the select few. Witness the long debate about whether the common man should be permitted to read Scriptures. Witness, too, the fact that when literacy became more prevalent, its primary exercise was in reading the Bible. The first primer printed on this continent began: "In Adam's Fall/We sinned all./Thy life to mend/This book attend." The real value of reading for our ancestors lay in its unique—near-magical—power to help those who mastered it gain salvation.

Fortunately for many children, the first books read to them—while they no longer deal with the greatest wonder of all, eternal life and salvation—contain enough magical events to convince them that by learning to read, they too will learn more about the supernatural. Stories that contain rich fantasy-stimulating material provide imaginary satisfactions which demonstrate the value and merit of reading.

The time is long gone when learning to read was directly related to learning about the supernatural and magic, about the dangers of sin and the hope of salvation. That is why many children, although they have all the requisite intelligence for learning to read well, fail to do so. Even if they do learn, reading remains emotionally empty and unappealing to them. This is the reason all too many children do not turn to reading out of their own desire. For them reading is not supported by its power to stimulate and satisfy their imagination in respect to what to them are pressing and urgent issues, nor has it created a strong id appeal through its magical meaning. If it has not become attractive during the child's formative years, it may never seem attractive, even when its practical value is recognized. On the other hand, after reading has been well learned on a potent and eminently attractive unconscious basis, it can slowly be divorced from this as the child, from his own experience, becomes convinced of the many real merits of literacy beyond the stimulation of the imagination and the provision of vicarious satisfaction through fantasy, which will always remain important elements. But if reading is too soon and too radically deprived—or never was imbued—with magical meaning, it will not be strongly invested.

But even the magic of reading will not sufficiently affect many children if their parents do not place high value on "book learning." The great emotional investment of parents in reading makes it uniquely attractive to their child, since then reading forms another link tying the parents closely to the child. I am sure that Jewish literacy was helped by the fact that it was customary on the day the child entered one of the yeshivas (Talmudic schools) for the father to carry his son, who was by then well able to walk, on his arms into the school. This symbolized to the child that learning in this school did not mean relinquishing closeness to the parent or primitive satisfactions in general, such as being cuddled.

It would benefit all children if schools—and parents—would make it clear to them both through symbolic gestures like that of Orthodox Jewish fathers and through their actions and attitudes that doing more grown-up things in school and in the world does not mean they now have to give up all childish behavior or be deprived of more childish satisfactions; and that learning in school will not curtail their chance to have their fill of play, nor will being able to read eliminate their parents' reading to and with them. The fear that this is so lies behind many early academic failures; by not learning in school, the child believes he will fend off the loss of more infantile pleasures. For this reason it is a bad idea to try to motivate children by appealing to them that they are now "too grown-up" to do something. While every child likes to be told how grown-up he is, he does not want to have to pay a high price for it, and if the price seems too high, he may want nothing of it. On the contrary, we ought to impress on our children that they now have a double advantage: they can do more grown-up things, and they can still also enjoy all the more primitive satisfactions.

Of course, merely saying this won't work unless our behavior proves to the child that we mean it. We must make sure that our children continue to enjoy more primitive pleasures even though they now can also achieve on higher levels. If we do this, these more infantile types of behavior will recede more and more, to reappear only in moments of stress, when they provide much-needed relief. But if the child has to give up on them because he is now older and can do more grown-up things, then he won't like these new things as much as he could, and the desire for older types of satisfaction will sour him on higher achievements.

After this digression suggesting how paradigmatic learning through playing is for *all* learning and that for true success in learning it must satisfy unconscious pressures and needs in line with the requirements of reality, let us consider further what can be and is learned by playing. There is no end to this subject, as there is none to the games children invent, nor to those they hand down from generation to generation, inventing and reinventing them anew in each age. The kernel of psychological wisdom inherent in even the simplest traditional games may be illustrated by Mother, May I, in which the "mother" tells the "child" how far and how fast he may advance, while the "child" tries to cheat as soon as the "mother" turns her back. It is almost impossible to overestimate to what degree "putting things over" on one's real mother is rendered unnecessary by this game; it makes obedience acceptable in reality because in the game, one is permitted to rebel and even rewarded for it.

This game also ritualizes every child's suspicion that his mother doesn't want him to advance as fast as he would like. On the other hand, the child playing the mother's role experiences, at least in token form, what it feels like when children attempt to get the best of their mother as soon as her back is turned. But despite all this "disobedience," at no time does the game deny the mother's paramount emotional importance to the child. The very purpose of the game is to get to her as quickly as one can; she is the ultimate goal, the center of the child's life. All group games children spontaneously play can reveal equally deep psychological meanings, if we look for them.

Engrossed in the free give-and-take of such a game, children learn how to fit themselves easily into the roles various situations demand, enjoying leadership at one moment and participating as part of the group in the next. They learn to wait their turn when the game requires it, and to take the initiative when the opportunity arises. Most of all, they may learn what too many children in our society fail to learn—the importance of being a good loser. Children become able to take losing in stride without being defeated by it, because they recognize that in a game, as later in life, we cannot always come out on top. However, for this to occur their participation in the game must be spontaneous and free from outside pressure.

Merely telling a child that it is "playing the game" which counts does not get this message across with any real impact. No one acquires attitudes merely by being *told* they are desirable. A child can make such attitudes part of his life only by participating in situations which both naturally require them and also demonstrate their advantage to him.

For example, it is easy for a child to learn to accept defeat through a game in which the loser automatically becomes the leader at the very moment of his downfall. This is the pattern for many tag games, in which the child who gets caught immediately becomes the powerful one who has the right to chase everybody else. Fear of being caught changes in an instant to the powerful feeling of being the chaser whom all others fear. And if one is not caught, there is satisfaction too in having outwitted the catcher.

Waiting patiently in line is another very difficult lesson for children to learn. But when, as in the game Last One First, the waiting child can see how every other player's move brings him closer to last place and his turn, then waiting makes sense. With such built-in possibilities of role change, one can learn to wait one's turn and to obey the rules of the game, since these guarantee that soon one will be in the leading position. Compare this with the concept of waiting a child is supposed to learn in school—a setting which offers no prospect of reversing the roles of leadership, or even any inherent promise that waiting one's turn will be rewarded.

Learning by doing what the situation requires, such as taking and keeping one's place in line because nothing else will work in the game, is much more effective and pleasant than listening to lectures about lining up to go to the lunchroom in school. Many children come to resent, most often in silence, the discursive teaching and preaching of cooperation and social responsibility with which they are bombarded. They dislike the parent's or teacher's moralistic fervor. It is futile to tell a child that these virtues are desirable, because he feels he would be much better off if he were simply to follow his egoistic tendencies. But if he tries to do that during a game, the game disintegrates, so he learns to control himself.

The ability to pay attention to what is going on and to control oneself are the basic skills that underlie all later learning in school and in life. Without them, one cannot cooperate, stick to a task, wait for results, or go on trying even if one lost this time. These abilities are quite different from each other and difficult to learn, but through playing games, they can be gained in an enjoyable, even exciting way. In practically all active group games, the child learns to pay attention to who is "it," to who is being caught. In many games he learns to control himself—most of all, to control his aggression—and to endure the limited aggression of others. He learns this from the tap games, where one must not hit too hard, and even more directly from games that involve specific and limited aggression. For example, in Battle Royal one player must knock a paper bag off another's head, but he is "out" if he touches the head in doing so. Such games teach the advantage of controlled discharge of aggression, because if one does exercise self-control, one wins, whereas if one fails to exercise it, one loses.

In many games, not only war or heroic games, winning *per se* is less important than winning through fair play. The rules, whether in board games or on the playing fields, are designed to promote such sublimation.

The more popular games ingeniously speak to unconscious quandaries and derive their appeal from positing solutions to them. For example, Careers is won by preselection of the right combination of points to be earned for money, fame, or love. Which of the three to concentrate on is quite a problem to the child at the age at which he finds this game attractive. He is honestly confused about what he wants most for himself: acclaim by others, earthly possessions, or being loved. The game permits him to explore all the options. For instance, it gives the child who feels unloved a chance to win without being loved; alternatively and in another mood, he can try to gain every possible point for love, thereby using the game to counteract his fears about his real-life situation. "Will I win out over my competitors by being more skillful in combining what life may have to offer me?" "Will amassing large sums of money enable me to purchase what life has not given me freely?" These are just a few of the questions the child unconsciously tries to answer by playing the game.

LEARNING THE RULES OF THE GAME

Piaget stresses the importance of the child's learning the rules of the game in the process of socialization because he must become able to control himself in order to do so, controlling most of all his tendency to act aggressively to gain his goals. Only then can he enjoy the continuous back-and-forth interaction with others that is involved in playing games with partners who simultaneously are also opponents. Thus in many ways the mastery of objects which the child acquired through handling them in play becomes slowly extended to self-mastery through the playing of games, and most important the mastery of his own aggression. The transition is gradual from play (characterized by spontaneity, fantasy, and sudden switches in content from reality to imagination) to game activities, which require considerably more self-control to wait one's turn and conform to the rules of the game, even if obeying them leads to one's defeat.

Obeying the rules and controlling one's selfish and aggressive tendencies is not something that can be learned overnight; it is the end result of a long development. When he begins playing games, a child tries to behave as he could in his earlier play: he changes the rules to suit himself, but then the game breaks down. In a later stage he comes to believe that the rules are unalterable; he treats them as if they were laws handed down from time immemorial which cannot be transgressed under any circumstances, and he views disobeying the rules as a serious crime. Only after the child has thus learned to obey rules and to be able to contain his selfish and aggressive tendencies to the degree that he can avoid bending or flouting the rules does he become able to comprehend and accept the fact that rules are followed not for any abstract reason, but because only if they are can the game proceed in an orderly fashion. Only then, and this is usually quite late in the child's development—often not until he has become a teenager and sometimes even later than that—can he comprehend that rules are voluntarily agreed upon for the sake of playing the game and have no other validity, and that they can be freely altered as long as all participants agree to such changes. Democracy, based on a freely negotiated consensus that is binding only after it has been formulated and voluntarily accepted, is a very late achievement in human development, even in game-playing.

For this reason Piaget insisted that learning to play by the rules is one of the most important steps in the socialization of the child. When children are free to do as they like in games not supervised by adults, more often than not the arguments over which game they will play, and how, and what rules they should follow take up most of their time, so that little actual playing may get done. Left to their own devices, it may take children hours of fruitful deliberations until they agree on the rules and related issues such as who should begin the game and what is to be the role of each child in it. And this is how it ought to be, if playing games is to socialize children. Only by pondering at great length the advantages of various possible games, and their relative appropriateness to the situation in which they find themselves, such as size of the group, conditions of the playing area, etc., and what rules should apply and why, will they develop their abilities to reason, to judge what is appropriate and what not, to weigh arguments, to learn how consensus can be reached and how all-important such consensus is to the launching of an enterprise. Learning all this is infinitely more significant for the child's development as a social human being than mastering whatever skills the child may develop by playing the game itself. Yet none of these socializing abilities will be learned if adults attempt to control which games are to be played, or if they prevent experimenting with rules (which they fear may lead to chaos), or if they impatiently push for the game to get started without further delay.

When adults step in to organize the game, they deprive the children of the personal growth they could gain through these engrossing preliminaries. All too often adults overlook the vast difference between the social situations of planning for the game and actually playing it. While they discuss what to play and why, and how to play it, the children are equal partners in a decision-making process, and they enjoy their ability to participate in a free give-and-take atmosphere. When they do this, they cooperate together, and a most enjoyable spirit of camaraderie is maintained. They feel accepted and secure with each other, because they are being friends who share a lot with each other.

All this changes the instant the game gets started. Then the friends and cooperators become competitors who feel they have to show themselves superior to those who only a moment before were their equals. This makes them feel insecure and tense, where before they had been secure and relaxed. Now not only do they wish to defeat those who were so recently their comrades and friends, but even the members of one's own team tend to be critical when a player does not live up to expectations (which are often unreasonably high because of the wish that their team should be victorious). Although the discussions before the game began were friendly, those following it are more often than not fault-finding and acrimonious, and on the part of the winners sometimes even gloating. The mood is just the opposite of that which characterized the period of anticipation.

While the winners may feel elated at the moment of victory, they also know that those they have defeated will resent it, and them; thus whatever security they gained from winning will be marred by having alienated those who were their friends only a short time earlier. The good feeling which was created and reigned during the discussion that anticipated the playing of the game largely evaporates once the contest gets under way. Children know this very well, and this is why, if left alone, they like to spend most of their time planning for the game, preferring that the period of their cooperation should be longer than that of their competition.

So long as the game has not started, everyone can imagine himself victorious, but once it is under way, this is no longer possible. If adults cut short these anticipatory pleasures and insist that a game must be played according to *their* rules, they only succeed in arousing the children's competitive emotions to a high pitch. Then they turn around and expect the children—whom they have urged to play to win—to accept that it is all "just a game" which should not lead to feelings of dejection at a loss or of superiority when one wins. Often such adults are themselves unable, despite their much greater experience, to accept defeat with equanimity and without loss of self-esteem. Nonetheless they expect of their children greater maturity than they themselves possess. Children cannot—nor should they be expected to—possess such mature control over their emotions, particularly when adult intervention has raised feelings to a fever pitch.

Parents must decide which is more important: for their children to settle down quickly to playing by adult rules, or to work at becoming thoughtful, self-determined human beings through planning for the game, even though much of the available time may be spent on this difficult process. We need the experience—over time and through repetition—that we can determine how to spend our time, as well as which rules should determine our conduct; we need also the feeling that such decisions are serious matters requiring much deliberation and experimentation. It is the combination of all these elements that makes for true self-respect. Only the slave has to obey rules that are imposed on him without his being able to question them.

Of course, it is simpler to be told what to do and to obey such commands than to struggle with making up one's own mind; obedience does not require learning to weigh choices, to reach agreement freely with one's fellow human beings, and to test in practice the workability of rules decided upon in theory. The child who plays as he is told may improve his skill in a particular game, but he will not learn how to cooperate well with his peers, nor what is involved in working out rules for his own conduct in cooperation with others; the game may be learned well enough, but the child will not be socialized by playing it.

THE CIVILIZING FUNCTION OF GAMES

Contrary to adult fears—the usual motive for many parents to supervise and regulate their children's games—even aggressive play in childhood serves often crucial civilizing functions. This is true if children are left to their own devices, in which case it only very rarely leads to mishap. Iona and Peter Opie, to whom we owe the most sensitive and comprehensive study of the games modern British children play on their own and under supervision by adults, write:

> . . . when children are herded together in the playground, which is where the educationalists and the psychologists and the social scientists gather to observe them, their play is markedly more aggressive than when they are in the street. . . . At school they play dodge ball, wolf and lambs, indulge in duels such as knuckles, in which the pleasure, if not the purpose, of the game is to dominate another player and to inflict pain. . . . Such behavior would not be tolerated amongst the players in the street.

When the Opies asked children what games they played in adult supervised playgrounds, they were often told, "We just go around aggravating people."

When self-regulation is taken away from children, to be replaced by adult insistence on what and how they should play, the play becomes both more vicious and less satisfying. When the spontaneous stickball play of children on the street and in vacant lots was changed into adult-organized and -coached Little League baseball, a previously delightful activity turned into a serious endeavor. Winning in competition began to take precedence over the enjoyment of the game.

When thinking about organizations such as Little League, we should keep in mind that the most important functions of play and games for the well-being of the child are to offer him a chance to work through unresolved problems of the past, to deal with pressures of the moment, and to experiment with various roles and forms of social interaction in order to determine their suitability for himself. All these purposes are negated when adults impose their standards of "seriousness" on the child's activities. The pernicious effects of such adult-imposed criteria have been described in the story about stamp collecting; in that instance the boy was as serious in regard to what it all meant to him as his father was, but their differences lay in the purposes their hobby served.

To stress playing "properly" and winning, as in Little League competitions, is to impose adult earnestness about baseball at the expense of what makes the game important to the child. The difference can readily be seen if we visualize what happens when a group of children get together for a spontaneous ball game. The course of such a pickup game is apt to be very uneven indeed, because sudden changes can occur as dictated by a child's need to act out some wild fantasy, using the game to deal with an emotional problem of past or present.

A freely organized ball game looks very ragged, and it *is* very ragged. The children use the game to serve their own individual and group needs, so there are interruptions for displays of temper, digressions for talking things over or to pursue a parallel line of play for a time, surprising acts of compassion ("give the little guys an extra turn")—all acts outside adult game protocols. If adults want to see a polished game of baseball played according to the rulebooks, they need go no farther than their television sets. But in imposing their notions of order on a child's game, they ought to think twice about what they are doing and its likely consequences, and what they are depriving their children of.

This is why most children prefer to play on the street rather than in an adult-supervised playground. Nor is it only the conditions of modern urban living that force children to play in the streets. They apparently did so in Biblical times; we read in Zachariah that the city of God "shall be full of boys and girls playing in the streets." The prophet could not think of a better image to suggest the freedom and happiness which would reign in the city of God, although children even in his day doubtless did not play in orderly ways only. While we have no eyewitness testimony about what went on when children played freely in the streets of Biblical Jerusalem, we do have reports from medieval cities. To quote the Opies again:

> In 1332 it was found necessary to prohibit boys from playing in the precincts of the palace at Westminster while Parliament was sitting. In 1385 the bishop of London was forced to declaim against the ball play about St. Paul's. . . . In 1447 in Devonshire, the bishop of Exeter was complaining of "young people" playing in the cloister, even during divine service, such games as "the toppe, queke and most atte tenys, by which the walls of saide Cloistre have be defowled and the glas windowes all to brost."

Thus, while some restrictions were found necessary, it did not occur to people in past times to rule that children should not play in the streets and enjoy themselves there in their own ways.

What makes the street or an empty lot so much more attractive than the playground? In such places, children can create their own environment—a very important consideration when the rest of their day is spent in adult-created settings. In this sense the bombing of London was a blessing for one generation of children. As late as 1955 one child wrote, "The sites of Hitler's bombs are many and the bigger sites with a certain amount of rubble provide very good grounds for Hyde and Seek and Tin Can Tommy." Another wrote, "Ours is a good park—there are still places in it that are wild."

When children can arrange things for themselves, their games teach them self-control. This was common knowledge in 1834 when *The Boy's Week-Day Book* remarked, "It is a pleasant sight to see the young play with those of their own age . . . in these boyish amusements much self-denial and good nature may be practiced." Even earlier, John Locke noted that "there can be no recreation without delight, which depends not always on reason, but oftener on fancy; it must be permitted children not only to divert themselves, but do it after their own fashion." How fortunate would it be for our children if we adults would heed the advice of this great philosopher!

UNCONSCIOUS MOTIVES

The runner who times himself or tries to increase his distance and speed, while consciously exercising for his health, is subconsciously trying to prove himself to himself, and unconsciously trying to prove his worthiness to his parents or whoever has taken their place in his unconscious. With good reason the first great athletic competitions were religious festivals, or were intrinsically connected with them. The Olympic games at their inception in classical Greece were not designed to encourage healthy exercise or to test athletes' prowess in meeting reality challenges. Transcending these considerations was the fact that the games were a religious ceremony in honor of the Olympian gods who lent their abode's name to the competition. An athlete brought himself to the punishing rigors of Olympic competition out of a sense that his participation served religious, magical ends. The gods took a special interest in the man who won in fair competition; or, depending on how one reads Pindar's *Olympian Odes*, the gods revealed which men they took a special interest in by permitting them to win. In either case, the victor's laurel wreath was a symbol of far more than victory in an athletic contest.

Although sports have now become secularized, they have not lost their important "magical" dimensions of serving unspoken unconscious needs. There is reason why the modern Olympics stress their connection with the religious games of ancient Greece in which the gods' choice of the winners indicated the people and city they favored above all others. Today we no longer live in city-states, but all this has been extended to the nations. The athletes in our Olympic contests compete not only as individuals but also as national representatives. Individual victories are celebrated by raising the flag of the winner's country, which in this way seems to demonstrate its superiority to others. It is obviously a symbolic superiority, but it suggests that we have not moved all that far away from feeling (and perhaps thinking) that winning in these competitions has a meaning far beyond what happens in reality, and that it shows some nations superior or favored over others for whatever reasons. All international competitions seem to take on such meaning, as illustrated by the world chess championships, which have now become widely viewed as events having political relevance.

Given that adults assign such far-reaching symbolic significance to the winning of competitive games, how could it be otherwise for children, who are even more ready to see magical meaning and connotations in nearly everything? Psychoanalytic examination of the meaning of sport competitions has shown that in many cases, people use them for externalizing inner conflicts. By projecting such conflicts onto the game, one need no longer repress them or feel torn by them, but can act out these feelings more or less directly either as participant or vicariously as spectator. The danger threatening from within—inner conflicts—is displaced onto the outside world through the game; neurotic anxiety is converted into conscious anxiety about defeat in a game and is thus easier to accept and to live with.

That we are dealing here with unconscious conflicts is demonstrated by the degree of tension and excitement that sports events produce in participant and spectator alike, and by their intense personal involvement in what is supposedly just a game. Witness, for example, the acute excitement generated in spectators who often cannot even clearly see what is going on because of the immensity of the arena. Witness too the pride of persons who don't even care about sports whenever the local or national team wins, and their fury and dejection if it loses, and the violence that sometimes erupts at the end of a hotly contested game. And what of the millions who spend their Sundays watching ball games and other contests on television? Their devotion is but another indication that much more is at stake unconsciously in such games than a contest to determine which team is better.

The child who plays Hide and Seek is experimenting with vital issues such as: "Is it safe for me to leave home?" "Will I be able to return to the security of home if I leave?" The parallel problem of the adolescent is to free himself from parental dominance, to prove his mettle and his chance of success with his peers in the wider world. As he tries to achieve the first he often attacks what his home stands for, whereas to succeed in the latter he still needs its safety; thus he is deeply ambivalent about home and parents. While the adolescent no longer plays Hide and Seek, or only rarely, he does avidly play ball games. In many of these, for example in soccer, the issue is to attack and invade the other team's home base or goal by means of a ball, and to defend your own territory against such danger at all costs.

Aggression and the defense against it are what soccer is all about; but in particular, it is about the attack and defense of the home base. Only one player—the goalkeeper—stays within this home base, and special rules of conduct apply to him only. As the one who is in the home and who must directly defend it, he may symbolize the father or the parents. All the other players, both attackers and defenders, must remain out in the field, outside the home area. The teams are like two groups of brothers—their number limited to how many siblings one may have in reality—who no longer reside within the home. Like adolescents in real life, they attack the home base and the father (of the other team) and simultaneously defend their own. So in the game they can have it both ways, as the adolescent so often wishes he could in reality: to attack, and to defend, a home and a symbolic father.

The winning players gain public applause and approbation both for their attack and their defense, which assures them that it is all right to discharge some of their aggression within set bounds. Winning enhances their self-esteem, something adolescents need even more than other age groups. While it seems doubtful that the battle of Waterloo was won on the playing fields of Eton, there is good reason to assume that the eternal battle of the adolescent of all times and places is symbolically acted out on all kinds of playing fields.

We attach many psychological or symbolic meanings to our teams, irrespective of whether we are players or spectators, and these are the source of much of the game's interest for us. For example, there are a number of successful athletes who suddenly lose interest in competing, although they continue to enjoy their sport. When these cases are investigated psychoanalytically, an interesting pattern emerges. The athlete seems to have cherished a magical belief that winning would prove something about him or predict what would happen in his future (but not in terms of the realistic consequences of winning or losing). When he loses this belief, he loses a powerful motive for exposing himself to the rigors and dangers of competition. One of the most common of these magical beliefs has to do with the indestructibility of the body; the wish to believe in it and to prove it through repeated testings accounts for many deeds of athletic daring. When such irrational motives are gone, neither the acclaim of the crowd nor financial rewards are compelling enough reason to continue competing.

GAMES OF CHANCE

To games of chance we give the unconscious meaning that fate will indicate who is its favorite, and whether the gods—those superlative stand-ins for parents—will smile on us. Addictive gambling is usually the consequence of efforts to force one's luck in order to confirm one's worth. On the other hand, continuing gambling in the face of persistent loss is a form of self-punishment; unconsciously, the loser feels he is not worthy of being lucky, and that losing is deserved because of some guilt. Some gamblers believe that winning will prove that they are finally forgiven for some earlier sin and returned to a favored status. And some get permanently stuck trying to use such magic devices to correct their fortunes in real life. These excesses do not alter the fact that in gambling the power of the unconscious is husbanded to serve at least some of the requirements imposed by reality, such as considering the odds at cards, dice, or roulette.

When a child subjects himself to the rules of a game, he does not do so just to win the competition. As a matter of fact, even adults could not engage in games so fiercely if all that were at stake were the winner's realistic gains. Always and everywhere there is an unconscious element also involved. For this reason we can compete "as if our life were at stake"—something we can do only if we really believe on some level that it is so.

To the child (even well into adolescence), winning means having been made one of the elect. For example, children often play solitaire, in strict obedience to the rules, not just because they wish to win a hand and not just to kill time or develop skills of attention. Rather, they play because they believe that the outcome will magically bring about, or foretell, for example, that they will pass an exam or win a desired friend, or that some other secret wish will come true. But this idea requires that they do not cheat at solitaire, because then the outcome would not predict anything.

Through such experiences the child learns to make his powerful unconscious and irrational sources of energy serve tasks imposed by reality. This is one of the most important learning experiences he can gain from games—the ability to use unconscious pressures and desires to give him the strength to meet realistic tasks. But this is not all. Through playing games the child learns not only to funnel the irrational forces of his unconscious into realistic activities—as in playing solitaire to make his wish come true—but also that he must control these forces to gain his goal: "I must not let myself be carried away to cheat in solitaire because then it will not permit predicting anything." This is why playing games is a most important, well-nigh indispensable step in becoming civilized, because civilization requires its members to use unconscious forces for realistic goals and at the same time to exercise a reasonable control over them. Once the child has acquired the capacity to make his unconscious serve the requirements of reality, he can apply its energies to other tasks. Having learned both to use and to master the forces of his unconscious, he has become his own master, and he has done it through playing games.

21

Beyond Winning and Losing

Man is a gaming animal.
—CHARLES LAMB, "Mrs. Battle's Opinions on Whist"

FOR YEARS, the growing child moves back and forth between the many demands that playing games imposes on him. It has been mentioned that at first he tries to bend the rules of the game to favor him; then he believes that authority forces him to obey the rules; finally, he realizes that it is to the players' advantage to voluntarily accept those rules.

When all goes well, a child can do full justice to whatever the game requires. But when things become psychologically too bewildering or frustrating for him, he may revert back to spontaneous play. Although he may still understand the rules governing the game—even insist that others follow them—he himself cannot obey them and may assert that they do not apply to him. For example, a young child may know perfectly well *how* to play checkers. All will go smoothly until he realizes, or believes, that he will lose. Then he may suddenly request, "Let's start all over again." If the other player agrees and the second game goes more in the child's favor, all is well again and the game will continue. But if things look bleak for the child the second time around, he may repeat his request for a fresh start, and do so over and over again. This can be frustrating to an adult, who may decide that the child should learn to finish a game once he has started it, even if he is about to lose. But if the adult is able to be patient and agrees to repeated new beginnings, even though the checker game may never be concluded, the child eventually learns to play better.

But if the adult insists that the child continue playing when he is likely to lose, too much is demanded of the child's still weak controls. If he could articulate his position, he might say, "Obeying the rules when it seems I'm going to lose is just too much for me. If you insist that I go on, I'll just give up on games and return to fantasy play, where I can't be defeated." Then the checker, which had been accepted as a marker to be moved only according to established rules, is suddenly moved as the child's fancy determines, or in a way which seems to assure his winning. If this is not accepted, then the marker may become a very personal missile to be hurled off the board, or even at the winning opponent.

The reasons for the child's behavior are not difficult to understand. Feeling himself momentarily defeated by the complex and painful realities of the game—he is losing, and thus his extremely tenuous self-respect is about to be damaged, something to be avoided at all costs—he reverts back to a play level at which the rules no longer pertain, in order to preserve inviolate his endangered feeling of competence. If his opponent is also a child, he will intuitively understand (although not applaud) his companion's action. The child opponent may say in response, "Come on, now, you're acting like a baby," as if recognizing—probably from his own experience in similar situations—that what has taken place is a regression to an earlier stage of development, because the higher one has proved too painful, and thus not worth the effort to maintain. Or he may suggest, "Let's play something else," knowing that checkers has become too difficult.

If the opponent is an adult, however, such intuitive understanding may be missing. Some parents are unfortunately too eager to see their child behave in a mature fashion before he is ready for it. So they become unhappy with his behavior when he reverts back to simple, unstructured play. But criticism and insistence on mature behavior just when the child feels most threatened merely aggravates his sense of defeat. We ought to recognize that a child may be forced by as yet uncontrollable pressures to disregard or even to pervert the rules of the game in an instant, and that if he does, he does so for compelling reasons.

Again we must remember that for the child, a game is not "just a game" he plays for the fun of it, or as a distraction from more serious matters. For him, playing a game can be, and more often than not is, a serious undertaking on whose outcome he rests his feeling of self-esteem and competence. It has been discussed in various contexts how very important his play is for a child, and pointed out that the world of play is in many ways his real world. To put it in adult terms, playing a game is the child's true reality; this lifts it far beyond the boundaries of what its meaning is for adults. Losing is not just a part of playing the game, as it is for adults—at least most of the time— but something which puts the child's sense of his own competence in question and often undermines it. Losing is then no longer merely part of playing a game; it is something which not only is an insult but, by putting his self-worth and with it his integrity as a person in question, puts his very existence in jeopardy, and this must be prevented at all costs. By making the child fear that he may lose his self-worth, losing can actually cause his composure to disintegrate to the degree that he becomes suddenly unable to separate the reality of the game from the reality of his life.

This is why the child who knows the rules of the game and insists that his partner follow them, as long as he hopes to win, is the identical child who flouts the rules with determination when he thinks he is losing. This often confounds adults—if the child can play so well by the rules when he is winning, why can't he so when he is losing? For an adult, both are the same play situation; but for the child, both are reality. When he wins, he is elated beyond reason, given that it is "only a game." When he loses, he feels destroyed and reacts accordingly—his maturity disintegrates, just as it does for many adults in situations when they feel confronted with utter destruction.

What makes it all so confusing is that now and then, the child is easily able to finish a game, even though he has been aware that he is losing. So if he can accept defeat on some occasions, why not always? Because he could do it yesterday, adults expect him to act equally mature today, and try to hold him to it, or are critical if he does not. What they overlook is that they themselves do not act all that differently in real life. They are able to accept defeat with relative equanimity when they feel very secure in other important respects; at other times, defeat temporarily disintegrates them, it makes them depressed, and unable to function. Their reaction depends on the details of the situation in which they find themselves at the moment of defeat—how secure they are in themselves and with others and how well they can counterbalance their defeat with strengths they possess in other matters of importance. This is true in real-life situations for most adults. Since game-playing is for the child a real-life experience, he behaves accordingly: when feeling relatively strong and secure, he can master defeat in a game without falling apart; but when insecure, he cannot. Because a child's inability to accept defeat in a game is a sign that at that moment he is quite insecure, it becomes even more important that we do not add to it further by our criticism of him.

TACTICAL RETREATS: THE CHILD'S NEED TO WIN

Some children—and most children at some stages in their lives—simply cannot afford to lose. So they cheat in order to win. From an adult standpoint, of course, cheating is highly objectionable and repugnant; but here, as in so many other instances, we must take care not to judge a child's feelings and actions by our own mature standards. Children who resort to cheating do so because of the enormous stakes involved—enormous, that is, to them—and it is then quite wrong to hold them to the rules of the game, because they may give up playing altogether and become utterly dejected, deeply disappointed in themselves. If instead of objecting to their cheating we silently accept it and in this way make it possible for them to win, they will enjoy the game and continue playing it. As a child continues to play—and to cheat—he slowly becomes more experienced in playing the game and needs to cheat less often, and less outrageously. This is why it is especially important for parents to play games with their child, because others are not so ready to let him cheat without at least remarking on it. But cheating may be necessary if the child is to play often enough to become sufficiently expert to win without cheating. Winning makes him more and more secure about his ability to hold his own in the game, and soon he will give up cheating altogether, although he will by no means win each time. That he can now win without cheating provides him with enough security in playing the game so that an occasional loss is no longer experienced as such a severe defeat that he must avoid the game altogether. But it takes a parent's time and patience until his child can become a good enough player not to feel devastated if he loses.

If we are observant, the child's behavior in the ways he tries to cheat will suggest to us the intensity of his fear of defeat and the all-consuming depth of his anxiety. Stopping the game is often not enough; sometimes not even manipulating his fortune by moving the pieces contrary to the rules is enough. Instead he may imagine that all his pieces are kings, which can jump all the pieces of his opponent. If such fantasies are accepted in good humor, the child's confidence may be restored, and he may try once more to play according to the rules. But if he is prevented from reverting back from the game to fantasy in order to shore up his threatened feeling of competence, he may lose all interest in games. When this happens, the child ends up short-changed of the chance games offer to learn higher degrees of socialization.

A child's expressions while he is intent on playing a game reveal his psychological state. As long as he believes he may win, he is wholly engrossed in the game, oblivious to what is happening around him. He is "all ego," entirely goal-directed, full of concentration on the task at hand and intelligently meeting its demands. All this may change in a second when he fears defeat. His face may become distorted; his voice may lose its even pitch; he may no longer be able to concentrate on the game but only on preventing defeat, no matter how outrageous the behavior this may require. The game and its rules may have been all that mattered a moment before, but now they count for nothing. Reality recedes in the presence of anger and frustration that possess him at the expense of everything else. In short, his ego, which has been in full command, loses its fragile integrity as his entire being is flooded by anxious dismay.

If a child in such a situation is permitted to indulge his feelings for the moment—that is, to let off steam, to vent his anger at the game that so frustrates him and threatens him with falling apart—the situation can be restored almost as quickly as it deteriorated, and ego control can again dominate. If his outburst is accepted by others in good humor as legitimate, and they say, "This one doesn't count—let's start all over," he may be able to settle down to another serious game, and in the process learn how to play more skillfully and even to cope with small amounts of frustration. Through such repeated experiences he learns a most important lesson: that he can compose himself anew, after temporarily losing control and being overwhelmed by instinctual pressures.

Losing, or fearing that he may lose are by no means the only situations in which a child becomes unable to view a game as such and obey its rules. Any game situation can arouse such strong emotional pressures that their control by the ego is impossible.

When a child gets hit by a ball during a game, his anger or anxiety may be aroused to the point where he takes it as a personal insult and a deliberate attack. He may become furious and counterattack in earnest, convinced that he was struck not as part of the game, or by chance, but deliberately. His ability to play by the rules may then collapse; but even more seriously, he may regress to an earlier stage of development when he believed that objects had purposes, such as to destroy him for their own reasons. The ball is then no longer an implement for playing but a dangerous missile. When asked why he reacts so violently at being hit by chance, the child may state his view of the matter by saying: "He did it accidentally on purpose," giving lip service to our view that it happened by chance while at the same time insisting upon his view that it was done on purpose.

We can take being hit as part of a game only as long as we can accept that it happens in an "as if" situation for which the rules of the game apply, rules which are not identical with those that pertain to the rest of life. To be able to recognize "as if" situations and to accept that they differ from real life requires a relatively high degree of sophistication and maturity. When emotions overwhelm the child, he can no longer maintain such maturity, and for him the "as if" situation collapses. Then being hit by a ball becomes the result of an aggression directed against him, against which he must defend himself. He then reacts exactly as many of us would if we were deliberately insulted and attacked.

But if we don't become critical of the child for responding as if to a purposeful attack, and if we recognize his predicament by agreeing that he felt gross injustice was done to him—because he had only meant to play a game and found himself in a situation which seemed to him to put his bodily integrity in jeopardy—then our support of him will help him to feel more secure again, and he usually is able to return to the game soon enough. But if we criticize him, this adds to his insecurity, which was already powerfully stimulated by feeling attacked, and he may be unable to continue playing, even be turned off the game altogether.

By granting validity to what (from our perspective) is a distorted view of what happened, we give the child the feeling that in his distress he has found a compassionate friend who sees things as he does; this feeling does more than anything else to restore security. It creates fertile soil for efforts to induce him to see things our way, because we have been so willing to see them his way; he may then listen to us when we explain that what happened was but a mischance, not the life-and-death threat for which he took it. Listening with sympathy and understanding to the child's view of the situation and according it validity often enables the child to return to the "as if" situation of the game. The more he has such experiences, the more he learns the lesson mentioned earlier: that he can still compose himself after he has been overwhelmed for a time by anger or anxiety. Gradually he will learn to handle "as if" situations as such; being able to do so is a major step in reaching a higher degree of comprehension and maturity.

THE ELEMENT OF CHANCE

Whatever the nature of a given game may be, some youngsters will not be able to accept or deal with the demands of reality symbolized by the rules of the game. Therefore, some children cheat or stop playing because they are unable to lose without suffering a severe drop in their self-esteem. They can feel content with themselves only when they can maintain a fantasy of omnipotence. This is usually because they can visualize only two possibilities: either power and control over everything, or total helplessness.

The same psychological mechanisms can also be observed in a child's attitude toward learning and study, when he either pretends to possess knowledge he does not have or approaches learning with anxiety and resistance, convinced he can never succeed. For him, cheating may represent a compromise between his emotional need for omnipotence and his growing recognition of the limitations imposed by reality.

Games of chance are the first ones through which a child learns the "rules of the game." Such games offer the young child an opportunity he can ill afford to pass up: he can beat older opponents despite their superior strength or skill. However, even when mere blind luck determines who will win the game, the child must still obey the rules: he cannot move more spaces than the throw of the dice determines. If he lands on a place where there is a penalty, such as to have to move back a few spaces, he must do so. Of course, the young child does often object and try to improve his fortune through cheating, by taking an extra turn, or by making errors in counting.

In games of chance, even a young child can honestly win over his older competitors, including his parents. In all other human endeavors he can win only if those older people make allowances: give in, pull their punches, pretend. So the child is willing to learn to obey the rules of the game of chance, because by respecting them, he may come out the winner. Once he has learned to play in an orderly fashion because the game of chance offers him this unique opportunity, it will be easier for him to conform to the rules even of games of skill in which he is at a competitive disadvantage.

For a long time many children remain unwilling to test themselves against reality; they will play only games of pure chance. Reliance on luck represents a very primitive view of how the world works and reduces all activity to a matter of fate. But gradually, the child begins to see that skill and knowledge can exercise some influence in games which combine skill with "pure" chance. Consequently he is encouraged to pursue higher learning and to sublimate his primitive drives.

Today in both the social and physical sciences, some of the most complex problems are solved by means of statistical analysis. Because comparing the likelihood of an event with what actually happens helps us to understand phenomena, whatever the youngster learns about statistical probability from games of chance is of great value. In large areas of life, success or failure depends entirely on the ability to have a realistic notion of the rules of probability, and games of chance can teach children important lessons about these. The child who is deeply involved in such games will learn such lessons well.

More highly structured games which combine chance and skill provide the opportunity for open competition within a reassuring framework, settings in which friendliness coexists with overt competition. The more a game depends on skill, the more the rules and not fate control the conditions of rivalry, and the more likely it is that the "best man" will win. But the element of chance, also very much present, reduces the tension of conscious competition and helps keep things on an even keel.

The winner, although he can inwardly congratulate himself on his skill, can still outwardly demur and modestly tell the loser, "Oh, I was just lucky." In this way he can defeat his friend and yet not alienate him. The loser, on the other hand, can console himself with a consideration of how extensively "bad luck" contributed to his downfall, so he need not feel hostility toward his winning opponent. Therefore, a child need not feel unduly guilty or worthless by virtue of winning or losing such a game. A child at this stage of reality adaptation in playing games may be upset by the suspicion that his opponent is "not trying," and also by the occasions when an opponent demonstrates unsportsmanlike behavior in response to winning or losing. Both of these attitudes tend to negate the value of the game for the committed player—the first by suggesting that the game was not serious, the second by implying that it was not friendly.

Monopoly, which reenacts financial operations, may serve as an example of what a child can learn through his participation in games. The neophyte player may initially hold on to all his money, anxiously hoarding it and refusing to invest it in houses or hotels. But he quickly learns that this approach does not work, that being the puppet of his anxieties leads to defeat. On the other hand, rash investment is not the answer either. This eventually becomes clear to the child who invests all his money on one high-priced property, mistakenly convinced that his fellow players will of necessity land on it. He too will find himself bankrupt.

In this way games (as distinct from free fantasy play) force a child, if he wishes to win, to restrain his wishful or anxious thinking and to seek viable compromises between the pressures of his conscious and unconscious desires and the demands of reality. Abiding by the rules of board games is analogous to getting along in the world by seeking satisfaction of one's desires within society's limits of acceptability. No one strategy gives success all the time, because our luck and our opponents change, but the child learns to improve his chances.

THE SYMBOLISM OF WINNING

Feeling threatened by what is taken for a personal attack or by impending defeat is not the only setting in which higher integration collapses and temporary regression occurs. Children sometimes feel compelled to give up a higher achievement for very particular reasons. One girl, quite proficient in chess, regularly defeated her mother fair and square and thoroughly enjoyed her success. Then she became quite ill. For entertainment one day she and her mother played a game of chess, as they often had done in the past. But this time the girl made what seemed to be deliberate mistakes, despite which she won. Instead of rejoicing in her victory as before, she burst into tears and began to berate her mother for letting her win.

The poor mother, who had actually played to the best of her rather limited ability, was flabbergasted. Why had her daughter, who always loved to win, suddenly become depressed by victory and so angry with her? In this case the daughter was frightened by her illness and wanted to use the game of chess for purposes other than distraction or for proving her own competence. At that moment, rather than experiencing chess as a game good for proving her skill, the girl now needed to see it as proof of *her mother's competence*. Frightened by her illness, she needed profound reassurance that her fate was in the hands of a person more competent and more knowledgeable than herself. Like all children she needed to be able to put her faith in the person who protected her life. In this instance she wished that her mother would turn out a winner in the battle against sickness, and she wanted her mother's superior abilities demonstrated by her success in chess.

When the mother lost and revealed herself as less competent than the daughter, the girl's victory defeated the purposes for which she was playing at that moment. She knew that in normal circumstances she could defeat her mother in chess. But what she needed right then was reassurance on a virtually magical level of her mother's superior power. This reassurance was not forthcoming, despite her efforts to play poorly. So her reaction to victory was to feel let down; she was angry at her mother for not showing herself a more powerful person, able to win when the daughter felt she herself was losing—in regard to her illness. Under the extraordinary circumstances of her illness, the girl tried to use the game of chess to gain a childlike assurance of being well protected by superior, benevolent powers.

This girl's story, taken in conjunction with the earlier description of a child who could not afford losing in checkers, illustrates why in some game situations a child needs to win, in others (but much rarer situations) to lose. Taken together, these examples suggest why it is wrong to give parents rules about what to do when playing games with their youngsters. What is best in one situation may be a poor way to proceed in another, or even in the same situation on another day. We need to sense this and to be guided by what is happening at the moment. Even the parent well attuned to his child will not always be able to know beforehand what course is best. But we can trust the child soon to show what he needs, and he will do so more clearly the less we force him to act in ways we think are correct. We should let the child proceed as he wishes, and his behavior will give us his message.

In the example of playing checkers, the child could not afford to lose, and so his behavior indicated this. If we understand the message, we can take it from there. On the other hand, the sick girl did not really need to lose in chess. She needed reassurance about other matters: her mother's ability to be capable and strong and wise when the girl felt so vulnerable, and her mother's willingness to treat her as the small helpless child she felt

275

herself to be at the moment. If the mother had understood the message inherent in her daughter's behavior, she still could have lost the chess game, but have addressed herself directly to the anxiety caused by the girl's illness and given her the assurance she so desperately needed at that point. Fortunately the mother understood soon enough what was going on and could relieve her girl's anxiety about being sick.

22

Becoming Civilized

> *The purpose of all civilization is to convert man, a*
> *beast of prey, into a tame and civilized animal.*
> —NIETZSCHE

THEORIES OF PERSONALITY DEVELOPMENT agree that the child moves through play and games from lower stages of development to higher ones (although explanations of why and how this may be so vary from theory to theory). The child will either earlier or later in life run into difficulties if he is prevented as he grows up from mastering *any* of the important developmental stages which, in their totality, make for full human maturity. These stages seem to parallel and in various ways relate to analogous stages which the human race has undergone in order to arrive at its present state.

Those who have studied the role of games in human development have arrived at two differing theories as to how they achieve these purposes and meaning. Karl Groos, in line with the purposeful rationalism prevalent at the beginning of this century, sees in play and games the child's preparation for his future life activities. Jean Piaget, along the same lines, finds in play various steps in cognitive development, moving from lower to higher stages of understanding and intellectual achievement. Freud, although he did not discuss play systematically, was deeply impressed by how much of our archaic heritage we still carry within us. He stressed repeatedly his conviction that ontogeny repeats phylogeny, that is, that the individual in many respects recapitulates the development of the species. So rather than seeing play activities as a preparation for the future, he saw them as evidence of how beholden we are to our collective past.

The rages of a small child, the way he hurls objects in his anger and frustration, are not all that different from what we imagine the behavior of primordial man to have been. Bertrand Russell remarks: "It is biologically natural that children should, in imagination, live through the life of remote savage ancestors."

The processes of biological, intellectual, social, and emotional development never permit us to omit an important stage entirely. Every stage in the individual's maturation must take place at its appointed time; if it does not, or if it is aborted before it can run more or less its full course, maladjustment will result. That is, for example, why some adolescents will try to live for a time "the life of the savage"—whether as hippies or revolutionaries, or by just "dropping out"—if they did not have sufficient chance to do so in childhood. In adolescence they try to throw off the yoke of parents who have tried to bring them up without recognizing that this process must encompass the playing out and working through of the "savage stage" at the right time, so that it can be transcended. Even if deprived as children of the chance to live out and work through important developmental stages, they can no longer do it the way they would have done it in childhood, because as adolescents they live in the world of reality to a much greater degree than children do. So they usually use contemporary events to serve as the external framework for their acting out and trying to master inner pressures—aligning themselves, for example, with the conflicting camps of contemporary extremist ideologies, some of them supporting thoroughly good causes for reasons quite irrelevant to those causes. The inner problems they are thus trying to work out are revealed through the "savage" ways they embrace some ideology, although these ways may be quite antithetical to the cause in question.

One of the greatest steps in human progress was the domestication of animals. So we should not be astonished when children repeat this experience as they "domesticate" and make a close companion of a dog or cat. Older children love taking care of and riding horses. They would make companions of other and bigger animals if it were feasible. The bigger the beast, the more feral its nature, the greater the child's desire to tame and befriend it. Many children's stories (and a significant number of adult fables and parables) are based on the (unconscious) recognition of this fact.

Anthropologists tell us that man made a huge leap toward civilization when he settled down in a definite territory that he had staked out for himself. We can see, understand, and appreciate echoes of this process in our children when they insist that a certain territory—their hideout, their bedroom, their backyard, their part of the street or neighborhood or city—be theirs alone, a place into which no one may intrude without permission. If provoked, they will band together to defend their "turf." Even quite young children play such territorial games; hopscotch is a typical example. Primitive men got together in groups and learned to communicate and cooperate for the purpose of more successful and pleasant living; children form gangs for similar reasons.

Some historians tell us that the main business of the Greek city-states was to wage warfare, and that higher social and political organizations were formed for this purpose. The Homeric myth tells that the Greeks discovered their identity as a people through the common enterprise of the war against Troy, and it is this myth that formed the basis of their civilization. The city-states attained the heights of their achievements when they got together as a kind of temporary nation to defend their territory against the Persian invaders. We can see a parallel development when rival juvenile gangs call a temporary truce and form an alliance to defend against a common enemy. Nor does the analogy end there. We should not overlook how much political and technical progress, including the formation of language-group national states—Italy, for instance—and the development of such technological refinements as atomic fission and fusion, has been due to or related to war.

Because I am deeply committed to the conviction that it is high time we dispensed with our archaic heritage of war, I believe that not only as a race (we do not seem to be succeeding well on that front) but as individuals we ought to work through all these primitive remnants within ourselves, so that we may be free of them. This is just what war games can achieve for a child. For everything there is a season; to engage in warfare as adults is no more seasonable than it is reasonable. Childhood is the time when we should be able to act out and permanently lay to rest this ancient heritage, and do it through symbolic actions only, as children play at warfare in which their aggressions, insecurities, and anxieties find outlets in ways that do no serious and certainly no permanent damage to anyone.

The child develops a moral code by acting out his aggressions, at the same time moving from indiscriminate pretend shooting and the effort to establish dominance at whatever cost to a battle of good against evil following organized rules. This progress forms a curriculum on how to control, educate, and sublimate chaotic, destructive strivings until they are so tamed that their energy can be made to serve social goals. It is a curriculum which children spontaneously invent and reinvent, if given the chance to do so.

WAR GAMES

War games are different from the simple gun play discussed earlier; they allow expression of an entire range of feelings, from oppressive self-assertion to emotional discharge of frustration and hostility. Through such games, these assertive tendencies are turned into age-correct, constructive play. In the earliest forms of war games, a child sees himself as a mighty warrior who will win every battle; reality plays hardly any role in these fantasies. When he advances to playing Cowboys and Indians with others, some historical elements enter in and certain reality aspects of the cowboy or Indian position usually are respected. Still, the game can easily deteriorate into a free-for-all.

Simply by playing with toy soldiers, a child distances himself from his aggression; he no longer fights, but rather his conflicts find symbolic expression in historical events. In his play, he becomes a great general, and at this juncture a more specific identification with a cultural hero may take place. When reenacting great battles, he sets up his toy soldiers in some accord with history; he can no longer simply follow his wishful fantasies. These more complicated games involve many factors such as geographical formations which have to be taken into account. As the child sets up the opposing forces, he learns to assess one and the same situation from the differing viewpoints of two opposing forces, with their relative strengths and weaknesses. Rational considerations begin to dominate over aggressive wishes. Setting up a complex battle formation with toy soldiers requires much persistent effort and patience—difficult attitudes for the young child to master, but invaluable qualities for attaining success in life.

Visitors to Blenheim Castle see there the elaborate battle scenes that the young Winston Churchill set up with his tin soldiers. To see these is to realize how a great statesman unknowingly prepared himself for his future tasks and how his childish pleasures nourished later adult achievements. In his early play, Churchill began to develop the perseverance and concern with details that maintained him and the British nation in their time of greatest adversity.

Aggressive and self-assertive tendencies are harnessed in war games and developed into attitudes of serious application. At the same time, the wish to be a powerful person and to have one's way begins to be modified by ego and superego identifications with a historical figure—Washington, Napoleon, Grant, Lee, or whomever. The child may study the life of his favorite general or hero, wanting to emulate him. Learning about history enlightens his war games. The fight is no longer one for sheer ascendancy, or to rid oneself of aggression, or to deny the defeats one has experienced in life. The game now becomes a battle for a purpose: to gain independence as in the Revolutionary War, to defeat another country and benefit one's own. The more elaborate such games become, the more erudite they are: facts of history increasingly dominate the play. In global games such as Risk, alliances are formed and broken, as it may seem to the player's advantage. Now the qualities of skill, planning, and foresight can modify results that were directed by pure chance before.

In some board games designed to recreate actual battles, the player's identification with a general extends to reliving in fantasy particular events of a real war. A knowledge of history and strategy increases and realistically strengthens the child's feeling of competence; identification with great historical figures serves both ego and superego needs. In this way the child begins to do what Freud found to be the essential process of becoming ever more humane: where originally there was id, there shall be ever more ego. When the war game is permitted to evolve from its aggressive and chaotic start to an increasingly more intricate undertaking, the id elements continue to provide the motivating energy, but the actions become ego-controlled as the soldiers are lined up in complex formations and moved only according to careful plans.

In addition, war games, like all childhood play, have other important dimensions. They serve a child to deal with and solve emotional and growing-up problems of the moment, but there is much beyond this. The Revolutionary War lends itself to exploring crucial issues of independence, for instance. A Civil War game, on the other hand, may serve as a vehicle for quite different matters which a child needs to approach and try to comprehend. Since the Civil War was the war of "brother against brother," it lends itself readily to problems of sibling rivalry. But a game around the Civil War can also serve as an imaginative representation of other dissensions within the family, such as the battle between father and mother, or between parents and children.

Of course, the Civil War was fought around the issue of slavery and ended in freedom for former slaves. A child feels more or less enslaved, since his life is controlled by his parents, so any war of liberation also represents the child's desire and fight for freedom from parental control The battles back and forth seem to mirror progress and setbacks of his own struggle for self-determination, while the final outcome of the Civil War—freedom for black Americans—seems to promise his victory as well. With such ideas and identifications underlying war games, how natural it is that many children are deeply involved in playing them.

Further, children may also use the Civil War setting on a more primitive level, for dealing with fears and aggressions, as soldiers are moved about, pushed over, shot. At the other extreme, a child with no particular family problem at the moment may play the game largely as an exercise in historical thought, testing his mental agility and social ability to perform well within the rules. Children with widely varying motivations may play together at the same war game quite amicably, each deriving from the game itself those aspects which suit his own needs and purposes. Also, certain children will strive to win, others to lose as self-esteem or a sense of guilt or worthlessness may dictate, regardless of the imaginative or symbolic uses they make of the Civil War setting.

There is a specific aspect to Civil War games which nicely illustrates the interrelation between reality and fantasy in games. As noted, the Civil War was a war within a family, a war of brother against brother. Within his own family the child experiences sibling rivalry and witnesses arguments—if not also fights—which he fears will threaten his own existence, as the Civil War threatened the life of the nation. Such familial battles jeopardize the child's sense of well-being more than anything else, for if there is no security within the family, where can it be found?

Here reality enters in its most reassuring form, for today, the ravages of the Civil War are healed and the United States appears more powerful than ever before. In fact, despite the Civil War—a true disaster at the time—the country survived, and grew very strong indeed. Thus historical facts offer a much-needed assurance: despite all the fighting, despite the hurt we inflict on each other, we have not broken apart; in the end, we will stick together and be better off than ever before.

A game about the Civil War, though it may be structured in a highly intellectualized, "educational" fashion, nevertheless appeals to our deepest emotions. It speaks to our greatest anxieties and engages us because of the unconscious reassurance it offers. As Aristotle said of tragedy, which we rightly call a theatrical "play," it educates our mind as it cathartically cleanses our emotions. In a sense this is true of all constructive human activities.

Many peace-loving parents object to their children playing with toy soldiers, so it might be worthwhile to quote what George Orwell, certainly a man deeply opposed to violence, had to say about this. He wrote: "The socialist who finds his children playing with soldiers is usually upset; but he is never able to think of a substitute for tin soldiers; tin pacifists somehow won't do." And indeed they won't; although children spontaneously play at being nurses and doctors, they never play at being pacifists, much as some parents might like them to. Pacifism is a sophisticated adult concept. When thinking of play and games, we have to remember that the underlying motives for children's play are inner conflicts which press for expression and resolution. Toy pacifists, even if they were available, could not lend themselves to the expression and resolution of one's inner conflicts; this is why they "won't do," whereas toy soldiers are admirably suited for this kind of play.

Since many conscientious parents do not object to board games which duplicate the battles of Waterloo or Gettysburg, but do prohibit shooting games, it may be useful to turn to the latter once more. Those who condemn such directly combative games out of hand as exercises in violence or irrationality fail to take into account the duality of our human and our animal natures, and the distance between them. Certainly there is a great deal of the animal—and with it violence—left in human beings, and sometimes these irrational forces do appear in children's games, and this makes many parents uncomfortable. But more often, it is actually the child's developing sense of humanity that motivates what seems to the uninvolved and uninformed parent to be mere "brutality." Since ancient times children have played out war games in which *we* fight *them*, *them* being the enemy of the historical moment. Classicists tell us that in fifth-century Greece, children studied Homer's *Iliad*. I would venture to guess that they also enacted the Trojan War in their games, as my friends and I did in our childhood, making age-appropriate use of the classical education partly forced on us and partly embraced by us.

But it was during those barbaric war games with cardboard or wooden swords, shields, and helmets that what we learned in class became real to us. Achilles and Hector became alive, as did Odysseus, whose trials and tribulations we also reenacted. In this way, the Homeric poems became a real part of our life. From acting out the war of the Seven against Thebes we could move on to appreciate, understand, and even love Greek tragedy, and then Greek art and culture. At that age, none of this would have had much substance for us had we not played it out. As we did this with Greek myths, the classical heritage became our own and it civilized us.

Children of the Middle Ages surely played at being knights and infidels, just as our own children play at being cops and robbers. Elizabeth I is said to have inquired whether the boys were now playing the war of the English against the Scots. In Europe early in this century, much play involved the Foreign Legion against the Arabs. And as soon as the wall went up separating West from East Berlin, German children began shooting at each other across miniature walls. The important common denominator of such battle play is that it invariably features the conflict of good and evil in terms and images that a child can readily grasp.

GOOD GUYS VS. BAD GUYS

In games such as Cops and Robbers, a child explores and experiments with moral identities. Such games permit him to visualize his fantasies, and he gives them "body" by playing the cop or the robber. Acting out these roles permits him to get closer to the reality of these characters and how they "feel," which reading or watching television cannot provide. A passive, receptive role is no substitute for active encounters with experiential reality.

In games featuring the conflict of good and evil, it augurs poorly for the child's social adjustment to reality and morality if the conditions under which he grows up do not permit him to clearly perceive the "cops" as the good guys. This may happen in the slums where those who outwit the police are considered, if not "good," at least more clever than the police. If these are the conditions of his reality, then a child will have difficulty developing a clear moral identity. But even such a child will have a much easier time succeeding in life if the final identity he chooses is that of those who uphold the moral order. But whoever the "good" guys are, the child must finally adopt their identity as his own.

Psychoanalytically speaking, such conflicts between "good and evil" represent the battle between the id's asocial tendencies and those of the diametrically opposed superego. Such battles—either dramatized by two groups of children warring against each other, or acted out by one or more children manipulating toy soldiers—permit some discharge of aggression either actually or symbolically, through conflict. Only after such discharge of anger or violence can the forces of the superego gain ascendancy to control or outbalance those of the id; with that the ego becomes able to function again.

As we watch the progress of aggressive activity in our child, we can gradually discern a developmental move from free play, which permits direct id expression and satisfaction (the unstructured free-for-all shooting match, in which aggression is freely discharged), to a more structured game setting in which not mere discharge of aggression but a higher integration—the ascendancy of good over evil—is the goal. So *we* destroy *them*, the Greeks defeat the knavish Trojan wrongdoers, the Christian knights destroy the infidels, the cops corner the robbers, the cowboys crush the savage Indians.

As objective adults we may know that the Trojan culture was perhaps superior to that of the bronze-age Greeks, or that the case of the Indian was at least as good as that of the cowboy. But such objectivity is the end product of a protracted intellectual and moral struggle, a long process of cleansing, tempering, and refining the emotions. For the child such objectivity cannot be quickly or easily attained, because emotions, not intellect, are in control during the early years. Our children *want* to believe that good wins out and they *need* to believe it for their own well-being, so that they can turn into good people. It serves their developing humanity to repeat the eternal conflict of good and evil in a primitive form understandable to them, and to see that good triumphs in the end.

When play and game have firmly established the ascendancy of good in the child's mind, so that the outcome of the fight is no longer at issue, he can turn to other humanitarian refinements of the original war game. Then the issue expands: it is no longer merely a case of order against chaos, of good versus evil, but of sublimation of violent emotions.

At this point, it is no longer the problem of whether the knight will win out over the infidel (of course he will), but whether he will be able to do so with elegance according to the protocols of the ring, or of knightly virtue. The problem posed and solved by the game is determining not merely which is the stronger—id or superego, my primitive I or my socialized I—but whether the ego can assure the victory of the superego in ways that enhance self-respect in the process. Not only must good triumph over evil, but it must do so in a fashion demonstrating the value of our higher humanity. The knight errant not only slays the monster, but does so to free the captive maiden. Good has prevailed, but it has prevailed for a purpose, gaining erotic (id) satisfaction as part of the bargain. Thus ego and superego combine to promise the id a reward if it does their bidding. Serving the good becomes reinforced by the motivating force of a higher purpose.

When a child acts out this understanding, he begins to appreciate a lesson which cannot be taught to him convincingly in a purely didactic fashion: that to fight evil is not enough; one must do so in honor of a higher cause and with knightly valor—that is, according to the rules of the game, the highest of which then has become to act with virtue. This, in turn, will promote self-esteem, a potent spur to further integrate id, ego, and superego—that is, to become more civilized.

PART THREE

Family, Child, Community

23

Ideal and Reality

Nobody's family can hang out the sign "Nothing the matter here."

—Chinese proverb

WHATEVER THE LEGAL DEFINITION of a family may be, common usage agrees with *Webster's New World Dictionary* that it is "a social unit consisting of parents and the children they rear." If a husband and wife have no children, they are a married couple, but hardly constitute a family. We recognize this fact when we say of a couple's first pregnancy, "They are starting a family." Because each member of a family carries a different mix of genes, and since the natural endowment with which we are born is immutable, and since also each person has a different history, despite the members' many common experiences, the social unit formed by every family is made up of quite different components. Contrary to Tolstoy's assertion, by no means are all happy families alike. It is this diversity that makes their functioning as a social unit difficult. A great deal depends on how sensitively parents can adjust themselves and their child-rearing efforts to the specific endowments of their children, to their personality differences, and to their different life experiences. For example, it makes an enormous difference to the child whether his parents can truly accept that their child is physically much stronger—or much weaker—than the parent; or that one child is intellectually very quick and another quite slow. If they do, they will modify their behavior accordingly. The happiest family is the one in which each member, given his age and level of maturity, acts with consideration and respect for the unique and individual nature of every other member.

The family in a psychological sense is formed by the interactions of all its members, their feelings for one another, and the way these are integrated into daily life. Since books on child-rearing (such as this one) address themselves to parents and not to children, the emphasis is placed on the way the parents think and feel and react to their children. But such emphasis usually neglects the great impact that children—especially first children—have on the development of their parents, and this effect extends to their roles both as parents and as individuals who are married. Because a family is a *social unit*, all its members influence one another mutually.

The arrival of the first child is a watershed, even for those who are responsive to what becoming parents implies. The change is often much greater than they anticipated or at first realized. Quite a few modern parents initially try to go on about their lives just as before, but they soon become aware of how their days are altered. These new external arrangements mirror more important internal changes in new parents, deep-seated and far-reaching modifications in their views of themselves and of their purposes in life. So from the very beginning, a child exercises a significant and formative influence on his parents, and therefore on the entire family. At first he does this passively, simply by his arrival and presence, but soon he does so also through his actions, through the way he responds to what his parents do to and with him.

During the child's early life, his parents determine what goes on within the family; they make all decisions, whether these are consciously determined or manifestations of their unconscious. Their thinking, particularly in regard to family life, is strongly influenced by their feelings for their child and about themselves as actual parents. Their ideas and the feelings they experienced before the child's arrival are usually based on fantasies both happy and anxious. It is a rare exception when an event like the birth of the first child conforms to the fantasies which have been woven around it before his arrival. Such fantasies have their origins in the parent's own childhood; thus they have little to do with present-day reality and a great deal with how the parent wanted his parents to behave toward him. Having a baby and taking care of him revives our memories of infantile experiences and feelings long buried in the unconscious, and the parent is forced to deal with these anew, but in a very different form—as different as unexamined fantasies are from reality. Many an individual, before he becomes a parent, indulges in fantasies of how wonderful he will be, how he and his child will have only marvelous times together, how nothing will ever interfere with their happiness together. Even if we admitted to reasonable doubt about our ability to make this come true, it would not reduce our wish that things should turn out this way.

Reality gives the lie to such illusions without entirely eradicating them. When we are forced to realize that we are not all that much different from our parents, or better parents than they were—despite our vows and good intentions—we are usually shocked and dismayed. Such a realization is not easy to cope with. We are torn between the wish to live up to our idealized fantasies about how we "should" act and the reality of how we do act as parents; the two are often quite different.

The situation is not made any easier by the fact that contradictory hopes or values coexist peacefully beside each other in these fantasies. This was the case with one brilliant woman, a professor of human development, who, from as early as she could remember, had been convinced that she would be such a wonderful mother that her child would immediately and permanently recognize this and feel nothing but happy love for her. At the same time she had also been certain, probably since early adolescence, that her child would have a forceful, unique personality and a strong mind "of her or his own."

All these wishful fantasies of perfect family bliss had become strongly activated during her first pregnancy. When her newborn daughter was put into her arms, she lovingly put her to her breast, expecting the baby to snuggle up happily and begin to nurse. Instead, to her great disappointment the baby started to struggle against her, trying to wriggle out of her arms, clearly uncomfortable. In an immediate and spontaneous reaction this mother, who used to be very candid with herself, thought to herself as she held her baby for the first time in her arms: "This is not what I bargained for!"

Fortunately for herself and her baby, this woman soon thought the situation over carefully: "Here I always wanted a child who would have a mind of her own, do things her own way, and be a unique person; but now when my baby from her very birth shows that she does things her own way, which is not necessarily my way, I'm disappointed." Acknowledging this paradox, she could then gladly accept that her daughter would grow into her own person, someone who would not entirely conform to her mother's wishes, especially when those wishes were incompatible with her own. This mother wisely permitted her wish for an independent daughter to win out over the fantasy of perfect maternal and infantile bliss with nary a struggle; and as the infant grew into a person quite different from her mother, they were happy with each other in their own ways. Personally and professionally the mother found her very first experience as a mother so typical, amusing, and instructive that she later used it in her teaching.

It is by no means all that rare that a mother harbors similar contradictory fantasies when anticipating her child. So it is also common that there are many more mothers who, particularly when they see their first child for the first time, are quite taken aback that he is not a replica of themselves, but is already at birth a completely different individual, in many ways a stranger.

Most mothers are soon delighted by how beautiful their baby is, happy that he is healthy and well formed; unfortunately there are others who are disappointed that he does not conform to their ideas of infantile perfection, and this original disappointment can unhappily cast a shadow on the parent's relation to his child.

Every child is received into the world by parents with a variety of feelings, some often very complex, about him. Those of his mother can be particularly fateful. In the fairy tale "Sleeping Beauty," many wise women (or fairies), delighted to be invited to the christening, bestowed on the little princess their magic wishes for beauty, happiness, and all good things in life. But the christening was attended by an uninvited guest, an evil woman or fairy whose destructive wish threatened to destroy the life of the infant at an early age. In all the various versions of this fairy tale, these figures who decide the child's future are females; this fact symbolizes the ancient wisdom that the fate of the child is largely determined by mother figures, i.e., by the child's own mother.

What "Sleeping Beauty" tells, in fairy-tale fashion, in symbolic form, is only too true. Every child is received into this world by many spirits, good or bad. Unluckily, some few children are haunted from birth onward by some of these bad spirits, but the good spirits—the parents' happiness at having this child, their love and tender care for him—prevail most of the time. Of these good spirits parents are quite aware, even though they usually do not know how these spirits came to inhabit them, but they are at any rate able to shower the infant with all the good things life can offer. Both the good and the evil spirits come from the parents' past. Unfortunately, parents suppress any knowledge of the existence of the latter, which makes it impossible to cope with them, to neutralize them, so that the child will not have to suffer their destructive impact.

These "spirits" are the residues of the parents' own childhood, and because of the parent's influence on his child, they determine what the infant's life will be like. The decisive quality of these spirits—the spirit in which the child is treated by his parents—is not so much whether or not the parent's own childhood was happy or unhappy, although it is much easier for a parent's good spirits to originate in a happy childhood. The saving grace here is that even when a parent had an unhappy childhood himself, if he is able to be aware of it and cope with the feelings it created in him, he then wishes to protect his child from a similar fate and will do his best not to permit the impact of his childhood deprivations to interfere with the happiness of his child. He might overdo certain things to compensate belatedly and vicariously for what he had to suffer, but this is all and need not be harmful. To give his child a happy life may be a little harder for such a parent, but he may nevertheless strive to do it. The parent who had a happy childhood and remembers it with pleasure will have an easier time arranging for a parallel childhood for his children. However, in either case all will be well.

Things can easily go wrong with those parents who are either not familiar with or entirely unaware of not their bad childhood experiences, which they may remember and even in detail, but of the feelings and reactions these cause. What they do not remember, what they have so deeply repressed that they remain completely unaware of them, are their own childhood feelings of anger and dejection. These form the "evil spirit," which is destructive because it mars their relations to their children. Since they are not cognizant of these feelings and have completely alienated themselves from them, these emotions remain encapsuled in their unconscious and act there like an evil incubus which makes parents do things which they would never do if they could just be aware of their own feelings. Even when such a parent wishes to reach out to his child, something stops him and turns the intended positive move into a negative one, and he does not know why and how. The long-repressed anger and despondency of his childhood interfere with his ability to form a positive relation to his child, because these ancient repressed feelings interpose themselves without his knowing it or being able to control it. He wants to be a good parent but cannot, which utterly frustrates him. This frustration is often blamed on the child, which makes matters worse.

When it becomes possible for such a parent to recall and reexperience in his mind these repressed childhood agonies, he is nearly always able to lay these ancient evil ghosts to rest and begin to relate in good ways to his child; this good relation finally helps him overcome the evil residues of his destructive childhood experiences, which then no longer are able to exercise their destructive influence on his relation to his child. Thus if all goes well, having a child can compensate for the parent's own bad childhood, but only after he is able not only to recall what was objectively bad in his childhood, but also to overcome his angry, desperate reactions to it.

For example, a mother who remembers how unhappy she was that as a child she had no toys to play with, that nobody played with her, and how terrible she felt about it—how she resented her parents for not giving her toys or being interested in playing with her—is the one who is most likely to be delighted to see her infant happily playing with toys and will greatly enjoy playing with her child. By vicariously participating in her child's pleasure in playing with toys, and by directly enjoying playing with her child, she will in this manner make up, to a considerable degree, for her own earlier unhappiness. Remembered deprivations and remembered feelings about them can thus become good spirits wishing the child well and taking pleasure in his happiness.

Quite a contrast is provided by a mother who remembers her childhood as deprived but does so in a distant manner, in a matter-of-fact way, because she has repressed her feelings of unhappiness and anger. This mother unconsciously fears that her child's happy play would arouse her repressed feelings of unhappiness and anger, to the degree that they can no longer remain repressed but break out into the open, with possibly devastating consequences. So to keep the repression going, she may either see to it that her child is not too happy and thus does not rouse jealousy in her, or she may distance herself emotionally from her child, so that what he does will not make so strong an impact on her that it would break down her repressions. Thus it is the *not-remembered* ghost of one's own unhappy childhood which can become the source of the evil spirit which will spread gloom in the nursery such a mother creates for her infant. The reason is that not being cognizant of what her true feelings then had been, she must for entirely unconscious reasons avoid being confronted with her child's happy feelings, because these would arouse in her emotions that she is completely unable to cope with; so she shies away from having feeling contacts with her child.

In those relatively rare cases in which it was possible to bring such a mother in touch with the angry and depressed feelings she had experienced as a child, it then was as if an evil curse of nonfeeling had been removed, and she became able to enjoy her child's happiness and permit it to make up in some measure for her own misery, which she now could remember not only as a fact, but also as a feeling. What had been missing was a feeling response to her child; the mother had to remain indifferent to her child as long as she had to remain indifferent to what had been her own childhood feelings, from which she had completely alienated herself because otherwise they would have overwhelmed her with their depressive quality. Lucky is the child and the parent if the parent, through his relation to his child, can disinter the evil ghosts of his past and lay them to rest as he gives his child the happy childhood he himself craved but never had.

There are countless child-rearing experiences that unexpectedly activate in us the remnants of our own childhood experiences, many of them partially forgotten and repressed. Thus when considering methods by which to toilet-train a child, few mothers are aware that doing so will reactivate forgotten but unresolved conflicts which they had when being toilet-trained. Similarly, cleaning up a baby after he has soiled his diapers cannot help but activate some of one's reactions to elimination and being cleaned up, whether or not one is at all aware that this memory has been aroused.

Whether or not they show it, all children resent being toilet-trained, are angry about it. Those parents who are able to remember any part of their own childhood anger about it will have sympathy with their children when they are being toilet-trained and be able to accept their resistance gently and with good humor, and things will go rather easily. The parent who has repressed his resentment at being toilet-trained will respond with annoyance (if not outright anger) to his child's angry resistance to toilet-training because the child's anger threatens to undo the parent's repression of his own childhood feelings; this is unconsciously experienced as danger, and consciously as annoyance at the child's resistance. With such feelings, toilet-training the child will be difficult for both parent and child.

Being a parent thus subjects one to the reliving—partly consciously but largely unconsciously—of many of one's own childhood experiences and problems and tempts one to try to solve these by doing things in certain ways with one's child. This can be one of the blessings of parenthood, but also the source of many problems! The less we are aware that this is going on in us while we care for our baby, the more we are apt to act out ancient unresolved problems in our relationship to our child. Actually, this challenge is inherent in being a parent—having to deal in some fashion on a conscious and much more on an unconscious level with one's own childhood experiences—and is what makes family life distinct from all other human experiences. The mere presence of the child and the necessity of taking care of him force the parents to deal with these issues; thus living with a child involves much more than reality-testing against one's fantasies of how good a parent one might be, how wonderful or troublesome one's child will be, or what kind of a parent one's mate will be. Most important of all, parenting makes it necessary to measure one's fantasies about what a family can and should be against the everyday reality of family living.

As soon as the first baby arrives, one's spouse is no longer seen and experienced only or mainly as one's mate, but simultaneously also as the parent of one's child. It would be tedious to enumerate in detail how this extends to all daily activities within the family, and it is hardly necessary, since many of these changes are obvious. One example is the husband's experience of seeing his wife also as a mother who feeds their child, or who leaves the marital bed to take care of the crying infant; this cannot help arousing new and different feelings in him. The wife's loving care for the infant can evoke stronger and different feelings of tenderness for her; or it may do the opposite and arouse feelings of resentment toward her, even jealousy. Here again, it matters a great deal whether such feelings are permitted to come to awareness or whether they are repressed; or if they are acted out, whether one or both spouses are conscious of what is going on (which is rare), or whether a father is more or less unconscious that he is acting out, and why. And it makes a great difference whether these feelings are directed toward wife or child.

All this, combined with inner developments from reactivation of their infantile and childhood experiences, causes major changes in the personalities of the parents, usually without their being aware of them. Whether they resist or embrace these developments within themselves and their mates or, as is most frequent and natural, resist some of them and embrace others, new adjustments are started in their personalities and in their relations to each other. These developments may take years to be completed, recognized, accepted. Much depends, for child and parents alike, on whether the changes are experienced by the parents as essentially an enrichment of their lives so great that the sacrifices required recede into insignificance, or whether the new situation demands of them to give up something that is experienced as a major loss, despite the pleasure derived from having become a parent.

Many years may elapse before a child begins to wonder consciously what becoming and being a parent may have meant to each of his parents, and he may never really do so. Most of us simply take our parents for granted. But practically from birth on, the child's feeling of self-importance and emotional well-being depends upon his parents' conviction that the enrichment coming from being the parent of this child radically compensates for whatever they may have given up to become parents. Infancy is the narcissistic stage of development, when the infant believes that the world is there only to serve him. Because of this, it may be objected that every infant is convinced of his self-importance. This is true enough, but it is of greatest impact on the infant whether such narcissistic feelings are given the lie by parental reality or are supported by it in the sense that his parents feel positive about parenting.

With the single exception of the child's natural endowment, nothing shapes a child's personality more than the experience of family living—the feelings it arouses and the attitudes it inculcates. His views of himself are likewise influenced, as are his relations to others and his expectations of the wider world. What he observes about the way family members, particularly his parents, live with each other and how he interprets these observations determine whether in his life he will successfully seek intimacy with others, or be afraid of doing so. If his parents—despite occasional irritations with each other, and the real difficulties that are part of everybody's life—are essentially well satisfied with their marriage, their contentment will form the firm basis for a deeply satisfying relation to their child, who is experienced by them as a symbol of their union. As his parents rejoice together in his well-being, or share their worries about it, the child becomes convinced of his importance and great value to them; on this basis, he develops his convictions about his own value as a person.

On the other hand, if parents are unhappy with each other, although they may try to keep their dissatisfaction hidden, it will cast a shadow on their relations with their child. Even when one or both of the parents deeply love the child and try to protect him against being drawn into their conflicts, he will nevertheless suffer from their unhappiness. If they seek to find compensation for what is missing in their marriage through their relation to their child, this will benefit nobody. In such situations, a parent may wish to gain too much or the wrong kind of satisfactions from the child, which either makes too heavy a demand on him or leads to an unhealthy relationship between parent and child. One familiar example of this is the parent who is disappointed with some aspect of his life, such as its economic conditions or his social status, and who wishes and pushes his child to do better. Understandable as such desires are, they lay a heavy burden on the child, who must then pursue his parent's goals rather than determine his own.

One of the unfortunate contradictions of life is that a parent who misses companionship and love in his marriage and seeks compensating satisfaction from his child will actually find less there than the parent who is well pleased with his marriage. No child of any age can provide mature love or adult companionship to a parent, and if (consciously or much more likely unconsciously) a parent makes these inappropriate demands, the child will be vastly confused and hampered in his efforts to offer his own childish love to his parents. Further, feeling rightly that more is wished for than he can possibly render, the child will resent his parents' demand, and this will interfere with their mutual attachment.

A parent cannot also be his child's friend, as much as some parents today wish for it. Friendship requires a different type of relationship than does parenting. When a parent hopes that his child will become a close friend, the result is a relationship based on relative immaturity. The parent is seeking friendship from a person who is immature when compared to him; the child is led to seek friendship from a person who is poorly suited to offer it in a satisfactory manner, because of the constellation of parent-child emotional experiences that have taken place during the child's formative years.

Even under the best of conditions, the only place in a parent's life which a child can fill well, and be happy in doing so, is that of a child. He cannot, in addition, make up for something that may be lacking in the life of the parent, no matter how fervently the parent may desire it. Further, all a parent can be to his child is exactly that: a tender and concerned parent; that is, a mature person who lovingly and caringly accepts the child's immaturities, protects him against feeling bad about them, and also guards against their having any evil consequences, while at the same time providing the child with examples of maturity that will guide him in the course of his own growth.

REALITY VERSUS THE MYTHS

The human family evolved to provide sustenance for all of its members and to afford them protection, first against the adversities of nature and ferocious animals, and later also against the dangers originating within the wider setting of society. Security provided by parents permitted a prolonged period of childhood during which the young human did not need to take care of himself. During this time he learned from his parents what he needed to know and do in order to mature into a self-reliant, self-supporting, and finally family-supporting adult. Whatever the family offered in the way of love and affection was merely a consequence of this basic social unit working together to survive and raise their young.

While parents today still have to provide for their children's physical well-being, this obligation has now receded in importance so far as the cohesion of the family is concerned. In part, this is because since World War II, American society has accepted the obligation (at least in theory) of aiding children whose parents fail to provide for them. With greater affluence, middle-class parents have fewer worries about whether they will be able to feed and clothe their children, and if the children are in good health, there is little fear for their lives. These paramount anxieties have been replaced by worry about children's psychological and emotional well-being; parental anxieties center around drug use, delinquency, sexual aberrations, and academic and social failures. With this major shift of concerns, the predominant feeling is that the tie that binds the family is no longer dire necessity, but emotional satisfaction. What was once the mere by-product of a social process assuring survival has taken on paramount importance in the minds of parents, who tend to see their main function as providing for the psychological well-being of the family. This has had the most far-reaching consequences for family life.

One consequence of this radical shift in major parental concerns is that now when emotional problems arise within the family, husband and wife have a tendency to blame either themselves, or each other, or the children for the difficulties, as if problems could always be avoided. Instead, we must realize that many difficulties are inherent in the conditions created by family life in our time, just because it is based less on survival and more on emotional support. The erroneous modern conviction is that problems should not occur, and that someone has to be at fault when they do; this causes untold misery within the family unit, aggravating the original difficulty and sometimes even putting the validity of marriage and family into question.

It is an ancient wisdom that "misery loves company," because we expect that in sharing our difficulties we can find relief. But the one whom we believe to be the cause of our misery cannot also serve as our confidant and companion. A family whose members blame each other for the hardships they have to endure will not be a source of support and consolation. Yet the conviction that members of one's family will provide this companionship in misery is what makes for a happy family. In such a family the members feel that whatever may happen, they will find the emotional support they need. But if one is convinced that there should never occur difficulties within the family, and that their occurrence is one individual's fault, this hypercritical attitude will destroy the family's inherent support structure. In some ways, life was easier when people believed that hardships were the will of God— to be endured, not questioned—and thus the family members pulled together in times of trouble.

An ancient Chinese proverb says that no family can hang out the sign "Nothing the matter here." This reflects the reality that family living inescapably creates its own difficulties. Some are attributable to the particular personalities of the family members, and to the ways in which they behave toward each other; other troubles are but the consequence of their living under one roof. Many familiar problems are inescapable, such as the conflicts which arise from a child's simultaneous craving for unlimited gratification and independence, or from each parent's wish to have some life of his own while also living up to the many demands placed on him by family obligations. A better understanding of what expectations are reasonable and what unreasonable in marriage and family life can greatly alleviate these difficulties; it can prevent us from placing blame where it does not belong, such as on oneself or other family members, and it may help to free family members from feeling disappointed when someone doesn't live up to unrealistic fantasies about how things could or ought to be.

The pattern for these exaggerated expectations of unlimited and continuous satisfactions from family life is formed in infancy and childhood, when no realistic comprehension of what is actually possible interfered with the belief that all of our wishes could be satisfied. While later acquaintance with harsh reality modifies some of these childish expectations, it is amazing how many of them remain active, at least in the subconscious; this explains why many deep dissatisfactions hold sway where a realistic analysis would show that none are justified.

The myth of the "good old times," of a golden age, or of paradise, which can be found in so many cultures, is still pervasive in our society, and continues to be persuasive when even the simplest reflection would show that life was much harder for parents and child alike in every bygone era than it is today. The naive belief in a golden age marks the beginning of every person's life, as the infant expects that all his needs will be satisfied effortlessly and without question. Of course, the infant must indeed be given a great deal to assure his survival and not be expected to give anything in return. Thus, since there does seem to have been such a golden age in each of our lives, it is understandable that at some deep level, we believe in the myth of a golden age and also harbor hopes that it will occur again. Further, since as infants we experienced within our family what appears in retrospect to have been a problem-free existence, we subconsciously believe that we can reproduce such a utopia with our present family. This very common, haunting childish desire is of course not consciously recognized by most parents, but it persists in some degree in the parents' unconscious; the same expectation exists in a larger degree in the children's conscious and unconscious minds, and it interferes with their finding true satisfaction in the reality of family life. Today's widespread tendency to seek ultimate satisfaction in recreational activities rather than in more serious and responsible adult pursuits is but one expression of this feeling that only childish pleasures are truly worth having.

Another aspect of this myth is the notion that in ages past, family life was much more satisfying than it is today. In this imaginary and nebulous past the family is supposed to have smoothly provided the gratification of all the emotional and other psychological needs for all of its members. Since this is supposed to have been the norm until only quite recently, it seems obvious that something must have gone very wrong for today's families, including one's own.

All the terrible hardships which our ancestors suffered throughout recorded history are conveniently forgotten in the face of this myth, because they would give the lie to it. The dreadful rigors which characterized life for so long are overlooked because we are no longer subjected to them. We also forget that in most cases, the family's greatest psychological satisfaction came from the fact that only through the members' working together and helping one another was the family able to make a go of things. And we further disregard the short life span, less than half of ours, of even that small minority of our ancestors who survived into adulthood. Even in civilized countries, life was lived under the specter of omnipresent dangers: frequent epidemics, for which there were no medicines as protection or remedy; recurrent famines, which killed vast numbers of people outright and left the survivors so weak in health that many succumbed to the next hardship; and also the deaths of women in childbed, and of many children at birth or in infancy.

Finally, there was an almost total absence of physical comfort and ease for most people; backbreaking labor was the common lot from childhood on. Little wonder that under these conditions, which we would consider unbearable, any small comforts the family members could provide for each other were highly valued; often they were the only positive thing life could offer to assuage slightly what to us would seem nearly uninterrupted, unmanageable distress.

During the last few generations, technological, social, medical, and scientific progress have done away with many of the causes of suffering which mankind bore throughout history, so these ancient agonies are no longer of concern to us, so much so that we pay hardly any attention to how easy life has become by comparison. Instead, we now concentrate our full attention on the psychological problems that have replaced in our minds the physical hardships of which our lives have been freed. And these elusive emotional and psychological problems seem to us as intractable and as troublesome to our hope for the good life as were the tangible physical and social hardships in the past. Yet there is one very important difference: although in the past hardships were considered the inescapable condition of life and *not* the fault of family members, these new problems are considered both avoidable and attributable, so we blame either family members or ourselves for them. Thus we have turned against the unit that has nurtured and protected us, and against ourselves as well, through guilt.

This is not to suggest that we ought to count our blessings and be happy that the problems which beset our ancestors, and threatened their very existence, are not those from which we suffer today. Such a notion, while it may contain more than a kernel of truth, hardly ever persuades anybody to change his mind. But the fantasy that family living was much more satisfying in the past, and that it should be that way now, is contrary to the facts. What is much more serious, this myth makes us unreasonably dissatisfied with the present. I do not propose that we ought to take lightly the psychological problems which now loom large in our experience of family living; however, we could try to view these within a more reasonable perspective.

Since the unity of the American family, if not in large measure its *raison d'être*, now rests on the emotional ties of its members to one another, they make much greater emotional demands of one another; they also have much higher psychological expectations of the satisfactions with which family living ought to provide them. It is these much greater, while at the same time much less tangible, demands and expectations that make family relations so precarious and thus cause some of our most severe difficulties. If we accept this fact with a clear realization of how it came about and what is involved in it, we may go a long way toward finding the right solutions to these problems, or at least become more tolerant of them and make their impact less disruptive.

24

The Ties That Bind

The silver link, the silken tie,
Which heart to heart, and mind to mind,
In body and in soul can bind.

—SIR WALTER SCOTT

IN ORDER TO FEEL CONFIDENT that we are doing a reasonably good job as parents it may be helpful to consider what gave sustenance to the family in the past and what has changed in this respect. Barely two hundred years ago the average life span in the Western world was some thirty years; in the rest of the world it was, and in many places still is, much shorter. The average time a married couple lived together was seventeen years, for the simple reason that, in most cases, either the wife or the husband had died. Today, even with all the separations and divorces, the average marriage lasts longer, which also gives more opportunity for occasional serious trouble. Further, in the past, economic necessity and religious constraints against separation often induced a couple to make a go of their marriage despite their incompatibilities; convinced that they had to manage somehow because divorce was unthinkable, they did. Today, divorce offers a fairly easy way to stop living together, and society accepts it.

But this is by no means all. With a much longer life span, married couples today have many years left after the children are grown up. Thus in many cases the need to take care of the children and the desire not to be separated from them no longer militate against divorce. In fact, quite a few of the couples who split up today have already lived together for as many years as people did in the past before one of them died.

We know that divorce often disrupts family life and severely interferes with the good relations between parents and children. Whatever the legal arrangements, the child suffers from being forced to divide his loyalties, and cannot help wondering what is wrong with his parents that they could not live well together; in addition he often feels deprived because one parent chose not to live with him. With increasing affluence, and the fact that both men and women can achieve independence and support themselves and their children, life is easier for all of us. Among many other amenities, this permits us to provide our children with many more years of learning, and has also opened up vast new opportunities for making choices, many of which are very difficult.

Since the biggest events in an individual's life used to take place in the home and were celebrated there with one's family, these events tied one symbolically and in one's deepest feelings to the family. This was so much so that in one's feelings, home and family were practically identical. Few of us have experienced the security and stability that accrued from living one's entire life in the house where several generations of one's ancestors had done the same. Although to some this was a hardship, the inner security and the stability experienced in such childhoods made it possible to bear up well under the burden of ancestry. Today, only a small fortunate minority spend their entire childhood and growing-up years in the same house; most people experience several relocations, each of which is disruptive to some degree.

In my family, I was the last child to be born at home; my mother was comforted and helped in her labor by a midwife, as she had been earlier during the birth of my older sister. After me, so far as I know, all children born to members of my family saw the light of day in hospitals. My paternal grandparents were the last members of my family who died at home in their beds, surrounded by all their children. My other relatives died either in hospitals or at home, but neither their children nor their grandchildren were present; the family assembled after they had died for their funerals. Thus the emphasis has shifted from the rite of passage in which the death of a loved one is actually witnessed to the comforting of survivors.

Traditionally, in many of the old countries, funerals were elaborate ceremonial events, even in families that could ill afford the often considerable expenses. The body of the dead person was not embalmed and displayed in a funeral home, but laid out and visited in the best room of his home, which was appropriately decorated in black (as was the entrance, if not also the rest of the house). After the visiting, the body was escorted by an elaborate cortege of family and friends to a place of worship, in anticipation of the actual burial at the cemetery. After the interment, a traditional period of mourning began, during which members of the immediate family wore mourning attire for many months. For days after the funeral, members of the extended family visited to console the bereaved—the family thus showing its support in times of need, the home being the place where it was received. The Irish custom of the wake and the Jewish custom of sitting shiva are traditional examples of effective ways in which those who are most immediately affected by a loss are helped to bear their sorrow by the wider circle of family and friends.

Birth and death were not the only events that highlighted the central value of home and family when I was a child. For example, the birthdays of my paternal grandmother were celebrated in her home by a pageant prepared weeks ahead, in which her many grandchildren performed for her and the assembled family; taking part in one of these pageants is one of my earliest memories. In fact, until quite recently, *all* the big occasions of every person's life—birth, marriage, celebrations, death—took place within the confines of the home and the womb of the family. The feeling was that one came into being as part of a family and experienced the main events of life within it; and as one left life, one did so in one's home, surrounded, attended, and comforted by those who would carry on where one had to leave off.

This was true in the past when living conditions forced members of the average family to spend most of their days in close physical proximity, perhaps even in a single room or, at best, in just a few rooms of a small house. In addition, family members often worked together during the day at the closely related activities of a family farm or shop. They had to rely on each other in sickness, but also in health; in good times and in bad times. True, sometimes they fought with one another, but they also depended on one another for information and entertainment. There were fewer opportunities and temptations to seek satisfaction outside of the family. Nearly all of life unfolded within a much narrower sphere, centered on the home or the church, which the family also attended together.

Today, when the great value of the family for its individual members is essentially based on providing psychological satisfactions rather than on the fulfillment of basic physical needs, it is regrettable that many experiences which gave deeper meaning to life are no longer shared by the family. For example, in former times religion tied family members to each other as they took part as a family in religious events, such as regular visits to the church and in its festivities. This is still true for some families, or among confessing Mormons and Mennonites, for example. This gave stability to the family and security to the believers. But now, for many people church attendance and the symbolic expressions of life's major events—the family celebrations—have been much reduced in importance and often removed from the home. To balance this, parents today can emphasize the symbolic meaning of family events such as birthdays and other special occasions, so that these events will give their child the feeling of security which the family, and only the family, can provide.

Our children are much healthier and mature much earlier than those several generations ago; through early inoculations and medical care, most debilitating childhood diseases have been eliminated or controlled and reduced in their impact. As a small child, for example, I had dysentery, scarlet fever, diphtheria, measles, mumps, and other ailments, not to mention several bouts of influenza and tonsillitis, which kept me in bed for many weeks at a time. With preventive inoculations and the availability of sulfa drugs and antibiotics, all this has changed.

Despite my many serious and prolonged illnesses as a child, I never spent a day in a hospital; I was treated at home by the physician, as were all other members of my family. Visits to the doctor's office became customary only after World War I. Few things can highlight better how things have changed than the fact that at the beginning of his practice, Freud made regular house calls. Today good medical care requires visits to the doctor's office and, if necessary, spending time in hospitals; these have become the place of treatment for many ailments which used to be taken care of in the home. Thus, the home has lost some of its function (and identity) as the best and most secure haven one can seek when faced with serious physical problems such as illness and childbirth.

In infancy, my ordinary daily care was entrusted to my nurse and later on to maids or governesses. But whenever I was sick, my mother attended to all my needs. She spent many hours caring for me and entertaining me, and she fed me all my meals. During the many nights when I was seriously ill, my mother sat at my bedside, sponging my feverish body and changing the cold compresses to give me relief. In moments like these I learned to understand and appreciate that a mother makes all the difference in the world when one is in need, in great pain, deeply worried, or even desperate.

Not for a moment do I suggest that we should relinquish any of the great advances in medical care made since my childhood, nor the advantages of hospital treatment (when indicated) over home care. Hospital care has to a great degree done away with childbirth complications, improved infants' health, vastly reduced birth injuries, and so forth; receiving hospital care in serious illness has prolonged and saved many lives. Modern medicine protects children from many of the serious childhood diseases which kept me in bed for such long periods of time. Still, I believe that there are few other occasions when children feel well cared for and realize how much a parent cares for them as when they are sick in bed, especially during the night.

This is true not only in sickness. As an infant, when I could not sleep, I was carried in my mother's—and sometimes my father's—arms until I fell asleep. Later if I woke up terrified by a nightmare, one of my parents came and sat on my bed, talked and played with me, comforted and reassured me, read me a story. To the best of my knowledge, these were the times when my parents and I formed the close ties to each other that later in life sustained us. My parents knew, perhaps from their own childhood experiences, that for children to have nightmares is nothing unusual, although at that time the reasons children have nightmares and their universal occurrence at certain ages had not yet been elucidated by psychoanalysts. Even today, when all this is widely known, for some reason many parents believe that a child should *not* have nightmares. And if he has difficulty falling asleep, all too many parents—often on the advice of their pediatricians (sometimes because they fall in with parental wishes, or because it seems the simplest solution)—rely on tranquilizing drugs to quiet the child, rather than on the security their presence provides, or the comfort that stories and warm drinks can offer. Drugs work, but using them in this way teaches the child at an early age to rely on drugs for comfort, rather than seeking comfort through satisfying human relations. Little wonder that as adolescents many youngsters rely on drugs to quiet their anxieties, as had been true in their infancy. At that point it is no use to preach about the dangers of drugs, because from their experiences as infants, they carry embedded deep in their unconscious the knowledge that drugs are the simplest way to gain relief. Such modern shortcuts, while convenient and less demanding of the parents' time, deprive a child of receiving human comfort in a situation when he most needs and desires it. Also, it deprives the parents of experiencing how desperately their child needs them, and of receiving gratitude when the child appreciates their care. There is great satisfaction for parents in the realization that because of their efforts, their child feels safe, where he did not before; that thanks to them, their child sleeps well and feels at peace with the world. It is this reciprocal experience of parent and child that makes them both feel so much better, that becomes a strong tie binding them together.

BREAST-FEEDING: A PRIMAL LINK TO HUMAN CLOSENESS

Breast-feeding ties mother and child together in an intimate bond that is at once physical and emotional. Perhaps a personal experience will illustrate. I was breast-fed well into my third year, but not by my mother—she was much too much the Victorian lady for such a role. However, she was deeply concerned about the well-being of her children and took great care to select wet nurses for us who were happy to meet all our physical and emotional needs. Even though I did not receive from my mother those bodily satisfactions which go with being nursed from the breast, the attention I got was sufficient. My nurse while she lived with us was very much part of the family, and therefore my relation to her tied me closely to my home and the security it stood for, as represented by my nurse and her good care. The respect my nurse had for my parents and her happiness at being part of our home (it was very important to my parents that she should be healthy and happy, so that she would have plenty of good milk, and enjoy taking care of me, so she received excellent care) were important elements in convincing me how lucky I was that this was my home.

Speaking in retrospect, I was probably also impressed that my parents had chosen to give me a person who was entirely devoted to my care, and who had no other tasks to detract her from concentrating entirely on me. By custom at that time a wet nurse had no other obligations than to take care of the infant; all housework was done by a live-in maid and a cook, and the nurse devoted herself entirely to me. On the other hand, if my mother had nursed me, she would have had to continue to meet her other social obligations and hence would not have been able to devote all her time only to my care, as did my nurse. Also by custom, a wet nurse who had done well by the infant was provided at the end of the nursing period with a generous dowry in addition to the small salary she had received, which would permit her to get married and go back to her own life, which very frequently included providing a home for the infant she had left behind in her village when she went to the city to seek employment as a wet nurse. Thus she had a great personal stake in my well-being. Needless to say, even after my nurse had left our home and had married, she remained for many years an important person in my life. Nevertheless, I have sometimes thought that I would have liked it even better if my mother had nursed me.

Breast-feeding is the archetypal example of what ties us simultaneously to another person and to life itself. Until relatively recently, when bottle-feeding became safe through modern hygiene and the pasteurization of milk, breast-feeding was the only way to nourish a baby and keep it alive and growing; there is, of course, the important additional advantage—even more important before inoculations—of transmitting to the infant some of the immunities and resistance to disease that the mother has acquired during her life. But breast-feeding does much more than simply assure the infant of the nourishment he needs: being fed is his central experience in life; it sheds its light on all his other experiences, which in turn derive much of their meaning from it. Being nursed is the nuclear event in the infant's existence which, when all goes well, serves as the firm basis on which the child's trust in himself, in the significant other persons in his life, and by extension in the world will be built. If things go badly for the infant as he is being fed—when it is an unpleasant, frustrating experience for him—then this experience of being fed in disappointing ways will be the seed of deep mistrust in himself and in the world. If the experience that should give the infant greatest satisfaction fails to do so, it can become the cause of severe disappointment and thus set the stage for general distrust and dissatisfaction.

What ties mother and child securely to each other in breast-feeding is the fact that in it each is getting and giving the other gratification of physical needs, relief from tension, and emotional satisfactions. In this interaction, both mother and child are at the same time active and passive; they are entirely themselves and serve themselves, but are also closely bound to and serve each other. The mother is active in offering her breast to her child, in holding him, in talking or making reassuring, encouraging noises and gestures to him, smiling at him; but she is passive in letting the infant nurse from her breast. The infant is active in rooting for the nipple, in sucking from it, in adjusting his body to the way his mother holds him, in looking and smiling, in taking in the image of his mother. He is passive in letting himself be held and cuddled. As he actively nurses, the infant satiates his hunger and thus gains relief of a pressing physical need, while the mother gains relief from the pressure of milk in her breast. The pleasure which each in this way provides for himself and the other is the bond "which heart to heart, and mind to mind, in body and in soul can bind," as the poet puts it.

After so much has been said in favor of breast-feeding, and since many mothers for one reason or another are unable to breast-feed their children, it should be stressed that bottle-feeding, when well done, can go a long way toward substituting for breast-feeding, and children who have been bottle-fed can do in life every bit as well as breast-fed children. The reason for this is that the basis for the child's trust in himself and the world is the mother's love for him; as she cherishes him, he learns to cherish himself, and her, and the world she represents to him. The messages the baby receives through being lovingly fed at just the right moment, with the right amount of food, which will last about the right length of time; his being held in a comfortable but secure manner, the pleasant contact between his skin and that of the mother—these in their combination and interaction convince the infant that he is well, and that all is right with the world. When the infant hears the regular heartbeat of his mother as he is held against her breast—as he did in her womb before he was born—this is a link between his pre- and postnatal existence; it gives him the feeling, vague and incoherent as it is, that his mother's heart continues to beat with and for him. All these elements which the infant is unable to sort out, or to perceive as such, form a universe of experience of the world that makes an indelible impact on his innermost feelings, and will strongly affect all later experiences.

For this to work and to work well, feeding must not be viewed by the mother as a time-limited, task-oriented activity whose main objective is to deliver (and for the infant to ingest) nutrition and which ends as soon as this purpose is achieved, as seems much too often the case among us. In many other countries, such as in Japan, skin-to-skin contact is prolonged well beyond the feeding experience; the infant is permitted to fall asleep on the mother's breast, with the nipple in his mouth, and his mother is pleased when he does so. All this is greatly facilitated when the infant shares a bed with his mother, or with both of his parents, as is true in many cultures.

The circumstances in which the infant is bottle-fed ought to approach the conditions just described as much as is possible and appropriate. For example, the flow from the bottle should not be too easy or too fast, because this deprives the infant of the experience of actively working at getting his nourishment. He works for his dinner, so to speak, and this is his first experience of getting something important through his own efforts. The infant should be held comfortably and securely to his mother's breast, whether he is being breast-fed or bottle-fed. There is no need to deprive the infant of the kinesthetic pleasures which feeling his skin against the warm skin of his mother give him, nor of his hearing his mother's heartbeat. When bottle-feeding was introduced in Japan, mothers typically bared the upper parts of their bodies and cradled the naked infants in their arms against their breasts as they gave them the bottle, exactly as they would have held him naked against their naked breast had they breast-fed him. What these mothers did instinctively, the modern American mother who bottle-feeds her child can do as well. She only needs to understand that her love for her baby is transmitted to him through closest bodily contact.

Since I mentioned Japan, I might add that there, as in some other cultures, important symbolic forms are used which give expression to the infant's close bonding to his mother. In one old and venerable custom, the mother of a newborn child is presented with a preserved portion of the umbilical cord which originally bound mother and infant to each other. Japanese mothers often kept the cords of all their children in an ornate box in an honored place in the home. In some regions when a child married, he was given his cord to take to the new home as a symbol of the continuing bond with the mother.

Today, as pointed out earlier, children are no longer tied to their family by dire necessity, nor to their home as the only secure haven in an alien world. All the old centripetal forces which closely bound the child to his family have been replaced by countless centrifugal forces, such as the tempting stimuli coming from the wider world—the importance of school (beginning at a very early age with day-care and nursery schools) and care by persons who are not part of the family, and the influence of the peer group. Now mainly emotional ties have to serve as anchors for the child to his family. Therefore it is particularly important that at a time when the wider world does not yet interfere with his experience, the infant be provided with contact of the most intimate physical and emotional sort from the persons who care most for him, so that the security gained in this way will counteract the alienating forces which are all too abundant in modern life, even within the family. Thus the right kind of feeding experiences and all other aspects of infant care such as diapering, bathing, and playing—always done with the right emotions—are needed to instill trust in the infant as well as a feeling of belonging, so that he will know that we belong to those who lovingly care for us, and that they belong to us. For our emotional well-being we need to feel that we belong, and that those to whom we belong *want* us to belong to them, and them to us. If we do not experience this, and at an early age, we feel lost, even amid plenty.

THE CREATION OF ADOLESCENCE

Better health and nutrition have given us greater longevity; we not only live much longer, but live much longer together as a family. This is a blessing, but it also makes greater demands on both parents and children, who now live with each other for many more years, which in itself creates certain new problems; and it continues long after the children have outgrown their childhood, which causes severe strains. Improvements in health have brought about greater physical strength in each new generation, as well as earlier physiological and sexual maturation; while affluence permits, and the increasing complexity of the modern technological world requires, a much longer period of learning and training for young people. Consequently, our children, although they mature much earlier than ever before, have to accept going to school for many more years than was once thought feasible. This, in turn, requires that they live for a much longer time in economic and to a large measure also social dependence on their parents. The strain affects parents and children alike: parents have to provide for their offspring long after they have outgrown childhood and have ceased feeling and acting as children, which had made supporting them relatively easy and much more rewarding emotionally. Having to support adolescents, who resent their dependence on their parents when they rightly feel quite grown-up, is psychologically much more demanding and troublesome.

Relations between parents and children are rarely beset by serious difficulties before the children reach adolescence. Some two centuries ago, and up to considerably more recent times, the average age of a child losing one of his parents through death was about fourteen—that is, at an age when modern children and parents usually begin to run into serious difficulties with each other. While the death of a parent created serious difficulties for the child, these were very different from those we and our adolescent children are apt to have with each other.

Actually, adolescence is neither a God-given stage of development, nor one that comes with our very nature—it is the consequence of recent social conditions. How recent it is may be seen from descriptions of life even in the most advanced countries of the world as late as the end of the last century. Writing of country life at that time (where a much larger segment of the population lived than today), Flora Thompson, in *Lark Rise to Candleford*, tells how in the English village where she grew up, "a stranger would have looked in vain for the sweet country girl of tradition, with her sunbonnet and hayrake. . . . There was no girl over twelve or thirteen living permanently at home. Some were sent out to their first place [of employ as a servant] at eleven. The way they were pushed out into the world at that tender age might have seemed heartless to a casual observer. As soon as a little girl approached school-leaving age [which was around thirteen, but out of economic necessity many children left school before they reached this age] her mother would say, 'About time you was earning your own living my gal.' . . . Her brothers, when they left school, began to bring home a few shillings weekly [as hired farm labor]." In other places children were apprenticed out of the home equally early to work and learn a skill, if they did not already work in mines or factories.

Adolescence as we know it now existed a century ago only among upper-class families who could afford to maintain their offspring beyond childhood, and it exists even today as a common stage of development only in the advanced countries of the world, where affluence and longevity permit a long period of schooling.

Obviously when life expectancy was less than thirty years, it was economically impossible for the vast majority to spend half of their lives being provided for. Even today, for the economic process to function in technologically advanced countries, most citizens have to be contributing members of society for considerably more than half their lives. Thus only affluence and a much longer life span permit our children and young people to spend their first eighteen years, if not longer, being educated. Philippe Ariès, the French historian of family and childhood, writes in *Centuries of Childhood*: "People had no idea of what we call adolescence, and the idea was a long time taking shape. One can catch a [first] glimpse of it in the eighteenth century. . . . Awareness of youth [i.e., adolescence] became a general phenomenon, however, [only] after the end of the First World War."

Although adolescence is a socially created developmental phase, puberty is a natural developmental phenomenon, the consequence of the physical changes that occur in the body as one attains sexual maturity. Exact data on the onset of puberty in times past are hard to come by, but there are reliable reports that the age of menarche in Europe in the seventeenth century was about seventeen years. In this country it has dropped from an average age of fourteen years and three months in 1890 to a present average age of about twelve and a half years. Since the beginning of this century, the age of menarche has dropped each decade by nearly three months, and so has the age at which boys reach sexual maturity. Thus our children mature sexually much sooner than people did at the beginning of the century. And over the same period, the time most young people spend in school has increased by at least the same number of years, if not by many more.

Earlier physical and sexual maturity, combined with a much longer period of dependence, leads inevitably to tensions within the individual and between him and his family. With earlier sexual maturity, it is little wonder that quite a few of our children become sexually active at an early age—however, now one may question whether it is correct to call such mature individuals children. In this connection, it might be worth considering that in Roman law (the Corpus Juris Civilis of Justinian of the fifth century) the age of legal majority was set at the time children reached sexual maturity, a view that was confirmed some thousand years later by the Council of Trent.

In the Jewish tradition, the coming of age is celebrated at the age of thirteen, at which time boys (and lately also girls) are ceremoniously introduced into the community of adults, at least as far as religion is concerned. In many Catholic countries, the first communion is observed at about the same age. Up to the time of the Second World War in most Western countries, free schooling ended at between thirteen and fourteen, depending on the country. While children who left school were not yet considered fully adult, they became working members of society who, in many cases, lived more or less independently of their parents. Only a relatively small minority, mostly upper-class and upper-middle-class children who were university-bound, continued their education beyond the age of fourteen.

Recently, a group of intelligent, sensitive twelfth-grade high school girls were asked whether they wanted to have babies; practically all hands were raised immediately to indicate yes. Asked whether they also wanted to have teenage children, most lowered their hands. When the question was re-phrased to ask if they wanted to have adolescents, not a hand was raised. Finally questioned whether they hoped eventually to have grown-up children, most hands went up again. These young people knew from their present experience of being adolescents that things are not easy for the parents of teenagers struggling to find themselves. Nevertheless they hoped that when their turn came, they would find in the total experience of raising children enough compensation for the difficulties encountered during the adolescent years.

If the same questions had been asked of young women a century and a half ago, the vote would surely have shown different results. Much as girls then wanted to have children, their fear about what might happen during childbirth, when so many women died, and their justifiable anxiety about infant mortality common back then might have made them hesitate to say that they wanted to have babies. Once out of infancy, a child's chance of surviving to maturity was vastly increased, and so in those times, young women most probably would have wished to have older children. In those days adolescence was not regarded as a separate stage of development, since by the age of thirteen most young people were working full-time alongside adults. But everyone would have wished for grown-up children, because in old age, people depended almost totally on them for help and support.

Thus when children as adults returned to their parents the care which had been received in childhood, there was a reciprocity of relations which tied the generations together psychologically, as their economic dependency on each other bound them together in fact. But in this country we have become accustomed to a family setup in which parents have to take care of their children much longer than ever before, while at the same time children are no longer expected, and in most cases no longer need or want, to take care of parents in their old age. The Social Security system was set up in the mid-thirties, but we as a society tend to forget how recent is this turn of events: only in this century have affluence and disease control permitted, for the first time in history, a large segment of the population of the most advanced countries to accumulate during their working years something at least approaching a sufficient surplus to allow them to take care of their own needs in infirmity and old age.

Thus only a few generations back, the reciprocity just mentioned gave parents a feeling of security about their future which they owed to their children, while the children derived their childhood feelings of security from their parents. This arrangement offered deep mutual feelings of security but often was not tested in its working for very long; the average life span was too short for this. However, as long as the parents lived, the children believed they would live up to their own part of this arrangement, and parents hoped that they would. Since they firmly believed that when their turn came they would take care of their parents, children then had little reason to feel guilty about what their parents did for them.

This is no longer true. While many adolescents readily recognize their resentment of their long period of dependency on their parents, they do not speak openly about their feelings of guilt about all their parents did and do for them; many are not consciously aware of this guilt feeling because they repress it as too painful, particularly since they can do nothing to change the situation which causes it. But this does not mean that the guilt ceases to work inside of them. To a considerable degree, adolescent rejection of parents (or of their way of life) is motivated by this repressed guilt, which remains unconscious and is often openly denied by defying the parent, or by being critical of him and his ways. One blatant expression of this guilt feeling is when the child believes or asserts that the affluence expended on himself was ill-gotten gains. The implication of this assertion is that one need not feel guilty about spending money or having it spent on one when it was gotten the wrong way.

In addition to feelings of uneasiness and guilt about the fact that their upbringing was and continues to be so expensive and demanding, children also feel awkward about having to accept so much from their parents without any chance to give something in return. Yet under our social arrangements and conventions this is unavoidable. In many cases all this prevents children from showing gratitude for all their parents do for them, because to do so would mean that they have to recognize how much has been given to them, a recognition that would be too heavy a burden to bear for the child who can do nothing that would appreciably lighten it.

The absence of expressions of appreciation, much more than the actual giving and doing, is what from time to time causes some resentment in the parent. This feeling is usually quickly repressed; the parent knows that the child does not ask for most things but is simply supplied with them because middle-class living conditions require it. Most parents are very glad, and even proud, to be able to do so much for their children. But often they cannot help feeling a tinge of resentment when their children seem to take it all for granted or, even worse, respond with criticism of the parent for doing it at all. (This may happen in adolescence, as mentioned before, to escape a burden of guilt that has become too heavy.) Thus in a strange way it is the child's feeling of guilt, or rather its repression and denial, that deprives the parents of their (unconsciously hoped-for) appreciation.

Until recently, the expectation of being well provided for by one's children in old age balanced the giving between parent and children; it created a strong bond between them, based on a recognized reciprocity. This particular bond has disappeared and its place has been taken by an interaction of unacknowledged guilt in the child and equally unacknowledged resentment in the parent. What used to be a tie that provided reciprocal social and economic security, and because of it psychological satisfactions to child and parent alike, has become a source of irritation—if not outright dissatisfaction—because the rendering of services is so onesided. While these negative reactions remain mostly underground, they are nevertheless detrimental to those good feelings between parents and children which benefit both so greatly.

Today the adolescent age is a much too prolonged period of social and economic dependence imposed on youngsters who mature earlier than ever before physically and sexually, and who are in all probability much more advanced intellectually than youngsters of the same age in past times. These contradictions create so many strains between adolescents and their parents that it is particularly important for parents to build up a strong enough "tie which heart to heart and mind to mind in body and in soul can bind," to quote once more the poet. The bond between parent and child, which can be created only by the parent's devotion, must be a firm one, so that the difficulties of adolescence won't break it in ways that are dangerous to both generations. Because of his great inner insecurity, the child desires nothing more than that his parents should create such strong ties between them. The good enough parent will be able to rely on the continuing strength of such a bond and on its resilience; if so, the whole family will successfully steer its course through the storms of adolescence.

25

Seeking a Rightful Place

Belong: *In English usage when* belong *is followed by
a preposition, it is followed by* to. *American usage,
retaining the basic idea of "having a rightful place,"
permits any preposition that indicates place.*
—BERGEN AND CORNELIA EVANS,
A Dictionary of Contemporary American Usage

THE FEELING OF BELONGING develops first and foremost within our family and our home, and only on the basis of this early experience extends later to the neighborhood, the nation, the ethnic group, and the religion to which our parents belong. We grow our first and our deepest roots within family and home; strong positive feelings about ourselves and firm emotional ties to others will anchor us in life, nourish our security, and permit us to weather successfully the adversities of our existence.

It is an unhappy reflection on the alienation of many modern people that they search for their "roots" in the distant and faraway past, and even in countries across the sea. The seeds of a tree can be carried far away from the place where it grew, but the trees which grow from these seeds can have their roots only where they grow; the same is true for man. Our roots are first and foremost in our family; this is where we belong in the deepest sense—to the family that raised us from infancy, and later also to the family that we create for ourselves and our children.

According to the dictionary, "to belong" means to have a rightful place. A rightful place is not one that is granted by the powers that be, not even by parents; this is too shaky a source for a true feeling of belonging. A rightful place is the place we gain for ourselves, first through loving and being loved in the right way, later through one's own efforts. This alone makes the place secure, one's very own.

Throughout history, the family has been a necessity for the survival of each of its members. Unless everyone in the family worked long and hard, all were likely to suffer severe deprivation. As long as there was enough food, shelter, and clothing and the rudiments of learning, all was well in the family and everyone knew his rightful place in it. To provide the family with the essentials of life was proof enough of the family's merits in general and of parental worth in particular. Parents and children had to apply themselves seriously to their tasks to survive, and they derived justified pride and satisfaction from their accomplishment. Children worked from an early age on to help secure the ecomomic well-being of the family; whatever their own contribution might be, they could not doubt that there was purpose and meaning to their lives; they felt that they were good persons because they did their share of important work. After long and hard hours of labor—in most families much too long and too hard hours—in the fields, the shop, and the home, the child was convinced he had done all he could, and could be expected to do. He knew his rightful place in the life of his family, and that he earned it every day; and with this knowledge came a strong and secure feeling of belonging, as well as self-esteem. And if his parents did not appreciate his contributions—as happened occasionally even then—then the child knew that it was not his fault, and that they wronged him.

The modern child of whom no physical labor is expected and whose workload seems so much lighter can never feel a similar security about himself. There is always more studying he could do; there is always someone else with whom he suffers by comparison. The child's academic responsibilities are by no means clearly defined, their purpose at best so distant in time as to seem pointless at a given moment. So the modern child can never feel sure he has met all his tasks and met them well. He cannot feel certain about himself if his value is determined by a teacher's estimation of his efforts, or depends on his ability to give emotional satisfaction to a parent by forming his personality in ways that please the parent, rather than in line with his own inclinations, personal talents and experiences. Thus the child lacks confidence about how well he is doing and is uneasy about the conditions of his work and life; he does not realize that this is due not to his own shortcomings, but to modern conditions that do not let him gain certainty about how well he is doing or what he should rightfully expect of himself. He only knows what others expect of him, and often this is not made clear; moreover, when expectations are spelled out, these often fail to make good sense to him. Objectively speaking, it may seem that much less is asked of the modern middle-class child compared to times past, but frequently children end up deeply dissatisfied with themselves and the world, without quite knowing why, which makes such feelings more disconcerting.

Parents and teachers may tell a child that learning well in school is meaningful because it will lead to a better job or more important work many years later, but this carries little conviction for the child, to whom even a year sounds like forever. In the past, a child who worked at growing crops to feed the family saw the meaning of his efforts, as he also did when he helped fabricate objects that took shape and were completed before this eyes. Thus when the child applied himself to his tasks in the past, this proved his worth to him; but at present the results of his application are intangible at best, with all the doubts and uncertainties that adhere to intangible things. Conviction about self-worth comes only from feeling that we have met our tasks well, and that the tasks are meaningful in themselves *at the time* we work at them. It is not only boredom nor the inequities of social conditions which lead a youngster to seek distraction or oblivion through music so loud that it drowns out all thought, or, worse, to escape through drugs, but a dominant feeling of uncertainty, or a dissatisfaction with himself, so painful that he wants desperately to be free of it, at least for the moment, no matter what the cost to himself.

Some parents expect their child to perform chores around the house, but even when well executed these cannot give the modern middle-class child any of the security which a child in the past could derive from his contributions to the family's well-being. Doing chores makes things easier for the parents, but such work does not contribute significantly to the family's and—most important in this context—to the child's well-being. He does not see how his work around the house makes life better for *him*. Worse, he knows that these chores require labor that his parents do not highly value as such; the work does not contribute significantly to the income or security of the family. Labor which is disliked—and the child usually dislikes performing these chores—cannot add to our feeling of worth and self-respect.

While we all have to attend to some chores or routine tasks, we manage to do so without resentment if these are connected with more important activities, of which they are the consequences. For example, in many families, children are required to take turns washing the dishes. Having to wash dishes is the consequence of having prepared a meal and eaten it from them. Planning and preparing the meal may be viewed as a creative enterprise; choices, decisions, and skill are involved in it. If a person is in charge of these decisions, then the chore of cleaning up after the meal is but the logical consequence of all that went before. But nearly always the child has little or no role in the decision-making processes and in the satisfaction which creating a pleasant meal provides. Thus cleaning up afterward is not an integral part of a process, but simply a chore. If we have to do the dirty work after someone else has done the creative work, we feel that ours is a servant's labor, even when well performed, which tends to reduce one's status in the whole process rather than to enhance it. Only if we also help with the creation can we derive self-respect from what we are doing. To be told that we have to do something, and also when and how, tends to further reduce the pleasure in what we are doing and the satisfaction we can derive from doing it. In relation to play it was mentioned that the child who is given the freedom to decide on the timing of his activity and on the manner in which he wishes to do it has a much better chance to derive some pride from doing it well than the child who has a little freedom to make his own decisions at least in these respects. The same applies to whatever the child is asked to do in his home as a contribution to family life.

Some parents think that requesting their child to perform labors around the house will teach him responsibility. Unfortunately, we do not become responsible by being told that we have responsibilities. This remains true even if a child's parent insists that some tasks are a child's responsibility and holds him to them. The child will learn to act responsibly—as opposed to obeying orders—only out of his own conviction that self-respect requires him to meet certain obligations, and also to meet them well. If a child has this conviction, it is hardly necessary to tell him what his obligations are, or his responsibilities; he knows it from his own decision. If he is *told* that doing something is his responsibility, this tends to arouse negative attitudes; he is obeying an order, whereas it ought to be his free choice if he is to gain self-respect from doing it. And if a parent—the main authority in a child's life—reminds him of his responsibilities, or worse, forces him to do what the parent declares is his responsibility, then the child understands that the parent does not trust him to behave either in accordance with his convictions or in accordance with his self-respect.

For example, many parents tell their child that it is his obligation to take care of his room because it is *his* room, and to some degree they get away with it, because they shame or force the child to do as they want. Nevertheless, this argument is not really effective, because it fails to convince the child of its soundness or fairness, although parental insistence may induce him to obey. The argument does not carry conviction, even if the parent's power to enforce his will gains results, because from an early age the child knows that one of the main aspects of having a possession is that one can do with this possession as one pleases, with the one exception that it cannot be used to harm others. This qualification is stretched beyond reason if a parent insists that a child's messy room endangers the well-being of the family. Thus the statement that the child is responsible for the condition of his room, and must keep it in a shape which conforms to the parent's views of orderliness and cleanliness, contradicts the essence of his ownership, because it is *his* room. Telling a child what he has to do with his room denies that it is really his, because if it were, he could do with it as he liked. Although the child may not consciously know that the parent's argument is faulty, he feels that it is, and this lowers his trust in the parent's fairness, a feeling that is not likely to make the child learn responsibility.

If, on the other hand, the parent makes it clear to the child that all of the home is the family's, including the room he uses as his own, then the parents, as heads of the family, have a say on how all rooms are to be used and kept. However, when all rooms are the family's rooms, there is no reason why it should be a child's responsibility to take special care of some special room; taking care of all rooms is then something all of the family ought to be concerned with, not just one child with one particular room. If this room needs some cleaning or straightening up, then it is not only one child's but also the parents' responsibility; and since they are usually those who feel most strongly that something needs to be done about this room, it becomes their obligation to do most of the required work. Of course, it seems reasonable that the child should participate in the task, since it was probably he who created the need for it; thus he could be expected to give a hand. In my experience, this seems reasonable enough to a child who has a good relation with his parents; and once the parent takes the lead, the child is usually willing to help and often genuinely enjoys it, particularly if his opinion is invited on how to go about the work. This he then usually does and is pleased when his ideas are followed. Although this gets the room in order, it does not teach responsibility, but neither does it permit taking care of the room to become a focus of dissension between parent and child.

Given the life-style of the modern middle-class family, there is hardly any regular labor left which is so intrinsically meaningful to a child that he feels it an obligation to do it and gains self-respect from doing it well, except in unusual situations such as emergencies—for example, when a parent is incapacitated by sickness, or when an older child feels responsible for the well-being of a younger sibling. But by and large such situations are rare and usually short-lived. Thus about all a parent can do is to be aware of how much more difficult it has become for our children to develop the inner security that comes from the feeling that one is needed and is making a significant contribution to the well-being of the family. These feelings have now to be gained from much less tangible experiences, very much including the feeling of obligation which comes with the conviction that a task is so important that it must be performed, and performed by the child because nobody else can do it, or can do it as well.

ALONE WITHIN THE FAMILY

In times past, not only did the child from a very early age on feel needed and therefore that he had a rightful place in his family—and with it felt that he truly belonged to it—but by having to work with others day in and day out, year after year, he was never alone. Loneliness, the feeling that one has no roots—this is the curse of modern man, while blood, sweat, tears, and a short and brutish life and backbreaking labor were the hardships our ancestors and their children bore. But our ancestors did not have to endure these hardships without the support of those closest to them. The modern family usually enjoys its togetherness only around the dinner table or during the evening, on weekends, or on vacations, when no activities essential for its sustenance occur. Consider, for example, how much time suburbanites spend riding in the car, and how children are forced to remain passive during the ride. Even when the purpose of the trip is to take the child where he wants to go, the fact that an adult must drive him there means that the parent is the one who decides whether and when it is possible for the child to do what he wishes. He depends on the goodwill of the parent for it, and during the car ride he has to sit still; he can only watch the parent do the important work of driving without which his own activity could not take place. Parent and child riding in a car are physically confined to a narrow space, which hardly, or only rarely, makes for a feeling of togetherness that they thoroughly enjoy. On the contrary, long car rides often make for feelings of edginess or tenseness and also boredom for the child, while the parent who drives is usually fully occupied.

Things may be pleasant enough once one has arrived at the destination, but the enjoyable aspects of leisure activity do not make up for its lack of importance as compared to doing something necessary for survival. As some students of the family have put it, throughout past history family coherence was based on producing things which secured the family's well-being, but now the main activities of the modern family consist of consuming things together. But it takes more than this to create a feeling of belonging; important as consumption is, it does not give one the conviction that one has a rightful place in the order of things. We all know that we have an easy time getting along when things are going well. Then we do not need our family to be able to enjoy ourselves. Even strangers will share our good times; there are plenty of fair-weather friends. But what we need for our security is to feel and know that somebody will stick with us and work either with us or for us and share our sorrows and difficulties when things do not go well. One is not likely to experience this on a vacation.

All through history, right up to the beginning of this century, a child could see with his own eyes that his parents worked hard to earn the family's livelihood, and he could and did respect them for their toil and skill. No child could fail to be deeply moved by watching a mother's labor in bringing a child into the world, and by her nursing and tending the infant. Her children could not be insensitive to the way she took good care of home and family and often also of many more people, such as hired hands or apprentices. All this required great skill and very hard labor before the days of labor-saving machines, ready-made clothing, and factory-prepared food. In addition, the child's mother usually rendered a wide variety of other services to the family; she cared for the sick, she frequently helped with the animals when they gave birth, she worked in the farmyard and vegetable garden, and she often helped with the farming itself. It was usually she who went to town to sell their produce in the market, and it was she who brought home the money earned from selling it. All this impressed the child with the great contributions his mother made.

From an early age, a peasant's child could not help admiring how his father was able to hitch up a team of strong oxen and then plow a straight furrow; soon he also admired his father's other skills, such as in repairing the house and the farming implements. A blacksmith's children watched with awe as their father took a piece of iron, heated it in the red-hot flame, and hammered it into the shape of a tool. As for craftsmen such as carpenters or shoemakers, their children marveled at the way they shaped the most complex objects out of what had looked like unpromising raw material. These children hardly needed the Biblical commandment to honor their parents; this was the logical and nearly inescapable result of observing their parents as they attended to the daily routines of work which so clearly served the well-being of the family.

It has always impressed me that in contrast to the modern family which tries to rely on *love* as the cement to bind it firmly and securely together, the one commandment that directly refers to children and parents orders us to *honor* our parents. We are not commanded to love our parents. Obviously, to honor one's parents was regarded as sufficient for establishing the right relations within the family; no more seemed needed.

In most cases to honor a person is an unambivalent feeling, especially when compared to the often ambivalent emotion of love, which is nearly always also demanding, if not fickle—not to mention that where there is love, there is often also jealousy. And, as Freud has shown, love for one parent often breeds jealousy of the other, whereas honoring one parent does not. When parents live well with each other, support and complement each other in work which sustains the family, then it is practically impossible to honor one parent without also honoring the other.

But it was not only the admiration for his parents' skill and knowledge, as they provided the family's livelihood, which made a child honor them. Living and working so closely with them, he formed an opinion of them as persons. Also very important was the fact that the parents were the child's prime educators before public schooling replaced them in this function, as happened only fairly recently. Before that time, even when children went to school for a few years, formal education played only a minor role in the lives of the vast majority of children. Working along with their parents took precedence in everyone's mind over schooling; this is indicated by the fact that even today the period of the long vacation is still the season when children were needed to help with the crops and the harvest, although today very few children do.

What the parents taught their children as they worked alongside each other formed a strong bond between them; such teaching and learning were important at a time when the tacit expectation was that children would largely follow in their parents' footsteps. We all love it when someone appreciates what we are doing well, and the more important such a person is to us, the more valuable is his appreciation. To most parents their children are of tremendous importance, as well as how the children feel about their parents. Thus when a child admires his parent in what he is doing—and often on this basis also as a person—it gives great satisfaction to the parent. Technically speaking, we all need what are called "narcissistic supplies" to sustain our emotional well-being; when others think highly of us, it makes us not only think highly of ourselves but also feel good. The more important a person is to us, the more sustaining are the narcissistic supplies we receive from him, and the more we will do our best to keep these supplies coming. Thus a child's admiration for his parent makes the work for which he is admired all the more valuable; it makes up for many hardships. Whether or not we realize it, we are grateful for being given these emotional supplies we need so much. Thus the parent is beholden to his child, who provides him with the feeling that he is admired—who, in the words of the Bible, honors him. This makes it easier and more rewarding for the parent to extend himself to his child by teaching him; and the child, in his turn, feels more secure, important, and loved when his parent devotes himself to teaching him anything that is very important to the parent. Thus the parent who is admired, who is "honored" by his child, cannot do otherwise than to love such a child, and he will do so, unless there is something very wrong with him. I believe this is why the Scriptures tell us that all we need for the well-being of the family is that children honor their parents; the parents' love for their children is the natural result of it.

But there was even more to the parent-child relation at a time when most children followed in their parents' footsteps. When a son inherited the father's farm or shop, or when the father expected him to do so, the father could feel that his son would carry on where he had to leave off. In this way his life's work would be continued; it would not end on his death. He was promised continuity not to his life, but to his life's work; and thus he would not have labored in vain. The mother's feelings were the same; she expected her daughter to bring children into this world and raise them, as she had done. The child was grateful to his parent for being taught how to gain his livelihood, and the parent was grateful to his child, believing that the child's work would give continuity to the parent's life. Thus they felt a satisfying reciprocity in their lives and their relations.

Today, when the lives and occupations of children are so different from those of their parents, there is rarely the feeling that they will carry on our work after us so that our labor's fruit will continue to accrue to our families. Our labors have lost much personal meaning, for it rarely seems that the results of our work will extend beyond our lives, and so in some fashion extend our lives beyond the grave.

Not being able to observe us in our daily work, not understanding its meaning from their own observations, modern children find it much more difficult to honor us for it. Since we are not honored by them in the same way as in the past, it is much more difficult for us to love our children with the depth which came easily and naturally when their admiration for what we were doing gave us unique dignity in their eyes, and with it in our own.

The modern middle-class child hardly ever has a chance to observe his parents at work or, given the complexity of many modern occupations, to understand why the parent's work is important in itself, as well as for the survival and well-being of the family. The child who in the past saw his father bring in the harvest could have no doubts about the fact that the father labored directly for the well-being of the family, nor could the child who saw his mother prepare the meals, sew the family's clothing, and tend the vegetable garden. This is still true today for some children, such as those who grow up on a family farm. But their number becomes smaller each year. On the other hand, selecting clothes in a department store, picking up cans and boxes at the supermarket, and seeing parents drive back and forth from work do not suggest to the child that his parents work hard for his welfare. He has only their statements that they do so, and statements carry little weight compared to what a child sees all day long. Most of the time the modern middle-class child observes his parents when they are engaged in leisure activities, or in consumption, conspicuous or otherwise. This hardly impresses him with the importance of what his parents are doing. Even when a parent cleans the house or does the laundry—necessary work which benefits the family—many a child fails to be impressed by the value of such work, because in his mind it is too directly connected with parental criticisms of him: he does not keep his room orderly enough; he leaves his things around and makes cleaning difficult; he fails to keep himself or his clothes clean. His resentment of these remarks makes it difficult for him to see much merit to housework.

Things are quite different when a child sees a parent repairing things around the house, or in other ways improving the home. This makes excellent sense to him, and so he is impressed by his parent's skill in doing it. He is usually delighted to be permitted to help, and takes pride in his contributions, provided his parent is satisfied with them. It is thus the child's own conviction of the value of what a parent does that makes him admire and respect the parent, or how he conducts his life. The latter is often difficult for him to evaluate correctly when he sees his parents only at times of leisure. But only the child's respect makes it easy for him to take seriously what a parent says; without it the parent's requests carry little weight.

The affluent society has separated the child's life activities from those of his parents; moreover, it has put a great deal of physical distance between them. The worst aspect of this is that many modern middle-class families consist of persons who, as they grow up, do not learn what it takes to live successfully with each other. Parents who themselves have not acquired the ability to get along well with others in hardships and in close living, and to cope well with the problems and difficulties which it creates, cannot teach it to their children. Then all suffer from living at an emotional distance from each other. Thus at a time when for the family to make sense we need to be close to each other emotionally, because what holds a family together now can only be the emotional ties formed within it, all too many have lost the art of living well with each other in close physical contact. But there can be no emotional closeness where physical distance is desired. Although "out of sight, out of mind" is not necessarily true, it is more true in children than in adults. Of course, physical closeness does not automatically make for emotional intimacy; many of our young people have learned this to their disappointment, as they remain lonely within themselves even though they live together in communes, or shack up together. Despite all this, without a period of physical closeness, intimacy is often impossible.

HOW CLOSE IS TOO CLOSE?

The ability to form close human relationships has to be acquired early, when things come intuitively to us, if it is to sustain us all through life. The infant learns it as he cuddles against his mother. The warmth which her body radiates to him can never be so well provided by his warm blanket. His body will feel warm under blankets, but without human warmth there is no emotional warmth inside the child, the very thing that makes him feel good about himself.

An old German saying claims that the biggest lesson one has to learn in life is to "stretch according to the cover." This adage goes back to the time when not only the children but the entire family slept under one blanket in one bed. In those days children indeed learned from an early age to adjust to living in close proximity to others. If one child pulled the cover too much over to his side, his sibling would wake him up to retrieve his share. If one child kicked, the other would protest that he was robbed of a night's rest. If one had a nightmare, the other helped him fall asleep again if there was to be peace in the bed without any anxious screaming or thrashing around. Thus if they wanted to sleep peacefully without interruption, children learned early and almost intuitively the give-and-take and the mutual adjustments which are as necessary for successful living today as they were then.

The philosopher Schopenhauer compared the human predicament to that of two porcupines who are trying to survive a cold winter. To keep from freezing to death, the porcupines hole up in a cave. Because it is very cold even in their cave, they seek warmth and creature comfort by drawing closely together. But the closer they come to each other, the more they prick each other with their quills. Bruised and annoyed, they draw widely apart to avoid pricking each other. Alas, now they lose all the comfort and warmth they can give each other and are again threatened with dying of cold. So once more they draw closer together. Eventually, as they move back and forth, they learn to live with each other so that neither is pricked badly but they are still close enough to live in reasonable comfort. This suggests that we must learn how to live close together without getting under each other's skin. If we fail to learn this, we are either too close for comfort or we freeze emotionally in isolation.

Man's life used to be bound by tradition, because necessity permitted him no leeway to arrange his life as he wished. As the conditions of life changed over the centuries, man learned the optimal distances to avoid being either enslaved by or too isolated from others. Many traditional arrangements were thus established and obeyed without question—including those regulating the relations between husband and wife, their roles in society, the relations between parents and children, the relations between social classes, and all those other relations which for so long were considered God-given. All were the result of centuries of trial and error to find the right human distance in any given condition of life. Often the experimentation ended in an uncomfortable, restricting, but nevertheless livable compromise between individual freedom (of which there was very little, as we conceive it today) and social dependence on each other, along with a sense that one must keep to one's place (on which we feel there was far too much insistence then).

The affluent society has changed much. In the cave of the porcupines there is now central heating. Reacting to our past suffering from pinpricks as we tried to escape freezing to death, we tend now, in our well-appointed caves, to draw far away from each other, to our very own private corners. There we live by ourselves, so that we do not prick others anymore, or get pricked. This is our headlong flight into emotional separateness, a flight based on former anxieties about imposing, or being imposed upon. But it has led in many persons to an inability to live successfully with others, because this has not been learned in childhood, which forces on them a social isolation that nearly always eventually leads to existential despair. These people have not lost but have never learned the mutual giving of warmth of the kind forced on the porcupines who lacked central heating. They shiver not from the cold but from loneliness in their large, overheated caves and do not understand why they shiver.

No wonder that people brought up in emotional loneliness, and whose living conditions never forced them to learn to stretch according to the cover, find it very difficult to establish lasting relations. They seek what they have been missing, but are unable to find it, because they have not learned to cope with the difficulties which close living together often entails. Having had no or too little experience with intimacy as they grew up, they are unable to enter into it with others as adults. Hence the many broken marriages, marriages they made hoping to find in them the intimate closeness they missed in childhood. Unfortunately, many such marriages turn out disappointing, because the partners are unable to give to each other the intimacy they so much desire.

Children from broken marriages often are afraid to form intimate relations, because the one they formed to one of their parents ended in painful disappointment. Fearful of a repetition of this experience, they do not dare to commit themselves deeply to another person, and so their marriages, too, fail. Children who had such experiences cannot develop a feeling of belonging, because they have been robbed of the "rightful" and permanent place they expected to have not only in one but in both their parents' lives.

Instability in the life of the child makes it difficult if not impossible for him to develop a feeling of belonging. Such instability need not always be the result of broken marriages. Too many moves from one place to another, with the breaking of ties to friends, can have the same result; even changing schools too frequently can have a deleterious influence on a child's ability to develop a strong feeling of belonging. This is all so obvious that it hardly needs further discussion.

Here also things used to be different. In times past it was often a great hardship to be bound for life to the place where one was born. But that one expected to spend all of one's life there and that the same in all likelihood would be true for one's children helped create a strong feeling of belonging to a particular place, if not also to a small group of people who also spent all their lives in the same place.

In this connection, it is enlightening to visit reconstructions of the villages in which our ancestors lived before the Industrial Revolution. These villages were often small, and all villagers lived close to one another. Not only that, even in the houses of the very affluent, the physical confines were very narrow. The house of a prominent citizen in Sturbridge Village in Massachusetts, for example, consisted of a downstairs with a small kitchen, dining room, and parlor. Each room was perhaps a fourth of what we would now consider a good-sized room for its purposes. The ceilings were low—only in this way could the rooms be kept warm in winter—and this gave them a cozy feeling. The upstairs was essentially an attic divided into two rooms: the bedroom of the parents, and that of the children. These two rooms were separated by a thin wooden partition through which children could easily hear what went on in the parental bedroom, and the parents what went on in the children's room. No need for an intercom system there.

Each bedroom was barely large enough for two beds and a very few pieces of furniture. The children slept in trundle beds, and as far as one can guess, at least four children of both sexes lived together in one room. Interestingly enough, living arrangements of this kind did not then lead to any sexual acting-out, as it does not today in the Israeli kibbutzim, where four children who are not blood-related, usually two boys and two girls, share a small bedroom until the age of eighteen. On the contrary, sexual mores were then, and in the kibbutzim are now, much more stringent than they are among our middle-class youth, who sleep each one in his own room.

More important, two or more children often shared a bed. As mentioned, sleeping together this way taught children at a very early age how to find warmth, security, and companionship in each other without disturbing the other's sleep and, more important, how to comfort each other when one awoke in the middle of the night out of an anxious dream. Children still comfort each other thus today, for example, in the Israeli kibbutzim, where one child will say that he is the protector of a roommate when he gets anxious in the night.

In the children's rooms at Sturbridge Village one would find perhaps a rocking horse, a doll's cradle, and a doll. These were the only toys. There were probably very few arguments about picking up toys, because there were none around to pick up. There would be no battles about what to wear, because there was only one set of clothes for everyday and one for Sunday. With nothing breakable around, there was little occasion for "don't touch." And since water had to be fetched from the village well, there probably was little insistence on the children washing their hands several times a day before eating and after using the toilet, because fetching water was simply too difficult and onerous a task. A single outhouse served the entire family nicely.

The American historian Daniel Boorstin has made a most perceptive remark about reconstructed Williamsburg—that it became acceptable only when indoor plumbing was installed in its tourist accommodations. If the open sewage ditches and outhouses of colonial Williamsburg had also been reconstructed for use, their stench would have driven the modern visitor away. But these odors were very much part of one's living conditions a few generations ago. There was no recoiling then from body odors, no alienation from one's own body because of a too rigid toilet training. In fact, excrement itself was not an object of disgust but was carefully collected for use as fertilizer, just as "night soil" is still used in China today, and by nomads as fuel. Toilet training in those days could never lead to the same distaste with one's own body which is all too frequently the case now, because the body's waste products were valuable and treated with respect.

This natural closeness to one's own and others' bodily functions used to be equally true of sexual matters. Modern concepts like infantile sexuality could not even have been "discovered" very long before Freud; historically, the adult's estrangement from the sexual life of the child (which then resulted in the child's alienation from his own sexuality) came about slowly. This estrangement reached its full height only as recently as Victorian times.

The modern tendencies in our affluent society are not the result of careful planning for good family living, but a reaction to the cramped living conditions amid narrow confines which were typical not so long ago. Private space used not to be available to most people; today, in reaction to this, we aspire to give each child his own bedroom and if possible his own bathroom, so that we need never meet each other in the course of caring for our bodies and are not forced to learn to share our intimate doings with each other. It is a life of considerable comfort, but also of relative isolation from each other virtually from birth, since most infants no longer sleep in their parents' bed, or at its foot, as they once did.

Parental intimacy is usually carefully hidden from the child today. I do not for a moment mean to suggest that our children would be better off if they could observe parents in their sexual intimacy. But we have made it nearly impossible for our children to learn intimacy with their own bodies, or with others, from infancy on; nor do they learn it in a step-by-step process as they grow up. And this at a time when social and economic conditions have forced us to try to build family cohesion on emotional intimacy alone.

Our adolescents recognize this physical isolation as a deficiency and react to it. Unlike their Victorian and post-Victorian parents, when given a choice, they do not hold their parties in huge, well-lighted rooms with ample space to separate the groups. Teenagers today like to huddle close together in dim discotheques, pressed against each other with little space to move. Belatedly they reconstruct the close living of colonial times. But adolescence is too late to begin to learn intimacy, and usually all that they get for their effort is a physical but not an emotional closeness.

26

The Supportive Family

Large family; quick help.
—SERBIAN PROVERB

N O SOCIAL ORGANISM requires more cohesion than the family if it is to ensure the well-being of all its members. This is especially difficult to achieve in modern times, and even more so because of our commitment to the individuality of each member of the family. Parents want to have children and feel that they will enrich their lives, but many parents today also fear that parenthood will rob them of their individual freedom; this ambivalence often sets in even before a child is conceived. A young married couple put it succinctly when they told me why they were planning a trip abroad: "This is our last chance to be human beings. After we return, we are going to be parents." They knew quite clearly that they wanted children, but they also knew this would require them to relinquish things that were very important to them.

As long as the roles and activities of each person were bound by tradition— that is, as long as individuation was not considered possible, desirable, or important—family solidarity was fairly easy to maintain. Although it imposed considerable restrictions on the freedom of each individual, this was viewed as absolutely necessary, and was taken for granted as the given order of things. But once it became accepted that each individual should not only be permitted but had an obligation to be truly himself, to develop his own personality as he wished—seeking satisfaction of his goals in life as a person rather than as part of a family, tribe, or caste—tensions among the members of a family increased and in extreme cases became well-nigh unmanageable.

Social solidarity within the family is as deeply desired as before, but it ·is difficult to achieve because of the intensity of the emotions—if not also of the conflicts—generated by people who live together, each striving for his autonomy. Still, we feel a need to be assisted in our striving to become uniquely ourselves and resent it if we are not. As long as social solidarity prevails within a family, its members are happy to live together, not because they do not encounter problems and difficulties, but because rather than blaming their troubles on each other or on themselves, they meet them as a unified group. The practice of psychiatry has mainly the purpose of alleviating the anguish of those who suffer from not having experienced such social solidarity within their families. This, then, is the paradox: although solidarity of the family alone makes individuation emotionally safe, personal uniqueness tends to define itself in contrast to others—mainly in contrast to those we know best—and this is disruptive to social harmony.

There is only one antidote, one cure, for this: security. To the degree that we feel important to those who are significant in our lives, we do feel secure; and in the same measure, the pressures of jealousy are reduced. A family is happy living together if, when things go badly for one of its members, he is supported by all the others, who make his misfortune their common concern. A happy family is not one in which nothing ever goes wrong; it is one in which when something does go wrong, the one who caused it or suffers from it is not blamed but is supported in his distress. For if anyone in a family feels downcast and is not uplifted, how can he feel that his family is his haven of security?

So what is the modern middle-class family to do? We cannot and must not look to outside threats to unite us. No longer does the sheer fight for physical survival force everyone to work long, hard hours together so that the family has enough to eat. I implied before that love and affection were the frosting on the cake of necessity—additional bonds grafted on a basis of sheer need. Now they have become the essential bond that ties the family together. Since physical security is no longer the main service which the family renders to all of its members, emotional security must take its place. Despite all experiments, human society has never found a better way to raise its young than within the family, nor any better arrangement to provide us with emotional well-being, or a better framework within which the child can become truly intimate with his parents—a relation that will give him inner security for the rest of his life.

Security as provided by society is fine, but it cannot give one inner security—neither emotional warmth and well-being, nor self-respect, nor a feeling of worthwhileness. All these only parents can give to their child, and they can do so best when they also give them to each other. And if one fails to get them from one's parents, it is extremely difficult to acquire these feelings later in life, and they will remain shaky, at best. Thus everything depends on whether the modern family can provide this emotional security based on personal intimacy and the mutual love and respect of all of its members.

Let us consider a typical example of what happens when the middle-class child desperately needs the emotional security which he should and can only find within his family. A child in a middle-class family comes home from school, dejected because he got some failing marks; he feels that he is worthless, that life holds out no hope for him, that he has been badly treated by his teacher and perhaps also by the world. Does his parent then heed the Biblical injunction to uplift the downtrodden, or does he further discourage the child, who already feels that he cannot hold up his head, by blaming him for his failure? This is the moment when the child most needs to experience his family's support, to know that they will stand by him when he suffers the agonies of his young life. How many parents feel with his misery, and encourage him not to see himself defeated? And how many aggravate his feeling of worthlessness by their criticism?

On the other hand, if he comes home delighted with the good marks he got, his parents rightly express their pleasure, as they should. But if he receives approval and support only when he already feels good, and experiences disapproval when he feels bad about himself, how can he help feeling that his parents are only fair-weather friends, and not to be counted on in time of dire need?

What happens in the middle-class family when a child suffers from a deep disappointment because of the breaking of important emotional ties? For example, a teenager may have experienced a shattering disappointment in his life: he was very close friends with a classmate, but suddenly, as happens so often at this age, he feels betrayed by his very best friend. Adolescent relations are much more fleeting than those of adults, but they are never-theless as deeply experienced at the moment. Such a teenager may feel unable to face his former friend who has so seriously hurt and disappointed him. Do we, who must try to build our family on the basis of satisfying the emotional needs of all its members, show our appreciation of the importance of his feelings, so that he will understand that these emotions are indeed the main essence in forming ties to other persons, most of all his parents and siblings?

If we experience such a blow, we usually avoid meeting the person; we do not want this traitor to see our anguish, nor watch the successful rival gloat over our misfortune. I have known adults who, after the breakup of an intimate relationship, or after a severe disappointment in a close friend, avoid meeting for months or years the person who so badly injured them. But when an emotional shock devastates our teenage child and he is projected into the deepest misery, do we encourage him to concentrate on the hard work of mourning the relationship? Do we keep him from school for a few days of rest and rehabilitation because he is desperately sick in his soul? If so, the wound will have time to scar over sufficiently before he has to reencounter the one who hurt his feelings. Or do we insist that he go to school again the next morning, although he will certainly meet his former closest friend who has just turned against him, as if losing a best friend is something much less important than an ordinary cold, for which we are quite ready to let him stay home? Parents will do this even to a child who is a very good student and would not be set back by a few days out of class, thus demonstrating to him that academic achievement—or worse, not having him hang around the house—takes precedence in their scheme of values over giving his deepest emotional wounds time to heal. And these same parents want to build the family on emotional ties, the significance of which they have given the lie to through their actions.

Even if the youngster tells his parents why he is upset, they usually try to persuade him not to take his feelings so seriously, as if merely saying he should not feel so hurt would take away any of his distress. Sympathy with his feelings that extends to letting him avoid meeting those who have inflicted such pain on him is the least they could do to convince him that they are truly concerned with the importance of emotional ties, and do not only give lip service to their value.

When we insist that he go to school, we show by our action that we want him to be serious only about his emotional ties to us as parents, but not to others. But emotions cannot be so schizophrenically split into "important" ones relating to one's family and "unimportant" ones such as to a friend. Either close ties are important or they are not—and the child assesses what we believe on the basis of our reaction to his emotions. If we do not respond appropriately to our child's feelings—not just with nice words but also with actions—he may decide to keep his feelings to himself in the future, thus preventing us from helping him with them.

One child had become deeply attached to his first-grade teacher, who suddenly died of a heart attack during the winter months. The child cried all day and refused on the next to go to school. But the parents insisted that he go, so that he would not lose out on learning or fall behind the rest of the class. Thus forced to act against his feelings, the child hated the new teacher and all others who followed her, remaining faithful to his first teacher-friend. As a consequence, he did not progress in learning at all. True, this is an unusual case, but had this child been allowed to work through his loss, which would have required all his emotional energy for at least a few days of mourning, he probably could have accepted the teacher's replacement and continued to learn. Even more important, though his parents wanted

335

him to love them, even as a grown man he was never able to forgive his parents for having shown so little respect for his desperate feeling of loss as a child. All this because they did not permit him even one day of respite in respect for his feelings of grief. A child's grief must be taken seriously. When I have talked with parents about their unwillingness to take their children's grief seriously, I have been tempted to remind them in the words of Shakespeare, "Everyone can master a grief but he that has it."

When responding or failing to respond to their child's grief and sorrows, many parents act as if because the child is small and immature, his afflictions are also small and immature. If they would just think about it, and observe their children in their unhappiness, they would know that this is not so. But usually it is not insensitivity which makes people disregard children's sorrows or think that they could easily overcome them. Much more frequently the parent has a deep wish that his child should be spared such unhappy feelings. Understandably, he wants his child to be happy, not to suffer at such an early age from the pain life inflicts on all of us. These wishes entrap parents unknowingly into believing the false and empty cliché of the happy childhood. Also because of the widespread idea that it is a parent's obligation to make childhood a happy time for his child, we have difficulty accepting that our child may be at times very unhappy; it seems to reflect on us as parents, and so we wish to believe that our child's grief is only a relatively small matter which he can easily overcome. But any observation of children shows that their lives have their full measures of pains and sorrows as does any other age of man. Not to accept this fact and behave accordingly is to belittle the child.

Even those who wish their child to be able to be serious about serious matters often do not act any differently, because in most cases this only applies to matters the parent takes very seriously. It rarely extends to matters the child views as serious but the parent does not, such as the loss of a friend or a teacher in the examples just mentioned. This attitude is readily illustrated by parents who worry about the dangers of atomic warfare, but who also draw their child into these adult concerns. Such parents may be pleased that the child shares their concern, is so serious about what his parents consider a most serious matter. But this anxiety about a destructive war clearly interferes with that happiness the same parents wish their child to enjoy. Children obviously can do nothing to prevent a nuclear war.

It is unfortunate when parents think they can decide what matters a child should be serious about and what others he should not. Parents who project their own uncertainties or anxieties onto their children are usually unwilling to give credence to the depth of the child's feelings and are unable to appreciate how much he suffers when they think he has little or no reason to do so. But whatever one's age, the decisions of others (even of our parents) about what we should and should not feel deeply are experienced by us as a demonstration of how little they know us and how little they care about *our* feelings.

As a consequence of such attitudes, parents often try to cheer a very sad child out of his unhappiness; and they often succeed, because he is in a poor position to resist them, and because their wish to make him happy is a very important indication to him of his importance to his parents. Also, a child's feelings are more volatile than those of most adults; he can fairly easily move, or be moved, from dejection into a more cheerful mood. But this does not mean that he feels less deeply than adults, and his deep feelings about, for example, the loss of a friend continue to work in him, even if he seems to have forgotten them for the moment. The grief soon returns, and the child then feels even worse that he could for a moment forget what are his deepest feelings. The parent, on the other hand, who succeeded in cheering up his grief-stricken child for a moment decides on this basis that the child's feelings do not run very deep, and will make it a practice to try to get his child out of a depressive mood by not taking it seriously. But even if his misery is temporarily alleviated, on reflection the child is very hurt to think that his feelings have been considered to be so superficial that he could readily be cheered out of them.

If we really take our child's feelings seriously, then when he is unhappy and grieves at a loss we will not try to cheer him out of it. When we mourn the loss of a loved one, we would think it callous if a friend of ours tried to cheer us out of our mourning. We expect a true friend to respect our feeling of loss, mourn with us, and in this way to try to help us cope. We would be appalled if he tried to jolly us out of our distress, and so are our children if we try such maneuvers on them. However, they cannot tell us how much they resent it when we take their loss too lightly to mourn with them; they cannot tell us how hurt they are that we are able to make light of it. If we do try to get them out of their unhappiness in this way, they feel as deep a resentment of our behavior as we would if our friends tried to joke us out of our unhappiness.

The loss of a friend is only one of the many situations which can make a child unhappy. Whatever his overt behavior may be, his inner reaction to our effort to cheer him up rather than to try to join him in his feelings is experienced as a demonstration that we are concerned only with our own feelings, namely our wish that he should not be unhappy, and not at all with his feelings, which at the time are those of deep distress.

If we want to build a firm basis for family life out of the emotional ties its members form to each other, then we must take feelings very seriously, and particularly unhappy ones. The reason for this is, as mentioned before, that when we are in good humor nearly everybody enjoys our company. Therefore it is very important that we pay the greatest attention to and have the deepest sympathy for our children when they are miserable; that we show them that we do not consider them so empty-headed as to be able to overcome deep unhappiness in short order. We also need to emphasize from the start the importance of emotional ties in our lives, and nurture them as assiduously as possible. We must be as concerned with them as our ancestors were with seeking salvation and survival. We must spend as much time and effort on them as parents in previous times spent working together with their children to keep the family going economically. These were then the essentials which bound the family together, and when the family managed to make a go of life, this made each of its members happy to belong to his family and gave him security. Today it is the emotional ties which must do all this. The stronger we make these ties, the more likely will our children grow into strong and secure persons.

FAMILY LOYALTY

Working together to earn the family's livelihood was serious business. Life itself was always hard and often very difficult, although people tried to forget this and make up for it on festival days. The good familiy supported each member in the big and small hardships of life. No one expected that there could be happiness other than as a part of such a good family, nor that life was anything but difficult.

Many of the most vexing problems in the day-to-day life of the modern family have their source in an expectation that life should be, if not happy, at least smooth-running, and that serious hardships should not mar family life. Thus what in the past was the touchstone of the family's merit—that when something went wrong, the good family pulled together to survive— has only in fairly recent times become the reef on which many a family founders. This is due to the erroneous belief that when serious difficulties arise in a family there must be something wrong with the family itself, and hence one must discover what or who is to blame.

The modern middle-class family has lost much of the belief in itself as a coherent unit for survival; moreover, it suffers a great deal from the tendency of its members to blame themselves or other members of the family when difficulties are experienced, even though this is precisely the time each needs to support the other, for the well-being of all. Of course, there are valid psychological reasons for this tendency of family members to blame each other when things go wrong. One reason is the commonly accepted idea

338

that if a child gets into serious trouble, it must be due to the way he was raised. Against such openly expressed or silently implied criticism, the family defends itself by asserting that not it but only the culprit is at fault. Being blamed for his actions makes the family angry with him. Now there is nowhere for the troubled child to turn to to find respite, while in the past, soothing support was readily forthcoming from within the family.

Most parents in earlier times concentrated so entirely on mastering the difficulties of securing their child's survival and physical well-being that they gave relatively little thought to their impact on his psychological development. They simply knew that they had to set a good example for their child to follow, and teach him right from wrong. Given the hard work necessary for survival, once they succeeded in providing the physical necessities, they did not fear that their child—or someone else—might criticize them for failing to take proper care of him. Thus they could deal with many psychological problems—which of course did occur, as they do in all intimate relations—with an equanimity based on their own inner security; and this reinforced the child's feeling of security.

These conditions of times past still prevail in much of the world; but in our families it has become difficult and complex for parent and child to feel secure with each other. One reason is that parents see as their most important task and obligation to create in their child the inner conditions for his psychological and emotional well-being—and this not only for the moment, but for all of his future! The intricacies of these psychological phenomena and uncertainty about how such elusive goals may best be achieved tend to make the parent diffident in what he is doing; naturally, this insecurity increases that of the child. Thus the parent is trapped, because providing the child with inner security is now viewed as one of the prime requirements of good parenting.

Every child is deeply affected by his parents' insecurities, but to make matters worse, he has his own insecurities which originate in his limited understanding of the world, his doubts about his ability to cope with the problems of life, and most of all his doubts about his lovability. He can manage these insecurities only to the degree that he is propped up by his parents' belief in him and in his ability to manage life successfully, if not right now then when he is grown up. These are the only guidelines he has and can trust, because he knows that his parents are much more knowledgeable about the world and its problems. But when these parents are dubious how well their child is faring and will fare in the future, then he is in double jeopardy: threatened by his own insecurities, and at the same time by the lack of reassurance from his parents. Since his parents are so much more competent to assess reality than he is, their worries about him and his future seem to him to be based on their having discovered shortcomings of which he has been unaware. Worse, he does not know what these problems might be, or what remedies might be available to him. No insecurity is more distressing and perturbing than those whose source remains unknown to us; by comparison, those the nature of which we know remain circumscribed. Thus the parent who worries a great deal about his child and his future creates exactly that which he worries most about: a deeply insecure child. By contrast, the parent who feels confident about his parenting by this very fact combats the insecurities of the child and helps him to feel more secure.

Naturally, every parent worries about many things regarding his child; such worries are inseparable from being a concerned parent. As is true for so many issues in child-rearing, everything depends on the right balance between worry and trust: worrying about oneself as a parent and about one's child, and trusting that since the child is ours, he is and always will be a good person, able to cope with life's challenges. The inner conviction that one is doing as good a job as one possibly can in being a parent naturally results in the connected conviction that because of this, one's child will do well, whatever temporary or minor shortcomings he may show at times. Since the future is always uncertain, we cannot know what particular problems our child will encounter in life; therefore the best we can give him on his way into life is our trust in him and a sense of his own great worth.

A small example may illustrate. When I was still a boy in Vienna, a cousin of mine went astray. Naturally this was viewed as a terrible misfortune, but in those times, nobody blamed his parents. On the contrary, everybody told them how unfair it was that such a thing should happen to such fine people. Then, to meet the emergency, our large clan of about two dozen families gathered together to help and comfort those immediately afflicted; money was collected to send the youngster abroad and get him started in the new world. If he was criticized at all, it was tacitly rather than openly; he was sent off with everybody's heavy heart, but supported by their goodwill and best wishes.

Given the means to begin a new life in a new country, away from the parents whose nagging pressure and marital discord had weighed heavily on him, and encouraged by the unexpected support he had received from so many relatives, my cousin took heart, and soon succeeded where he had failed before. Because his parents had also received emotional support from the wider family when they needed it most, it was easier for them to send their son away with blessings rather than recriminations. That support, and their need to arrange for their son's departure, got his parents to cooperate more closely instead of fighting with each other, and their marriage improved, at least temporarily. Supported by their relatives, and not blamed by the family at large, the parents had no reason to become angry at themselves or their son, and they managed not to be overcome by the inescapable pain that comes from having one's child get into trouble. Thus the family structure proved of great value to one and all.

Things worked out so well because of the family's conviction that none of its members could possibly be really bad. They were so certain of the essentially good character of everyone who belonged to our family that this belief successfully overcame the self-doubt of the boy's parents, as it did that of the boy. The high opinion that the family held of all of its members was of paramount importance to the favorable outcome of this episode. At that time the ancient Serbian proverb that a large family is tantamount to quick help was still valid.

Some twenty years later, this was no longer quite so true. Another relative of mine failed at home and was sent abroad, but unfortunately the family structure had weakened and the good opinion was lacking. This second boy had not been delinquent, as had been my cousin, but he could not hold a job and spent more money than he had; without doing anything very wrong, he seemed unable to make a go of life. By that time, many factors of modern life had combined to loosen family cohesion, and nobody outside his nuclear family knew of his troubles. Although the clan would have helped as it had two decades earlier, the boy's parents feared—not without reason—that the wider family would be most critical of him and of them, his parents; so they kept his problems to themselves. This young man, too, was sent abroad, this time not to North but to South America, to seek his fortune there. Because he lacked the support and good wishes of the wider family, this boy's low opinion of himself was not allayed; further, he felt the doubts of his parents, who also resented him because they felt ashamed of him. Without the family's belief in him, he did not manage to do any better in the new world than he had in the old.

It can easily be objected that the two boys involved in these stories were different and so were all the other details, and that this may explain the changed outcome. This may very well be true, but also by that time it was a fact that in many other situations big and small, the wider family no longer supported its members so readily in times of stress or difficulties. The attitude of "my family, right or wrong" may be objectively questionable, but subjectively it used to provide a shield against the worst consequences when things went wrong, and a respite that greatly facilitated recovery.

In similar cases today, parents frequently do not receive the support they desperately need from the wider family, and they suffer additionally from guilt and from the opprobrium of those who in the past were the source of their comfort. This in turn makes them angry at the family member who caused the difficulty, which only aggravates matters. Thus one of the major causes of the modern family's difficulties is the great change in the perspective by which its troubles are viewed and responded to.

This change in perspective is in large part the consequence of our having recognized the importance of individual psychology: that phenomena originating in our personalities and in intimate relations cause our most severe difficulties in facing life and in living with each other. What is not as readily accepted is that only affluence has made this emphasis on psychology possible. So closely related are psychological insights and social and economic conditions, particularly where family relations are concerned, that it is a distortion to consider the former in isolation. As long as we were unable to survive physically without the support of other family members, we had a reason to blame all our problems on outside forces, so as to be able to continue living well with each other and ensure mutual survival. Today we can afford to recognize the difficulties we experience as psychological in nature, and perhaps caused by family members—something we could not afford to see before.

There is good reason to assume that it is the shortcomings of his parents, or their manner of parenting, which cause many of a child's difficulties. But subscribing to this view benefits child and parent *only* if it induces them to change themselves; otherwise, it can create much additional misery. For example, the child who for unconscious reasons manages to get into trouble—fails in school, drops out, and acts delinquent—often acts this way in order to punish his parents, knowing they will feel hurt and guilty and be blamed for his misdeeds. Parents, on the other hand, rightly resent the idea that their child may prove them to be bad parents. Anxious about this, they tend to overreact to his normal inadequacies and other shortcomings, because they see these as ominous signs of worse things to come. The child then has to cope not only with his own anxieties about his inadequacy, which is difficult enough, but also with his parents' anxieties, which is an unwarranted and thus rightly resented burden. It is hard enough for him to prove himself; the idea that in addition he ought to prove the merit of the parenting he has received is something children correctly resent. How much easier it was to settle parent-child disputes when the troubles could be attributed to a young person's ignorance of the world, which led him astray, or to a stroke of bad luck, which we must accept as part of our human heritage.

Anticipating hostile and rejecting attitudes in their child makes the parents feel insecure, afraid, and often angry long before he gives them any cause for it. In the past, when a child in his high chair spilled milk or porridge all over the floor, it did not occur to his mother that this might be an expression of his anger at her or his dissatisfaction with the world, or a presaging of his future failure to cope with life. She was sure that it happened because he was immature and clumsy; to many mothers such incidents seemed to show his great need for her to help him get his food, and this made her feel that she was even more important to him. (Of course, since in times past the plate from which the child was fed was made of wood or pewter, it did not break when it was pushed to the floor; further, the floor was usually coarse and did not suffer from spills, while an expensive rug or fancy carpet is easily damaged by food spilled on it.) Here, as in so many other situations, affluence is a mixed blessing for the child, and often makes it hard for the parent to take his antics in good humor, or at least with tolerant indifference. Today, when we suspect that the mishap may be a deliberate act of annoyance or defiance, all the goodwill created by our feeling that we are important to our child is marred by the possibility that he has rejected us or the food we have prepared so carefully for him. Feeling thus rejected, we may in turn react to his spilling, dropping, or breaking things with annoyance or anger, instead of accepting such actions as instances of childish awkwardness.

Although ignorance never was or is bliss, a little knowledge can be a dangerous thing, as the Talmudist knew. Before it was understood that children not only love but also reject their parents, knowing that without their parents' ministrations children would perish, it never occurred to people that this could be so, for a child's existence depended on the goodwill of his parents. So they did not ascribe a child's actions to rejection. Today we know that children both love and reject their parents, and hence are ready to attribute what we view as their negative behavior as due to the child's rejecting us. This may occur, but it is much more rare than many a worried parent believes, and this is the little knowledge which can be dangerous. More complete knowledge tells us that many things which look like rejection of the parent are really nothing but the child's frustration with his own inadequacy. In the example of his spilling his food, he does so more often out of frustration with himself because he is not better able to feed himself, or to make his own choice as to the nature and the timing of his meal. Thus, much of what the modern parent may take for rejection is nothing but the result of the child's deep disappointment in himself. Often the naïve parent who ascribed it all to the child's clumsiness was closer to the truth than is the modern parent who is anxious about whether he is a good enough parent and who, out of this anxiety, is often all too ready to see negative attitudes if not rejection of himself in the child's action. Being a good enough parent hence requires that we ourselves be convinced that this is what we are.

It is this inner security about ourselves and about our love for our child which today must protect us against feeling rejected by our child when he is only or mainly frustrated with himself and the limitations which his inadequacy imposes on him. Where the parent of the past saw only the child's inadequacy, greater knowledge ought to permit us to also see the depth of the child's frustration because of it and to realize that this is often the mainspring of his action. This is an example of the truth of Gratian's statement that knowledge without wisdom is double folly. Wisdom about ourselves: while we are not perfect, we are indeed good enough parents if most of the time we love our children and do our best to do well by them. This wisdom, or truth, can protect us against the folly of reflecting that everything a child does reflects only upon us. Much of what he does has mainly to do with himself and only indirectly or peripherally with us and what we do. Wisdom about ourselves and our child will permit us to understand that what seems like hostility directed against us—which, when we view it as such, we cannot help resenting and hence in our turn reacting negatively to—is often actually due to the child's unhappiness with himself. When we recognize this, our heart will go out to him and we will do our very best to help him in his distress. If we do, we will feel good about our ability to help him in his need, he will know how nice it is to be part of a family that helps those who are in need, and then all will be well with our family.

27

Magic Days

*Young and old come forth to play
On a sunshine holiday.*

— MILTON, "L'Allegro"

I T IS VERY EXHILARATING to feel that one is the special cause of a celebration, as a child may experience on his birthday. Such personally significant moments are truly to be cherished, for they provide us with great happiness at the moment and also with a sustaining hope for the future. The more significant and insecure we feel about our place in the world, the more we need the affirmation of our importance—if possible from the whole universe, but at least from those persons who mean most to us.

Children especially need this experience, as we recognize when we celebrate children's holidays, both individual ones such as birthdays and others when all children are made to feel very special, such as Christmas. On these occasions children stand in the center of affectionate attention and are made to feel important; the gifts they receive prove to them that they are loved and also that they are worthwhile persons. If such occasions are celebrated in the right spirit, the glow from these days can spread out over the rest of life. The regular repetition of these events is the child's guarantee of his continuing importance; holidays punctuate the child's year and with it his life; they are the highlights of the year for him, which demonstrates that such organization of one's life is best achieved around happy events.

We do not know exactly what the first holidays expressed symbolically, but there is little doubt that they were celebrations of life and of that which sustains it; thus the ample, festive meal is still the centerpiece of any true holiday and often symbolizes the holiday spirit. A distinction must be made here between religious *holy days* such as fast days and days of contrition— which to the believer are important spiritual observances—and the more secular occasions experienced as *holidays* by children and often the whole community, universal festivals when even a deeply religious person like Milton felt it was appropriate for young and old to "come forth to play."

The first organized and regularly observed holidays were ritual evocations meant to assure the fertility and with it the birth and rebirth of plants, animals, and men. Others were rites of passage to secure, solemnize, and glorify stages in the maturing of man, or seasons of the year. In the ancient Judeo-Christian tradition, religious festivals were manifestations of communal joy. In fact, the Hebrew word for holiday or festival, *chag*, is derived from the root word *chug*, which means to dance in a circle, and this is the way the Hasidic Jew still celebrates religious feasts; the Hebrew for Passover means literally "the feast of leaping." Today our greatest holidays, whether religious or patriotic, solemnize and celebrate birth: that of the Christ child; the Resurrection— the rebirth—of the Lord; and the birth of nations, just as the child's birthday celebrates his own birth. (That the Christian church decided to commemorate the unknown date of Christ's birth at the time of the winter solstice indicates the close symbolic connection between the birth of the Savior and the reawakening of nature's yearly life cycle in the Western world.) Passover also celebrates not only gaining freedom from slavery, but also the birth of the Jewish nation. It led to the giving of the Ten Commandments, the basis of Jewish law. The Last Supper, which was the Passover meal, began the sequence of events which led to Redemption and the Resurrection on Easter Sunday with its chance for "a new life."

All these festivals are magical events, for what could be more magical than the birth of a child, or the rebirth of the world? What holds more magic for mankind than the promise of a chance for a new beginning? Originally, the celebration of these holidays included donning of vestments of ritual or magical significance; new Easter finery and the funny hats people put on at birthday or New Year's parties are the last vestiges of this practice. The presents a child receives at Christmas and on his birthday are symbolic of the gifts of the three holy kings; and fireworks are symbols of a new sun which will bring the light and joy of freedom and a new life, a hope that the lighted Christmas tree also symbolizes.

Long before the lighting of the Christmas tree became part of the celebration of this holiday in northern Europe, huge bonfires were started in pagan times on the mountaintops on the day of the winter solstice to symbolically or magically encourage the sun to increase the length of days and again warm the earth. The bringing in and lighting of the yule log is a remnant of this custom, reduced to just one large log. Even more ancient than the lighted Christmas tree is the Jewish custom of lighting candles during the feast of Hanukkah, which celebrates a magic event: namely, that the lamp in the Temple in Jerusalem continued to burn although its oil supply had been exhausted. Thus, as often happens, the magic ritual (in this case consisting of lighting trees and candles) continues, while with the passing of time, different meanings are attached to the ritual. Whatever the meaning of the rituals which have entered our Christmas celebrations may have been in the past, now they symbolize the wondrous birth of a child who created a new era—our own—and gave a new meaning to all of human life.

Children's holidays have one unique feature: distinctions of rank or authority are obliterated or reversed. A child is king on his birthday; he can make demands of adults or even make them fear him on Halloween; and he is allowed to fool them on April Fools' Day. These status reversals and magical connotations are important reasons why holidays are especially meaningful and pleasurable for children. A child is badly deprived if he cannot fully enjoy special holidays or benefit from what these symbolize; such symbolic meanings are built permanently into our unconscious experience of the world. Thus while holidays are here for all of us to enjoy, how they were celebrated when we were children can and does have the most far-reaching consequences over the rest of our lives.

"Holidays are the secret anniversaries of the heart," the poet Longfellow reminds us, speaking as an adult to adults. And when we were young, these yearly recurring days were joyously and eagerly awaited, their festive pleasures anticipated for many weeks, if not for months or even all year long. Holidays most pleasantly punctuated our lives and gave a positive meaning to the ongoing days. As mature adults, we often decide that we no longer ought to give in to such childish views of what makes life worth living, so many of us tend to keep our feelings about holidays secret, not only from others, but also from ourselves. Their meaning to us, however, remains deeply anchored in our unconscious; this is why Longfellow called them secret anniversaries of the heart. Our feelings about these special days thus become internalized as part of our hidden inner life.

THE SYMBOLIC MEANING OF HOLIDAYS

The way we celebrate many holidays has changed quite a bit. For example, Christmas, from being an essentially religious festivity, with the giving of gifts only to children, had developed during the last century into more and more of a family holiday, in which all members participate equally—now everybody gives presents to everyone else. There is certainly nothing wrong with any sort of family holiday; in fact, it would be most beneficial if families were to celebrate such holidays more often. Older generations can remember when in their childhood almost every Sunday was a family holiday—the occasion for a gathering of the clan; this might mean twenty people or more all together, because families tended to be larger then, and also because kinfolk lived physically, emotionally, and socially much closer to each other. Even when there were occasional arguments, these added excitement to the enjoyment and were soon amicably settled, as everybody had a good time around a plentiful meal. The adults enjoyed each other, the children played together, and family problems could be discussed and resolved.

Among the happiest memories of my childhood are the times when I and the cousins near my age—we were called "the little ones"—played under the huge table around which a dozen or more adult members of the family had gathered, often forgetting that we were literally underfoot. We would play together in the cozy darkness, hidden by the huge tablecloth that hung down nearly to the floor; as we played we listened to the talk and arguments of those we called "the big ones." We and they, each group on its own level, thus had a grand time every Sunday.

The closest many of our children and our families come to this type of experience is at Thanksgiving. To the young child, Thanksgiving means first and foremost the turkey dinner with all its trimmings, and secondly, the family getting together to enjoy a very special occasion. Teachers and parents might explain the history of the holiday, but what stands out in the child's mind—and in adults' minds as well—is the plentiful food and the spirit of good fellowship. On a conscious level, such holidays are meaningful to the child mainly because of the warm feelings evoked in him by all the festivity, and this may later reflect a pleasant glow onto the more abstract ideas connected with the celebration. However, on a subconscious level, some of what the day symbolizes continues to exercise its influence.

Fear of physical and emotional deprivation are the two greatest anxieties of man. Hunger and starvation are the basic forms of the first, desertion—of which death is only the last and ultimate form—of the second. The young child does not understand death and thus does not fear his own, while that of his parents is feared in the form of permanent desertion. Although in our society children do not actually starve, everyone experiences more or less severe pangs of hunger at one time or another; and all children suffer temporary desertion when their parents are not available. These two forms of the first real deprivations most children experience become greatly magnified in the unconscious, where they come to stand for, and are symbols of, all anxiety. (Even fears of dangerous animals, so frequent in the nightmares of children, are experienced by them as special cases of the fear of desertion, because these ferocious animals are dangerous only because of the absence of parents, who otherwise would chase them away and thus fully protect the child.)

Family holidays celebrated around a table set with an ample and festive meal thus combat the child's greatest anxieties, both as real experiences and, what is much more important, also on a symbolic level. The "gathering of the clan" reassures the child that for his security against desertion he need not rely solely on his parents, that there are many other relatives who would be available in a crisis and would protect him against desertion. The ample meal similarly provides security, both on the real and much more important on a symbolic level against starvation anxiety. In this way such family holidays are, both as a conscious experience and on an unconscious level, one of the most reassuring experiences the child can have in regard to his most fervent anxieties. They are among the most constructive experiences we can provide for him to buttress his security.

Thus, with good reason the story of Thanksgiving stresses that a successful harvest saved the Pilgrims from the starvation and privation they had known the winter before. In this way the holiday symbolizes a rescue, and the beginning of a better and more secure life, a symbolic rebirth on a better plane. At base, all our most important celebrations—Christmas, Easter, Fourth of July, birthdays—commemorate births or rebirths. The hope inherent in this symbolic meaning continues to reverberate in us, whether we know it or not.

Throughout the history of man, holiday ceremonies themselves and the happy feelings attached to them have outlasted the specific event or idea which originally sparked the holiday; as noted before, these ideas alter over time. For example, Christmas was at first a pagan ritual celebrating the rebirth of the sun and of nature, long before the idea of the birth of Christ became attached to it. Similarly, the most ancient holiday rituals, those carrying the deepest unconscious and emotional significance, have a way of reappearing in different form, sometimes after a lapse of centuries. So the huge fires lighted on high mountaintops at the winter solstice to encourage the sun to start remaining longer in the sky reappear after centuries, as lights on the Christmas tree. Such celebrations are simply too important to be relinquished, because they serve deep, often unconscious needs. As the way these traditional celebrations have been observed has changed over time, and different ideas have become attached to them, so too do we as individuals alter the way we celebrate holidays over our lifetimes. From our own experience we all know how the ideas we connect with Christmas changed as we matured, from Santa and his reindeers to the spirit of giving, from the enjoyment of receiving presents to that of giving them to others.

Thus, the tangible celebrations and rituals are permanent and paramount; the abstract ideas they presently center on may alter, but nearly all these abstract ideas had concrete precursors, without which the abstract ideas would have reminded empty shells. For example, according to the Bible, God forbade the Jews to make a likeness of him, just because the desire to imagine him in concrete ways, such as an old man with a beard—not to mention as a golden calf—is so overwhelming; not visualizing him in a definite form is very difficult. Nevertheless, hardly any modern child thinks of God in any other form than that of a most exalted, immortal, very old person. As we mature, for most of us this image is replaced by the abstract idea of a formless supreme being, or essence, or first cause, as the case may be. Nevertheless, we continue to admire how God was rendered in human form by great artists, such as Michelangelo did in the depiction of the creation of Adam on the ceiling of the Sistine Chapel. And in some such form God appears to us in our dreams, which suggests that however far we have removed ourselves from our childish imagery, in our unconscious it continues as we had visualized it and thought of it as children.

So why should we worry about our children visualizing Christmas in the form of Santa? Even if we as parents do nothing, as our children mature they will free their ideas of Christmas of such concrete imagery. But for about the first six years of their lives, most modern children firmly believe in their magical visualizations such as Santa and the Easter Bunny, no matter what lip service they may feel obliged to give to their parents' view of the matter. Then for a year or two they feel uncertain, although they still would prefer to give full credence to their former convictions. Thereafter, it all becomes a pretend game which they thoroughly enjoy; and they resent it when their parents try to disillusion them. If the parents tell them what they consider to be the "truth," as children see it they do it because they are begrudging children their fun. This fun depends on children being able to pretend to believe in these magic figures, while also feeling at the same time that they really are smarter than their parents give them credit for. They enjoy being able to fool their parents into thinking that they, the children, still have full belief in the reality of these imaginary figures, while actually they do not. In such make-believe, the original feeling for magic that was connected with these figures continues to evoke happy emotions and experiences, tying parents and children to each other in the most enjoyable ways.

A recent American study demonstrates how the belief in imaginary figures is directly related to a child's needs. It showed that while practically all four-year-olds believe in Santa Claus and the Easter Bunny, only 20 percent of them also believe in the Tooth Fairy. The reason for this discrepancy is that at the age of four, not many children had lost, or even were about to lose, their first teeth. By the age of six, only about two-thirds of the group studied still believed in Santa Claus and the Easter Bunny. But, having by then begun to lose their baby teeth, the same number who believed in the first two magical figures now also believed in the Tooth Fairy. Two years later, when the children were eight years old, the number of those who still believed in the first two magical figures dropped to a mere third of the group, while two-thirds of them still believed in the Tooth Fairy. As children continued to lose their first teeth at this age, they held onto the belief in the Tooth Fairy. Thus there is a direct connection between the somewhat scary experience of losing a tooth and belief in compensatory magic.

The need, or possibly more correctly the desire, of children to pretend that they believe in these and other magic figures—maybe to ensure that their parents will continue to provide presents, but more likely to enjoy the pretense discussed above—is suggested by the fact that although by age eight only a third of the children claimed that they continued to believe in Santa Claus, three-fourths of this age group still left food, drink, or some other token such as a drawing they had made for Santa to enjoy upon emerging from the chimney, and they faithfully and carefully hung up their stockings at the fireplace for him to fill with goodies.

The need to grasp abstract ideas by means of concrete images is by no means restricted to early childhood; it holds equally true for most adults. Few of us are able to get a real grasp of beauty unless we can think of some object the perfection of which gives emotional meaning to the abstract idea. Only if a child has come to love objects that he considers beautiful—never mind what adults may think about their merit—will he later grasp the idea of beauty in the abstract, and come to love it. If we dispute, on the basis of our adult refined and educated standards, the loveliness of an object which embodies the child's idea of beauty, then the child may be turned away from the enjoyment of beauty forever, because we made him mistrust his judgment of it. He may still come to think highly of beauty as an abstraction, but he won't be able to love it when he meets up with it, because he was prematurely forced to separate his value judgments from those emotions which alone can make beauty deeply satisfying. Speaking to a young child about it in the abstract does not aid him in learning what beauty can do to and for him. Though he may learn to speak intelligently about beauty, it will fail to warm his soul the way loving a certain object which is beautiful to him does.

Thus the young child should be allowed to believe in Santa, the Easter Bunny, and the Tooth Fairy because these are precursors which continue to give emotional fervor to important concepts he will develop as his mind matures. To the young child the Tooth Fairy, who brings him a coin for a lost tooth, is both a guarantee of justice and its embodiment; it also symbolizes the goodwill of a world that does not want a child to lose anything without effort at compensation.

By contrast, the reality of a parent's giving the child a coin for a lost tooth compensates little, for the child already knows that his parents can give and take away. It is scary to the child to lose some part of his body; his parent's giving him a present to make up for it is very nice—but can he rely on it, and will it always be this way? Can a parent make a new tooth grow in replacement? But if the supernatural enters in the guise of the Tooth Fairy, then the child can feel more secure that there is a higher world order, one which sees to it that his loss will not go unrelieved. It is out of such experiences that his sense of justice and fair play is built up. The majesty of true justice cannot be instilled in a man's mind at any age without being based on childish beliefs which continue to carry deep emotional conviction long after the immature and fanciful ideas from which they were derived have been forgotten and have sunk into his unconscious. Moral fervor will be weak if one's conviction is the consequence of cold reason alone, since rationality develops much later in the growing child.

The wonderful thing about the positive magic of holiday happiness is that it can provide security all during the year when it is most needed, even under life's worst circumstances. Children know this, and when given the chance, they use the symbolic security which the holiday spirit offers to provide themselves with moral support when they need it most desperately. A story told by the Swedish psychoanalyst Stefi Pedersen may illustrate this:

When the Nazis occupied Norway, Pedersen served as a guide for a group of refugees, including several children, who made their escape by fleeing in deep winter over the high mountains into Sweden. Nobody could take more than he could easily carry on his back, because the climb was difficult and speed was of the essence. For most of the group it was not their first escape from the Nazis, since a few years previously they had fled from Germany or Austria into Norway. Thus these refugees had experience with what it means to have to abandon almost all of one's possessions, taking along only what is most important. The group took its first, desperately needed rest only after reaching safety within the Swedish border. Once they had eaten the small amount of food they had taken along, very little was left in the children's small knapsacks. Pedersen happened to look into one child's bag, and there she found among the pitifully few objects a small silver star, the sort people hang on Christmas trees. She picked it up in surprise, but then she sensed that the child was staring at her in embarrassment, as if she had discovered a most precious secret. Without saying anything, Pedersen put the star carefully back in the child's bag.

Since she would be responsible for the children once they reached their destination in Sweden, and since as a child psychoanalyst she was deeply interested in what might provide psychological safety for them there, Pedersen decided to explore what else the children might have chosen as their most valuable possessions to bring along on their flight from home. So she looked into the bags of the other children, and again and again she found cheap Christmas-tree decorations—stars and bells made out of cardboard, covered with silver glitter. This was what these children—most of them of Jewish origin but raised in assimilated families who celebrated Christmas as a family and mainly a children's holiday, though not as a religious event—had chosen to take with them from Norway in preference to all else. Otherwise, they owned nothing but the clothes they wore. Pedersen concluded that they had taken along these symbols of a happy past because these alone could cast a spell of safety over the anguish they felt as they embarked on a trip into the fearful unknown. On their journey out into nothing, the tinselly little ornaments—symbols of a happiness they had once known in their homes and with their families—assuaged their feeling of loneliness and impotence and held out a promise of hope.

The same evening, when they had reached a Swedish border village, a young Norwegian woman joined them. She had had to make a frantic escape to save her life, without even a half-hour's notice to pack a few essentials. Her flight had entailed several days of travel through the wilderness, so her knapsack could not be heavy. Now for the first time, she had the leisure to unpack her things. Besides a minimum of clothing, all she had carried with her was a heavy brass music box. Her apologetic explanation was: "Well, I had to take something nice with me since I was going to leave forever."

The Danish actor Texiere once reported that the only thing he had managed to take with him on his flight to Sweden was a little snuffbox that had belonged to Hans Christian Andersen. Of little value in itself, the snuffbox was a symbol of the abundant life he had to leave behind. And a woman carried, among a few sturdy sports clothes appropriate to a trek over the mountains, a pair of high-heeled gold shoes. Again and again among the scant belongings that these refugees took along when leaving their homes forever there were things which, viewed objectively, would have seemed peculiar choices, completely inappropriate when considering what a refugee would need most. None of these objects related in any rational way to the situation of these refugees. But they were objects which had come to represent symbolically what had been best in their lives, and as such were both last remnants of a good life and the promise of a continuing life that would have its happy moments.

Anyone who has had experience with people in similar desperate situations could easily duplicate these stories. Most remarkable here is the difference between what adults and children trusted to sustain them in extreme adversity. Adults typically took along some object that symbolized for them experiences of happiness with real people. The heavy music box, it turned out, had been given to the lady by someone who had loved her, and whom she had loved. The woman who took along the golden shoes had worn them on the happiest day of her life, when she had felt particularly beautiful and successful. On the other hand, the children sought and found comfort in something that reminded them of a happy occasion they had shared with their parents, but which at the same time symbolized powers even higher than their parents. Most of all, their tokens stood for a predictably recurring, particularly happy day for children. Desperate as their situation was at the moment, these Christmas decorations seemed to assure the children that in the future, happiness would again be theirs.

This, then, is probably the deepest and most reassuring meaning of Christmas for a child: a memory that sustains him in situations of adversity, as it did the young refugees in their extreme distress. The symbolic promise contained in the little Christmas ornaments spelled hope to these children, when everything seemed utterly hopeless. Children feel this subconsciously; that is why they hold on to the fiction of Santa Claus, who is the carrier of a very special symbolic meaning.

ANNIVERSARY REACTIONS TO UNHAPPY HOLIDAYS

The poet in his insight about "the secret anniversaries of the heart" anticipated what psychoanalysis painstakingly had to discover: these phenomena shape our views of life, both positively and negatively. The destructive force of negative reactions highlights the importance of holidays perhaps more impressively than do the benign positive influences. Although the latter are thoroughly enjoyed, adults often do not take seriously the effects, but repress into their subconscious what they consider childish reactions.

The study of severe pathological types of behavior has shown that these are frequently cyclical, recurring on the anniversaries of significant events, usually but not always without the person knowing why this is so. In the psychological literature these are known as anniversary reactions, and they always have unique personal meaning; they are days—or times of the year— on which some event of great unhappy import took place, such as the death of a parent, or of a child. Sometimes these reactions are particularly marked around holidays, especially Christmas. Suicides are often associated with such anniversary reactions, be they centered around a holiday or a personal calamity, showing that subconsciously, we remember very well what happened to us on a certain day or at a particular time of the year. The aftereffects of happy events are equally strong, but since there is no reason to suppress these memories as too painful to be consciously remembered, our positive anniversary responses are much less dramatic, and so less easily observed. For example, persons who as children had unhappy Christmas experiences tend to suffer because of it from severe anniversary depression all through their lives at Christmastime, while those who as children had happy Christmases do not later become depressed at this season, even when their life has become lonely or deprived. Memories of their happy holidays continue to permit them to bear up well under present hardships.

I knew a woman, successful in her own life, who nonetheless became deeply depressed every year around Thanksgiving. She would feel terribly lonely and deprived in reaction to the holiday, though she was quite aware that her present condition gave her no reason to feel this way. But she was haunted by her memories of childhood when—at least so she remembered— she could never be sure whether there would be a Thanksgiving celebration in her home, for she could not be certain whether her father would return in time for a feast and bring the turkey, or even come at all to join the family. Although her father usually did arrive at the last moment, and more often than not brought a turkey on Thanksgiving, her anticipatory anxiety continued to ruin the holiday for her completely. Anxiety felt in anticipation, as much as anticipatory pleasure, is thus of great psychological consequence in the way we experience later anniversaries. Unfortunately, as this example indicates, such anxiety is not undone when it turns out to be unjustified, and anticipatory pleasure can be utterly destroyed when the event runs counter to the expectation.

On his special days a child feels more alive and more himself than on most other occasions, an experience that benefits everyone. Children's birthdays are the most special celebration days for them, assuring them that their arrival in this world, their joining their family, was indeed a happy event for their parents. No wonder they need to feel very special on this day. Whenever it is not made a cause for a feast, the child suffers. I mention briefly just two examples. A boy born on December 21 resented it all his life that his parents, to avoid two celebrations in short succession, combined both on Christmas day. Another boy born on Christmas day could have felt very special because of it, but instead felt very acutely deprived because instead of having two special celebrations, experiencing twice a year his importance to his parents, he had only one. In the first case it would have been quite easy to celebrate the boy's birthday on December 21, and that this was too much trouble for his parents he correctly interpreted as demonstrating that it seemed not worthwhile to them to put themselves out for him twice within a few days. Things were more difficult for the parents of the child born on Christmas day, but with some ingenuity they, too, could have found a solution. They might have celebrated his name day, for instance, a day which is made much of in some other cultures. Here, too, we have the example of the birthday of the king or queen of England, which is officially celebrated on a day other than the one on which he or she was born. Thus it would have been possible to designate some day on which if not the child's birthday, the child himself was made a special occasion. Children enjoy it very much when, just for the fun of it, another day is made the occasion for a substitute or additional holiday. Thus, for example, a "Christmas in July" party reminds those children whose parents make an occasion of it of the happy times they had at Christmas; it also impresses them with the fact that their parents go out of their way to make a happy event for them where other parents do not.

Bitterness about spoiled holidays or being deprived of them altogether is in some cases not restricted to a particular time of the year, but can cast a deep shadow over a whole life. One girl's younger sister was born a few days before her own birthday. So, to simplify matters, her parents decided that both birthdays would be celebrated on the same day rather than two within a week of each other. The parents also thought it would be better for the children to receive presents sooner rather than later, and so both birthday celebrations were combined to take place on the birthday of the younger child. The older girl felt terribly cheated because, as she put it, she was "robbed" of her own birthday, and had to invite her friends "on my sister's birthday, to her birthday party." She had resented from the very first the arrival of this sibling, who had deprived her of being the only child in her family, and now she hated this sister with a vengeance, since she had to share her birthday with her. She felt she had no real birthday of her own. To her, this was evidence that her parents cared only for her sister and not for her. In consequence she could not enjoy her presents, although she was rational enough to realize that they were quite as good as those her sister received.

As the girl grew a bit older, she refused to invite anybody to the celebration of what to her was not her birthday, but her sister's. I do not know how the younger girl responded to having to share her birthday and its party with her older sister, but the older one never forgave her parents that she had been deprived of her birthday for their convenience. In anger and in depression she remarked, "I received my presents on my sister's birthday." Even as a fully grown person this woman could not overcome her resentment of her sister, although she knew that it was not her sister's fault that this combination of birthdays had occurred. But the event was demonstration to her that her parents did not recognize her as a person in her own right. On this issue she blamed her lifelong feelings of inferiority and deprivation, which began to lift in some measure only when she could arrange beautiful birthdays for her own children.

The latter development is an example of the positive consequences for anniversary reactions which celebrating the same event with one's child can have. The woman who fell into depression every Thanksgiving managed to keep her spirits up when she began to arrange a specially nice Thanksgiving for her children. I have known quite a few Jewish children who suffered from depressions around Christmastime because they did not have a Christmas celebration, but who did much better after they began to arrange nice Christmases for their children. This helped them, while it had been of no help to them in their childhood that their parents had celebrated Hanukkah. Part of the reason for this is that while both are religious holidays when children are given presents, Christmas symbolically celebrates the birth of a child and thus extols childbirth and with it childhood, while Hanukkah does not. The other part is that Christmas is celebrated all over the place, and its festive spirit permeates all of life. Thus reexperiencing with one's children in a happy frame of mind an unhappy event from one's own childhood can correct and improve in considerable measure the aftereffects of bad childhood experiences.

Unfortunately, such corrective emotional experiences are not always possible. Several examples are reported in the literature of persons who had severe depressive anniversary reactions around the time of the year at which they had lost one of their parents in childhood. When their own child—either the favorite child or the child of the same sex—reached the age at which the parent had lost his parent, the unhappy adult, reminded by his child's behavior and frame of mind of himself at the same age, fell into a deep, even a suicidal depression, or suffered a schizophrenic break. In these parents' cases, vicariously reexperiencing through their child what had been going on in them at what was now their child's age reactivated a psychological trauma with which they had been unable to cope when it had happened. Realizing this now increased the severity of the anniversary reaction in the most damaging way. Thus, anniversary reactions can be exacerbated, or mitigated, or even overcome entirely. It all depends on how the distressing event is relived. Unfortunately, sometimes vicariously reliving through one's child experiences which were destructive to the parent can increase their destructive impact.

All this is just one more example of how children, by their very existence and by living with their parents in emotional closeness, can exercise the most far-reaching influence, both positive and negative, on them, and parents invariably have an even greater impact on their children's lives, for good and for bad. We would be wise, then, to arrange good special days for our children and also to enjoy these events ourselves to the full, since as suggested, such happy events can make up to a marked degree for our past deprivations.

28

✦

Not Believe in Santa Claus?

> *Virginia, your little friends are wrong. They have been*
> *affected by the skepticism of a skeptical age. They do*
> *not believe except they see. They think that nothing*
> *can be which is not comprehensible to their little minds.*
> *. . . Not believe in Santa Claus? . . . No Santa Claus!*
> *Thank God, he lives, and he lives forever. A thousand*
> *years from now, he will continue to make glad the*
> *heart of childhood.*
> —Francis Pharcellus Church in the *New York Sun*,
> September 21, 1897

CHILDREN SUFFER ACUTELY if they are deprived of the few special days which are their very own, and they lose a great deal of their enjoyment of life if these days are diminished in importance. For most children in our culture, aside from graduations and religious ceremonies such as confirmations, only birthdays and Christmas remain as genuine children's days of the year. While the birth of Christ has deep religious meaning to all believers in Christianity, it is Santa Claus alone who caters to children in a way no amorphous "spirit of giving" can possibly do. To exchange presents as a symbol and token of love and goodwill can take place at any time and occasion, and it is certainly part of Christmas. But no child believes that Santa brings gifts to his parents, and most would think their parents foolish were they to hang up stockings on the mantel for Santa to fill. Likewise, Christmas, as the day on which the world's Redeemer was born, is a fast day for everyone to celebrate, but a fat and jolly Santa, who brings presents for children down the chimney and puts them under the tree, is only for children. This is why children who are allowed to believe in Santa and to enjoy this belief to the full will all their lives experience Christmas as a time of great personal happiness, much more so than those for whom it was mainly a matter of religious observance; and they are able later on, as parents, to make a joyous Christmas for their children, because the warmth of ancient feelings is still in them.

All holidays acquire their deepest significance through magic connotations. If we deprive a holiday of its magic for the child, it loses much of its symbolic and unconscious meaning; with such loss, the holiday also loses the reassuring and beneficial effects which it could exercise over the rest of a child's life. Further, stripping a holiday of its magic is no protection against the devastating consequences when the day has left unhappy memories. Premature rationality, like all other premature experiences, leaves us poorly equipped for dealing with the vagaries and vicissitudes of later life.

The parents of one bright six-year-old boy decided that it was time to let him know that Santa Claus was only a fiction. So at the appropriate time in the Christmas celebration when Santa Claus made his expected appearance, it was made clear to the child that Santa was a person well known to him. At this, the boy began to cry bitterly: "Why doesn't the *real* Santa Claus come to *me*?" The rational parents were flabbergasted. They did not see that being of an age when children still need the support of magic to be able to cope with life, their child could not believe their rational explanations but felt terribly deprived that he, of all children, had not been visited by the "real" magic figure. No assurance that other children were not visited by the "real" Santa Claus could shake this boy's conviction that only *he* had been singled out for rejection by Santa Claus. When he was told that the Santa who visited other children was a Santa like his own Uncle John, the boy logically replied: "Uncle John cannot visit all children!"—a reflection of the boy's intelligence and, for his age, sound logical thinking. It reflected equally his wish to hold on to his belief in Santa Claus no matter what his parents told him, even in the face of his knowledge that "Santa" was an uncle dressed in a red suit. When the boy was then told that their own uncles or family friends visited the other children, he still maintained: "But to some children, the *real* Santa Claus comes!"

Lest one think that this was a particularly stubborn boy, it should be mentioned that he was usually quite willing to listen to reason, except when he was deeply emotionally involved. In this he was not different from the rest of us. Highly intelligent and sensitive, and given the freedom to speak his mind openly, he did so. Many children think exactly as he did, but dare not speak up about the secret longings of their hearts, because they are convinced that their parents will ride roughshod over them. Thus many children agonize that the "real" Santa Claus does not come to them, but they keep this sorrow to themselves, secretly blaming their parents for it. They think that for some reason the good things in life, such as the "real" Santa, are bypassing them, and fear that this will always be their fate in life.

One five-year-old tried in a different way to keep the magic figure alive in his mind, despite his parents' efforts to have him accept a prematurely rational view of what Christmas is all about. Actually, these parents wanted their five-year-old child to celebrate the Christmas holiday in line with their views—as if the feelings of a five-year-old about holidays and those of his parents could be identical.

The mother of this boy decided to let him know that there was no Santa Claus because she felt he should know "the truth." She told him that Santa was not real, but just a nice story people tell to children. She then went on to talk about the "spirit of giving," which she said the figure of Santa symbolizes. The boy seemed to accept this explanation. But a little while later he asked, "What if there's a fire in the fireplace when Santa comes down the chimney?" This made no sense to his mother, because the family home didn't even have a chimney. She replied by telling him not to worry, because it was all just a story. But in the night the boy woke up and asked with distress in his voice, "Is there a Santa?" By then the mother no longer knew what her son believed: that Santa was real, as his question in the middle of the night suggested, or that it was just a story, as he seemed to have accepted during the day when she had told him so.

The boy's waking up and asking whether there was a Santa showed that he was not able to accept his mother's rational explanation that there was no Santa Claus, as did his worry about what would happen should there be a fire in the chimney when Santa came down. His mother thought it puzzling that her son should be worried about a fire in a nonexistent chimney, because she was unable to see the world as he saw it. She thought her son's worry about fires in the fireplace was senseless, but it made excellent sense to him, because he believed in Santa Claus, and he knew that Santa comes down the chimney. When the mother saw her boy become so confused, she began to wonder whether she had done the right thing in telling him there was no Santa Claus.

She was willing to accept her child's fantasies, but unfortunately for both of them only up to a point. She was hesitant about going along with his belief in Santa Claus, but she was completely unable to accept his conviction that Santa would come down a nonexistent chimney. Since Santa was real to her son, and since Santa comes down a chimney, it followed in the child's logic that Santa would come down the chimney, whether or not there was one in their home.

After all, why would magic spirits be stopped by some physical obstacle put in their way? Once we believe that reality can restrain spirits, we no longer believe in spirits. If a child believes in Santa, he believes that Santa must come down a chimney, even if there is no chimney present. To understand such logic is difficult if we approach it with our rational adult minds, but it makes excellent sense to children; and it did to us when we were children, although because of our adult wish to see ourselves as more rational than we are, we may have forgotten it.

It is hard to imagine how a five-year-old could be supposed to believe in the reality of a "spirit of giving," but not in Santa, who is so much more visual and tangible a spirit! For her own reasons, this mother wanted to have her child think of Christmas the way she thought of it. But what is the sense of celebrating a children's holiday if children have to experience it from our adult frame of reference? Why, then, should we bother to have children's holidays at all? This mother's quandary was that she wanted her son to accept her concept of reality; his difficulty was her unwillingness to accept the validity of *his* view of reality.

The mother said that all she wanted was for her boy to be happy. She had told him there was no Santa because she didn't want to lie to him, and because she was afraid other children might think he was a baby if he still believed in Santa Claus. But actually, she wished him to be more advanced intellectually and emotionally than he could be, since she wanted him to replace Santa by a spirit of giving, thereby relinquishing a childish symbol for an abstract idea.

Such intellectual constructs can never replace the emotional satisfactions of belief in a magic figure who brings all children gifts. What this mother meant by the "spirit of giving" and what her boy meant by Santa Claus were not at all the same. She wanted him to replace his belief in Santa with an appreciation of the spirit of giving; she wanted him to enjoy Christmas in the mature way of exchanging gifts and good wishes. But a holiday celebrating the spirit of giving requires all participants to give; the child, too, would have to become a giving person. Maybe Santa, or whoever invented him, understood better the nature of childish needs. As the story goes, Santa Claus works all year long at the North Pole to prepare presents for children. He is a good elf who does not want to receive anything in return, and that is why he comes in the middle of the night and remains unseen, even though we visualize him so thoroughly. We, as well as our children, know that there is a great difference between being given presents by some sprite who wants no return at all for his efforts and receiving presents from friends and relatives, who expect gratitude, at the very least.

Premature disillusionment in Santa Claus may cause a person to view Christmas in a rational way all his life, without those emotional overtones which only ancient memories of childhood experiences can give to our adult pursuits. The Christmas such a parent may then prepare for his own children may speak to their minds only, as the giving is motivated only by his mind. This leaves the irrational needs of a child's heart not only unsatisfied, but unawakened; no abstract "spirit of giving" can match the image of Santa coming down the chimney, which children see illustrated all about them during the holiday season anyway.

Young children can comprehend abstract concepts only in concrete forms; to them, Santa *is* the spirit of giving. Piaget gave a telling example of how the child's concept of reality develops, and how different it is from adults'. Walking with his little boy in the garden behind his house, Piaget asked him: "Where is Papa?" At this, Piaget's child pointed to the window of Piaget's study and said; "Up there." He was at an age when his security depended on his "knowing" that his father resided in his study. Had Piaget tried to convince his son at this stage of his mental development that his father could not be in two places at the same time, he would not have increased the little boy's understanding of reality, but made him confused and insecure about it. To know that his father resided in the study gave the boy security in the world, while being told that his father could not be in his study at that moment since he was right there in the garden would have shaken the child into believing that he knew nothing for certain.

Piaget's story illustrates how in the young child's reality, Papa in the body and the spirit of Papa can have independent existence; and far from detracting from each other, they are mutually enriching. For the young child, important figures exist in many places at the same time, both in spiritual and physical forms. This is why parents find it so difficult to understand why a child is not disturbed by the many Santas that appear all around him at Christmastime, which he enjoys, vulgar though they may appear to us. The reason is that the child has begun—though he has not yet completed this development—to separate abstract ideas from their physical embodiments, as Piaget's son separated the idea of the Papa who is doing serious work in his study from the one who is playing with him in the garden. For adults, these street Santas may destroy all the beauty and mystery of Christmas. To the young child, they are a reassurance of the reality and of the omnipresence of the mystery. Piaget's observation also shows how a young child can believe that one and the same Santa can bring presents to all children, all over the world, at the same moment.

Even drastic experiences cannot shake a child's wish or need to believe in Santa Claus if he is not yet ready to give up this friendly image for cold reality. This was illustrated by a Jewish mother's experience with her five-year-old son. Since the family was Jewish, there was no talk of Santa Claus or Christmas in their home, but the boy had been exposed to it all in school and on television. While his mother was busy doing her errands in a shopping center, the boy got bored. So she told him to go look around and come back to meet her at a certain place when he was ready. To her surprise, the boy returned a while later and said, "I went to see Santa." His mother asked him what he had said to Santa. "I asked Santa how he knows which are Jewish children and which are Christian children, and what kind of presents he was going to bring the Christian children." Then he added, "You know, Mom, Santa was all mixed up." Though his family did not celebrate Christmas, this boy was still sure that there was a Santa, one who came only to Christian children. Happily, his mother didn't have the heart to tell him otherwise.

ACCEPTING AND GIVING GIFTS THROUGH SANTA

There is a reason why the myth of Santa Claus was so readily accepted when it became attached to Christmas, which was originally a universal religious and not a special children's holiday. Only with Santa did Christmas become truly a children's holiday, because believing in him is the only way some children can permit themselves to enjoy their presents. There are many children who feel that they don't deserve to receive gifts from their parents, because of the way they have behaved, or because of negative thoughts they have had about their parents. There are many more children who feel that receiving presents from parents or relatives makes them beholden to these people, as if they must feel gratitude toward them even if they have no wish to do so. But children know they have harbored no negative thoughts about Santa, and that he expects no gratitude; thus they can accept gifts from him without ambivalence.

Presents received from parents are tainted by feelings connected with them. This is why children may have ambivalent feelings about such gifts and are unable to enjoy them fully, or feel guilty when they play with them. Some children even reject presents their parents give them, and if it is not the right present, they believe this shows that their parents do not care enough for them to know better. But no child rejects Santa's gifts or feels ambivalent about him. Even if a present Santa brings is not quite the expected one, the fact that Santa made a mistake and did not know better will not reflect on the parents.

Maybe making Christmas for our children and enjoying their belief in Santa was easier when the holiday was not so much of a production. Persistent commercialism has raised children's expectations to such a pitch that reality often fails to come up to their hopes, and this frustrates parent and child alike. The Christmas fanfare seduces parents to do more for their children than they can well afford, both psychologically and economically. Further, since parents try to make Christmas an ever more glorious event for children, it has become increasingly difficult for them to forgo receiving their children's recognition of their efforts. When presents were modest, it was easy for parents to pretend that the gifts came from Santa; but when so much money and effort is expended, parents, despite their best intentions, want to see recognition and gratitude from the child. This unconscious wish on the part of the parents for recognition and possibly also for gratitude makes the child only more eager to believe in Santa Claus, so parents and children are then at cross-purposes.

Of course, all children know that their parents have an important share in making Christmas, as they see all the cooking and baking and other preparations for the holiday going on in their homes. What can make Christmas into such a lovely festivity is exactly this blending of fiction and reality, which enhances both. Whether or not the child will experience it in this way depends entirely on the spirit with which the parents prepare for the reality of the holiday and its magical meaning. For the holiday to be fully significant for the child, both fantasy and reality must be involved.

Children are so keenly attuned to the deeper meaning of Christmas that the more we adults involve ourselves in its reality, the more a child's fantasy is aroused and satisfied. Most meaningful is the tree; any parent who has brought home the Christmas tree with his children can observe this truly magical (because it is based on the child's magic beliefs) transformation of a real pine tree into the realization of a wish-fulfilling dream, when the child first beholds the decorated tree in all its splendor of glimmer and light. This is why the Christmas tree is so unquestioningly accepted as the right symbol: it is obviously a real tree, yet it is so clearly what no real tree can ever be. The parents have transformed its everyday reality for their child into a children's wonderland. As mentioned earlier, the present the parent has worked on making is also something very special. No store-bought Raggedy Ann doll can compare with one sewn for the child. Homemade wooden blocks become transformed into an object of fancy: such blocks form the child's very own castle; the homemade doll becomes the child's own baby.

The true wonder of Christmas, aside from its religious meaning, is the miracle of the child's mind, which permits him to turn the thin disguise which hides his parent behind the image of Santa Claus into a promise of a benign, gratifying world. To the child, in addition to all other symbolic meanings, Santa symbolizes not only his parents' generosity, but the goodwill of the whole world. This goodwill cannot be guaranteed by a certain number of presents or by their elaborate nature, but is indicated by the parents' readiness to create for their child, once a year, a world that is in accord with his wishful and magical thinking. The presence of Santa Claus, this symbol of goodwill and devotion to the happiness of children, gives greater security to a child than any number of presents his parents could give in their own identity.

In our society, Santa Claus represents in many ways the last remnant of an ancient belief in a golden age when we were given everything, without being expected to do anything to deserve it or give anything in return. This myth, of course, is a projection of the world of the infant. Santa's big belly seems pregnant with all the good things he is going to give away, and in this sense is symbolic of the happy uterine existence. Despite our growth into adult rationality, it is amazing to what degree we remain captivated by this ancient image of a blissful existence—a golden age which reality shattered for us as soon as we realized that we are not given unendingly, but only by parents whose ability in this respect is quite limited.

Children are only too keenly aware of parental and reality limitations every day of the year. Thus they have every reason to wish to believe that at least once a year, fairyland—or the paradise of infantile existence—can be regained, at least in make-believe for a few hours. These experiences are most reassuring to children, because they mean the golden age is not lost forever. This gives them the strength to go on with the difficulties of the present and holds out hope for the future. Parental insistence that this dream has no basis in reality, not even as a once-yearly return of Santa, makes the world a very unfriendly place.

One ten-year-old said when Santa Claus was discussed: "I know there is no Santa, and no Tooth Fairy who puts a dime under my pillow." And then she broke down, sobbing, "I hate reality." Her hatred of reality was the consequence of being forced too early to give up her wish-fulfilling fantasies. Far from bringing her closer to a healthy understanding of reality, as her parents intended, their rational explanations had alienated her from it, because without some fantasy relief, some specially satisfying events or rituals, unrelieved reality becomes just too unbearable for the young—and for quite a few of the not so young. Belief in magic and the use of magical thinking to bind anxiety (such as belief in a guardian angel or in good fairies) and also to rekindle and sustain hope for good things to come (belief in Santa and the Easter Bunny) are needed by the young child to help him master the rest of reality.

Normally, the need for magic of this sort is greatest for about six years, typically from ages four to ten or so—exactly the time when the child has to learn to cope with the real world. Magical thinking eventually goes into decline, but in normal development this should not happen before grade-school age. When early rationality is pushed, the need to think magically can become repressed. It is not given up, however, but remains encapsulated, full-force, in the unconscious. When it is thus repressed, magical thinking is prevented from undergoing the normal process of slow disintegration under the ever stronger impact of rational thinking. It may then assert itself with full power in adolescence, when the child becomes free of parental domination. Children who were told too soon that there is no Santa Claus, who were brought up not on fairy tales but on realistic stories, often go off to college believing in astrology, trusting the *I Ching* to provide answers for life's problems, or studying Tarot cards to predict the future. The adolescent who thus engages in magical thinking tries to make up for what he was forced to lose out on at an earlier age.

Normally, magical thinking is gradually given up as the child's widening experience with reality takes over and he becomes more able to cope. There comes a time when the child will not believe in the reality of Santa Claus no matter what a parent says, although Santa can then turn into an enjoyable make-believe game for parents and children alike, in which they temporarily recreate a childish world of fantasy that both enjoy, each on his own level. But this deep enjoyment of the Santa fantasy is possible only if Santa Claus was indeed once a reality to the child, and if he was not pushed to accept prematurely an adult view of such fantasies.

So if we wish to help our children have a healthy understanding of reality and ability to cope with it, we must not only make it possible for them to hold on to their fantasies for some time, but make their fantasies become reality for them at significant moments. This is the important function holidays serve for children's psychic economy: to strengthen them for the tasks of living.

29

❧

The "Real" Santa, the Easter Bunny, and the Devil

> Above all else he loathed the homily,
> The slogan and the ad. . . .
> . . . .The Christmas tree,
> The Easter egg, baptism, he observed.
> —KARL JAY SHAPIRO,
> "Elegy for a Dead Soldier"

A FEW GIFTS can actually be more satisfying than an overabundance—that is, if the commercialization of Christmas and the ubiquity of television advertisements have not aroused a child's expectations beyond all reason. The giving of a few presents eliminates the ambivalence a child may feel about giving and receiving (discussed earlier). This issue is recognized by a children's holiday which is celebrated in many European countries including Holland, from where it was brought to New Amsterdam and thus the New World: Saint Nicholas's Day. On this day, December 6, children are given a very few inexpensive things so that even the poorest parent can afford to participate in the holiday spirit and celebration, and no child needs to feel guilty about receiving, even if he believes he was bad and undeserving.

While this holiday is not now celebrated in the United States, a discussion of it here may aid the understanding of the figure of Santa Claus, and what he subconsciously means to children. Santa speaks to some of our most important emotions, and it is through this figure that we can best gain access to the fullness of meaning which Christmas has today for children.

For a very long period, much longer than our present form of celebrating Christmas has been in existence, Saint Nicholas was the most venerated and celebrated, the most popular saint within both the Western and the Eastern churches. During the many centuries when Christmas was strictly a religious holiday, Saint Nicholas's Day was probably the most popular secular holiday.

As far as the saint himself is concerned, records indicate that there may have been two holy bishops of this name in Myra, an ancient city in Lycia in Asia Minor. The first supposedly lived in the third or fourth century; many miracles are ascribed to him but nothing concrete is known about him, not even whether he actually existed. The evidence suggests more strongly that another bishop of Myra named Nicholas lived in the sixth century, but about him, too, very little is known for certain. The two became merged into one, Saint Nicholas of Myra, and many and various miracles are ascribed to him. This saint became so venerated that as early as the eleventh century expeditions were sent to Myra—which by then had been destroyed—to secure his relics. A church in Bari, Italy, was founded in 1087 to receive some of these relics; its importance is indicated by the fact that it became one of the four Palatine churches of Apulia. Since that time many great and small churches all over Europe have been dedicated to this saint, and his feast day has been amply and widely celebrated ever since.

Some of the numerous miraculous deeds attributed to Saint Nicholas are pertinent to our discussion. He rescued many children out of mortal danger and revived others, and thus became the patron saint of children. Having inherited great wealth, he gave it away freely, in one instance to three virtuous maidens who could not marry for want of dowries. The legend goes that he dropped three bags of gold, one for each of the maidens, at their sides while they slept, so that they would not know the origin of these gifts. This element of the saint's story—that he chose to remain anonymous by depositing his gifts in the middle of the night when everyone was asleep— has become an important element of Santa's role.

Saint Nicholas was the patron saint not only of children, whom he protected and rescued, but also of parenthood and human fertility. This aspect probably goes back to much older pagan fertility cults, some features of which accrued to the saint. As the patron of the family and of fecundity, Saint Nicholas was invoked by married couples who desired to have children, particularly by women who wished for them. Similarly, virgins who needed dowries prayed to him. His propensity for assisting a woman to become pregnant was so well known that in Alpine countries, saying that a woman had prayed to Saint Nicholas was tantamount to saying that she was with child. When it was said that Sant Klos—which is Saint Nicholas's name in certain dialects and may well have been the origin of his being known as Santa Claus—had come to a family, this meant that a child had been born to it.

In parts of Switzerland it was not the stork which was said to bring children but Smichlaus, another dialect name for Saint Nicholas. In Brittany, women who wished for children went to a chapel dedicated to the saint, in which a figure of him was suspended from the ceiling by a rope. Supposedly, when they rubbed this statuette over their bodies and prayed to Saint Nicholas, they would get pregnant; this is one example of how pagan fertility customs entered rituals centering on this saint. So from as early as the eleventh century, the cult of Saint Nicholas was intimately related to pregnancy and fertility, to the bringing of children and also of presents in the middle of the night. In some districts it was said that on his name day, the saint rode in the middle of the night on his white (or dapple-gray) horse over the rooftops and dropped down, as the case may be, either newborn infants or presents for children. Here is an origin of the legend of Santa Claus driving his sled and reindeers over the rooftops. During the pageants celebrating Saint Nicholas's Day, the person representing him might wear the garb of a bishop, since he was one, or on occasion the attire of a cardinal; this may possibly have been the origin of Santa's red costume.

What are the features of Santa Claus which may appeal to a child's unconscious mind, particularly in connection with other events or features of the celebration of Christmas? Many elements evoke subconscious responses in their combination and totality, as much as in their individual aspects. For example, every child wonders about what his arrival meant to his parents, and many worry whether or not they were welcome. Therefore any celebration fêting the arrival of a child is reassuring, and it is this event which Christmas obviously celebrates. The joy with which the Christ child was received into this world, not only by his parents but also by the shepherds and the three holy kings, is taken by the child as a sign that his birth was an equally joyous event for his parents and even for the wider community, since everybody celebrates Christmas.

The period before Christmas is a time of happy anticipation, as is that before a child is born. Everybody waits for the happy moment to come. In preparation for a birth the house is rearranged, as it usually is before Christmas. The coming of Santa in the middle of the night is mysterious enough, and so is the birth of a child, most of whom are born at night. Santa comes down the chimney and enters the home through the fireplace, which provides the home with life-giving warmth, and Santa's big belly is like that of a highly pregnant woman. As the infant on his birth descends through a narrow and dark channel and from there emerges into the light of the world, so does Santa. A legend of long standing is that the stork brings newborn infants and drops them down the chimney—another parallel between Santa and the Saint Nicholas of legend. Last but not least, parents know the true story of conception and birth, but children are not supposed to know and are told a different story; in the same way, parents know the truth about Santa but tell their children something different. Finally, both Saint Nicholas's Day and Christmas, each in its own way, celebrate the rebirth of the year and fertilization. Even though Saint Nicholas's Day is not actively celebrated in the

United States, it would be a very insensitive child who did not respond, at least to some degree subconsciously, to all these parallels between the coming of Santa and the birth of children. In their combination these symbolic meanings make Christmas probably the most important happy event in the child's life.

When I was a child in Austria, Saint Nicholas's Day was celebrated, there as in many other countries, in much the same way it had been over the centuries, and as it is still celebrated now. On this day, two male adults visit the homes of children. One is dressed up as a bishop, playing the role of Saint Nicholas; the other is either his helper and servant, or his counterpart—a figure variously dressed and named, depending on local custom. He is often called Ruprecht when he is merely a servant carrying a bag of presents, but more frequently he is called Black Peter, Krampus, or Grampus, in which case his face is blackened and he represents the devil. Then he wears a mask with horns, a tail, and even hooves; he is dressed in black and carries a sack or some other receptacle. Black Peter's sack, however, does not contain gifts—it is there to carry away bad children. Nearly always he carries chains and rattles them, threatening to chain bad children. But while this evil figure looks and acts ferocious, he is in the power of the good bishop Saint Nicholas, who always soon stops him and—as in the legend—rescues the children.

On Saint Nicholas's Day these two, who are neighbors appropriately dressed up, go from door to door, asking the parents (who have expected them) whether their children have been good or bad. In most cases the answer is "mostly good, though not always." At this the devil steps forth and tries to grab the child to give him a few strokes with his switch, but the child nearly always manages to escape with great shrieking. In any case, after a perfunctory effort on the part of the devil to punish the child, the good saint comes to the rescue and puts the devil in his place, making it clear that he will protect all children. Then Saint Nicholas admonishes the child to be good and gives him small presents, usually some pieces of fruit and candy. But one of his more traditional gifts is particularly meaningful: branches like those which were made into Krampus's switches, but Saint Nicholas's are covered with gold or silver glitter, and from their branches hang small fruits or candies. Saint Nicholas's branches are turned into a token candy tree; they are a close parody of the instrument with which children are occasionally punished, a transfiguration of the instrument of punishment into one giving pleasure that is much appreciated by the children. Thus, on Saint Nicholas's Day, through a little drama much enjoyed by all, first the negative side of parental ambivalence and children's guilt about their bad behavior (if not also bad thoughts) are satisfied by the threats or token punishment meted out by the devilish figure, and then the positive side of this ambivalence wins out, and the gifts are given which are much more immediate and real than was the symbolic punishment. (For the sake of completeness I might add that at the end, when the children are fully occupied with enjoying what they have received, the parents surreptitiously give the visitors some money to compensate them for their expenses and usually add a gratuity in recognition of their efforts.)

The two characters of Saint Nicholas's Day always appear as a pair, reflecting the two sides of our personalities in a way that everyone understands. They symbolize that in the child as also in adults, neither the good in us nor the bad exists in isolation. The parents' answer to their query shows they know that their child is neither all good nor all bad, and thus the child can enjoy his small presents to the fullest without guilt. Of course, the impressive bishop's costume with his miter and staff and the flamboyant and ingenious getup of Black Peter (Ruprecht or Krampus) add a great deal to the fun, as does the red costume of Santa Claus at Christmas. Since adults dress and act this way for children with full parental cooperation, they thus give body and reality to the child's fantasies, both the fearful and the wish-fulfilling ones, according them obvious adult approval.

FUNDAMENTAL CHANGE IN HOLIDAYS

Christmas is not the only children's holiday which symbolically celebrates childbirth, fertility, and the rebirth of nature; May Day, which is hardly celebrated anymore in the United States, with its dance around the Maypole also used to be an occasion for festivities enjoyed particularly by children and youth, although with the active participation of the entire community. It was truly a day when "young and old came forth to play." (Today May Day is still celebrated by the socialists in the old sense of heralding a new beginning.) The other great holiday celebrating a new beginning is Easter, the day of the Resurrection, a feast day celebrating rebirth. Without it, the story of Christ would end with his death by crucifixion, but with Easter, there is the beginning of a new life, of a new era, of new hope. Like Christmas, Easter was originally mainly a religious holiday, but it has now become an important children's holiday.

As its ancient name and many of the rituals connected with it show, Easter also has deep symbolic meanings in connection with birth, rebirth, and fertility. The name Easter is derived from that of the German goddess Ostara, who was the goddess of spring and fecundity. Her symbol was the egg and her messenger the hare; this was the origin of the Easter egg and the Easter hare, or rabbit. The egg features prominently in creation myths all over the world to signify birth, and as early as the fourth century, eggs became connected with Easter ceremonies. In the twelfth century the Roman Catholic Church legitimized this connection by introducing the Benedictio Ovarum, authorizing the special use of eggs on the holy days of Easter. Ever since, the egg has played a prominent role in Easter celebrations, from the custom of egg-rolling to the hunt for Easter eggs by children and the giving of decorated eggs as special presents. The hare and later the rabbit were natural symbols of fertility because these animals reproduce so abundantly. The first German reference to the hare in connection with the Easter egg appears in 1572, but by then it was already an old custom. Many rituals, as well as common sense, attest to the symbolic connection between egg and birth. For example, among the Hungarian Gypsies, when a woman was enduring painful labor, her relations came to visit and one of them dropped an egg on her while they all sang: "The egg, the egg is round / And the belly is round; / Come child in good health! / God, God, calls thee!"

So all the great children's holidays—birthdays (in some parts of the world the child's name day), Christmas, Easter—are days which commemorate and celebrate birth and in this way assure the child that his arrival on this earth was a happy occasion, eagerly wished for by his parents and the world. The more we celebrate these occasions, the more certain the child can feel about being loved.

In order to gain emotional security, a child needs not only to be loved and cherished, but also to feel that his darker aspects can be accepted. The traditional Saint Nicholas's Day ritual gives recognition to the fact that children cannot be good all the time, and so do certain customs around Eastertime when children's asocial tendencies are allowed some scope. In Oxfordshire, England, for example, in times past, during the week before Easter gangs of boys and girls used to go around from house to house, extracting presents. When after they had sung some Easter song no gift was forthcoming, they would cry out: "Here sits a bad wife / The devil take her life / Set her upon a swivel / and send her to the devil." Then the children would cut the latch of the door, stop the keyhole with dirt, or leave some other token of their displeasure in front of the door.

Another day used to give expression to the negative side of children's ambivalence was April Fools' Day, which was at one time a most joyous holiday in the juvenile calendar. All kinds of tricks were played on adults, who had to accept them in good humor. In addition, there were other such days depending on local customs, such as New Year's Day, Valentine's Day, or Shrove Tuesday, which was the occasion for cockfights, for rowdiness and rebellion. But Saint Nicholas's Day was a particularly popular time for youngsters to let loose their negative attitudes. Black Peter or Grampus was the expression of adults' negative feeling toward children, but after the visit—or procession, as the custom might be—of Saint Nicholas had ended, later that evening and at night gangs of boys and girls who had blackened their faces boisterously roamed the streets, chasing everybody they met, smearing walls and windows, and in general playing havoc. This behavior, which had to be accepted by adults in good grace, was especially widespread in Holland.

Although in the United States we have no children's holiday which centers so clearly and delightfully on ambivalence, we used to have one which ritually celebrated and discharged the negative component of children's ambivalence about the world of adults: Halloween. This holiday's origin was in a Celtic festival at the far end of summer, connected with the return of cattle from pasture and the rekindling of fires in the home.

In more modern times, on Halloween children could act out their resentment of those adults who all year long expected them to act more civilized than they wanted or were able to be. Children feel that adults always want them to be better-behaved, cleaner, and neater than feels good to them. Halloween was the one day when they could threaten adults, as they feel threatened by them all year round, and scare them, as they are scared by adults. It was the one night when they could smear windows and doors to their heart's delight, vent their anger at having had to submit to an all too rigorous toilet training by turning over the outhouse, move fences and so do something about their feeling of being fenced in. In short, on this one night children could band together against the world of the adults, which they felt was banded together all year round in its common demands on children.

Of course, what made Halloween so significant an experience for children was that adults entered into the spirit of the occasion by acting scared, and by buying off the child's threats by giving him goodies in response to his demand of "trick or treat." On this one night adults had to accept the children's urge to be "bad" or "wild"; they had to comply with the children's demands and behave as if they felt threatened by them—a reversal of normal life. This reversal is what made Halloween so delightful to children: this grand admission by the adult world that children, too, have a right to get even—a right to act out their negative feelings. Anyone who did not enter into the spirit of the holiday and would not go along with the children's mischievousness was a spoilsport, like those who denied Santa's existence to the child who wanted to believe in him.

The permanent underlying positive ties between parents and children were strengthened at Halloween—after all, adults made this outburst of naughtiness possible and encouraged it, with their merriment barely hidden behind their pretense of being scared. This holiday told children that deep down, despite adult demands to socialize the child, their parents did not totally reject the negative side of the child's feelings toward them. They knew it existed and had to be given its due, at least symbolically, one night a year. Having freed themselves of their hostile feelings on Halloween, the children could then fully concentrate during the Christmas season, a few weeks later, on positive feelings toward their parents.

Halloween, like Christmas, was once a religious holiday, and like Christmas it was an ancient pagan tradition onto which Christian meanings were grafted. Like Christmas, the rites of Halloween are anchored in the deepest layers of the unconscious, where our emotions run strongest. Santa Claus, as mentioned, represents infantile fantasies of the benevolent parent of the golden age, when all our wishes were satisfied immediately; thus, to some extent, he is the reincarnation of the all-good mother who gave birth to the child. Halloween, on the other hand, represents the opposite aspect of our basic ambivalence. Christmas symbolizes the satisfaction of all our hopes, but Halloween symbolizes our persecutory anxieties. The witch on her broomstick, so central a symbol to Halloween, is the reincarnation of the bad mother, the hostile-destructive one. The devil, a figure which in every way symbolizes phallic aggression (the hoof, the tail, the horns), represents the bad father. Halloween used to present a unique, important opportunity for boys and girls aged three until adolescence to act out some of their aggressive wishes and in doing so not only to become acquainted with them, but to some degree to master them.

Before Halloween was bowdlerized, children were able to attain power for one night. To be able to dress and act like a witch, a devil, or a ghost means that one shares by proxy in the secret power of these figures. Haunting adults was not done entirely in play; it was not merely the acting out of a wish to turn the tables on the adult world. It reached much deeper into the unconscious and satisfied a primitive need to identify with these primordial powers. But in order to exorcise these extremely primitive layers of the personality, children had to be free to run wild for a few hours, and adults had to make sure that they could do so safely.

What even as recently as a generation ago was an orgiastic and therefore deeply cathartic experience has been turned from a haunting event into a fancy-dress party. The true function of Halloween has been denied and abandoned. What was formerly a symbolic acting out of man's most anxious and destructive drives, breaking out of repression, has become totally de-mystified and civilized. Now among nice middle-class families, this ritual reappearance of devils and witches—all the dark forces in man—has been watered down to an ever-so-gentle extortion for the nicest of causes, such as collecting for UNICEF. If we thus try to civilize our children by denying everything strong and wild in them, it is little wonder that some of them grow up into young adults who hate civilization, which robbed them of even one night a year in which they could give free rein to an important aspect of their natures.

Recently, in some parts of the United States, such as in California and New York City, adults, too, have taken to dressing up as ghosts and witches on Halloween, thus depriving children of their exclusive holiday by making themselves part of it. No longer do children try to scare adults on this night; when adults act the same as they do, children are robbed of their one chance a year to assert their dominance. Children rightly interpret this as adults being jealous of their fun and thus changing its meaning. Adults who act in this way were probably deprived of fun when they were children, perhaps forced to collect for worthy causes instead of running wild and scaring adults, giving once-a-year expression to their asocial tendencies and getting rid of them through acting them out. So as adults, they try to make up for what they lost out on as children. But in doing so, they make it impossible for their own children to turn the tables on their parents and all other adults at least once a year.

The same process of destroying the deeper emotional meaning of a holiday has been at work in the changing nature of how we celebrate the Fourth of July. All along, it was a patriotic family event and not just a children's holiday; since it celebrated a revolution, it used to be a chaotic, raucous occasion. On the preceding night of July 3, firecrackers were set off. Then on the day itself, the orators at community festivities could successfully concentrate on the American Revolution's positive achievement—the creation of a new form of government. But now that the rougher aspects of the celebration have been done away with, there is little patriotic fervor left either. As always in life, when we do away with the negative aspect of human ambivalence, the positive loses its emotional strength as well.

Our effort to take the ambivalence—our recognition of both the light and dark sides of human beings—out of our celebrations by trying to make them pretty and civilized has divorced them from the deepest sources of our human existence and turned them into empty events. As Aristotle knew, we can free ourselves for our higher purposes only if we first purge ourselves of the dark forces within us. This catharsis has traditionally taken place through our participating emotionally in the performance of both: an elevating classic tragedy and a satyr play or raucous comedy; or a Dionysian holiday celebrating chaos. Having denied the dark forces their due at Halloween, we now make the redeeming forces seem unnecessary. By creating bland holidays for our children, we have created a vapid world for them, a world which does not recognize their and our deepest fears and most satisfying wishes. What is additionally unfortunate is that by making the world bland for them we also contribute to making their feelings for us bland, something from which we and they suffer alike. If, on the other hand, we could restore magic to their world, it would also be restored to our relations, which would become greatly enriched by it.

This book's purpose is to encourage parents to do their own thinking about some aspects of child-rearing in the hope that these examples will help them to find good solutions to whatever problems they may encounter in raising their child. Their struggles to do so will make them good enough parents, to their own and their children's benefit. The good enough parent will always be aware that conceiving and bearing a child and bringing it into this world are the most wondrous events in the lives of parents. To be born is the most wondrous event in the life of a child. The more they can enjoy together, each in their own ways, what follows from it—the parents raising the child, the child being raised by his parents—the happier their lives will be.

If this book, in some small way, contributes to such potential happiness becoming a reality, it will indeed have achieved its purpose

Gordon Bourne FRCS FRCOG
Pregnancy £5.95

Having a child can be one of the most exciting and fulfilling experiences in a woman's life, provided she has the confidence that comes from knowing exactly what pregnancy involves.

This comprehensive guide is written by Dr Gordon Bourne, Consultant Obstetrician and Gynaecologist at one of London's leading teaching hospitals. It provides full information, guidance and reassurance on all aspects of pregnancy and childbirth. An indispensable aid to the expectant mother, it will also be of great interest to her husband and family.

'Sets out in a clear, factual and reassuring way every possible aspect of pregnancy . . . I would recommend this book to anyone who can buy or borrow a copy' MARRIAGE GUIDANCE

Dr Stephen Davies and Dr Alan Stewart
Nutritional Medicine £3.95
The drug-free guide to better family health

Nutritional medicine is based on the assumption that many illnesses, mild and chronic, are caused by nutritional imbalance, and can be cured or alleviated by correcting the patient's biochemistry. In this important new book, Drs Davies and Stewart, whose pioneering work in nutritional medicine is in line with the latest scientific, well-proven information, reveal why these imbalances occur – addiction to caffeine, tobacco and alcohol, use of the Pill and other drugs, eating over-refined foods, exposure to chemicals and pollution – and how nutritional medicine can effectively treat a wide variety of conditions, from arthritis to hyperactivity or even schizophrenia.

They explain how we can all become healthier by taking certain measures, dietary ones included, to make us more resistant to the stresses of modern life – especially important in pregnancy, childhood and old age – and how a doctor who practises nutritional medicine will assess how a patient functions best, adjusting their needs carefully, scientifically and without the use of drugs.

Drs Andrew and Penny Stanway
The Baby and Child Book £5.95

A complete handbook of child care for the crucial first five years covering all aspects of health, child psychology, toys and play, clothing and equipment, pre-school education (including playgroups) and day-care that concern parents in the 80s.

The sensible and practical information is arranged alphabetically to make it as easy as possible to find exactly what you need to know when you need it. An important and innovative feature is the Medical Action Chart which aids speedy and accurate identification of illnesses common in early childhood and refers you to the relevant entry in the text for more information.

'The Stanways have one overriding advantage over most experts on childbearing: they have done it themselves recently! It is this, combined with their wide-ranging professional expertise, which gives this book a down-to-earth reliability lacking from many similar publications'
MOTHER AND BABY

'Splendidly practical . . . the doctors really understand what *you* want to know' WOMAN'S OWN

Breast is Best £2.99

More and more doctors are emphasizing the important advantages of breastfeeding for mothers who are anxious to give their child the best possible start for a healthy life. There's immunity from infection, less chance of obesity and less risk of dental decay . . . just some of the advantages of natural feeding. This comprehensive guide explains how breastfeeding works, how to prepare for it and look after your own health while coping with the rest of the family.

Dr B. Robert Feldman with David Carroll
The Complete Book of Children's Allergies £3.99

'Runny nose, watery eyes and a sore throat, all may be due to hay fever. Or they may stem from a cold; the symptoms are identical. A breathing problem could be the result of pollen sensitivity. Or perhaps it's just lingering bronchitis. The whole area of symptoms can get downright confusing. How do you as a parent decide whether or not an allergy is behind it all?'

The Complete Book of Children's Allergies is packed with information, advice, support and tips to help you identify your child's symptoms with ease and provide real, effective relief.

All aspects of the allergy war are explored and explained in a practical, easy-to-follow format. Subjects include asthma, hay fever, skin reactions, food sensitivity, visits to the doctor, testing for allergies and, of course, the treatments available. There is also a handy question-and-answer section at the end of every chapter covering in a realistic and reassuring manner the most common questions that parents ask.

Sharon Faelten
The Allergy Self-Help Book £3.50

Self-help can do more for allergies than for any other form of disease. The more you learn about the cause of your trouble – and exactly how to avoid whatever irritates you – the less likely you are to need constant medical supervision.

This comprehensive, easy-to-use guide – based on first-hand interviews with and reports from some of the world's most experienced allergy doctors – will help you identify the specific food or environmental substance that's the cause of your discomfort or your child's – and tell you what you can do about it. It includes a special no-allergy diet plan and expert advice on how to decode lists of ingredients on food labels to avoid hidden food allergens, how to manage food allergies in children, and how to choose safe household cleaning products and cosmetics.

There are plenty of helpful, practical tips on how to escape harmful airborne particles, some of which you may not even know exist, and the book ends with a unique A–Z of allergic reactions that can mimic any of over 50 different health complaints, including arthritis, depression, eczema, insomnia, migraine, sinusitis and vertigo.

Barbara Griggs
The Home Herbal £2.99

A handbook of simple remedies

When it was first published, this book was hailed as an informative and authoritative guide to simple herbal remedies for home use. Now completely revised and updated, it is even more valuable and deserves a place on every family bookshelf.

The Home Herbal makes no claims for miracle cures. But it does offer a sensible and systematic guide to herbal remedies for a whole range of ailments where conventional medicine can often fail to provide relief or produces unpleasant side-effects, and for those minor medical problems such as sunburn, coughs and colds and hangovers which can benefit from natural, gentle treatment by herbs.

The book is organized alphabetically under medical problems, from acne through depression and insomnia to whooping cough, and herbal remedies are suggested under each of these headings. In addition there are chapters on the preparation of herbal medicines, where to find your herbs and how to stock your family medicine cupboard. A new feature of this edition is the section devoted to children's ailments.

Dr Barbara Evans
Life Change £3.50

A guide to the menopause, its effects and treatment

Dr Barbara Evans, a former medical correspondent of *The Sunday Times* and consultant editor of *World Medicine*, explains what's happening to your body, your emotions and your relationships . . .

How the menopause affects you

How to cope with it

Understanding your body changes

Good news about hormone treatment

Sex and the menopause

Preventing osteoporosis

Now fully revised and updated in line with the latest medical research, Barbara Evans' practical, sensible and sympathetic advice will bring hope and understanding to every woman suffering the physical and psychological problems of the menopause.

Foreword by John Studd, FRCOG, Consultant Obstetrician and Gynaecologist, King's College and Dulwich Hospitals, London

Oliver Sacks
Migraine £3.95

Understanding the common disorder

'Written by one of the great clinical writers of the twentieth century, *Migraine*, intended for the general public, should be read as much for its brilliant insights into the nature of our mental functioning as for its discussion of migraine' NEW YORK TIMES BOOK REVIEW

A new revised edition of Oliver Sacks' classic book on migraine, this is a full and penetrating insight into that most distressing of common illnesses. The symptoms, treatments and psychological effects are all discussed in detail, making it an essential guide to the migraine sufferer who wants to know exactly what he or she is up against.

'Informative, well-written and entertaining . . . includes a good review of specific drug treatments and can be read by all those who have to deal with migraine' THE LANCET

'A most excellent survey . . . must be the definitive book on the subject' NURSING MIRROR

'Well organized, original, constructive . . . deserves a wide readership' MENTAL HEALTH

'His commentary is so erudite, so gracefully written, that even those people fortunate enough to never have had a migraine in their lives should find it equally compelling' NEW YORK TIMES

Dr Richard Mackarness
Not All In The Mind £2.50

In this new vitally important book, Dr Richard Mackarness, doctor and psychiatrist, shows how millions may be made ill, physically and mentally, by common foods such as milk, eggs, coffee and white flour.

He relates case after case from his clinical practice where patients with chronic ailments resistant to other methods of treatment were cured by identifying and eliminating foods to which they had developed unsuspected allergy.

Peter G. Hanson M.D.
The Joy of Stress £3.99

The mismanagement of stress can be fatal. Under stress, people don't feel at their peak, they don't perform at work to the best of their abilities, they are more likely to be sick, and ultimately they are most likely to die before their time.

But you can make the stresses in your life work positively for you. Dr Hanson's easy-to-read and entertaining book shows you how to harness stress productively. It distils scientific facts into practical advice for everyone – making sense out of the confusing and often contradictory advice we've all been subjected to on stress, body management, longevity, productivity and nutrition.

The key to surviving and thriving on stress is control. The Hanson Method teaches you how to ignore what you can't control, and to control what you can. It's a *practical* plan that you can put to work immediately and continue to use forever. So don't hide from stresses; go out and challenge new ones. Take the *thrill* from stress, but leave the *threat* behind. Thrive under pressure and learn the true Joy of Stress!

Donald Norfolk
Farewell to Fatigue £2.95

The 28-Step Vitality Programme

Fatigue plays an increasingly destructive part in our lives by making us less efficient at work, more prone to accidents and diseases, irritable and miserable and less able to enjoy life to the full. But chronic fatigue, this modern plague, is not a natural part of life and you can banish it completely with the *Vitality Programme* . . .

Osteopath Donald Norfolk's 28-step *Vitality Programme* has worked wonders for his political, business and showbusiness patients. It's fun, easy-to-follow, and you don't have to turn your life upside down to benefit from it. All that's required is a series of subtle habit changes. If you're going to breathe, you might as well discover how to breathe well. If you're going to walk, why not learn how to walk efficiently, with minimum strain? If you're going to eat, why not eat a nourishing, healthy diet? You will find that once these habits become part of your daily routine you will be automatically programmed for health and vitality for the rest of your life.

The *Vitality Programme* is not only a prescription against fatigue, it's also a blueprint for healthy living. By following it you'll gain a slimmer figure, greater strength, better posture, sounder sleep, relief from tension, an enhanced sex life and a reduced tendency to disease. And the energy you possess will enable you to enjoy a richer, fuller life than you've ever known before. Start now . . .

D. C. Jarvis MD
Folk Medicine £2.50

The late Dr Jarvis lived and practised among the tough mountain folk of
Vermont for over fifty years. This unique and remarkable book – which has
sold over 500,000 copies in the Pan edition alone – is the result of his deep
study of their way of life, and in particular of their concept of diet and time-
honoured folk medicine.

It offers a novel theory on the treatment and prevention of a wide range of
diseases and nagging complaints:

The common cold

Hay fever

Arthritis

Kidney trouble

Digestive disorders

Overweight

High blood pressure

Chronic fatigue

and many others which often defy conventional diagnosis and treatment.

'There is not a family in the land who won't find its theories – and
propositions – fascinating' DAILY EXPRESS.

Arthritis and Folk Medicine £2.50

When *Folk Medicine* swept through Britain and America with its amazing
message of relief from countless diseases, the author received innumerable
letters from sufferers from arthritis, lumbago, gout and muscular rheumatism,
enquiring what *Folk Medicine* had to offer them for their misery.

Now Dr Jarvis replies – explaining step by step a simple, sensible method
of treatment, evolved through generations of trial and error by the rugged
folk of his native Vermont and meticulously tested against his own medical
experience.

Malcolm Jayson and Allan Dixon
Rheumatism and Arthritis £2.50

This excellent, readable and highly informative book covers every aspect of rheumatic and arthritic conditions, and offers a survey of the very latest techniques of treatment. It examines recent developments in this area of research where hundreds of millions of pounds are spent annually, and the possibilities of the breakthrough thousands are waiting for. Dispelling the medical mystique that disturbs so many patients, here is well-informed, commonsense advice for sufferers from one of the most common diseases.

'One copy of this book is worth at least ten copper bracelets'
NEW SCIENTIST

Mary Laver and Margaret Smith
Diet for Life £3.50
a cookbook for arthritics

Written by an arthritic for sufferers everywhere, this cookbook explains the principles of a dietary regime that offers new hope of a normal active life free from the crippling pain of arthritis. A step-by-step guide to almost two hundred recipes, avoiding animal fats and fruit and using the minimum of additives; varied and interesting eating to take full advantage of the range of fresh vegetables as they come into season.

Dr Felix Mann
Acupuncture £2.50

how it works and how it is used today

Today, thousands of European and Russian doctors practise acupuncture in conjunction with Western medicine. Dr Felix Mann is an expert in the field and in this illuminating book he dispels the mystery of this ancient science and art. This new edition of a classic guide has been revised and updated to include the latest information on the use of acupuncture and how treatment can be obtained. With a foreword by Aldous Huxley.

Irwin Maxwell Stillman, MD and Samm Sinclair Baker
The Doctor's Quick Weight Loss Diet £2.50

Vital truths about effective dieting. Over sixty quick reducing diets to fit every problem and taste . . . This book contains no way-out theories or strange concoctions. Its instructions are simple to understand, easy to follow – and have been proved dramatically effective by the eminent and experienced doctor who wrote this highly acclaimed work.

All Pan books are available at your local bookshop or newsagent, or can be ordered direct from the publisher. Indicate the number of copies required and fill in the form below.

Send to: **CS Department, Pan Books Ltd., P.O. Box 40, Basingstoke, Hants. RG21 2YT.**

or phone: 0256 469551 (Ansaphone), quoting title, author and Credit Card number.

Please enclose a remittance* to the value of the cover price plus: 60p for the first book plus 30p per copy for each additional book ordered to a maximum charge of £2.40 to cover postage and packing.

*Payment may be made in sterling by UK personal cheque, postal order, sterling draft or international money order, made payable to Pan Books Ltd.

Alternatively by Barclaycard/Access:

Card No.

Signature:

Applicable only in the UK and Republic of Ireland.

While every effort is made to keep prices low, it is sometimes necessary to increase prices at short notice. Pan Books reserve the right to show on covers and charge new retail prices which may differ from those advertised in the text or elsewhere.

NAME AND ADDRESS IN BLOCK LETTERS PLEASE:

....

Name———————————————————————————

Address—————————————————————————————

————————————————————————————————

————————————————————————————————

————————————————————————————————

3/87